PHILADELPHIA

IN THE

CIVIL WAR

1861–1865

A Complete History Illustrated with
Contemporary Prints and Photographs

FRANK H. TAYLOR

WESTHOLME
Yardley

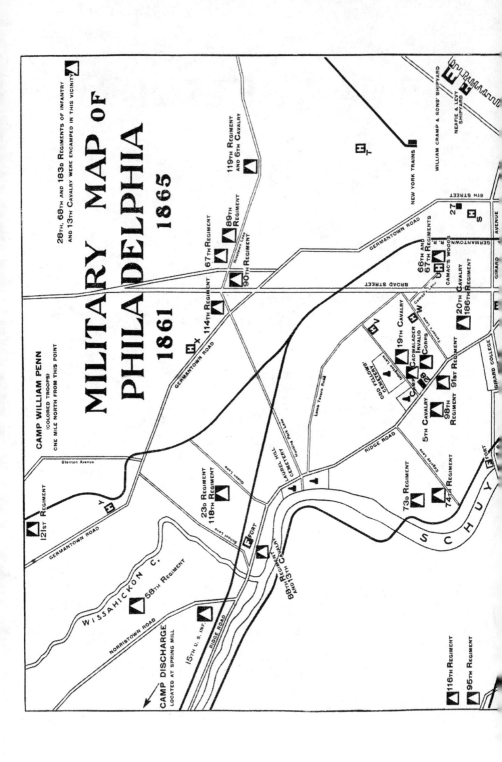

MILITARY MAP OF PHILADELPHIA
1861
1865

CAMP WILLIAM PENN
(COLORED TROOPS)
ONE MILE NORTH FROM THIS POINT

28TH, 68TH AND 183D REGIMENTS OF INFANTRY AND 13TH CAVALRY WERE ENCAMPED IN THIS VICINITY

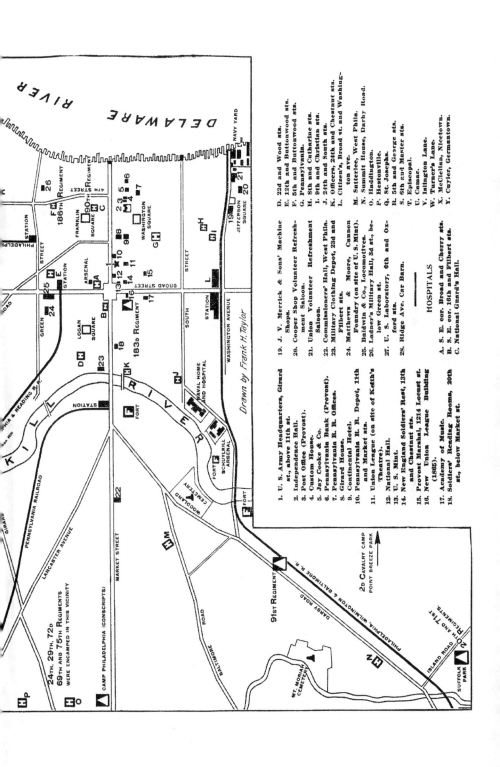

Drawn by Frank H. Taylor

THE TRIBUTE OF WAR

THERE is "a theme of martial music which represents the approach, the presence and the departing march of a body of soldiery. The first faint notes grow clearer and louder until, amid the acclaim of trumpets, the brisk beat of drums and with the quick stride of an aspiring movement, the troops sweep by in all the brilliance and panoply of war, and then their tread slowly recedes away."*

So the Union volunteers of the great American war came, in proud array, along the flag-draped corridors of our national history, passed on to their mission, consecrated to the cause of national integrity. Whatever may now be told of their heroism and triumph can be but an echo of the music which led them on; which stirred the souls of all loyal and patriotic men and women of that far-gone time.

Written half a century beyond the days of which it relates, this book is, at best, only an outline of events, guiding the student of our local annals to those abundant sources of information, the numerous regimental histories, official records and personal narrations to be found in the libraries, wherein the glory, suffering and sorrow of war are depicted, and where the names and deeds of all soldiers and sailors of Philadelphia who had a part in the great conflict are inscribed. There has been but scant room between these covers to portray the ardor of the men, the sacrifices by women, the patriotic toil of children in the schools. It was a time of all-pervading self abnegation, changing the fortunes of a whole community. Out of the travail of this loyal city has arisen her prosperity and greatness of to-day.

Monuments are erected to the honor of our heroes of the Civil War, but the greatest of memorials is the splendid fact of a Union restored and perfected, looking out upon the world unafraid, based upon the rock of enduring Freedom, an example for the patriots of every nation to follow, and in the consummation of which the people of Philadelphia had an honorable part.

---

* From an address by Colonel William McMichael upon the placing of the corner-stone of the First Regiment Armory, April 19th, 1882.

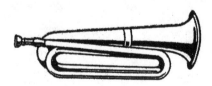

4

PENNSYLVANIA VOLUNTEER AND MILITIA ORGANIZATIONS COMPOSED OF, OR INCLUDING, PHILADELPHIA COMPANIES WHICH SERVED IN THE COURSE OF THE CIVIL WAR

Washington Brigade, 1st and 2d Regiments, Gen. William F. Small, not mustered in.

THREE MONTHS' SERVICE, 1861.

17th, 18th, 19th, 20th, 21st, 22d, 23d, 24th Infantry; Commonwealth Artillery; First Troop Philadelphia City Cavalry; McMullen Rangers.

THREE YEARS' SERVICE.

23d, 26th, 27th, 28th, 29th, 31st, 32d, 33d, 36th, 41st, 56th, 58th, 61st, 66th, 67th, 68th, 69th, 71st, 72d, 73d, 74th, 75th, 81st, 82d, 88th, 90th, 91st, 95th, 98th, 99th, 106th, 109th, 110th, 114th, 115th, 116th, 118th, 119th, 121st, 147th, 150th, 157th, 183d, 186th, 187th, 188th Infantry; 2d, 3d, 5th, 6th, 8th, 9th, 11th, 12th, 13th, 14th, 15th, 16th, 17th, 18th, 19th, 20th Cavalry; 2d and 3d Artillery; 2d Provisional Heavy Artillery; Schaffer's Battery A; Independent Company Engineers.

Colored Troops.

3d, 6th, 8th, 22d, 24th, 25th, 32d, 41st, 43d, 45th, 127th Infantry; colored troops. These regiments were raised as a part of the United States Army and were not credited to the State of Pennsylvania.

ONE-YEAR SERVICE.

192d, 198th, 199th, 203d, 213th, 214th, 215th Infantry, and Keystone Ind. Battery.

NINE MONTHS' SERVICE.

154th and 179th Infantry.

SIX MONTHS' SERVICE, 1863.

20th Cavalry; First Battalion Infantry; Third Battalion Infantry; Woodward's Ind. Battery.

MILITIA EMERGENCY SERVICE, 1862.

7th (not mustered), 8th, 9th, 20th, 21st, 25th Regiments; Battalion (National Guards); Ind. Battalion Baldwin Light Infantry; Haine's Ind. Company Infantry; Wilson's Ind. Company Infantry; Robertson's Ind. Battery; Miller's Ind. Battery; Landis' Ind. Battery.

MILITIA, NINETY DAYS' SERVICE, 1863.

32d, 40th, 44th, 45th, 49th, 51st, 52d, 54th, 55th, 56th, 57th, 58th, 59th, 60th Infantry; Rich's Ind. Company Infantry; Frishmuth's Ind. Battery; Fitzki's Ind. Battery; Hasting's Ind. Battery; Dana Troop, Cavalry.

MILITIA EMERGENCY SERVICE, 1863.

20th, 31st, 33d Infantry; Mann's Ind. Company Infantry; Spear's Ind. Company Infantry; Campbell's Ind. Company Infantry; Landis Ind. Battery; Miller's Ind. Battery; First Troop Philadelphia City Cavalry.

ONE HUNDRED DAYS' SERVICE, 1864-1865.

196th, 197th Infantry; Keystone Battery; Stroud's Ind. Railroad Troop; Southard's Ind. Company Infantry (colored troops).

5

CONTENTS

6

7

7

PAGE

ILLUSTRATIONS

8

ALEXANDER HENRY, WAR MAYOR OF PHILADELPHIA.
From a painting by J. Henry Brown, 1859.

THE SHADOW OF ARMED CONFLICT
Ante Bellum Conditions in Philadelphia

I N the disturbed period preceding the actual outbreak of the Rebellion, Philadelphia, situated but a few miles above the latitude of the old divisional line of Mason and Dixon, was far from being locally united upon the problems of the time. Although this city, by reason of its Revolutionary shrines and traditions, is the very Mecca of the American patriot, there were important political and commercial reasons why she should hesitate to become actively arrayed against the South and its institutions. Twenty-three years before the commencement of civil war an uncontrollable riot, representing, in a degree, the sentiment of a large proportion of the people, had destroyed the new Pennsylvania Hall, "devoted to the rights of man," and driven from the city the little group of anti-slavery enthusiasts there assembled. New England looked upon Philadelphia as a southern rather than a northern community.

From early in the century a large percentage of the manufactured goods made here had been shipped, by sea, to every southern port. The completion, in 1838, of the Philadelphia, Wilmington and Baltimore Railroad, having its headquarters at Eleventh and Market Streets, in this city, provided another strong bond uniting Philadelphia to the South. The tonnage rates from this port to all southern points were far below those of New York and Boston. The South, long the most wealthy and luxury-loving section of the country, was Philadelphia's best customer. The extensive jobbing houses arrayed along Market, Chestnut and the river front carried, as a rule, profitable lines of slave-state accounts.

Every Southern belle considered Philadelphia-made boots as a necessity, while Philadelphia household furnishings were to be found in every southern store. Southern side-boards were inevitably provided with Philadelphia ales. This city, in turn, was a great consumer of the products of the South. Lumber and turpentine were especially required by our industries, and our mills were large users of southern cotton.

Prior to the completion of the Pennsylvania (Central) Railroad through to Pittsburgh, New York and New England commanded the Western trade. Philadelphia merchants were, it will be seen, by virtue of location and direct rail and water connection, driven to foster their traffic with the South and the West Indies, and to shrink from whatever circumstance might endanger it.

In the fifties the capital invested in Philadelphia factories exceeded, according to Freedley (the industrial authority of the city), $100,000,000 and our operatives numbered 132,000. We required a market for goods to the value of $145,000,000 annually.

Against this generally close relationship of business with the southern people there stood, almost alone, the conscience of the Society of Friends,

9

which was either passively or ac⁺'vely arrayed, upon moral grounds, against slavery. The main rou⁺e of the once famous "underground railway" led through this city toward the further north and freedom. Bryant, in his History of the United States, records that, in 1850 "Philadelphia was the only place in the country, probably, where any feeling upon the subject (of slavery) asserted itself and that there it was chiefly confined to Friends." The first anti-slavery society in America was organized by Philadelphia Quakers before the Revolutionary War.

In a pamphlet, recently from the pen of Ex-Attorney General William U. Hensel, relating to "The Christiana Riot and Treason Trials of 1851," it is stated that the "Vigilance Committee" of Philadelphia, which included Robert Purves, J. Miller McKim and William Still, had been instrumental, directly or indirectly, in effecting the escape, in the course of a few years, of not fewer than nine thousand slaves. The affair near Christiana, a small hamlet upon the main line of the Pennsylvania Railroad, close to the eastern border of Lancaster County, followed closely upon the enactment of the Fugitive Slave Law of 1850. A Maryland slave-owner named Gorsuch, with his son and several other persons, undertook to reclaim two of his slaves. In the ensuing fight he was killed and his son was wounded. Mr. Gorsuch was acting within the law, but the trials, held in Philadelphia, resulted in the acquittal of the two members of the Society of Friends and the blacks who resisted the Marylanders. Col. Alexander K. McClure, in his "Recollections," dignifies this as "the first battle of the war." It stirred the whole south, and further affected the southern trade of Philadelphia, which was drifting steadily toward New York City.

But all of the milestones along the thorny road of anti-slavery were regarded in Philadelphia, by the masses, with little more than passive interest. The "Underground Railway" was commonly spoken of as somewhat of a mythical joke.*

The New York Tribune of May 1, 1857, stated that "Philadelphia has at least twenty manufactories of textile fabrics where New York has one, and her superiority in the fabrication of metals, though less decided, is still undeniable." The most welcome patrons of our hotels came from the South. There were frequent interchanges of visits between our local military organizations and those of Baltimore, Richmond, Charleston and other southern cities. New Jersey's leading seashore resort, Cape May, was filled, in summer, with slave-holding families. Our medical colleges constantly graduated southern students, and many of the remedial preparations as well as the medical books, then in use all over the South, were made here.

Politically, the Philadelphia vote was almost uniformly of a shade

---

*The body of John Brown was taken through Philadelphia December 4th, 1859. The incident was attended with a pro-slavery demonstration at the railroad station, Broad and Prime Streets.

agreeable to the watchful southern people. Our congressional representatives affiliated, generally, with the southern members when at Washington.

Between 1845 and 1857 the vessels engaged in the coal-carrying trade from Port Richmond largely exceeded in number and capacity the whole foreign tonnage of the city of New York. Much of this traffic was coastwise southward.

In 1858 a list of twenty-five millionaires was compiled in Philadelphia. This was a rich showing for that period, and to such capitalists more business with the South spelled prosperity.* Baldwin locomotives were in use upon every southern railroad. Philadelphia wagons and carriages were common all over the South. Southern printers obtained their type from this city, and here also were made the Bibles and school books for the southern trade.

The spirit of the Mexican War, in which Pennsylvanians fought side by side with southern troops, was an influence, in this city, for the ensuing twenty years or more, in cementing southern affiliations despite the agitation of the anti-slavery group.*

The ascendency of anti-southern ideas in Philadelphia may be said to date from June 17, 1856, when the first Republican Convention assembled in the city.

The Union sentiment engendered by the excitements of the Buchanan-Fremont Presidential campaign remained aglow through the following years. It found expression in a variety of seemingly insignificant ways. But the business interests remained, as a whole, in an attitude of waiting and hoping.

In the closing months of 1860, although orders and remittances were still reaching Philadelphia merchants from their southern customers, there was a considerable falling off of demand from that portion of the country, and an equally evident hesitation upon the part of shippers to seek further trade in that field. Commercial bodies were greatly concerned and many good citizens still believed that Philadelphia's duty was that of an arbitrator between the extremists of both North and South. George William Curtis, of New York, was announced to lecture in the city, upon December 13th, as the representative of anti-slavery elements, but the threats of riot were so loud that Mayor Henry dissuaded him from the attempt. Instead, upon the same date, a monster citizens' meeting was held in Independence Square for the purpose of extending the olive branch to the South through promises of concessions. The resolutions adopted were sent to South Carolina, but evoked no reply.†

---

*In a list of two hundred and fifty-seven names of local citizens who paid Government assessments upon their incomes, thirty-one were taxed for $100,000 or more, thirty-three upon $75,000 or more, thirty-four upon $50,000 or more, and one hundred and fifty-nine for sums less than $50,000.

†At this meeting two hundred and fifty vice-presidents and secretaries, included nearly everybody then prominent in the city. Addresses were made

Another meeting, called by "one hundred and fifty prominent citizens," was assembled to devise measures "to remove all ground of complaint against the northern States and to secure the perpetuity of the Union." This meeting developed bitterness over the resolutions and accomplished nothing.

About the same time the Board of Trade met for a similar purpose with no effective results. Still another gathering, called by leading Democrats, met at National Hall, upon January 16th, to protest against "coercion." One of the speakers, Benjamin Harris Brewster, Esq., said that it was uncertain whether Pennsylvania "would go with the North or with the South or stand by herself." A resolution carried at this meeting claimed "the wrongs of the South as our own." Judge Woodward, afterward Democratic candidate for Governor, expressed the hope that Pennsylvania would also secede.

Among the wealthier families of the city there had always been a considerable infusion of southern blood. Southern men were engaged in business here and their wives and daughters had a conspicuous part in society affairs. *The Sunday Dispatch,* of April 14, 1861, stated that in a single square of Walnut Street, "occupying palatial residences," were twenty-two southern families, also that the commander of the First Division of Pennsylvania Militia owned one of the largest plantations in Louisiana; that the officer in command of Fort Delaware was a southerner. Many of these adopted Philadelphians continued true to the Union cause. Many such families were divided and subjected to great distress.

Upon the day when President Lincoln succeeded to his high office, of the 974 southern officers in the army and navy of the United States, but 172 had resigned. They, too, doubted the coming of the war and were slow to turn their backs on the old flag.*

Following the accession of the new administration there ensued a marked avoidance of mention, in the Philadelphia newspapers, of local military matters, although activity continued, all over the city, in recruiting and drilling. There was still a hope that the southern people, a large proportion of whom were not favorable to separation, might yet advance new propositions. It was thought well to give the President

---

by Mayor Henry, presiding officer; Joseph R. Ingersoll, Theodore Cuyler, and Judge George W. Woodward. The resolutions there adopted recognized the validity of the Fugitive Slave Law, deprecated all denunciations or interference with slavery and generally went to the limit of oratorical conciliation, an attitude which was soon resented by many who had been brought into the matter with the expectation of hearing something more patriotic in flavor.

*With the beginning of hostilities, 322 naval officers of southern birth or affiliations resigned from the national service, they were replaced by volunteer officers. Many southern officers remained loyal and served faithfully in the Union fleets through the war.

Twenty-five of the thirty Major-Generals and forty-two out of ninety Brigadier-Generals in the Confederate army were graduates of West Point Military Academy.

a chance to meet them half way. This policy of silence and waiting continued for several weeks. Meanwhile, Philadelphia merchants were responding to the urgent orders of retail customers in Charleston and other southern points, and were hurrying ship-loads of merchandise down the coast to reach destinations in advance of the date set for the enforcement of the Confederate import duty. Agents of southern bankers were scouring the financial quarters of Philadelphia and New York trying to find a market for Confederate bonds. In at least one Philadelphia factory rifles were being made, during March and the early days of April, for southern soldiers. Very little activity was seen at the Navy Yard. Upon April 6th the total number of workmen engaged there was two hundred and eighty-five. No effort had been made to refit the dismantled frigate St. Lawrence, long moored at the wharf.

The conciliationists, at this time, called themselves "Silver Grays." Their opponents stigmatized them as "dough faces." When the test of courage was applied many a "Silver Gray" went gamely away in the ranks and many of their defamers stayed safely at home.

A report having been spread about that the southern business men intended to repudiate their northern debts, numbers of them forwarded checks, with indignant denials, accompanied with friendly assurances that the South did not want war and her merchants deplored separation.*

Upon the twelfth day of April the Confederates opened fire upon Sumter, and Philadelphia, in common with all sections of the loyal North, awoke from her dream of peace. Upon April 15th the President called upon Pennsylvania for sixteen regiments of volunteers. At this time the number of uniformed militia of Philadelphia aggregated about 4,500 men. Several organizations had already tendered their services. The local regiments and battalions became the nuclei toward which the majority of recruits were drawn. The first of the recruiting posters, later so familiar, was pasted around the city on the 13th, inviting citizens to rally at Military Hall for the formation of a company.

The story of the patriotic support given by the city of Philadelphia to the cause of the Union during the following years of the great war begins here. It was a part of the supreme effort of twenty-two millions of people, living in the free and border States and the Territories, to compel less than six millions, in the slave States, to stay in the Union and submit to its laws. The emancipation of 3,700,000 slaves, which was to come later, was not a question at issue upon the commencement of the struggle. The impending conflict was purely a matter of saving the nation, The war was now on. Upon April 18th the Sixth Massachusetts

---

*However willing the southern merchants may have been to make payment to northern shippers of goods it was soon beyond their power to do so. Under the provisions of a Confederate Statute enacted upon May 21st, 1861, payment was forbidden upon all debts due to northern individuals or corporations. The money thus due was ordered into the Confederate treasury. (American Historical Review, October, 1912.)

regiment arrived and took quarters at the Girard House, which had been closed upon March 1st. At three o'clock, on the morning of the 19th, a body of Philadelphia recruits under General Wm. F. Small started, via Baltimore, for Washington. The Massachusetts regiment, which left at the same time, forced its way through Baltimore and reached Washington, but the attempt of the Philadelphians, without arms or uniforms, to traverse Baltimore resulted in disaster and humiliation. The scattering return of these demoralized volunteers was followed by the destruction of bridges upon the Washington route. This compelled the New York Seventh Regiment and the Eighth Massachusetts Regiment to embark from the foot of Washington Avenue, on April 20th, upon steamers for Annapolis. The honor of being first to reach the national capital was already held by the infantry companies from Allentown, Reading, Pottsville, and Lewistown, which had proceeded from Harrisburg via the Northern Central Railroad. Philadelphia now devoted herself, with characteristic energy and system, to the one great duty of providing the Government with soldiers properly armed and equipped as far and as fast as they were needed. In the course of the war which then began this city was represented in nearly 150 regiments, battalions, independent batteries, cavalry troops and other detached bodies (including emergency troops not called outside of the State), the majority of which were entirely local, and in addition to which were numbers of Philadelphia companies serving in regiments of other States, as well as thousands of sailors, marines and regular army recruits who cannot be accurately enumerated.

The effect of war upon business in Philadelphia in the early months of the struggle was a source of great anxiety among large employers. At the establishment of M. W. Baldwin & Co., where eighty locomotives had been built in the preceding year, matters were nearly at a standstill. Many of the hands were discharged and plans were considered for turning the plant into a factory for shot and shell. Unexpectedly, however, the National Government ordered many engines and the "war railroads" required many more. Between 1861 and '65 Baldwin's turned out 456 locomotives, many of them the heaviest and most powerful ever constructed. At the ship yards, machine shops, textile mills and in factories of many lines, Government contracts soon afforded abundant employment. Our workmen were able to provide heavy and light artillery, swords, rifles, camp equipage, uniforms and blankets in great quantities. This activity continued throughout the period of the war.

PRESIDENT-ELECT ABRAHAM LINCOLN AT PHILADELPHIA

A NIGHT JOURNEY TO WASHINGTON

MANY and widely different accounts of the journey through Baltimore to Washington, undertaken on the night of February 22d, 1861, by the President-elect have been published. The following story has been written after a careful study of the formal statements left by the officials who were participants in the event.

Upon January 30th, 1861, President S. M. Felton, of the Philadelphia, Wilmington and Baltimore Railroad Company, summoned Allan Pinkerton, a well-known detective of Chicago, to Philadelphia, engaging his services to assist in safe-guarding the railroad against threatened injury in Maryland. Mr. Pinkerton placed a number of his men along the line. One of these detectives, Timothy Webster, joined a disloyal company of cavalry at Perryman's, Maryland. It was through this source that Pinkerton learned the details of the proposed murder of Mr. Lincoln while en route through Baltimore. When Mr. Lincoln arrived at Philadelphia, from New York city, upon the evening of February 21st, a messenger summoned Mr. Norman B. Judd, of his party, to a conference with Mr. Pinkerton. Later in the evening the latter was introduced to Mr. Lincoln and told him of the plot. A similar warning was brought by Mr. Frederick Seward from his father in Washington. It was difficult to convince Mr. Lincoln that the danger was real. He insisted upon proceeding, with his entourage, to Harrisburg at once after the ceremony of raising the flag upon Independence Hall early upon the following morning. At the conclusion of the reception at the State Capitol a consultation was held at the hotel, where Mr. Pinkerton urged his story upon Judge David Davis, Capt. John Pope, Col. Ward H. Lamon, John G. Nicolay and David Hunter. There were also present G. C. Franciscus, General Agent of the Pennsylvania Railroad Company, and Henry Sanford, of the Adams Express Company. These officials finally induced Mr. Lincoln and his advisers to abandon the Northern Central Railroad train, scheduled for the journey to Baltimore, and to return to Philadelphia. Governor Curtin called at the hotel in a carriage, ostensibly to carry Mr. Lincoln to his residence. The only member of his traveling party who entered the carriage was Col. Ward H. Lamon. Unobserved, the President-elect boarded a special train which was hurried eastward. The persons with him were Mr. G. C. Franciscus, John Pitcairn, Jr., General Baggage Agent; T. E. Garrett, Col. W. H. Lamon, General Superintendent Enoch Lewis, and Allan Pinkerton. At Harrisburg, two officials of the American Telegraph Company, Messrs. W. P. Westervelt and Captain Burns, with Andrew Wynne, an employe, drove two miles out of the city and grounded the wires of the Northern Central line. No dispatches went out of Harrisburg that night.

Mr. Lincoln's "special" reached West Philadelphia late in the evening, but too soon for close connection with the train for Washington. The closed carriage containing Mr. Lincoln and Col. Lamon, together with Allan Pinkerton and General Superintendent H. F. Kenny, of the P., W. and B. Railroad, the latter on the box with the driver, proceeded slowly down Market Street, up Nineteenth Street to Vine Street, and thence down Seventeenth street to the P., W. and B. Depot. Chairs for the party had been arranged for by "Mrs. Warne," one of Pinkerton's agents. It was represented to the chair car conductor that one of the passengers was an "invalid gentleman" who must be admitted at the rear of the coach, and have a rear chair. The other engaged seats were occupied by Allan Pinkerton and his agents.* Two officials of the Company, Messrs. George Stearns and William Stearns, remained on guard throughout the night. So carefully were the plans consummated that none of the train employes of either road were aware that Mr. Lincoln was aboard. Col. Thomas A. Scott,† waiting anxiously through the night at Harrisburg in company with Col. Alex. K. McClure, was rejoiced to receive, soon after six A. M. upon the 23d, a dispatch from Washington assuring him of the safe arrival of Mr. Lincoln.

THE STATE MILITARY ESTABLISHMENT

THE report of the Adjutant-General of the State of Pennsylvania of January, 1861, estimates the militia of the State (men subject to service) at 350,000, enrolled as follows: Twenty divisions, sixty-seven brigades, three hundred and one companies, of which forty-seven were cavalry, fifty-four artillery, one hundred and twenty-five infantry and seventy-five rifle corps.

The actual organized and uniformed State force aggregated 56,500 and comprised four hundred and seventy-six companies. The arms owned

*This narration has been read and approved by Comrade Wm. B. Spittall, a surviving Pinkerton who was one of the guards upon the car.

Allan Pinkerton was delegated by Gen. McClellan to organize the Secret Service Corps of the Army. He held a commission as "Major E. J. Allen," this being the maiden name of his wife.

†Col. Thomas A. Scott, then Vice President of the Pennsylvania Railroad Company, acted for a time upon the staff of Governor Curtin. On April 27th, 1861, he was appointed, by the Secretary of War, Superintendent of Railways and Telegraphs, his immediate duties being the restoration of transportation between Annapolis and Washington.

PHILADELPHIA ZOUAVES PASSING INDEPENDENCE HALL.

A SOLDIER OF THE FIRST INFANTRY, National Guard of
Pennsylvania
(Gray Reserves), 1861-1911.
(Henry K. Bush Brown, Sculptor.)

by the State, chiefly apportioned from the Federal Government, were 12,080 muskets, many of them flint-locks, 4,706 rifles, 2,809 cavalry swords, 3,147 pistols and 60 six-pound bronze cannon. A large percentage of this material was unfit for service.

This condition accounts for the inability of the State to equip newly-formed bodies of soldiery with weapons for which they were constantly appealing in the winter and spring of 1861.

The inadequacy of the State military establishment in 1861 is evidenced by the Act of the Legislature dated April 12th, providing for the office of adjutant-general, which official was also designated to act as paymaster-general, inspector-general and judge advocate. He was bonded in the sum of $20,000. His salary was $500 per year, with an allowance of $3 per diem for each day "when actually engaged in the service of the State."*

The lessons of unreadiness upon the part of the State, taught by the experiences preceding the invasion of September, 1862, do not appear to have resulted in any legislative measures of improvement.

According to good authority, the State militia law in effect in June, 1863, had been in force since 1822. Under this law, when any portion of the enrolled militia was required for duty, it was the business of the Adjutant-General to notify the brigade inspectors who were to order officers of regiments or companies to divide their commands into ten parts by drawing names from a box. The first tenth was to be first called and the other parts or classes in the order of their numbers, but it was provided that men who had served in the War of 1812 should only be called out as a last resort. Amendments were made in 1849 and 1858 which enrolled all able-bodied men between the ages of 18 and 45 years, with the proviso that those who did not care to identify themselves with the uniformed militia might escape service by paying fifty cents annually.†

The effort to summon, muster and forward emergency militia through the operation of this antique machinery was largely responsible for the friction which now and then occurred between the officials at the State Capital and the military officers of Philadelphia.‡

It is only fair to reflect that Pennsylvania has never been, in times of peace, other than an example of a commonwealth founded upon high principles of humanity and devoted to the development of internal resources. It was the confidence of her strength as expressed in the minds of generations of her law makers, so largely of Quaker influence, that led to the neglect of the State military arm and of the martial spirit dormant within her borders.

---

*Report of Adjutant-General, State of Pennsylvania, 1866.

† Inquirer, June 24th, 1863.

‡The officials of the reorganized Pennsylvania State Military Establishment included Henry H. Smith, Surgeon General; Reuben C. Hale, Q. M. General; Col. William McMichael and Major Craig Biddle, all of Philadelphia.

2

PENNSYLVANIA MILITIA, PHILADELPHIA COMMANDS, 1861

THE Legislature of the State of Pennsylvania enacted a law "for the Regulation of the Militia of this Commonwealth," which was approved by the Governor, April 21st, 1858. Section First reads: "Be it enacted, etc., that in addition to the three Brigades of the First Division of the City of Philadelphia, authorized by the Act to which this is a supplement, there shall be organized within the City of Philadelphia another Brigade to be called the Reserve Brigade, which shall consist of four Regiments of Infantry and one Squadron of Cavalry, for the special defence of the city."

The Philadelphia militia regiments, when thus reinforced, consisted of the following organizations:

First Regiment, First Brigade, First Division, which includes the old National Grays.
Rifle Battalion, First Brigade, First Division.
First Regiment, Pennsylvania Artillery.
Second Regiment, Second Brigade, First Division.
First Regiment, Third Brigade, First Division, Philadelphia Light Guard.
First Regiment, Third Brigade, First Division.

The new Reserve Brigade, Brig.-Gen. Patterson, was composed of:

First Regiment, Gray Reserves, Col. P. C. Ellmaker.
Second Regiment, Blue Reserves, Col. Alfred Day.
Third Regiment, Gray Reserves, Col. C. M. Eakin.

*The Scott Legion, Washington Grays, and First Troop Philadelphia City Cavalry, were independent organizations.

THE RESERVE BRIGADE INFANTRY, PENNSYLVANIA MILITIA.

While the active members of the Artillery Corps Washington Grays, were preparing to accompany Col. Francis E. Patterson's new regiment into the field, a number of the retired and contributing members of this historic corps met, pursuant to a newspaper notice, upon April 17th, 1861, to consider the formation of a "Reserve Guard" "for the protection of the city and support of the Constitution and laws of the United States of America." At a second meeting, held two evenings later at Sansom Street Hall, an organization was completed which was, by resolution, entitled "The First Regiment Infantry, Gray Reserves, of the City of Philadelphia." Peter C. Ellmaker was elected colonel and was commissioned by the Governor of the State on April 21st.*

---

*The *North American and United States Gazette* printed, April 22d, 1861, a list of six hundred and fifty-eight names of citizens who had enrolled in this regiment, which included those of a large number of men then prominent in the official, business and professional life of the city. This list has been preserved upon the pages of the History of the 1st Regiment, of which Major-Gen. James W. Latta is the author.

As a part of the organized militia force of the State this regiment was known as the "3d." By Act of Assembly dated May 3d, 1861, and enforced by the Adjutant-General on September 7th, 1861, Col. Ellmaker's command was designated the "1st Regiment Infantry, Reserve Brigade."

Col. Ellmaker's regiment was quickly uniformed, and, in June, was armed, by special order of Hon. Simon Cameron, Secretary of War, with smooth-bore percussion muskets from the United States Arsenal at Frankford. Drills, occasional parades and escort duty provided plenty of work for the command throughout the year. Changes of personnel among the officers and men, due to a desire for volunteer service, were constant. Under the call for emergency militia the 1st Regiment served in 1862 as the "7th Regiment, Infantry Militia," this tour of duty covering two weeks. In 1863 the "Gray Reserves" were enlisted for the Gettysburg campaign into the national service as the "32d Regiment, Pennsylvania Ninety-day Militia." This command was on duty forty-two days. The 118th (Corn Exchange) Regiment, and the 119th, in the three years' service were both largely composed of both officers and rank and file of men connected with the "Gray Reserves."*

The old National Guards' organization, an effective and popular regiment, ready for any service required of it, was known in the Reserve brigade as the First Blue Reserves.†

The 3d Regiment, Reserve Brigade, commanded by Col. Constant M. Eakin, served as the 25th Regiment, under the emergency call of September, 1862, as guards at Camp Brandywine, Delaware, for the protection of the Dupont Powder works.

The 4th Regiment, known as the "Second Blue Reserves," was identified, under Col. Alfred Day, as the 8th Regiment in the Emergency force of September, 1862, and as the 33d Regiment, Col. William W. Taylor, in the Emergency Campaign of July, 1863.

---

*The militia of the State of Pennsylvania was re-organized by Act of Assembly dated April 7th, 1870, and by a supplement to the Act of 1864, as the "National Guard of the State of Pennsylvania," and thereafter the regimental commands were numbered serially. The 1st Regiment, Gray Reserves, retained its original number.

†"Historic Militia Commands of the City."

HISTORIC MILITIA COMMANDS OF THE CITY

FROM these well-trained bodies of State and independent soldiery hundreds of officers, many of whom gained high rank, were supplied to the volunteer regiments of Pennsylvania and of other States.

THE FIRST TROOP, PHILADELPHIA CITY CAVALRY

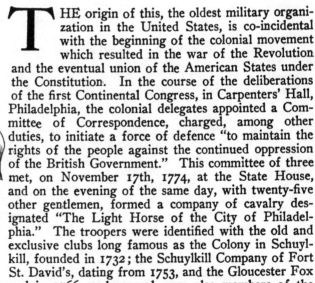

THE origin of this, the oldest military organization in the United States, is co-incidental with the beginning of the colonial movement which resulted in the war of the Revolution and the eventual union of the American States under the Constitution. In the course of the deliberations of the first Continental Congress, in Carpenters' Hall, Philadelphia, the colonial delegates appointed a Committee of Correspondence, charged, among other duties, to initiate a force of defence "to maintain the rights of the people against the continued oppression of the British Government." This committee of three met, on November 17th, 1774, at the State House, and on the evening of the same day, with twenty-five other gentlemen, formed a company of cavalry designated "The Light Horse of the City of Philadelphia." The troopers were identified with the old and exclusive clubs long famous as the Colony in Schuylkill, founded in 1732; the Schuylkill Company of Fort St. David's, dating from 1753, and the Gloucester Fox Hunting Club, formed in 1766, and several were also members of the Friendly Sons of St. Patrick and the Scottish St. Andrew's Society, which dates from 1749.

The Troop was the first to carry a flag bearing thirteen stripes. In the course of the Revolutionary War the Troop and detachments of its members performed many notable services in the patriotic cause. The command was also in the field in the course of our second war with Great Britain. The present title and the existing uniform were adopted in 1833.

Between the years 1793 and 1865 the Troop furnished to the Pennsylvania Militia (National Guard) eleven major-generals and thirteen brigadier-generals.

In the course of the Civil War seventy-three members of the Troop became officers in the Union armies. Eight of them were killed or died in the service.*

The Troop tendered its services to the Government upon each occasion of emergency, and was in the field in the summer of 1861, and again during the Gettysburg campaign, two years later. The command occupied its first armory, on Twenty-first street above Chestnut street, in 1874, and its present armory in 1901. The Troop is now identified with the Pennsylvania National Guard; but whether clad in khaki of the field and camp or the picturesque dress uniform familiar in our local military parades, its members continue to maintain the honorable traditions of readiness and self-sacrifice for which the command has ever been distinguished.

ARTILLERY CORPS WASHINGTON GRAYS

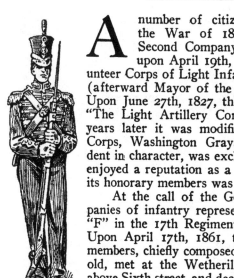

A number of citizens who had served, during the War of 1812, in Captain John Swift's Second Company of Washington Guards, met upon April 19th, 1822, and organized the "Volunteer Corps of Light Infantry," of which Captain Swift (afterward Mayor of the city) was elected commander. Upon June 27th, 1827, the title was changed to that of "The Light Artillery Corps Washington Grays." Six years later it was modified to that of "The Artillery Corps, Washington Grays." This command, independent in character, was exclusive in its *personnel* and long enjoyed a reputation as a "crack" organization. Among its honorary members was the Marquis de Lafayette.

At the call of the Government, in 1861, two companies of infantry represented the "Grays" as "A" and "F" in the 17th Regiment in the three months' service. Upon April 17th, 1861, the honorary and contributing members, chiefly composed of those over forty-five years old, met at the Wetherill House, upon Sansom street above Sixth street, and decided to form a "Reserve Corps" (see The Reserve Brigade, Infantry). At a second meeting, held upon the 19th, at Sansom Street Hall, an organi-

*The officers who perished while in the service were Gen. David B. Birney, Col. William Sergeant, 210th Infantry; Major Charles F. Taggart, 2d Cavalry; Major Robert Morris, Jr., 6th Cavalry; Capt. Henry J. Biddle, A. A. G.; Brevet Lieut.-Col. J. Penrose Ash, 5th U. S. Cavalry, and Lieut. J. Hamilton Kuhn, 27th Infantry.

zation was perfected which became the "First Regiment Infantry, Gray Reserves, Reserve Brigade of the City of Philadelphia." Every commissioned officer, with one exception, had been at some time a member of the Artillery Corps, Washington Grays.

The old command of the "Grays" continued to maintain its distinctive organization. From this well-drilled body, in 1862, Company "A" of the 21st Regiment Emergency Militia was recruited, and in 1863 the "Grays" furnished Company "A" and part of "B" to the 49th Regiment, Ninety Day Militia.

In the course of the Civil War the "Grays" were represented by members in the volunteer troops of seven other States, the District of Columbia, the Regular Army, Marine Corps, and the Navy. From a total of four hundred and forty-two members of the "Gray's" Battalion who volunteered, one hundred and eighty-one received commissions. Among these officers three became Major-Generals, nine Brigadier-Generals, eleven Colonels, fifteen Lieut.-Colonels, twenty Majors, sixty-one Captains and sixty-two Lieutenants. Twelve of these officers were killed or died while in the service.

In February, 1878, the corps was increased to a battalion of four companies. In 1879 the battalion lost its independent status as a military body, being then merged with the Weccacoe Legion and designated the "Third Regiment, National Guard of Pennsylvania." Subsequently, through the intervention of the veteran members, the active contingent was transferred, as Company "G," to the First Regiment. National Guard of Pennsylvania.

A fund having been provided, of which $2,000.00 was presented by Col. Edwin N. Benson, for the erection of a monument to the members who participated in the Civil War, it was dedicated at Broad Street and Girard Avenue upon April 19th, 1872. It was subsequently adorned with the figure of a soldier in the uniform of the corps at a cost to the Old Guard of about $5,000, and placed in Washington Square.

"GRAYS" WHO ENTERED THE REGULAR SERVICE.

Blake, George Alexander H...Brig.-Gen., U. S. Cavalry.
Blanchard, William...........1st Lieut., 2d U. S. Cavalry.
Burnett, Robert Lyon........Major, U. S. Army.
Brown, James M.............1st Lieut., 111th U. S. Colored Infantry.
Engle, Archibald Hill........Major, 13th U. S. Infantry.
Fagan, Louis Estell..........Captain, U. S. Marine Corps.
Harris, Enon M.............1st Lieut., 8th U. S. Colored Infantry.
Hough, Alfred Lacey.........Colonel, 9th U. S. Infantry.
Kneass, Charles L............Brevt.-Major, U. S. Army.
Pollock, William K...........2d Lieut., 1st U. S. Artillery.
Randolph, Wallace Fitz.......Major-Gen., U. S. Army.
Wallace, George W..........Lieut.-Col., 12th U. S. Infantry.
White, John Chester.........Major, U. S. Army.

THE NATIONAL GUARDS

THE National Guards Regiment of Philadelphia originated in a single company formed in 1840 under Capt. Thomas Tustin, who was succeeded in 1844 by Capt. Stephen B. Kingston. In 1846 Capt. Peter Lyle became commanding officer and recruited the company for the Mexican War, but its services were not required.

In 1856 the organization was incorporated as the "Infantry Corps, National Guards of Philadelphia." The armory built by the command, located on Race street, below Sixth street, was opened on November 16th, 1857. The "National Guards" first paraded as a regiment on December 11th, 1860.

As a part of the Reserve Brigade Militia the regiment was known as the "First Blue Reserves."

The regiment tendered its services to the Government on April 16th, 1861, and was mustered in on April 27th, for three months, as the 19th Regiment Volunteers. Following this term of service the 2d Regiment, National Guards, became the basis of the 90th Regiment Volunteers under Col. Peter Lyle. A large proportion of the three-year regiments originating in Philadelphia contained field and company officers who had been schooled in the National Guards.

Under command of Major Jeremiah W. Fritz the regiment was in the field, in September, 1862, during the Antietam Campaign.

In addition to its services as the 90th Regiment, the National Guards were active in organizing, and furnished officers for Baxter's Philadelphia Fire Zouaves (72d Regiment), the 196th and 213th Infantry, the 52d (2d Union League 90-Day Regiment, 1863), and other bodies of troops sent into the field.

The Old Guard of the Regiment, composed of veterans and retired members, has long maintained a distinctive organization.

LANDIS' BATTERY

ON April 19th, 1861, at a meeting held in the office of Chapman Biddle, Esq., it was determined to revive an old company of artillery dating from 1844 as the basis of a new organization, which became Company A, 1st Regiment, Pennsylvania Artillery, and of which Chapman Biddle was elected captain. This command included in its membership many of the best known and most affluent citizens of that period. Captain Biddle and Lieut. Alexander Biddle resigned in August to recruit the 121st Regiment of Infantry. Henry D. Landis, who had also been active in old Company I, was elected captain.

In addition to repeated service in periods of emergency, Company A (Landis' Battery) furnished from its membership many officers who were identified with the regular and volunteer service, among them Captain Frank H. Furness of the 6th Cavalry (Rush's Lancers); Captain T. C. Williams of the regular army; Captain James M. Lennard, Jr.; Dr. S. Weir Mitchell of the Medical Corps, U. S. Army Hospitals at Philadelphia; Major Harry C. Egbert of the regular army; Col. John M. Gries, 104th Infantry; Major A. G. Rosengarten, 15th Cavalry; Captain William Elliot Furness; Surgeon William F. Norris; Captain Charles Chauncey, 2d Cavalry; Joseph B. Blakiston, 15th Cavalry; Captain Charles E. Cadwalader, 6th Cavalry (Rush's Lancers), and Gen. Isaac J. Wistar.

Some other distinguished Philadelphians who were attached to this command and served in emergency periods were C. Stuart Patterson,* John G. Johnson, Judge Robert N. Willson, Judge F. Amedee Bregy, Charles Morgan, Charles G. Leland, W. G. Leland, A. A. Outerbridge, Edward W. Patton, C. Redwood Wright, Francis I. Maule, Clement Biddle, William H. Rawle, Samuel C. Perkins, Woodruff Jones, Edward C. Bullard, Thomas Hart, Jr., William D. Winsor, William S. Stewart, Richard S. Willing, Duffield Ashmead, Alexander Johnstone, Alfred C. Lambdin, Joseph Meehan, John B. Thayer, James D. Young, Rodman Wister, Thomas M. Newbold and Edward Pennington, Jr.

THE SCOTT LEGION

OF the Philadelphia militia companies which volunteered for service in the war with Mexico the City Guards, Monroe Guards, Light Guards, Cadwalader Grays, and Jefferson Guards were organized as the First Regiment. After the return of the survivors they formed the "Scott Legion," and this veteran body not only supplied many well-drilled officers to the Union forces, but became the nucleus of the 68th Regiment Infantry Volunteers, one of the most notable of Pennsylvania's fighting commands of the three-year enlistment.

*Dr. Charles K. Mills relates in a recent narration of his experiences as an infantryman at the shelling of Carlisle by the Confederates, that he saw Mr. Patterson, of the battery, wounded in the sword hand.

FRANKFORD ARSENAL, Bridesburg, Philadelphia.
1. Main Entrance.   2. Old Store Building.
3. Commandant's Residence.
(From war time photographs.)

SCENES AT THE SCHUYLKILL ARSENAL. 1862.
(The white horse is "Old Bill," Gen. Meade's war horse.)
From photographs in possession of Mr. Richard P. Barr.

THE STATE FENCIBLES*

THIS infantry corps dates from the martial period of our second war with Great Britain. It was organized in June, 1813, and served in the field during a portion of the following year under Capt. Clement Biddle as part of the advance Light Brigade. Lieut. Hartman Kuhn was elected captain in 1815, being soon afterward succeeded by John C. McCall. Two years later James Page became captain, remaining in this rank nearly fifty years, in the course of which the command enjoyed a national reputation as a "crack" drill corps.

When the Civil War impended, a second company of Fencibles was recruited, the two serving as Companies E and K, of the 18th Regiment of the three months' enlistment. Subsequent to this tour of duty the majority of the officers and men entered the three years' service, principally in the 72d and 82d Regiments. The reorganized Fencibles responded to the emergency call of 1862, serving in Col. Alfred Day's 8th Regiment, and again, in the Gettysburg campaign, the command volunteered, being attached to Col. W. W. Taylor's 33d Emergency Regiment. In the course of the war the Fencibles furnished to the army two hundred and five of its active and retired members, a large proportion of them holding commissions. After the war ended, the old military spirit was dormant, but in 1871, with the election of John Ryan to the captaincy, the State Fencibles entered upon a new and brilliant career. The command was increased to a battalion of four companies in 1877, and, under Major Ryan, attained the highest proficiency in precision of drill. Major Ryan died in 1886. Subsequent commanders have been Majors Wesley Chew, William A. Witherup, Thurber T. Brazer (to June, 1913), and Thomas S. Lanard. Incident to the Spanish-American War the State Fencibles formed a battalion of the 6th Regiment, N. G. P., but later withdrew from the National Guard, and is now an independent body, sustained by the city. A feature of the Centennial parade of the battalion in May, 1913, was the presence of the "old guard," under Major Emanuel Furth, costumed in uniforms of the type worn by the command a century ago.

---

*The list of organizing members, as they are given in the newly published history of the corps ("One Hundred Years with the State Fencibles," Lanard), includes representatives of a large proportion of the leading Philadelphia families of the time. The first public mention of the organization appeared in the American Daily Advertiser, July 9th, 1813.

THE UNITED STATES ARSENALS AT PHILADELPHIA

U PON April 3d, 1861, Capt. Josiah Gorgas, the commandant at the depot of military materials at Bridesburg (Frankford Arsenal), Philadelphia, who was a native of Pennsylvania, had resigned in order to cast his fortunes with the South, and had been succeeded by a loyal officer.*

This important establishment, generally called "The Frankford Arsenal," had been a part of the Government property in this city forty-five years. The reservation covered fifty-nine acres upon the shore of the Delaware River. The principal structures were the usual barracks, two large Arsenal buildings, two store-houses, a hospital, powder magazine and work-shops. At the opening of the war the materials on hand were supposed to include about 18,000 muskets, a great amount of saltpetre and sulphur, 50,000 pounds of powder, percussion caps, primers, cartridges and general military stores, of which horse equipments were the most important. These supplies were being sent away by the new commandant to "the front" as rapidly as possible, and space was being cleared for an augmented force of work-people to be employed in the preparation of ammunition.

A brief paragraph appeared in a Philadelphia newspaper upon January 30th, 1861, stating that, upon the preceding day twenty car-loads of rifles had been shipped from the Frankford Arsenal "to Washington." A few weeks earlier an attempt to ship munitions of war from the United States Arsenal at Pittsburgh to southern points had created a riot and the order was countermanded. It may well be doubted if that consignment of rifles from the Frankford Arsenal ever reached the national capital.†

In April, Gen. William F. Small, searching for arms for his "Washington Brigade," applied (after receipt of urgent telegrams from Washington) to the commandant of the Frankford Arsenal, and the latter

---

*Captain Gorgas was a Pennsylvanian, appointed cadet from New York. He went South, where he attained, in the Confederate service, the rank of brigadier-general and chief of ordnance.

†On November 1st, 1859, there were stored at the Frankford arsenal, as set forth in an official report of that date, 19,404 muskets. In the course of the year 1860 the traitorous Secretary of War, John B. Floyd, had caused to be sent from Springfield, Watervliet and other Northern arsenals to those of the South, or had sold to the Governors of the Southern States at $2.50 each, muskets and rifles to the number of 119,000. With his connivance, experts, some employed from abroad by the agents of the South, were openely allowed the use of models and drawings of weapons, field guns and machinery at the Northern arsenals, and were instructed in the making of shells and fuses at the Government armories. This continued to the date of Floyd's resignation at the end of the year. One of his last official acts was to telegraph to the commandant of the arsenal at Baton Rogue to deliver 5,000 guns to the Governor of Louisiana.

replied that he had no authority to issue anything to troops not mustered, and, in any event, could only provide fifteen hundred guns, a large proportion being of doubtful value. When, in May, strenuous efforts were being made to equip and forward the 18th, 19th, 22d and 23d (three months) Regiments, the officers of those long-suffering troops protested, with one accord, against the useless, antiquated and misfit muskets offered to them from this Arsenal.

The United States Arsenal, located upon Gray's Ferry Road, between Carpenter street and Washington avenue, and commonly called "The Schuylkill Arsenal," was established in the year 1800.* Adjoining it upon the north is the United States Naval Hospital and Naval Home. The Arsenal was, throughout the Civil War, an important depot for uniforms, blankets and equipments for the outfitting of the armies of the Republic. In addition to the large regular force employed in the several workshops and warehouses a great number of persons, chiefly from families of soldiers and sailors in the service or who had died under enlistment, were kept employed in thousands of the humble homes in this section of the city. The operations here were so constantly urgent that warehouses outside were leased by the Government. One of these "branch Arsenals" was the building adjoining the Custom House, upon the west, afterward replaced by the Post Office. Other storehouses for military clothing and equipment were created at William Gault's brew-house at Twenty-first and Spruce streets, at the old hotel building Twenty-fourth and Chestnut streets (built in 1833) and at Murphy & Allison's machine shop on the Schuylkill river north of Market street. In the "emergency" summers of 1862 and 1863 a company of the employees was recruited to assist in defending the State. At one period of the war the increase of the "contract system" in making uniforms threatened the employment of several thousand women. A committee of their number visited Washington and secured an order from President Lincoln ensuring a continuance of their means of support.

THE WASHINGTON BRIGADE, 1861

AMONG men of military experience engaged, early in 1861, in the formation of tentative bodies of volunteers in the City of Philadelphia were Col. William F. Small and Col. Charles Angeroth. Col. Small's battalion was known as the "Washington Guards." These organizations had headquarters at Military Hall, upon

---

*The official name of this Arsenal was changed in 1873, by order of the Government, to "Philadelphia Depot of the Quartermaster's Department, U. S. Army."

Third street, below Green street, and it was there, on January 19th, that the two commands resolved to unite as the "Washington Brigade," and elected Col. Small commander. The "First Regiment" was composed chiefly of recruits of American birth. The "Second Regiment" (Angeroth's) was strongly German in composition.

On January 28th, 1861, Gen. Small had offered to President Buchanan the services of eight hundred men for garrison duty, in order to relieve an equal number of regular troops for more urgent work in the South. On February 4th the "Washington Guards" organization was offered to Governor Curtin for any emergency service required. This tender was acknowledged, by order of the Governor, on March 2d, 1861.*

When the attack on Fort Sumter stirred the North to action, Gen. Small renewed his offer of assistance, and on April 15th received a dispatch from the Hon. Simon Cameron, Secretary of War, promising "acceptance if in Washington this week." This was followed by a dispatch from the War Department stating that arms and equipments would be furnished at Washington. On April 16th, Major George P. M'Lean, of the First Regiment, Washington Brigade, telegraphed from Washington, "The Governor (Curtin) expects your command here at once." Urgent messages were also received from Hon. Eli Slifer, Secretary of the Commonwealth, dated from Harrisburg the same day.

Under date of April 17th, Mr. Dickinson, Aide-de-Camp to Governor Curtin, forwarded to him a list of officers for the brigade, which had been prepared by General Small, for whom commissions were desired. Without waiting for these commissions, Gen. Small arranged with President Samuel M. Felton, of the Philadelphia, Wilmington and Baltimore Railroad Company, to entrain the brigade at Philadelphia, at midnight on the 18th, and to pass through Baltimore at daybreak. On the evening of April 18th, Gen. Small assembled his men at Jones' Hotel, on Chestnut street, above Sixth street. At the appointed time seven companies of the 1st Regiment and five companies of the 2d Regiment marched to Broad and Prime Streets Depot, from which they departed at 3 A. M. April 19th. A second train, carrying the 6th Massachussets Regiment, which had barracked the previous evening at the Girard House, closely followed. Before reaching Baltimore the train of the 6th Massachusetts troops, who were uniformed and armed, was given precedence. The Washington Brigade reached the Baltimore Station at noon upon the 19th, only to be surrounded by a dense mob, frenzied by the street battle incident to the march through the city of the Massachussets soldiers earlier in the day. The attack of the infuriated secessionists upon Gen. Small's unarmed men, who were

---

*Andrew Gregg Curtin, War Governor of Pennsylvania, was born at Bellefonte. Pa., April 28th, 1817. He became Minister to Russia in the Grant Administration in 1869.

without protecting escort, resulted in injury to many, the dispersal of others into the country, and the return of the balance, after long delay, by train, to Philadelphia. One of the recruits, George Leisenring, was repeatedly stabbed, as he sat in a car, and died four days later at the Pennsylvania Hospital, the first volunteer of Philadelphia who perished in this war for his country.*

Those of the Philadelphians who did not succeed in regaining the comparative safety of the cars were either temporarily concealed by friendly residents or made, in squads, for the open country. Some of these hapless fugitives experienced considerable hardship and indignity, but all eventually reached friendly territory east of the Susquehanna. Smarting beneath a certain amount of underserved ridicule the majority of the men sought enlistment in other regiments then forming.

Gen. Small was criticised severely in many quarters for his rash attempt to take his men through Baltimore without the means of defending themselves, but the records show that had the railroad company fulfilled its understanding regarding the hour of arrival there, he would probably have led his men into Washington and have been acclaimed a hero. The result of this mischance was the disbandment of the Washington Brigade. Gen. Small persisted, however, in his patriotic efforts, and, making his headquarters at the Montgomery Hotel, at Sixth and Willow streets, finally had the satisfaction of being mustered into the National service as Colonel of the 26th Penna. Infantry on May 25th, 1861. The mustering date was, however, moved back to May 5th, and this command became the first of the three years' regiments of the State of Pennsylvania. The Second Regiment of the Washington Brigade became the 27th Regiment Penna. Light Artillery under Col. Max Einstein, and was mustered for three years' service upon May 31st, 1861. The Washington Brigade appears in the official list of volunteer organizations in the National service, in 1861, as published by the War Department in 1885, and the 26th Regiment was permitted to inscribe upon its battle-flag the legend, "Baltimore, April 19th, 1861."

Nearly a year after the Baltimore incident the General Assembly of Maryland voted the sum of $7,000.00 to be distributed to the families of the three men killed and of the seventeen men wounded upon that date in the Sixth Massachusetts Regiment, but no indemnity or apology was ever offered by Maryland for the indignity placed by Baltimore upon the men of the Washington Brigade, or the murder of one of its members.

---

*Records of the Pennsylvania Hospital show that George Leisenring, aged 26 years, single man, born in Germany, was brought to the hospital April 19th, 1861, suffering from penetrating wound of thorax, and died on the 22d. This volunteer was a private in Company C, Captain Henry Ungerer, 2d Regiment Washington Brigade. No information regarding location of the grave in which he rests has been found after search among the city records.

THE CLOSED GATE AT BALTIMORE

A PRIL 18th, 1861, the Secretary of War, Hon. Simon Cameron, telegraphed to Governor Thomas H. Hicks, of Maryland, notifying him that the Government had reason to believe that Northern troops passing through Baltimore would be interfered with. Upon the same date Bvt.-Lieut.-General Winfield Scott informed Major Clark, Quartermaster, U. S. A., stationed at Baltimore, that two or three Massachusetts and one New York regiment would pass through that city "within two or three days." Meanwhile, the Baltimore and Ohio Railroad Company had refused to transport troops being forwarded by Ohio. Transportation was also refused to the 7th Regiment, of New York, and other volunteer organizations.

Like Philadelphia, Baltimore had assumed, in the winter of 1860-61, the role of mediator between the discordant sections North and South. In the preceding October a reform Mayor and City Council had been elected by a large majority. It was the "departing dynasty," according to J. Thomas Scharf, the historian of Baltimore, that led to the trouble that followed. Late in October, at the ceremonies incident to the opening of Druid Hill Park, several thousand children sang the "Star Spangled Banner," accompanied by the band of the "Blues."* This sentiment of love for the national song in the city where the words were first given to the nation was rudely shaken, however, by the election of Abraham Lincoln, of whose character and intentions the newspapers of the city reported nothing but evil.

The first of the rioting in Baltimore, in April, 1861, was that of a crowd angered by the display of a Confederate flag upon a vessel in the harbor. Four days later a mob captured a Confederate flag and a cannon on Federal Hill. The flag was destroyed and the cannon thrown into the harbor. But upon the same day another mob followed five companies of Pennsylvania Militia (the "First Defenders") across the city with jeers and insults.

Baltimore, as far as the excitable elements were concerned, was in a chaotic frame of mind. The city was persuaded, through its newspapers, that the State was "being invaded." The logical consequence was the mobbing of the 6th Massachussets Regiment upon April 19th, and the repulse of Gen. Small's helpless and ununiformed Philadelphians.

Whatever of loyalty to the Union then remained in Baltimore was dormant. It was only after the occupation of the city by Federal regiments (which included Col. Morehead's Philadelphia Light Guard and

---

*Among the citizens of Baltimore afterward arrested by the Union troops garrisoned in the city and placed, as a prisoner of war, in Fort McHenry, was Francis Key Howard, Esq., the grandson of the author of the "Star Spangled Banner." Mr. Howard was also detained nearly a year at Fort Lafayette and Fort Warren.

Col. Lyle's National Guards) and the arrest or flight of the secession leaders that the loyal people dared to come forth. *A committee of these citizens then published an address, in their effort to set the city right in the eyes of the North, which was distributed to all passing regiments. It was as follows:

"Soldiers, we welcome you to this city as men who are willing to defend the best Government on earth in the hour of its greatest need. We do not view you as barbarians whose only idea is hatred of the southern people, whose only intentions are to commit shameful crimes in violation of all law, as is charged upon you by the leaders of the Rebellion. We believe you to be actuated by a noble and honest patriotism, desiring only to preserve unimpaired the National Union. With this understanding, we wish you success and ask God's blessing upon your bodies and souls during your perilous marches. May we again behold this nation united and prosperous under one government and one flag."—The Loyal Citizens of Baltimore.

ORGANIZATION AND WORK OF THE "MILITARY DEPART-MENT OF PENNSYLVANIA

MAJOR-GEN. Robert Patterson was appointed on April 19th, 1861, to the command of the "Military Department of Washington," which included not only the District of Columbia, but also Maryland and Pennsylvania. A few days later this Department was limited to Pennsylvania, Delaware and a part of Maryland, and officially designated "The Department of Pennsylvania."

Major-Gen. Patterson, in his capacity of department commander, telegraphed under date of April 19th to Lieut.-Gen. Scott for authority to requisition arms and clothing from the Government Arsenals in Philadelphia. In response he was ordered to send 5,000 muskets to arm the regiments near Harrisburg. On April 19th Gen. Patterson telegraphed to Gen. Scott, saying "The law of necessity over-rides all laws. We must have arms, ammunition, clothing and equipments. Gen. Cadwalader is decided, as I am, that our men shall not be made inmates of hospitals for want of comfortable garments which the Government has at our doors and which may be taken by others." Still there was no equipment forthcoming.

President J. Edgar Thomson, of the Pennsylvania Railroad Company, wrote to Secretary of War, Simon Cameron, on April 23d, that "the people of Philadelphia are mortified that the Bostonians have got nearly a week ahead of them, and that few troops are ready." Four days later Simon Cameron wired Mr. Thomson as follows: " I am really gratified to hear from you that our military friends in Philadelphia have opened their eyes to the existing state of affairs in the country. * * * * All of my orders and wishes of the past week have been neglected."

Lieut.-Gen. Scott telegraphed to Gen. Patterson to send no troops deficient in equipment. Still the doors of the Arsenals remained locked. Gen. Patterson busied himself in establishing camps of instruction for his unarmed regiments at York, Chambersburg, Lancaster, Harrisburg and Philadelphia. In reporting these arrangements he added, "The impoverished condition of the Quartermaster's Department here in regard to tents, canteens and other camp and garrison equipment will prevent the execution at an early day of any plan of operations."

The Secretary of War sent an order to Gen. Patterson on May 5th as follows: "Send immediately six regiments of Pennsylvania volunteers to this city (Washington) via York, Pa."

Of the sixteen regiments being fitted for service in this State at that time but one had tents, and much of the ammunition did not calibre with the guns.

About this time Baltimore, having been roundly anathematized by the entire North, sent out word that the northern soldiers might go through their streets, but they would like to have some regular troops pass through first. In partial concession to this request, when the fine "1st Artillery" Regiment, armed as infantry, under the command of Col. Francis I. Patterson, left for the South on the morning of May 9th, the command was accompanied by a battalion of regular infantry (three companies) and a battery of regular artillery. Thus, three weeks after the passage through of the 6th Massachusetts Regiment, Philadelphia had a regiment in the field.

Every effort was now being made to outfit the 18th, 19th, 22d and 23d Regiments. When the muskets, so long awaited, were finally delivered to these commands, their respective Colonels, W. D. Lewis, Jr., Peter Lyle, Turner G. Morehead and Charles P. Dare, made a protest, stating that a large proportion of the guns were worthless, having broken locks, rusted barrels and misfit bayonets. Major Porter, A. A. G., wrote that "the guns are horrible, and if a collision should arise the responsibility is fearful. The officers will not take it."

With regard to the issue of these defective fire-arms to our patient and patriotic regiments of the three-months' service, the Department Commander, exasperated from his experiences and depressed by his heavy task, wrote on May 9th to his Assistant Adjutant General: "It appears that the regiments here are now entirely neglected by the State authorities, who are sending everything to the regiments in the interior."

Gen. Benjamin F. Butler, with the 6th Massachusetts and 8th New York Regiments and Cook's Battery, occupied Federal Hill, Baltimore, on the night of May 12th. Two days later the 18th, 19th and 22d Regiments left Philadelphia, in command of Gen. Cadwalader, for that city.

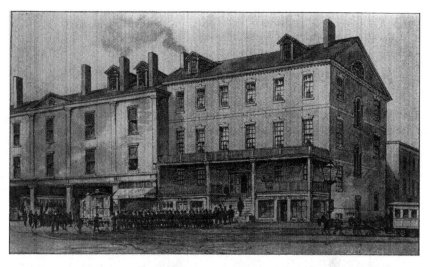

STATION OF THE PENNSYLVANIA R. R., ELEVENTH AND MARKET STREETS.

GIRARD HOUSE, 1861. Used as a barracks and factory for military clothing.

STATION OF THE PHILADELPHIA, WILMINGTON AND BALTIMORE R. R., Broad Street and Washington Avenue, 1861.

THE THREE MONTHS' VOLUNTEERS, 1861

THE traditions of the Pennsylvania militia are interwoven with those of the American Revolution and of subsequent wars in which the nation has been engaged. The various subordinate commands in the State have always been the nuclei of companies and regiments which have instantly responded to the call of the Commonwealth and the nation, and it was logical that the "three months' regiments" of the State, recruited under the first call of President Lincoln, should have been largely composed of these Keystone guardsmen. It will ever stand to the glory of Pennsylvania that five companies of her militia were the "First Defenders" of the City of Washington and the guardians of the Capitol building and archives in April, 1861.

That these "minute men" were all from interior cities does not detract from the spirit of military ardor and activity then pervading Philadelphia. All of the then existent State militia commands in this city were included in the volunteer regiments from Philadelphia, which served under the three months' call in 1861, and these organizations included many of the best, most patriotic soldiers which this State provided. A large proportion of the officers of the "three years'" regiments, formed later, had a part in the "three months'" campaign, and the majority of the rank and file, upon discharge, promptly re-enlisted for the long service that the war exacted from the "three years'" soldiers. The Pennsylvania militia organization was the school of the Pennsylvania volunteers.

In the confusion of the time, due to the necessity of protecting the rail route leading directly from Harrisburg to Washington, the process of mustering and forwarding to exposed points in Maryland the hastily-formed regiments at Camp Curtin, Harrisburg, had the earliest attention of the Government mustering officers. Thus it happened that the first of the waiting regiments at Philadelphia to become soldiers of the nation was numbered the 17th, although it was actually inducted into the volunteer army before some of the Camp Curtin regiments to whom lower numerical designations were given.

Pennsylvania regiments raised under later call by the Government were sent forward singly and brigaded from Washington. The three months' troops of the Keystone State formed a complete army of twenty-five regiments of infantry and a small force of cavalry, officered

3

by the Governor of the State. This force numbered 20,979 officers and men.

The services performed by the Philadelphia volunteers of the three months' campaign were most important, as they had an active part in guarding the routes leading southward and in keeping Maryland within loyal territory pending the formation of an army of the North under the call for "three years or the war." They also enabled the veteran Major-General Robert Patterson to enter Northern Virginia and thus prevent a strong Confederate advance upon Washington at that time. The task of the regiments along the upper Potomac river, under Gen. Patterson, in the early summer of 1861, was not battle, but a show of force.* Fifteen months prior to the event of Fort Sumter, ex-President Franklin Pierce had written to Jefferson Davis: "I have never believed that the actual disruption of the Union can come without blood, and if through the madness of Northern abolitionism, that dire calamity must come, the fighting will not be along Mason and Dixon's line merely. It will be within our own borders, in our own streets."† Although one great battle and eight minor engagements were fought upon the soil of Pennsylvania, and thirty battles and skirmishes occurred in Maryland, the "three months'" campaign, under the direction of Major-General Robert Patterson, determined that the chief theatre of the drama of war should be in the heart of old Virginia.

Jefferson Davis, in an address made at Stevenson, Alabama, in February, 1861, said: "Your border States will gladly come into the Southern Confederacy within sixty days, as we will be their only friends. * * * * * The grass will grow in the Northern cities where the pavements have been worn off by the tread of commerce. We will carry war where it is easy to advance—where food for the sword and torch awaits our armies in the densely populated cities, and though they may come and spoil our crops, we can raise them as before, while they cannot rear the cities which took years of industry and millions of money to build."‡

The best answer to this deliverance ever made was the salvation of Maryland by the soldiers of Pennsylvania under Patterson, with the approval and aid of the loyal citizens of that "border State."

Truly, the months of weary and nearly bloodless marches and countermarches of the Pennsylvania brigades through Maryland and Northern Virginia in 1861 were not in vain.

---

*Major-Gen. Patterson, then a prominent manufacturer of Philadelphia, was born in the county of Tyrone, Ireland, in the year 1792. He came to America while yet a boy. He served as a volunteer in the War of 1812-14, with the rank of captain. In the Mexican War he held a commission of major-general. As a result of his three-months' campaign and due to contradictory orders from Washington he was unjustly treated by the military authorities in 1861. He was afterward exonerated. His death occurred on August 7th, 1881.

†McPherson's History of the Rebellion.

‡The American Conflict, Greeley.

PHILADELPHIA COMMANDS OF THE THREE MONTHS' SERVICE, 1861*

THE eight regiments, one cavalry troop, one artillery company and one independent company furnished by Philadelphia under the first call by the President, dated April 15th, 1861, to serve three months, were as follows:

SEVENTEENTH REGIMENT INFANTRY.

COLONEL FRANCIS E. PATTERSON.

The First Regiment of Artillery was mustered upon April 25th, 1861. This organization included the Washington Grays, Philadelphia Grays, Cadwalader Grays, National Artillery, West Philadelphia Grays, Independent Grays, and State Guards. Col. Patterson had been, twenty years previously, a member of the Washington Blues of Philadelphia, organized by his father, Gen. Robert Patterson. After a brief business career in New Orleans he had joined the Texas Rangers, became a Lieutenant in Magruder's Regular Battery, of the First Artillery, U. S. A. Later he had held the rank of captain in the 9th Regiment Infantry (regulars), on duty in Oregon, finally accepting his present command, which, leaving Philadelphia via Baltimore, upon May 10th, 1861, was the first Philadelphia regiment to reach Washington. Upon May 15th the regiment was designated, by Governor Curtin, "The 17th Regiment, Penna. Volunteer Infantry." This regiment was, at first, quartered in the Capitol building, but later performed guard duty along the upper Potomac river, as a part of Gen. Patterson's column operating in that section. Companies B and C of the regiment were engaged in a skirmish at Edward's Ferry, Va., upon June 17th. Mustered out upon August 2d, 1861.

EIGHTEENTH REGIMENT INFANTRY.

COLONEL WILLIAM D. LEWIS, JR.

The old First Regiment Infantry Militia was mustered upon April 24th, 1861. This regiment included the State Fencibles, Washington

---

*General and Brigade Commanders of Patterson's Army, three months' troops, 1861, were Major-Gen. Robert Patterson, Major-Gen. W. H. Keim, Brig.-Gen. George Cadwalader, Brig.-Gen. James S. Negley, Brig.-Gen. E. C. Williams, Brig.-Gen. George C. Wynkoop.

Blues, Minute Men of '76, National Grays, Garde Lafayette and Zouaves. The officers whose State commissions dated from 1858 were continued in their respective ranks. Upon May 14th this command proceeded to Fort McHenry and upon May 22d entered Baltimore, then under military control of Major-General Benjamin F. Butler, and was here engaged in provost duty. Two companies were dispatched to the National Arsenal at Pikesville, from which they removed the Government property to Fort McHenry. The regiment continued in service ten days beyond the period of enlistment, and was mustered out at Philadelphia upon August 7th, 1861.

NINETEENTH REGIMENT INFANTRY.

COLONEL PETER LYLE.

The Second Regiment Infantry Militia, nine companies, mustered April 27th, 1861. Part of this regiment was already on duty at Perryville, guarding the railroad and the Susquehanna river bridge. The regiment, which had been increased from a militia battalion in 1860, was ordered to Fort McHenry and Baltimore upon May 10th, where it remained during and for some days beyond the term of service, engaged in the maintenance of loyalty and good order. Mustered out at Philadelphia August 29th, 1861.

TWENTIETH REGIMENT INFANTRY.

COLONEL WILLIAM A. GRAY.

The Scott Legion (an independent organization) was mustered April 30th, 1861. This regiment was barracked in the building adjoining the Custom House upon the west. The men were clad in the uniforms of the pattern worn by many members in the War with Mexico. Later, after a considerable stay at Suffolk Park, the regiment was sent to Major-Gen. Robert Patterson's command, with which it remained until mustered out July 20th, 1861.

TWENTY-FIRST REGIMENT INFANTRY.

COLONEL JOHN F. BALLIER.

"The German Rifle Regiment" mustered April 29th, 1861. Included were the Lafayette, Sarsfield, Washington, Philadelphia and Jackson Rifle Companies. From the 20th to the 29th of May the regiment was engaged in drill and target practice at Suffolk Park. It then joined Major-General Robert Patterson's command operating upon the upper Potomac river, and was mustered out August 8th, 1861. A majority of the enlisted men and officers subsequently became identified with the several distinctively German regiments raised for the three-year service in Philadelphia and New York City.

Twenty-second Regiment Infantry.

Colonel Turner G. Morehead.

This regiment was formed from the First Infantry Militia, Philadelphia Light Guard, and was mustered April 24th, 1861. Upon the day of the surrender of Fort Sumter, April 14th, this command had been accepted by Governor Curtin, and, with headquarters at the State Arsenal, had filled its ten companies at the date of muster. Logan Square was used as a drill ground. In company with the 18th and 19th Regiments the command departed May 14th, by rail, for Fort McHenry and Baltimore, where it remained to date of muster out, August 7th, 1861.

Twenty-third Regiment Infantry.

Colonel Charles P. Dare.

This command was originally the Artillery Battalion, Third Brigade, First Division, Pennsylvania Militia. It was mustered as infantry upon April 21st, 1861, and immediately sent to Perryville, Havre de Grace and other points near the lower Susquehanna river. It had been preceded to this section by Col. Dare, temporarily assigned to command of the 4th Regiment, from Montgomery County, who also took with him Company A, of the 23d (Continental Guards). This was, therefore, the first fully equipped Philadelphia company to leave for the scene of the war.* At Perryville, Col. Dare was placed in command of the post, which included regulars, volunteers, and a fleet of gunboats and transports. Relieved, upon May 11th, by the 11th Pennsylvania Regiment, the 23d Regiment proceeded to Chambersburg, Pa., and there joined the force of General Patterson, being engaged in the several movements of that campaign. The "23d" formed part of a force of Union troops composed of regulars and volunteers which met the Confederates at the action of Falling Waters, West Virginia, upon July 2d, 1861, and shares with the First Troop, Philadelphia City Cavalry, also present, the honor of participating in the first battle of the Civil War which was fought south of the Potomac river, in which Pennsylvania troops were engaged.† The regiment was mustered out upon July 31st, 1861. The "23d" was the first properly enlisted regiment of Philadelphia troops in the field. When the regiment re-enlisted in the "three years'" service it was allowed to retain its original number in the Pennsylvania line. Under the synonym, "Birney's Zouaves," the reorganized regiment was uniformed as zouaves, but when this showy costume was worn out it adopted the regulation blue of the infantry.

---

*Bates' History, Vol. I, page 40.
†Dyer's Compendium, page 1578.

Twenty-fourth Regiment Infantry.
Colonel Joshua T. Owen.

The "24th" was recruited from the old 2d Regiment of the Second Brigade. It was composed largely of men of Irish birth or descent. Being well advanced in its formation, it was accepted and mustered upon May 1st, 1861.

The command included the Irish Volunteers, Hibernia Greens, Emmett Guard, Meagher Guard, Jackson Guard, Shields Guard, Patterson Light Guards and United Guards. Company H was raised in Wilmington, Delaware.

Early in June this command arrived at Chambersburg, Pa., and participated in the several movements of Major-General Robert Patterson's troops, ending at Harper's Ferry. At the urgent request of the General in command the 24th Regiment remained on duty two weeks beyond its term of service, being mustered out August 15th, at Philadelphia.

The Commonwealth Artillery Company.
Captain James E. Montgomery.

This company was raised in Philadelphia and mustered upon April 24th, 1861, to serve three months. The command was promptly sent to reinforce the small garrison of regulars at Fort Delaware. At the end of its tour of duty the battery was mustered out upon August 5th, 1861.*

The First Troop Philadelphia City Cavalry.
Captain Thomas C. James.

Thirty officers and men of this Troop having been mustered into the United States service upon May 13th, 1861, at Point Breeze, Philadelphia, four weeks after its tender to the Governor of the State, reported at Carlisle, Pa. Upon May 30th, the Troop was attached to the Second Regular Cavalry, Col. George H. Thomas. The Troop had been provided at Philadelphia with regulation cavalry uniforms. Moving thence to Shippensburg and Chambersburg, the cavalry encamped at the latter point. On June 7th the command, with other troops, arrived at Greencastle, Pa., and then advanced to Williamsport, Maryland, upon the upper Potomac river. The division, under Gen. Cadwalader, here crossed the river into West Virginia. At Falling Waters, upon July 2d, the Troop was engaged with the enemy, thus winning the distinction of being the first body of Pennsylvania cavalry under fire during the Civil War. The Union column re-crossed the Potomac upon July 2d. Skirmishing upon the way to Martinsburg, Charlestown was reached upon the 17th. Here the objective point was changed to Harper's

*This command is not included in "Bates'" list, but is recorded by "Dyer" (pages 216 and 217).

Ferry, where the column arrived upon July 21st. While in the field the Troop was reinforced by forty-one recruits. The Troop was afterward stationed at Sandy Hook, Maryland, from which camp it returned to Philadelphia, and was mustered out upon August 17th.

Residence of Major-Gen. Robert Patterson, Southwest corner Thirteenth and Locust Streets

McMullin's Rangers.

This company was organized chiefly from the membership of the Moyamensing Hose Company, on May 20th, 1861, and served with Gen. Patterson's force in the three months' campaign. The McMullin Rangers are credited, together with the 23d Regiment, with participation in the action at Bunker Hill, W. Va., July 15th, 1861. (Dyer, page 970.)

The number of officers and men from Philadelphia in the three months' service of 1861 was about 5,700.

THE PHILADELPHIA HOME GUARD

BY authority of an Act of Assembly adopted upon May 16th, 1861, the Mayor and Councils of Philadelphia decided to form a Home Guard Brigade, not to exceed ten thousand men, to be composed of five regiments of the line, one regiment of light infantry, one regiment of riflemen, one regiment of cavalry and two regiments of artillery. These troops were intended to be distinct from the State Militia and to be subject to the orders of the city authorities. Membership in this organization did not exempt citizens from liability of draft. Philadelphia was empowered to collect a special tax to uniform and equip the Home Guard.

Brig.-Gen. A. J. Pleasonton was appointed in command. In November, 1861, the use of the market house, at Broad and Race streets, was given to the Home Guard as an armory. Many independent companies were absorbed into this organization. On February 22d, 1862, the Home Guard paraded the following troops:

First Regiment Infantry..........................Col. John M. Bickell.
Second Regiment Infantry........................Col. Charles P. Dare.
Third Regiment Infantry.........................Major William B. Thomas.
First Battalion, First Regiment Rifles..............Major Harry Pressner.
First Battalion, Second Regiment Rifles...........Major Charles E. Graeff.
Company B, First Regiment Artillery.............Capt. Matthew Hastings.
Company C, First Regiment Artillery..............Capt. Mark G. Biddle.
Company D, First Regiment Artillery..............Capt. E. Spencer Miller.
First Troop, City Home Guard....................Capt. John Bavington.
Washington Light Cavalry........................Capt. J. W. Hall.

In an official report to the Mayor, Brig.-Gen. Pleasonton stated that he had in line, upon that occasion, 2,096 men, all well armed and provided with uniforms, including overcoats. He reported as absent 2,162 men. At a later period the brigade commander claimed that the "Home Guard" had supplied to the army 3,000 infantry and a battery of artillery. A number of officers who afterward became distinguished in the volunteers graduated from this force, and it is probable that the most valuable results gained from this local attempt to maintain a municipal military body is to be found in the foregoing fact. During the Confederate invasion of the State, in September, 1862, nineteen companies of the Home Guard were sent to the Cumberland Valley and elsewhere.

ARMORY OF THE NATIONAL GUARDS REGIMENT,
Race Street below Sixth Street.

1. CITY ARSENAL, Race Street below Broad Street.
2. LADNER'S MILITARY HALL, Third Street below Green Street.

MAY AND JUNE, 1861. A SURPLUS OF ENLISTMENTS

IN the latter days of May a rush of enlistments, beyond all requirements, possessed the youth of the city.* New companies were constantly projected, each having its distinctive name and enthusiastic enrollment. The streets, public squares and suburban tracts were alive with drilling squads of recruits. The Philadelphia newspapers clamored at the injustice of the Government in allowing the State of New York to send fifty-two regiments into the field while accepting from Pennsylvania but twenty-six regiments. Hundreds of men, impatient of the uncertainty of local enlistment, went individually to New York City and there entered the National service. The agents of other States opened recruiting offices in Philadelphia. The regular army, marine corps and navy absorbed much of the best material.†

Many of the tentative companies, advertised in hand-bills and through the daily papers, were afterward merged, and others of the surplus finally became identified with the "Home Guards," the first company of which, the "City Grays," was enrolled at the Philadelphia Bank Building on May 25th, 1861.

The names of many colonels and lesser officers much in evidence in the newspapers of that period were conspicuously absent from the roster of the field and staff of the regimental organizations. The fighting colonels who were to lead many a regiment through historic campaigns were often, in the beginning, modest officers of the line or men in the ranks.

When a company had found its place and letter in a regiment, its recruiting title was generally forgotten, but every old soldier, who first handled musket or sabre in one of those ambitious formative organizations, has always held a sentimental interest in the original names by which they were known.

SEPARATE COMPANIES FORMING IN PHILADELPHIA IN 1861.

Spring Garden Minie Rifles, joined 71st Regiment.
Franklin Guards, joined 71st Regiment.
Pennsylvania Guards, joined 71st Regiment.
Marion Guards, joined 29th Regiment.
2d Company West Philadelphia Grays, joined 29th Regiment.

---

*Probably the most notable instance of enlistments from a single Philadelphia family was that of the seven Neilson brothers, six of whom served in the army and one in the navy. Of this group two are now living, one of the survivors being Gavin Neilson, Assistant Clerk of Common Council, who lost an arm at Spotsylvania.

†The first of the military funerals of which Philadelphia was destined to see so many was that of Lieut. John Trout Greble, U. S. A., a young officer of artillery, killed on June 10th, 1861, at Big Bethel, Va. The military burial, on June 14th, impressed the public greatly with the sad realities of war.

United Rifles, joined 29th Regiment.
Belmont Guards, joined 29th Regiment.
Koska Guards, joined 29th Regiment.
Wayne Artillery Corps, joined 29th Regiment.
Federal Guards, joined 29th Regiment.
Henry Clay Fencibles, joined 29th Regiment.
Morgan Artillery, joined 29th Regiment.
Dougherty Guards, joined 29th Regiment.
Lincoln Cavalry (3 companies), joined 1st New York Cavalry.
State Fencibles, 3d Company, joined 82d Regiment.
Read Guards, joined 4th Pennsylvania Reserves.
Able Guards, joined 4th Pennsylvania Reserves.
Dickson Guards, joined 4th Pennsylvania Reserves.
Quaker City Guards, joined 4th Pennsylvania Reserves.
Harmer Guards, joined 4th Pennsylvania Reserves.
Wayne Guards, joined 12th Pennsylvania Reserves.
Duncan Guards, joined 8th Pennsylvania Reserves.
City Guards (Schuylkill Arsenal Employees).
Wetherill Blues, joined 82d Regiment.
Penn Rifles, joined 2d Reserves.
Governor's Rangers, joined 2d Reserves.
Hibernia Target Company, joined 2d Reserves.
Governor's Rangers, 2d Company, joined 2d Reserves.
Governor's Rangers, 3d Company, joined 2d Reserves.
Taggart Guards, joined 2d Reserves.
Independent Rangers, joined 2d Reserves.
Constitution Guards, joined 2d Reserves.
Consolidation Guards, joined 2d Reserves.
Scotch Rifles, joined, 2d Reserves.
Germantown Guards, joined 3d Reserves.
Ontario Infantry, joined 3d Reserves.
De Silver Grays, joined 3d Reserves.
Philadelphia Guards, joined 7th Reserves.
Ridgeway Guards, joined 7th Reserves.
Douglas Guards, joined 7th Reserves.
Philadelphia Merchant Troop joined 3d Cavalry.
Curtin Hussars became 12th Cavalry Regiment.
Washington Troop joined 14th Cavalry.
Garde Lafayette joined 82d Regiment.
Gymnast Zouaves joined 23d Regiment.

Other companies then being recruited in different sections of the City were the Washington Rifle Reserve Guard, Minute Guards (from Jefferson Grammar School), Atalanta Guards, Henry Guards (city police), Kirkwood Rangers, Wissahickon Rifles, Brownell Zouaves, Light Infantry Corps (U. of P.), Commonwealth Light Infantry, Quaker City Artillery (1st and 2d companies), National Guard Cadets, Pennsylvania Cadets, Garde Lafayette Cadets, Boys' Own Infantry, United States Zouaves, Washington Zouaves, Philadelphia Cadets, Hamilton Rifles, Jayne Rifles, Bustleton Home Guard, Ellsworth Zouave Cadets, Penn Treaty Home Guard, Girard Home Guard, Ironside Guards, Union Artillery Guard, Municipal Guard, Buena Vista Rangers, Maennerchor Rifles, Blucher's Home Guards, Freeman's Rifle Corps, Gas Works Company.*

---

*As an example to the employees of the City Gas Works, the Board of Trustees took the Oath of Loyalty to the United States Government. It was subsequently administered to all of the workmen, who were represented, in August, 1862, by one hundred and eighteen men in the army, in addition to which two companies were afterward formed which joined Roberts' Artillery.

THE MILITARY DISTRICT OF PHILADELPHIA

The Military District of Philadelphia was commanded in the course of the war by the following officers:

Brig.-Gen. William R. Montgomery.
Brig.-Gen. O. S. Terry.
Major-Gen. N. J. T. Dana.
Lieut.-Col. William D. Whipple, U. S. A., and
Major-Gen. George Cadwalader.

The latter officer succeeded Major-Gen. Darius N. Couch in June, 1865, as commander of the Department of Pennsylvania and established his headquarters at Philadelphia. Later he was succeeded by Major-Gen. A. A. Humphreys. The provost headquarters in the city was stationed, under Capt. John Orr Finnie, at the old Pennsylvania Bank building on Second street near Dock. The site is now covered by the U. S. bonded warehouse.

The United States provost marshals for the several districts comprising the City of Philadelphia were:

1st District, Captain William E. Lehman.
2d District, Captain Edwin Palmer.
3d District, Captain Jacob S. Stretch.
4th District, Captain D. M. Lane.
5th District, Captain Mahlon Yardley.

In January, 1864, the provost guard at Philadelphia consisted of about two hundred and fifty men, detached from numerous regiments and under command of Lieut.-Col. H. A. Frink, with headquarters at Fifth and Buttonwood streets.

A provost company of eighty men, under Capt. Finnie, was stationed at this time at Fort Mifflin.

The District of Philadelphia was an important command. The provost marshal held supervision of the thousands of convalescent soldiers then in the local military hospitals, returning them to their respective regiments when again fit for further service. He provided hospital supplies and issued vouchers for the payment of soldiers in hospitals or on special duty. Good order among the multitude of soldiers always thronging the streets required his constant attention. His force was increased in the spring of 1864 to a full regiment, the 186th Infantry. The Military District of Philadelphia was discontinued in August, 1865.

43

WAR SERVICE OF THE RAILROADS

I N 1861, Philadelphia's rail connection with the South consisted of the Philadelphia, Wilmington and Baltimore, the Pennsylvania, the Northern Central and the Cumberland Valley Railroads.* The importance of the first and second, from a military standpoint, was recognized long before the outbreak of the war. The third and fourth became, in the course of the struggle, "bones of contention" between the Union and the Confederate forces upon many occasions. Although the burden of responsibility was heavy and constant, the officers of these corporations worked nobly to assist the National Government throughout the war. This patriotic attitude of the railroad officials had already been shown in the safe conduct of President-elect Lincoln to Washington upon the night of February 22d, 1861.

Realizing that the resentment of the disloyal element south of the Susquehanna River, because of this feat, would probably result in damage to the company's property, President Samuel M. Felton, of the Philadelphia, Wilmington and Baltimore Railroad, organized a select force of about two hundred men to guard the bridges, and act, if necessary, as a military body. A train was kept in readiness to concentrate them at any time, and in order to allay suspicion, they were put at work white-washing the bridges, some of which were given, it is said, six or seven coats, a very good protection against fire. Immediately following the transportation of the 6th Massachusetts Regiment and of the unarmed Philadelphians under Gen. Small into Baltimore, with the attendant rioting, the Mayor and Police Commissioners of that city ordered the destruction of the bridges. The work was entrusted to a force in charge of Isaac R. Trimble, formerly a superintendent of the railroad company. As a result, upon April 20th, the Harris Creek bridge at Baltimore, and the Bush River bridge were burned. The draw of the long Gunpowder River bridge was burned six days later. All telegraph wires leading from Baltimore were cut. It required twenty-four days of hard work to repair the damage, and in the meantime troops and supplies were carried from Perryville and Havre de Grace upon the large transport steamer *Maryland,* the Philadelphia ice boat and other vessels, to

---

*The Pennsylvania Central Railroad occupied the building upon the south side of Market street east of Eleventh street in 1852, when the Philadelphia, Wilmington and Baltimore Railroad Company vacated it upon completion of its new terminal building at Broad and Prime streets. It was here that the "Pennsylvania" was organized and it was, for a dozen years or more, its main point of arrival and departure, the cars being hauled to and from West Philadelphia by mules. The hotel on the site of the present New Bingham House was built in 1812 by Gen. Thomas Leiper, and was then quite out of town. In the Civil War period it was still called the "New Mansion House." It was conducted at that time by James London, and was practically an annex to the railroad "depot."

44

Annapolis, Md. With the occupation of Baltimore by an effective Federal force under Gen. B. F. Butler, and the arrest of the pro-southern leaders, the latent Union sentiment of the city again manifested itself. The only further damage to the P., W. and B. line was done in July, 1864, by a raiding party from Gen. Jubal Early's force, known as Gilmour's guerillas, which partially burned the Gunpowder River bridge and a few cars. The P., W. and B. was destined to become, in the following years, the greatest military highway in history.

Mr. Thomas A. Scott was granted leave of absence from the Pennsylvania Railroad in 1861, in order to serve the Government as Assistant Secretary of War. He was, at this time, thirty-seven years old, and endowed with great energy as well as experience. It was his task to facilitate the movement of troops by rail and to establish telegraphic service in the field. At his instance the first military telegraph station in America was opened in the office of Governor Curtin at Harrisburg, April 17th, 1861, by William Bender Wilson, who later became manager of military telegraphs at Washington.

Mr. Scott was given a commission, by President Lincoln, as Colonel of the District of Columbia Volunteers. Among the young men he summoned to Washington to aid him was Frank Thomson, who was not yet twenty years old, but who was well versed in the line of work assigned to him. Under the orders of Col. Scott he organized the Military Telegraphic Corps, the first auxiliary of its kind in the world, from among the dispatchers of the Pennsylvania Railroad. It was the duty of this corps to maintain the important lines used by the armies in the field in servicable condition.*

The Northern Central Railroad, in which the Pennsylvania Railroad Company soon afterward acquired a controlling interest, was operated as a separate corporation under President James Donald Cameron. Joseph N. Du Barry, superintendent of this line, Col. O. N. Lull, of the Cumberland Valley Railroad, and other officials co-operated with General Superintendent Enoch Lewis and Division Superintendent Samuel D. Young, of the Pennsylvania System, in maintaining a mounted patrol along the southern border of the State as a safeguard against raids. The members of this patrol made constant use of a line of telegraph extending from Chambersburg to Bedford, keeping the railroad officials at Harrisburg and through them the War Department, fully informed of predatory movements by the enemy. It was due to the energy of the Northern Central officials that the five companies of Pennsylvania militia, known in history as the "First Defenders" were promptly and safely conveyed to Washington when President Lincoln summoned troops for the defense of the National Capitol.

*In May, 1861, Major Fitz-John Porter, A. A. G., Department of Pennsylvania, acting under orders, had prepared to burn the bridges of the Baltimore and Ohio Railway and of the Philadelphia, Wilmington and Baltimore Railroad, if necessary, to impede any general advance of the Confederates northward.

Until the opening of the Civil War the railroad had never been a factor in army campaigns. The alternate destruction and rebuilding of tracks in the disputed territory in the earlier part of the war made it imperative to employ experts familiar with work of that character. In April, 1862, the Secretary of War called to Washington Mr. Herman Haupt, of Philadelphia, an engineering graduate of West Point, who had previously occupied the position of the Pennsylvania Railroad's first general superintendent, and was, at the time, engaged upon important work in Massachusetts. He was appointed Chief of Construction and Transportation, with the rank of Colonel. In recognition of invaluable services rendered the Government, Col. Haupt was promoted to the rank of Brigadier-General in September, 1862. Gen. Haupt and his subordinates performed heroic service in many times of need and danger.

Prominent among the railroad men who served in this branch of the army were W. W. Wright, of the Pennsylvania Railroad staff, who became Gen. Sherman's Chief of Construction upon the campaign through Georgia and the Carolinas; General Adna Anderson and E. C. Smeed formerly of the Catawissa Railroad. It was with the co-operation of such practical engineers that, under the active personal supervision of Col. Thomas A. Scott, Col. D. C. McCallum, successor to Gen. Haupt, was able to transport General Hooker's force of twenty-two thousand men with all of their impedimenta from Catlett's Station, Va., to Georgia and Tennessee, over a distance of nearly twelve hundred miles in eight days.

William J. Palmer, private secretary in 1861 to President John Edgar Thompson of the Pennsylvania Railroad Company, resigned to take command of the famous "Anderson Troop" of cavalry, and in 1862 recruited and took command of the 160th Regiment, better known as the 15th Pennsylvania Cavalry, which he continued to lead to the end of the war.

The list of officers of the line and field in the Federal armies who thus left the service of the railroads for that of their country was large and their achievements brilliant. One of the most distinguished instances was that of President George Brinton McClellan, of the Ohio and Mississippi Railroad Company, a former captain of the regular army.*

The patriotic attitude of the Philadelphia railroad officials is illustrated in a circular issued to all employees by the Philadelphia and Reading Railroad Company, proposing to them to devote one day's pay in each month to the purchase of Government bonds, the interest to be re-invested until the close of the war. This was very generally done.

---

*Capt. McClellan was a native of Philadelphia. He was attached to the Corps of Engineers, having graduated at West Point in 1846. He had resigned from the army in 1857. He was a son of Dr. George McClellan of Philadelphia. He was born at the southwest corner of Seventh Street (then Columbia Avenue) and Walnut Street, December 3d, 1826.

The Railroad Companies voted large sums of money to the relief of soldiers' families.* The Philadelphia and Reading Railroad Company performed valuable service throughout the war by the rapid transportation of troops and actively providing coal at its tide-water terminals for naval use. And while considerable rioting among the foreign miners in the coal regions, in resistance to drafts, required the presence of troops, that section of the State sent some splendid regiments to the front.†

Through at least a portion of the war period the official envelopes of the Pennsylvania Railroad bore the then popular device of cannon and flags. The subscriptions made at various times by the "Pennsylvania" for the help of the Sanitary Fair and the military hospitals amounted to $220,000, and for homes for orphans of deceased soldiers and sailors, $50,000.

---

*In later years a large proportion of the men who occupied important and responsible positions with the railroad companies centering at Philadelphia were returned veterans of the armies of the Union cause.

†In the summer of 1864 the wide-spread spirit of disloyalty, existing in the Pennsylvania coal regions, manifested by strikes and riots, induced the Government to take military control of the Philadelphia and Reading Railroad in order to secure the necessary supply of coal for naval purposes.

In September, 1863, troops stationed at Pottsville were the 10th N. Y. Infantry, 1st N. Y. Artillery and the Invalid Corps.

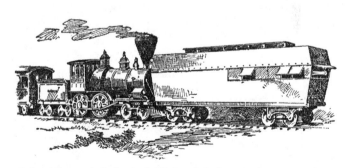

Railroad Battery built for the P. W. & B. R. R. Company by Baldwin & Co.

THE THREE YEARS REGIMENTS

IN the course of an address delivered at Orchard Knob, Tennessee, upon November 13th, 1897, Comrade John Tweedale, late of the Fifteenth Cavalry, Pennsylvania Volunteers, said: "It does not come to each generation to be privileged to offer life that a Nation may live. In our time the opportunity came and we accepted it." In the highest sense, the "three year" men of the Union Armies "accepted" their duty. There were among them recruits lured by large bounties, unwilling men who had been conscripted, some who had no higher motive than adventure, but the greater part were actuated by the purest spirit of patriotism, for which they willingly gave up education, business opportunity, trade and security, to face unknown dangers, death, disease and Southern prison pens. These men were paid, from month to month, and when the paymasters closed their accounts, at the end of the war, the Government owed them nothing in agreed-upon dollars and cents. What was this pay? The average monthly pay of the commissioned officers in an infantry regiment, not including commutations for rations, servants and forage, was $58.75 per month, or $1.82 per diem.

The pay of a captain of infantry, including allowances, when computed on a gold basis, which represented in 1864 its true purchasing power, was less than $60 per month, out of which he subsisted himself, bought clothing, equipments and paid his servant.

The enlisted men really received a little more than $8 per month.* It has been estimated that from depreciated money alone the three-year soldiers lost $250,000,000.

Three years away from the ordinary avocations of life was a handicap for the returned soldier, which many found a losing factor in his resumption of a civilian life. The "three year" soldiers did not figure out the cost—they "accepted" an opportunity to fight for the salvation of country and flag.†

---

*Army and Navy Journal, November 19, 1864, page 196.

†Seventy-two per cent. of all enlistments were for the term of three years.
The average strength of the Union armies, volunteers and regulars, during the war, was 809,777. This figure does not include the militia serving as State troops. The maximum strength of the land forces (not including militia) did not reach 1,000,000 men until May 1st, 1865, and the highest number reached was 1,000,516. ("The Soldier in the Civil War," Frank Leslie Reprints.)

TWENTY-THIRD REGIMENT INFANTRY
(Birney Zouaves)

COLONEL DAVID B. BIRNEY to February 17th, 1862.
COLONEL THOMAS H. NEILL to December 13th, 1862.
COLONEL JOHN ELY to December 6th, 1863.
COLONEL JOHN F. GLENN to September 8th, 1864.
Total Enrollment, 1,589 Officers and Men.*

THIS regiment was organized under the first call for troops, on April 21st, 1861, under command of Col. Charles P. Dare, being the first regiment that left Philadelphia fully armed and equipped. It was mustered out on July 31st and re-enlisted August 2d under command of Col. David B. Birney.†

Breaking camp at the Falls of Schuylkill, the regiment left in September for Washington. Soon afterward the regiment was recruited to fifteen companies, of which twelve were from Philadelphia and one each from Pittsburg, Wilkes-Barre and Columbia. Col. Birney was promoted February 17th, 1862, as brigadier-general, and Capt. Thomas H. Neill, of the 5th U. S. Infantry, became colonel of the regiment. At this time four of the companies were detached to the 61st Pennsylvania Infantry and a fifth was absorbed into the remaining ten companies. The "23d" first met the enemy at Warwick Creek, Williamsburg and Bottom's Bridge, losing a few men wounded. At Fair Oaks, Seven Pines and in the final movements of the Peninsular campaign the regiment saw heavy fighting with much loss, being engaged at White Oak Swamp, Charles City Cross Roads and Malvern Hill. The "23d" was next sent to the Bull Run Campaign, via Alexandria, Va., participating in the battle of Chantilly. In September it was part of an independent brigade under Col. Thomas H. Neill, detached to guard the fords of the upper Potomac,

---

*When Philadelphia companies are specified in headings the total enrollments apply to them only, in other cases the entire regimental enrollments are given.

†Col. Dare died soon after the return of his regiment. Col. Birney was advanced to the rank of brigadier-general on February 17th, 1862. He died while in command of the Tenth Army Corps on October 18th, 1864.

Gen. David B. Birney died at the Eagle Hotel on the West Chester turnpike, near Llanerch, a fact recalled by the newspapers in connection with the recent destruction of the time-honored hostelry by fire.

just crossed by Lee in the Maryland campaign. Here the regiment lost twenty-six men of Company B by capture.

At Fredericksburg, upon the night of December 10th, the "23d" led the army across the Rappahannock River upon the pontoon bridge at Franklin's Crossing. Col. Neill here took command of a brigade, and Lieut.-Col. John Ely became colonel. In May, 1863, the regiment, with the Sixth Corps, was again in front of Fredericksburg, where five companies, under Lieut.-Col. John F. Glenn, made a preliminary attack upon Marye's Heights, losing sixteen men. In the final charge the "23d" voluntarily rushed into a weak point, and entered the works, assisting in capturing, with the Sixth Corps, everything in sight, losing seventy-two men. For this feat one hundred silver medals were afterward presented to participants by Col. Ely. Upon the afternoon of the same day (May 3d) the "23d," with Gen. Sedgwick's Sixth Corps, again met the enemy at Salem Church. Skirmishing and marching through June, the 23d Regiment entered upon the famous forced march of the Sixth Corps, which brought all-important help to Meade at Gettysburg. Arriving upon the scene at 4 P. M., July 2d, they were promptly sent to the support of the Fifth Corps, near Little Round Top, but without actual engagement. In the conflict of the third day Shaler's Brigade, including the "23d," was sent to the Twelfth Corps at Culp's Hill, where they became engaged, driving Johnston's force back to their works, and in the afternoon it was marched, under the heavy artillery fire preceding Pickett's assault, to the left center of the battle line formed to receive him. The regimental loss in these various movements was two officers and twenty-nine men killed and wounded. The monument of the 23d Regiment at Gettysburg is located at Culp's Hill, where it was engaged.*

On July 5th the Sixth Corps followed Lee's retreating army in the direction of the Potomac River, capturing large numbers of prisoners. While in camp at Warrenton the regiment received a re-enforcement of one hundred and forty-six drafted men, and was assigned to the Second Division, Sixth Corps. Col. Ely returned and resumed command on September 2d, 1863, and soon afterward the regiment was again marching, guarding and skirmishing in the movements of the Sixth Corps, this period covering the affairs at Rappahannock Station, Kelly's Ford and the Mine Run. At the beginning of December, 1864, the regiment was back in its old camp at Warrenton, where, because of disabilities, Col. Ely resigned and Lieut.-Col. John F. Glenn was commissioned colonel. At the end of the year two hundred of the men re-enlisted as

---

*The Gettysburg Battlefield Commission first offered the regiment a monument site at either to the right of Little Round Top or to the left of Gen. Meade's headquarters. Eventually the "23d" proved its claim to the location on Culp's Hill and there erected its monument. After the State appropriation was made for the cost of regimental monuments the "23d" expended its share thereof in the addition of a bronze figure of a Zouave. When this had been done the monument was rededicated.

veteran volunteers. The balance of the regiment was dispatched, in January, under Major William J. Wallace, to Johnson's Island, Lake Erie, for guard duty over the prison for Confederate officers, the veteran contingent joining them on February 11th, 1864. The opening of the summer campaign found the "23d" again upon familiar ground in Virginia, and on May 14th the command was detailed to guard and convoy freshly captured prisoners, then very numerous. This work and the destruction of the railroad trackage was performed under command of Col. Isaac C. Bassett, of the 82d Regiment, Pennsylvania Infantry. The "23d" rejoined the Army of the Potomac at the North Anna. At Cold Harbor, on June 1st, the "23d" met with its most trying experience, losing, in the futile effort to break the Confederate line, nine officers and one hundred and eighty-eight men, killed or wounded. The remnant of the regiment remained on the firing line until, ten days later, the movement was made to the investment of Petersburg. Here the old Sixth Corps was kept busy, night and day. in the trenches. After a hot skirmish at Ream's Station, the scene again changed. The Sixth Corps was hurried away to Washington, then threatened by the tireless Early, who was followed to the Shenandoah Valley. While engaged in the Valley the term of enlistment of the "23d" expired. The veterans and recruits were transferred to the 82d Pennsylvania Regiment. At Philadelphia the command was mustered out on September 8th, 1864.

TOTAL LOSSES.

Killed or died from wounds ....officers, 6; men, 126.
Died from disease or other causes .... "   3; "   56.
Wounded, not mortally .... "   18; " 434.
Captured or missing .... "   1; "   78.

BATTLES AND ENGAGEMENTS.

Warwick Creek, Williamsburg, Fair Oaks, White Oak Swamp, Charles City Cross Roads, Turkey Bend, Malvern Hill, Fredericksburg, Marye's Heights, Salem Church, Gettysburg, Funkstown, Mine Run, Cold Harbor, Petersburg; also present at Second Malvern Hill, Chantilly, Rappahannock Station, North Anna, Hanovertown, Fort Stevens, D. C., and in Shenandoah Valley campaign to August 23d, 1864.

TWENTY-SIXTH REGIMENT INFANTRY

COLONEL WILLIAM F. SMALL to June 30, 1862.
COLONEL BENJAMIN C. TILGHMAN to July 26, 1863.
LIEUT.-COL. ROBERT L. BODINE to June 18, 1864.
Total Enrollment, 1,523 Officers and Men.

THIS regiment, recruited by Col. William F. Small, late commander of the "Washington Brigade," was the first of the "three years'" regiments of Pennsylvania. It was mustered in to date from May 5th, 1861. With the exception of a part of Company K it was composed of Philadelphia volunteers. *The regiment moved to Washington upon June 17th, where Company B, Capt. John B. Adams, was detached for special duty at headquarters of Gen. George B. McClellan. This company rejoined the regiment in February, 1863. The "26th" was attached to Grover's Brigade, Hooker's Division, Third Corps, and wintered in camp at Budd's Ferry, Maryland. In April, 1862, the "26th" was engaged upon the Virginia Peninsula, sharing in the actions of Yorktown and Williamsburg. At the latter battle Col. Small was wounded, necessitating his retirement from the service. Lieut.-Col. Benjamin C. Tilghman succeeded to the colonelcy. The regiment participated in the battles of Fair Oaks, Seven Pines and Malvern Hill, and in the movements leading to Harrison's Landing, on the James river. Leaving Yorktown by steamer for Alexandria, Va., the Third Corps was advanced to the Rappahannock river, met the enemy at Bristoe Station, and on August 29th, 1862, lost heavily at the second battle of Bull Run. In December, 1862, the "26th" was engaged in the attack upon Fredericksburg. At the battle of Chancellorsville it was again severely depleted. In this battle Col. Tilghman was wounded, and, later, resigned. Lieut.-Col. Robert L. Bodine assumed command. Early in June, 1863, the regiment was detailed to guard the wagon train of the Third Corps upon a march which finally led to South Mountain and Gettysburg. The Third Corps was engaged in the great battle at this historic field upon the second and third days. The "26th" went into the fight with three hundred and sixty-four rank and file, losing two hundred and thirteen killed and wounded. Of the eighteen officers, two were killed and nine severely wounded. Three color bearers were killed. At Beverly Ford, in August, 1863, the regiment was reinforced by one hundred and ninety-two recruits from Phila-

---

*Col. Small had served in the Mexican War as Captain of the Monroe Guards. Lieut-Col. Rush Van Dyke had also served in Mexico as captain of the Montgomery Guards. Both of these companies were from Philadelphia and numbers of their members were enrolled in the 26th Regiment.

delphia. A series of marches and skirmishes kept the regiment fully occupied through the autumn and the winter was spent in road construction and camp routine. At this time the Third Corps was disbanded and the "26th" became a part of the Second Brigade, Third Division, Second Corps. On May 4th, 1864, the regiment, under Major Samuel G. Moffitt (Col. Bodine having been promoted Bvt.-Brig.-General) was again on the march, and in the thick of the fight at the "Wilderness," losing twelve killed and twenty-seven wounded. On the 10th the "26th" charged the enemy at Spotsylvania, and two days later shared in a greater charge upon the same ground, capturing two Napoleon guns. Here the regiment lost twenty killed and forty-five wounded. Many of the casualties were inflicted by an attack upon the left flank of the army by Rosser's cavalry. At North Anna River a week later, the "26th" fought its last battle, and, its term of service having expired, was sent to Philadelphia, arriving upon June 5th, 1864. The men whose enlistments had not ended were transferred to the 99th Regiment, Penna. Infantry. After a splendid reception by the people of Philadelphia the regiment was mustered out June 18th, 1864.

TOTAL LOSSES.

Killed in action ....officers, 5; men, 77
Died of Wounds .... " 1; " 63
Died of disease or other causes........................... " 2; " 73
Wounded, not mortally .... " 22; " 398
Captured or missing .... " 65

BATTLES.

Yorktown, Williamsburg, Oak Grove, Seven Days' Battles, Manassas, Fredericksburg, Chancellorsville, Gettysburg, Mine Run, Wilderness, Spotsylvania and also present at Savage Station, White Oak Swamp, Glendale, Malvern Hill, Chantilly, Kelly's Ford, North Anna and Totopotomoy.

TWENTY-SEVENTH REGIMENT INFANTRY

COLONEL MAX EINSTEIN to October 2d, 1861.
COLONEL ADOLPH BUSCHBECK to June 11th, 1864.
Total Enrollment, 1,346 Officers and Men.

THE staunch German element of the Northern Liberties and Kensington districts which had been so largely represented in the Second Regiment of General Small's "Washington Brigade," proceeded, immediately after the Baltimore episode, to organize a regiment of light artillery. Col. Max Einstein, its commander, offered the services of his regiment to the Government, but the acceptance was accompanied with the proviso that the command should serve as infantry and as such it was mustered in, May 30th and 31st, 1861. The term of service was, however, dated to begin upon May 5th. Camp was established in Camden, N. J., from which the regiment proceeded to Washington June 18th, encamping at Kalarama Heights. Here it was assigned to the First Brigade (Blenker's) of the Fifth Division, Army of the Potomac. This division formed the reserve of the battle of Bull Run and being posted at Centreville Heights was not actively engaged. The "27th" was the only Philadelphia regiment identified with that disastrous Union advance and rout, and its men covered the retreat of the army like veterans. In August, Company F, Captain Chauncey Spering, was detached for duty at the Washington Arsenal and did not rejoin the regiment. Upon September 7th, 1861, Lieut. Col. Charles Angeroth and Major William Schoenleber resigned, their respective successors being Adolph Buschbeck and Lorenz Cantador. Col. Einstein resigned October 2nd, 1861, and the officers named were promoted as Colonel and Lieutenant Colonel. Colonel Buschbeck was soon afterward placed in command of the brigade. It was not until in winter quarters that the officers received their commissions, and the regimental colors were not provided until February, 1862. Under the McClellan organization the "27th" became a part of Lieut.-Colonel Stahl's Brigade, Blenker's (German) Division, First Corps. In the spring of 1862 Blenker's Division marched westward to join the Mountain Department, then commanded by Major Genl. John C. Fremont, with headquarters at Franklin, West Virginia. At Cross Keys and Port Republic, in the Valley of the Shenandoah, the regiment experienced its first duels with the enemy, with great credit to its officers and men. Through July, August and September, the "27th" participated in a retrograde movement, which led in the direction of Washington. Major General Franz Sigel had superseded Fremont in command of the Mountain Department. The First Corps crossed the Blue Ridge and the

54

"27th," with the 45th New York and a battery, now became the extreme outpost of the Army, and the rear-guard of Pope's retreat. At Rappahannock Station, Freeman's Ford and White Sulphur Springs the command was under constant fire. Skirmishing and fighting across the country to the vicinity of Centreville, the Confederates were encountered in force upon the old Bull Run field, upon August 28th, 1862, where, as usual, the "27th" was in the thick of the fight. This action was preliminary to the more important battle known as the "Second Bull Run," occurring upon the 30th, from which, after a hard day's work, the "27th," with a detachment of "Bucktails," covered the retreat, which led through Vienna to Falls Church, Va. Upon September 21st the brigade was moved forward to Centreville, Va.

Upon October 26th, 1862, the "27th" was attached to the First Brigade of the Second Division, Eleventh Corps. Between this date and February 5th, 1863, when the regiment was finally allowed to establish winter quarters at Stafford Court House, Va., it was constantly employed in building roads, clearing ground for defences and similar heavy duty, varied with picket duty and skirmishing.

The campaign of 1863 opened, in earnest, with the disastrous battle of Chancellorsville, in which the "27th" lost heavily. The Confederate success on this field was promptly followed by the invasion of Maryland and Pennsylvania. The Eleventh Corps was rushed into Maryland and, constantly watching the movements of the enemy upon its left-flank, was but little behind the First Corps in reaching Gettysburg, where it arrived at noon, upon July 1st, plunging at once into the conflict. In the melee many of the men were killed, wounded or captured. The balance of the regiment retired to Cemetery Hill, and there, at nightfall of the 2d, joined in the repulse of the famous "Louisiana Tigers." The "27th" remained upon this part of the field assisting in the defence of the right flank, upon the 3d, being exposed much of the time to a destructive fire. The command was among the first to enter Gettysburg upon the morning of the 4th of July. The regimental loss in this series of battles was two officers and twenty-two men killed, three officers and sixty-five men wounded, one officer and forty-four men captured.

Two months later, after having received an accession of one hundred and seventy conscripts, the "27th" entered upon a new chapter of adventure. With the Eleventh and Twelfth Corps it became a part of an army of twenty thousand men under Major General Joseph Hooker, dispatched to the assistance of General Rosecrans, who was beleaguered at Chattanooga, Tenn. The journey, by rail, was accomplished in eight days, traversing five States. On September 9th the Eleventh Corps marched from Murfreesboro, Tenn., to a point thirteen miles south, where the command fortified, but was advanced by rail to Stephenson, Ala., reporting here to General Hooker. The task of the troops was now to force a junction with Rosecrans. The way led through Bridgeport, Ala., twenty miles west from Chattanooga, via Shell Mound, beyond which, to Wauhatchie,

Tenn., the route was through the wild and picturesque valley of the Tennessee River. While in camp near Wauhatchie, Lieut.-Col. Cantador resigned, being succeeded by Major Peter A. McAloon. The brigade, including the "27th," marched into Chattanooga upon November 22d, and, with Sherman's troops, participated in the fight of Orchard Knob and in the assault upon Missionary Ridge. One officer and forty-five men were killed and six officers and eighty men were wounded. Among the latter was Lieut.-Col. McAloon, who died upon December 7th. The command of the regiment now devolved upon Major August Reidt. The remnant of the "27th" was immediately sent, with other troops, upon a forced march under General Sherman, without tents or blankets, to the relief of General Burnside at Knoxville, but was returned to Chattanooga in December. The "27th" was now placed in the First Brigade of Geary's Division. At this time the men claimed that the term of service of the regiment had expired, but, after considerable discontent had been manifested, the command marched away toward Atlanta, a part of Sherman's victorious column, to wage further battles at Rocky Face, Dug Gap, Resaca and Dallas. At the latter point the war-worn survivors received orders to proceed to Philadelphia, where they arrived upon May 31, 1864, and were soon afterwards mustered out, having served three years and two months. Lieut.-Col. August Reidt was the only original field officer of the regiment who remained to the end of the term of service. The total strength of the regiment, together with conscripts and recruits, was thirteen hundred and forty-six officers and men. Of these, three hundred and thirty-six officers and men, including those in Company F (detached), came home with the regiment, and a large portion of this remnant had been wounded in one or more of the many battles in which they had been engaged.

TOTAL LOSSES.

Killed or died from wounds...........................officers, 5; men, 73
Died from disease or other causes........................... "   " 62
Wounded, not mortally....................................... "   3; " 26
Captured or missing . . . . "   1; " 76

BATTLES.

Cross Keys, Rappahannock River, Groveton, Bull Run (second), Chancellorsville, Gettysburg, Hagerstown, Orchard Knob, Missionary Ridge, Rocky Face Ridge, Resaca, Dallas.

TWENTY-EIGHTH REGIMENT INFANTRY

COLONEL JOHN W. GEARY to April 25th, 1862.
COLONEL GABRIEL DE KORPONAY to March 26th, 1863.
COLONEL THOMAS J. AHL to March 18th, 1864.
COLONEL JOHN J. FLYNN to November 3d, 1865.
Philadelphia Companies C, D, I, K, M and P.
Total Enrollment, 975 Officers and Men.

I N June, 1861, Col. John W. Geary began the organization of a regiment of fifteen companies, six of which were recruited in Philadelphia and nine in the counties of Luzerne, Westmoreland, Carbon, Huntingdon, Allegheny and Cambria. Col. Geary uniformed and equipped the regiment at his own expense. The original uniform was gray, but this was afterward discarded for the regulation blue. The command was mustered in upon June 28th, 1861, as the Twenty-eighth Regiment. The camp was located at Oxford Park, Philadelphia. Ten companies were sent, upon July 27th, to Harper's Ferry, where Col. Geary was ordered by Major-General N. P. Banks to patrol duty along the Potomac River. This involved great vigilance and some desultory skirmishing. The "28th," with several Massachusetts and Wisconsin companies, under the command of Col. Geary, met and defeated a force of Confederates at Bolivar Heights, West Virginia, upon October 16th, and again, a few days later, at Loudon Heights. For these achievements the regiment was especially commended by the President, Secretary of War and Gen. Banks. Upon October 21st, the regiment was present at the affair of Ball's Bluff. A week later at Nolan's Ferry, Md., a Confederate column was repulsed in an effort to cross the Potomac and enter Maryland. For more than three months the bridges and ferries of the Potomac were protected and then, upon February 24th,. 1863, Col. Geary once more crossed the river and again drove the enemy from Bolivar Heights, and beyond Leesburg. On March 8th he occupied that point and pushed on to Snickers Gap in the South Mountain, and thence to White Plains, with several brisk skirmishes en route at Middleburg and Salem. Here, fifty miles southwest from Harper's Ferry, Col. Geary's force proceeded to repair the Manassas Railroad. Upon April 25th, 1862, Col. Geary received a commission as Brigadier-General of Volunteers. Lieut.-Col. Gabriel de Korponay now became Colonel of the "28th." The brigade, now under Gen. Geary, continued to guard and make effective the Manassas Railroad over a distance of fifty-two miles. At the western extreme of this line, at Front Royal, in the Valley of the Shenandoah, a portion of the "28th" was engaged with other troops in a defensive fight in which the infantry with Knap's Battery did effective work. Upon July 10th, 1862, orders

57

were issued constituting the "28th," and other troops of Gen. Geary's command, the Second Brigade, First Division, Second Corps. A month later the designation was changed to First Brigade, Second Division, Second Corps. Upon August 9th the "28th" was sent to dislodge the enemy from possession of Thoroughfare Gap (Cedar Mountain). Part of the regiment reached the field of Cedar Creek at night in time to participate in the battle at that point. In this affair Gen. Geary was wounded. At Bristoe Station the "28th," in the face of the advancing enemy, destroyed, by order, several locomotives, a large number of cars and all of the Government supplies stored there. The "28th" reached Bull Run upon the day following the second battle upon that field. From September 2d to the 16th the First Brigade was upon the march which was ended at Antietam, Md., a distance of one hundred and twenty-five miles in torrid weather. In the hard-fought battle of the 17th the regiment lost, in killed and wounded, two hundred and sixty-one officers and men, a record exceeded by but one other command present. The trophies of the "28th" were two guns and five flags.

Two days later the regiment found itself once more at the scene of its early victories, upon Loudon Heights, Harper's Ferry.

Five companies, including M and P, of Philadelphia, were detached on October 28th, 1862, to become a nucleus for the 147th Regiment, then forming at Harrisburg.

General Geary returned to duty and assumed command of the Second Division, at Bolivar Heights. Upon December 9th the Twelfth Corps was ordered to Fredericksburg, but the "28th" was left ot Dumfries, Va., upon the Potomac River, where it was attacked by a large force of Stuart's Cavalry. The latter were driven northward by Geary's Division, resulting in an engagement at Occoquan, Va., a few miles south of Mount Vernon. For four months, dating from January 1st, 1863, the "28th" enjoyed comparative rest at Acquia Creek. Then it was hurried away upon a forced march to Chancellorsville, and three days later counted its losses to be above one hundred killed and wounded of the three hundred officers and men in line. Among the killed was Major L. F. Chapman, who had been in command. Upon March 26th, 1863, Col. De Korponay resigned and Capt. Thomas J. Ahl of Company H was commissioned colonel. Up to this period the regiment had been armed with Enfield rifles, carrying sword bayonets. These were now replaced with Springfield rifles. Along with the hurrying army en route to head off the determined Confederates under Gen. Lee, in their break toward Pennsylvania, the Twelfth Corps began its northward march. It was destined to reach the scene at Gettysburg upon the morning of July 2d, 1863, being stationed at the "point of the hook" upon Culp's Hill. Being well fortified the "28th" lost in this great battle but twenty-five killed, wounded and missing. The regiment followed with other troops, upon the heels of the retreating Confederates seventy-five miles, finally reaching Sandy Hook, Md., upon the Potomac River, on the 18th. Geary's division next met the enemy at Manassas Gap, where the last of the "28th's" battles upon Virginia soil was waged. The Eleventh and Twelfth Corps had been selected, for their oft-proven fighting qualities, to go to the help of the Army of the Cumberland. The "28th" with Geary's Pennsylvanians speeded westward, over the Baltimore and Ohio Railroad, to the Ohio River and on through Ohio, Kentucky and Tennessee to Murfreesboro, Tenn., arriving in time to save the railroad connecting with Bridgeport upon the Tennessee River from the tender mercies of Wheeler's Cavalry. Upon joining the Army of the Cumberland Gen. Geary's Brigade became a part of the Twentieth Corps, through the merger into that organization of the old Eleventh and Twelfth Corps. The "28th" missed the battle of this division at Wauhatchie, after a twenty-eight-mile march. In this battle Capt. E. R. Geary, the eighteen-year-old commander of Knap's Battery), and son of Gen. Geary, was killed. Upon November 24th, the Second Division, including the "28th," was ordered to storm the heights of Lookout Mountain. All that historic day of the famous "battle above the clouds" the struggle continued. Around the rock-strewn flanks of Lookout the battle surged and the clouds were lurid with fires, but in the morning, when the mists had swept away, the host of soldiery in and around Chattanooga, saw the stars and stripes waving from the cliffs of the mountain. This splendid feat won the unstinted praise of Gen. U. S. Grant, who reviewed and thanked Geary's Division at Wauhatchie. The "28th" was in the action at Missionary Ridge upon November 25th, and on the 27th again met the enemy at Ringgold, Ga., where the regiment lost thirty-four killed and wounded, including among the killed Lieut. Peter Kahlor of Company E, a veteran of the Mexican War. In December the regiment, having re-enlisted, returned home for thirty days, at the expiration of which it rejoined the Army of the Cumberland. Upon March 18th, 1864, Col. Ahl resigned and Lieut.-Col. John J. Flynn was commissioned in his place. In April the regiment helped to punish the enemy at Guntersville and Triano upon the Tennessee River, and in May placed two more affairs to its credit at Snake Creek Gap and Dalton Road, Ga., followed by a week of continuous fighting near New Hope Church, Ga. In June the advance toward Atlanta was contested at Pine Knob, Pine Hill and Lost Mountain, Muddy Creek, Noses' Creek, Kolb's Farm, Kenesaw Mountain and upon July 3d the battle of Marietta, considered the key to the city of Atlanta, which was approached upon July 5th, 1864. This prize was not to be had, however, without further effort. It was necessary to chastise Hood and his cohorts at Peach Tree Creek. Atlanta fell upon September 2d. So constant was the battling all through this campaign that it has been called the "hundred days' fight," the progress of the Union forces being one of constant victory.* The "March

*The total losses of Sherman, in killed, wounded and captured, between Chattanooga and Atlanta were estimated to be 31,300.

to the Sea" began upon November 15th. This remarkable *tour de force* required five weeks of constant marching and skirmishing, out of all touch with the North and without reserve supplies. The Fourteenth and Fourth Corps formed the left wing of the army. The men seemed to know that they were making history. Savannah was occupied upon December 21st. The 28th Regiment captured and occupied Fort Jackson. The Pennsylvanians of Geary's Division were the first to enter the city. The troops extinguished the fires kindled by the Confederates and restored order and confidence. Within a few days Philadelphia was busy raising money for and sending food to the "starving people of the city."

The left wing started from Savannah upon the long, wet and muddy journey westward and northward upon January 19th, 1865. This occupied eleven weeks, up to the date of Johnston's surrender. As a result of the capture of Columbia, capital city of the "mother of secession," the city of Charleston, heroically defended for more than four years, was abandoned by the garrison under McLaws. Upon February 24th, 1865, Gen. Joseph E. Johnston was appointed by the Richmond Government to the command of the Carolinas, and that capable officer came into conflict with the Union forces in numerous skirmishes and in two severe battles, at Averysboro, N. C., and Bentonville, N. C. At Goldsboro, N. C., Gen. Sherman found, upon March 23d, Schofield's force awaiting him. Raleigh, N. C., was occupied upon April 13th, and here, upon the 26th, Gen. Johnston surrendered upon terms similar to those extended to Lee by Grant, seventeen days earlier, at Appomattox. In referring to the march of the Union force "from Atlanta to the Sea," and from Savannah to Raleigh, the Confederate Gen. Johnston said that "these troops were the toughest and most ready army since Julius Caesar commanded the Roman legions."

The 28th Regiment, including its re-enlistment, was in the field more than four years. "It served in twelve States and was engaged in as many skirmishes and battles as any regiment in the army."

The Philadelphia companies of the regiment were mustered out upon July 18th, 1865.

TOTAL LOSSES.

Killed or died from wounds...................................officers, 6; men, 151
Died from disease or other causes......................... "   3; "   124

BATTLES AND ENGAGEMENTS.

Pritchard's Mill, Berlin (September 19th, 1861), Point of Rocks (September 24th, 1861), Berlin (September 29th, 1861), Bolivar Heights, Point of Rocks (December 19th, 1861), Leesburg, Middleburg, Linden, Northern Virginia campaign, Antietam, Hillsborough, Lovettsville, Old Wilderness Tavern, Chancellorsville, Gettysburg, Fair Play, Lookout Mountain, Missionary Ridge, Ringgold or Taylor's Ridge, Mill Creek Gap, Resaca, Pumpkin Vine Creek, New Hope Church, Pine Knob, Kulp's House, Dallas, Kenesaw Mountain, Peach Tree Creek, Atlanta, Savannah, North Edisto River, Congaree River, Durham Station or Bennett's House.

TWENTY-NINTH REGIMENT INFANTRY

COLONEL JOHN K. MURPHY to April 23d, 1863.*
COLONEL WILLIAM D. RICKARDS, JR., to November 2d, 1864.
COLONEL SAMUEL M. ZULICK to July 7th, 1865.
Total Enrollment, 2,108 Officers and Men.

UNDER the name of "The Jackson Regiment" this strong command was recruited entirely in Philadelphia, by Col. John K. Murphy in May, June and July, 1861. Headquarters were located in the building adjoining the Custom House, upon the west. The ten companies were known as the Marion Guards, West Philadelphia Greys, United Rifles, Belmont Guards, Koska Guards, Wayne Artillery Corps, Federal Guards, Henry Clay Fencibles, Morgan Artillery Guards and Dougherty Guards.

Upon July 16th the regiment went into camp at Hestonville. The heavy expense of recruiting, and of uniforms and subsistence was borne by the officers. The uniforms, as in the case of many other of the early regiments, were of gray cloth. The companies were mustered during June and July and the command was designated the 29th Regiment of the line, and was the third of the five Philadelphia infantry regiments destined to win glory in both the eastern and western armies. Upon August 3d, the "29th" left Philadelphia for Sandy Hook, Maryland, there joining the army under Major-General N. P. Banks, being attached to the Third Brigade, First Division, Second Corps. The work and experiences of the "29th" under Gen. Banks were parallel with those of the "28th," involving the guarding of ferries along the upper Potomac River, and the occupation of the country westward along or south of the Shenandoah River, co-operating with Fremont's Mountain Department with almost constant skirmishes with Confederate cavalry parties. In a skirmish with the Louisiana Brigade at Winchester, Va., upon April 25th, 1862, Col. Murphy with a considerable number of the regiment were made prisoners. These, together with two companies captured on May 23d by the Confederates at Front Royal, aggregated a loss of seven officers and one hundred and forty-eight enlisted men. Three Companies, C., E. and F. of the "29th," under command of Major Michael Scott, were present at the battle of Cedar Mountain upon August 9th, but not actively engaged. Upon September 17th the regiment was at Antietam, but being upon provost and rear guard duty did not meet with heavy fighting. Col. Murphy and his fellow officers having been exchanged, returned to the regiment upon October 22d.

---

*In the War with Mexico Col. Murphy was captain of the National Artillery from Philadelphia.

After a period of provost duty at Hagerstown, the regiment rejoined the brigade near Fairfax Station, Leesburg, Va., of which Col. Murphy, as senior officer, took command. The brigade was then moved to Alexandria, Va. Following the experience of Burnside's famous "mud march" the "29th" went into camp at Stafford Court House, Va., where, in command of Lieut.-Col. William D. Rickards, winter quarters was built and the regiment devoted itself to the routine of drill and guard duty. Upon March 21st, 1863, the "29th" became a part of the Second Brigade, Second Division, Twelfth Corps. The new brigade was composed entirely of Pennsylvania regiments. Upon April 26th, 1863, the regiment moved from its camp toward Fredericksburg, arriving at Chancellorsville upon the evening of the 30th. In the battles of May 1st to 4th, the "29th" lost six men killed and thirteen wounded. With the general movement of the army toward Maryland and Pennsylvania, in June, 1863, the "29th" performed the long and exhausting march ending at Gettysburg, reaching the field, with Geary's division, upon the 1st of July, occupying Round Top. Upon the morning of the 2d, the "29th" was sent to the right of the line at Culp's Hill. At 7 P. M. the brigade was hurried away to assist the left flank, in the direction of Little Round Top. Returning to Culp's Hill it was hotly engaged in that wilderness of forest and rocks to the end of the battle, losing, altogether, fifteen killed and fifty-nine wounded or missing. The pursuit of the retreating Confederates led the Twelfth Corps back to the region of Harper's Ferry and the Shenandoah River and thence on to the South Mountain and Thoroughfare Gap, but the quarry had escaped. On September 23d, the regiment, proceeding to Washington, was entrained with the rest of the Eleventh and Twelfth Corps, and sent to join the Army of the Cumberland. At Murfreesboro, Tenn., Col. Rickards was ordered to the command of the Twelfth Corps regiments already arrived. While engaged in building a fort at Fosterville, upon the Nashville and Chattanooga Railroad, the force was ordered to Stephenson, Ala., by rail and there reported to Gen. Hooker. From this point the "29th" was sent forward through a wild and picturesque country to Wauhatchie Junction, the regiment being at once placed on picket duty. This precaution frustrated a night attack in which the enemy was badly beaten. This was the battle of Wauhatchie, in which the Union force consisted of four New York and three Pennsylvania Regiments and Knap's Battery. General Longstreet's troops, met here, numbered three to one of the Federal force.

Upon November 24th, at daylight, the "29th" occupied the right of Major-Gen. Geary's division in the picturesque action called the "Battle above the Clouds." The column advanced up the west slope of Lookout Mountain at a place about three miles south from the point which overlooks the Tennessee River. When the head of the line reached the vertical escarpment of rock the column faced left and swept along the slope, through the tangle of rocks and forest growth, followed by the supporting line of the Third Brigade. The enemy swarmed along the cliff and down the narrow gorges to the attack. Hundreds of the Confederates surrendered and were sent to the rear. In the midst of lowering clouds, here, eighteen hundred feet above the valley, the fight surged around the point, past the Craven house and on, to another defensive work, just south of the Summertown road, which leads up to the mountain from Chattanooga. Here the advance rested. To the thousands of spectators in the valley the scene seemed, indeed, a battle in the skies. The "29th" remained in the darkness, when friend or foes could not be distinguished, until 9.30 P. M. then being relieved. At dawn, the following morning, Col. Rickards, with a number of his men, ascended ladders found in a cleft of the cliff, and upon gaining the summit, discovered that the enemy was gone. While there an officer of the 8th Kentucky (Union) Regiment and several men came up the Summertown road and waved a flag within sight of the city and camps below. A party from the 111th Pennsylvania Regiment also ascended the ladders, and the incident is shown in bronze upon their tablet, affixed to the rock at this point. The tablet of the "29th," near by, does not refer to the circumstance.

Losing no time the brigade crossed the valley upon the Rossville Gap road and captured a brigade from Polk's left wing upon Missionary Ridge, and the next day, November 26th, fought his retreating rear guard at Rossville, then moving upon Ringgold, Georgia, where the enemy was encountered in force and a severe action was fought with his rear guard. This was glory enough for three days, and the regiment rested upon its honors once more at Wauhatchie. The "29th" was mustered out on December 8th and on the 10th two hundred and ninety of the officers and men were mustered into the first "veteran" regiment formed for further service in the Union Army.* Gen. Geary's Division passed in review of the "29th" and the General complimented the regiment upon its patriotic action.

This entitled the command to a visit home. The "29th" arrived in Philadelphia upon December 23d, 1864, where it was honored with a great military reception, with addresses of welcome at National Guards Hall and a dinner at the "Cooper Shop." Three months later, having recruited to a strength of twenty-one officers and five hundred and eighty-eight enlisted men, the regiment barracked at Chester, Pa., leaving for the front early in April. The regiment was now attached to the

---

*Under a general order dated June 25th, 1863, able-bodied volunteers who had served more than nine months in the United States forces, and who could pass the mustering officer, were eligible to re-enlistment as veteran volunteers for three years' service. Such veterans were allowed a month's pay in advance, a furlough and a bounty and premium of $402.00, payable in instalments at specified intervals. It was provided that the full sum thus awarded was to be paid to any veteran honorably discharged at any time prior to the full term of his enlistment. Veteran volunteers were distinguished by service chevrons upon the sleeve. General Order No. 191.

Third Brigade, Second Division, Twentieth Corps. With Gen. Sherman's army the "29th" fought its way through to Atlanta. At Kennesaw Mountain Col. William Rickards was so badly wounded that he was retired from the service and Lieut.-Col. Samuel M. Zulick was commissioned in his place. Under this officer the regiment continued from Atlanta to Savannah and thence to Goldsboro and Raleigh, a march of nearly one thousand miles. After a rest of four months with comparatively uneventful service the regiment was mustered out at Alexandria, Virginia, upon July 17th, 1865, after a service of four years and one month. The "29th" was engaged in the last great battle of the war, at Bentonville, N. C., on March 19th, 1865.

TOTAL LOSSES.

Killed or died from wounds	officers, 4;	men,	55.
Died from disease, accident and in prison	" 1;	"	66.
Wounded, not mortally	" 7;	"	125.
Captured or missing	" 7;	"	164.

BATTLES, ETC.

Harper's Ferry, Winchester, Campaign of the Shenandoah Valley, Woodstock, Edenburg, Stony Creek, Front Royal, Backton Station, Winchester, Bull Run (guarding trains), Antietam, Chambersburg, Maryland Heights, Fairfax, Mud March, Chancellorsville, Gettysburg, Pursuit of Lee, Movement with Hooker Detachment, Bridgeport, Ala., Wauhatchie, Lookout Mountain, Ringgold, Mission Ridge, Ringgold Gap, Atlanta Campaign, including Dalton, Resaca, Cassville, New Hope Church, Dallas, Allatoona Pass, Marietta, Pine Hill, Lost Mountain, Golgotha Church, assault on Kennesaw Mountain, Ruff's Station, Chattahoochie River, Peach Tree Creek, Atlanta, Expedition to Tuckum's Bridge, March to the Sea, Siege of Savannah, Campaign of the Carolinas, Bentonville, Bennett's House, Surrender of Johnston, Muddy Creek, Noses Creek.

THE RESERVE CORPS OF THE COMMONWEALTH OF PENNSYLVANIA

THE rapid formation of regiments for the National service, through Pennsylvania, in the spring of 1861, having deprived the State of its uniformed militia force, the Legislature, upon the initiative of Governor Curtin, enacted a law, upon May 15th, providing for the formation of a body of troops to be sustained by the State for defence against internal disorder and invasion. It was also provided that this "Reserve Corps" should be subject, at all times, to call by the Government. Under this Act thirteen regiments of infantry, one regiment of cavalry and one regiment of artillery were soon assembled and in camps of instruction at Easton, West Chester, Harrisburg and Pittsburg. Philadelphia was represented in this corps by twenty companies of infantry and four companies of artillery, in which were enrolled about 3,000 men.

The command of this Reserve Division was tendered by Governor Curtin to, and accepted by, Col. George A. McCall, a native of Philadelphia and a veteran officer of the United States army, who had retired from the service in 1853 and was residing upon his farm in Chester County. He was given a State commission as Major-General, and proceeded to organize the several camps.* Two regiments from this force, the Fifth and Thirteenth Reserves, were accepted by the Government for guard duty upon the upper Potomac river and in West Virginia. After the battle of Bull Run, responding promptly to the urgent call of the President for troops to defend Washington, the entire Reserve Corps enlisted in the United States service for three years. It was not until the reserve regiments were encamped at Tenallytown, upon Georgetown Heights, that they were brigaded. Maj.-Gen. George A. McCall having received his commission from the United States Government, selected as his brigade commanders Brig.-Generals John F. Reynolds, George Gordon Meade and E. O. C. Ord, all fellow cadets at West Point.†

The record of the Pennsylvania Reserves in the following years

---

*The command of the Pennsylvania Reserve Corps was tendered by Governor Curtin to Major-Gen. George B. McClellan before it was offered to Gen. McCall. ("McClellan's Own Story.")

†The staff of Gen. McCall included Lieut.-Col. Henry J. Biddle, A. A. G., Capt. Henry Sheetz and Capt. Henry Coppeé, all of Philadelphia.

forms one of the most brilliant chapters in the annals of the great Rebellion. Upon June 27th, 1862, Gen. Reynolds was captured by the
enemy, and three days later Maj.-Gen. McCall was made a prisoner at
the battle of New Market. A return of ill health, resulting from hardships before exchange, compelled the latter to resign. Maj.-Gen. Truman
Seymour then became the commander of the Reserve Corps pending
the return and appointment to that position of Maj.-Gen. John F. Reynolds. Just before the battle of Antietam Gen. Reynolds was detailed
to the command of the Pennsylvania militia. Maj.-Gen. George Gordon
Meade then commanded the Reserves until called to lead the Fifth Corps.
The last commander of this splendid corps was Maj.-Gen. Samuel Wylie
Crawford, who led the remnant of the division in its heroic work at
Gettysburg.*

In the critical days just before the battle of Gettysburg, when newspapers of other States were reproaching Pennsylvania because of her
inability to defend her State borders from invasion without help from
outside, the editor of the Philadelphia "Inquirer" wrote, July 1st, 1863:
"At the first call to defend the National Capital Pennsylvania's valleys
overflowed with volunteers, and the excess was embodied into a military
organization armed, equipped and maintained out of her own treasury.
Then she was capable of defence. But when McDowell's army was
overthrown at Bull Run the National authorities called again for instant
help, and Pennsylvania contributed her only State corps to the defence
of the Nation, for the whole war, fifteen thousand nine hundred men,
infantry, cavalry and artillery. That body is known to history by its
brilliant fighting in almost every battle since Bull Run as 'The Pennsylvania Reserves.'"

At the close of their term of service, in the summer of 1864, the
"Reserves" were accorded great honors at Harrisburg and Philadelphia.

PHILADELPHIA COMPANIES ATTACHED TO THE PENNSYLVANIA
RESERVE CORPS, THREE YEARS' SERVICE.

Thirty-first Regiment, Second Reserves. Companies A, B, C, D, E, G, H and K.
Thirty-second Regiment, Third Reserves. Companies E, G and K.
Thirty-third Regiment, Fourth Reserves. Companies A, B, D, G and I.
Thirty-sixth Regiment, Seventh Reserves. Companies E, G and K.
Forty-first Regiment, Twelfth Reserves. Company A.
Forty-third Regiment, First Artillery Reserves. Batteries C, D, G and H.

These troops were part of the Third Division, First Corps, and
the Third Division, Fifth Corps, Army of the Potomac.†

*Major-Gen. S. Wylie Crawford, of Philadelphia, was a surgeon in the small
garrison under Major Anderson at Fort Sumter in 1861.

†The traveler southward, after passing Fredericksburg may see upon the eastward side of the railroad a stone pyramid. It was erected by Confederates upon
the spot where they met the Pennsylvania Reserves. Just beyond is the house
within which Stonewall Jackson died.

THIRTY-FIRST REGIMENT INFANTRY (SECOND RESERVES)

COLONEL WILLIAM B. MANN to October 30th, 1861.
COLONEL WILLIAM McCANDLESS to June 16th, 1864.
Total Enrollment, 850 Officers and Men.*

THIS regiment was recruited under the direction of William B. Mann, Esq., and was taken by him to Camp Washington, the Reserve camp at Easton, Pa., of which Col. Mann was appointed commander May 27th, 1861. The eight Philadelphia companies were: Co. A, Penn Rifles; Co. B, Governor's Rangers; Co. C, Hibernia Target Co.; Co. D, Governor's Rangers; Co. E, Scotch Rifles; Co. G, Taggart Guards (partly from Lancaster Co.); Co. H, Independent Rangers; Co. K, Consolidation Guards

Responding to the call of the War Department, the command was moved from Harrisburg to Baltimore in the latter part of July, and thence to Sandy Hook, Maryland, reporting to Gen. N. P. Banks without the formality of muster into the United States service. This led to complications which resulted in the defection of a large proportion of the rank and file. Many of the men returned to Philadelphia and entered other regiments. By order of Major-Gen. Nathaniel P. Banks the regiment was disturbed by the disbandment of several companies.

This displaced a number of excellent officers, for some of whom other places were found. The regiment was active in the movements under Banks in the vicinity of the Potomac river, above Washington. Upon September 25th the Reserve Division was joined at Tenallytown, Md., and the "31st" was assigned to the First Brigade, commanded by Gen. John F. Reynolds. Entering Virginia with the Reserves, the brigade was near Ball's Bluff upon the morning of the unfortunate battle at that point, but was ordered back to camp by Gen. McClellan. Col. William B. Mann resigned upon November 1st, and was succeeded by Lieut.-Col. William McCandless, who was not, however, commissioned as colonel until the following August (1862). Late in May, 1862, the Reserves were sent to Fredericksburg to operate in the direction of Richmond, but were recalled, and upon June 8th embarked upon a steamer, landed at White House, on the Pamunkey river, and marched to Dispatch Station, within ten miles from Richmond. At Mechanicsville, six miles north of Richmond, upon June 26th, and at Gaines' Mill, the next day, the "31st" had its first battles, in which the command lost twenty-two killed, forty-two wounded and a number captured. The next move was through White Oak Swamp, where, in the close fighting at Charles City Cross Roads, the regiment lost heavily, and upon July 1st was in reserve at Malvern Hill, nine miles east of Richmond. Al-

*Philadelphia companies only.

67

68

though victors, the army was withdrawn by McClellan and the Reserves found themselves at Harrison's Landing, on the James river. The struggle was now transferred to the Rappahannock river, where Pope faced Lee, and where, on August 29th, the second battle of Bull Run was fought. Col. McCandless was among the wounded. The battle of South Mountain was fought on the way to Antietam. At the latter field the "31st" was under fire upon both the 16th and 17th of September. Here, out of one hundred and seventy-one men in line, the regiment lost twenty-six killed, wounded and missing. At Fredericksburg, in December, the "31st," on the left of the line, killed, wounded and captured the 19th Georgia Regiment. Of one hundred and ninety-five rank and file in the "31st" the loss was thirty-nine killed, wounded and missing. Being greatly reduced and war-worn, the regiment was ordered to the vicinity of Washington, where it went into camp under Maj. George A. Woodward. Upon June 17th, 1863, the officers of the "31st" signed a petition to be allowed to go with the Army of the Potomac, then hastening to Pennsylvania. Accordingly, the First and Third Brigades were attached to the Fifth Corps and started north. The Reserves reached Gettysburg upon the 2d of July at 5 P. M., plunging immediately into the battle in support of the Third Corps, in front of Little Round Top, driving the enemy back in confusion. In the afternoon of the 3d, the regiment, with the 3d. 11th and Bucktail Regiments, advanced and cleared the wheat field and woods, in front of Little Round Top, of the enemy, capturing many prisoners. The regimental loss here was forty killed and wounded. Early in September, 1863, Lieut.-Col. Woodward was succeeded in command (as Lieut.-Col.) by Maj. Richard Ellis. In the operations of the Army of the Potomac, early in 1864, the regiment was engaged in fights at Mine Run, Briscoe Station and New Hope Church. At Spotsylvania the regiment lost twenty killed, wounded and missing. Upon May 31st, 1864, six days after its term of service had expired, the "31st" fought its last battle upon the site of its first fight, three years before, near Mechanicsville, Va. In this last encounter the enemy was annihilated or captured. The regiment was soon afterward sent to Harrisburg and Philadelphia, where, with many honors, the remnant was mustered out June 16th, 1864.

TOTAL LOSSES (Regimental).

Killed or died from wounds ....officers, 4; men, 82
Died of disease .... " 2; " 54
Wounded, not mortally .... " 22; " 207
Captured or missing .... " 5; " 48

BATTLES OR ENGAGEMENTS.

Mechanicsville, Gaines' Mill, Glendale, Malvern Hill, Groveton, Second Bull Run, South Mountain, Antietam, Fredericksburg, Gettysburg, Bristoe Station, Rappahannock Station, Mine Run, Wilderness, Spotsylvania, North Anna, Totopotomoy, Bethesda Church.

THIRTY=SECOND REGIMENT INFANTRY (THIRD RESERVES)

COLONEL HORATIO G. SICKEL to June 17th, 1864.
Philadelphia Companies, E, G and K.
Total Enrollment, 338 Officers and Men.

A MONG the numerous companies of volunteers raised in Philadelphia at the outbreak of the war, which were unable to find places in the three months' service, were the De Silver Grays, of Holmesburg; the Germantown Guards and the Ontario Infantry. The captain of the latter was Horatio G. Sickel. These companies became respectively E, G and K of the Third Reserve Regiment which Capt. Sickel commanded as colonel throughout the three years of its service. The "32d" was organized at Easton, Pa., in May, June and July, 1861, and under its colonel, an officer of twenty years' experience, rapidly gained in efficiency. The command was mustered at Harrisburg upon July 27th, and sent to the Reserve camp at Tenallytown, near Washington, where it joined the Second Brigade under Brig.-Genl. George Gordon Meade. Entering Virginia with the Reserve Division, the movements of the regiment were identical with those of the 31st or Second Reserve Regiment. In the course of the several battles occurring at Mechanicsville, Gaines' Mill, White Oak Creek and Charles City Cross Roads within six days, the "32d" lost about two hundred officers and men, killed, wounded or missing, but it inflicted a heavier loss upon the Confederates. At Malvern Hill, upon July 1st, 1862, the regiment was in reserve and had no casualties. The Reserves were moved by water from Harrison's Landing to the Potomac in July, and pushed forward to assist Gen. Pope at Rappahannock Station. This led to the battle of the Second Bull Run, with a resulting heavy loss in the regiment. At South Mountain the "32d" was upon the edge rather than in the thick of the fight, but in the two days' conflict at Antietam lost, in killed and wounded, fifty-one officers and men. At Fredericksburg, on December 13th, the regiment had its part with the Reserve Division on the left, losing, in killed, wounded and missing, one hundred and twenty-eight. This was the regiment's last fight in Virginia. The remnant of survivors were placed in camp near Washington, and attached to the newly formed Twenty-second Corps. The "32d" remained here nearly a year, then, with the Fourth Reserves, both under the command of Col. Sickel, it was sent to meet further warfare in a new field. Under command of Maj. William Briner the "32d" was taken to Martinsburg, West Virginia, and in this section was subjected to an exhausting service far more trying than fighting open battles, as the mountains were infested with the guerilla cavalry of the enemy, and the railroads were in need of constant guarding. In March the Third and Fourth Reserves were sent to Harper's Ferry, but immediately returned to West Virginia, in the vicinity of Grafton, and upon April 22d, 1864, moved by steamers down the Ohio river to the Great Kanawha river, camping at Brownstown, West Virginia. Here Col. Sickel returned to resume command of his old regiment, but was placed by Gen. George Crook in charge of the Reserves brigade. The "32d" was then under command of Capt. Jacob Lenhart. The troops thus assembled formed an expedition intended to destroy the railroad line south of the Allegheny Mountains, over which Gen. Lee's army received the greater portion of its subsistence. This involved a forced march of three weeks in mud, storm and cold, through a wild and desolate country, but the task was accomplished. The chief features of this heroic raid were the battle of Cloyd Mountain, upon May 9th, and of New River, upon the 10th. At Cloyd Mountain the two Reserve regiments lost nearly one hundred officers and men. Among those killed were Col. Richard H. Woolworth, of Philadelphia, formerly Major of the Third Reserves, but, at the time, in command of the Fourth Reserves. The wounded were subjected to great suffering in the course of the march, which ended at Meadow Bluff ten days after the battle. Upon May 22d the brigade was ordered home, its term of service having expired. The return occupied nine picturesque, happy days by steamer and rail via Pittsburgh, the brigade reaching Philadelphia upon June 8th, 1864, and there the troops were mustered out upon the 17th of June. The recruits and re-enlisted veterans of the brigade still remaining in the field were formed into a battalion, which subsequently became a part of the 54th Regiment Veteran Volunteer Infantry. This battalion included, out of the two Reserve regiments, one hundred and three Philadelphians, who shared the fortunes of the "54th" to the end of the war.*

TOTAL LOSSES (Philadelphia Companies).

Killed or died from wounds.................................. men, 17.
Died from disease ....officers, 1; " 7.
Wounded, not mortally .... " 16.
Captured or missing .... " 8.

BATTLES.

Mechanicsville, Gaines' Mill, Charles City Cross Roads, Glendale, Malvern Hill, Gainesville, Groveton, Bull Run, South Mountain, Antietam, Fredericksburg, Cloyd Mountain, New River Bridge, Newport.

---

*These veterans experienced further service in the Shenandoah Valley under Sheridan and in the closing scenes of the siege of Petersburg. During the pursuit of Gen. Lee's troops after the fall of Richmond the "54th" was captured and held until the capitulation at Appomattox when, after considerable hardship, they regained their liberty.

THIRTY-THIRD REGIMENT INFANTRY (FOURTH RESERVES)

COLONEL ROBERT G. MARCH to October 1st, 1861.
COLONEL ALBERT L. MAGILTON to December 3d, 1862.
COLONEL R. H. WOOLWORTH to May 9th, 1864.
COLONEL THOMAS F. B. TAPPER to June 17th, 1864.

Philadelphia Companies A, B, D, I and G.

Total Enrollment, 497 Officers and Men.

FIVE companies from Philadelphia, the Able Guards, Quaker City Guards, Dickson Guards, Reed Guards and Harmer Guards were sent in June, 1861, to the Reserve camp at Easton, Pa., and enrolled with companies from Montgomery, Lycoming, Monroe, Susquehanna and Chester Counties to form this regiment. Fifteen of the field officers were from Philadelphia. The "33d" was mustered in at Harrisburg July 17th, and sent to Baltimore, encamping there at Carroll Hill on July 21st. Part of the command occupied the Stewart mansion in the city, assisting in the suppression of the disloyal element of the population. At the end of August the "33d" moved to the reserve camp at Tenallytown, Md., near Washington. Col. March resigned in October, being replaced by Albert L. Magilton, late Lieut.-Col. of the Second Reserves. Under this experienced officer the regiment improved greatly in drill.

The "33d" was, at this time, assigned to the Second Brigade, First Corps. The Brigade commander was Gen. George G. Meade. Eager for active service, the Reserves enterd Virginia upon October 9th. At the battle of Dranesville, Va., twenty-five miles northwest from Washington, upon December 20th, 1861, the "33d" was in the supporting line and not actively engaged, but in the movement under Gen. McClellan, in the costly "on to Richmond" campaign, between Mechanicsville and Malvern Hill the "33d" lost two hundred officers and men, chiefly during a desperate bayonet fight in defence of Randall's battery at Gaines' Mill. These inexperienced troops drove back the on-rush of seasoned Alabamians and saved the guns. Under Pope, the "33d" fought at the second Bull Run and at South Mountain, Md., on the way to Antietam. In the two battles of the Antietam campaign the regiment lost seventy-five officers and men, killed and wounded. Three months later, at Fredericksburg, Va., upon December 13th, the Reserve Division, led by Gen. Meade, charged the Confederate right wing with success. Here the "33d" lost thirty-eight killed and wounded. A few days later Col. Magilton resigned and Lieut.-Col. Richard H. Woolworth assumed command. This officer was commissioned as Colonel in the following March. The Reserve Division was placed upon routine duty in the defences of Washington, remaining here nearly a year. Upon January 6th, 1864, the "33d" was sent to join the force in West Virginia, then concentrating under Major-Gen. George Crook, in the Kanawha Valley. The services of the regiment, in the exhausting but successful expedition southeastward across the Allegheny Mountains, were identical with those of the Third Reserves. At Cloyd Mountain, Va., Col. Woolworth, leading the brigade, and Capt. Prosper M. Davis were killed. At New River Bridge, Va., May 10th, 1864, the "33d" had its final meeting with the enemy. After a few days of rest the regiment, with such of its wounded as could be transported, was sent via the Ohio river and Pittsburg to Philadelphia, where it was mustered out upon June 17th, 1864.

Just prior to the dissolution of the regiment a portion of the men re-enlisted in a battalion, which was subsequently merged with the 54th Regiment Infantry. This additional service included fifty-seven men from the Philadelphia companies of the Fourth Reserves.

TOTAL LOSSES (Regimental).

Killed or died from wounds ....officers, 2; men, 76
Died from disease .... " 1; " 60

BATTLES AND ENGAGEMENTS

Dranesville, Mechanicsville, Gaines' Mill, Savage Station, Charles City Cross Roads, White Oak Swamp, Malvern Hill, Second Bull Run, South Mountain, Fredericksburg, Cloyd Mountain, New River.

THIRTY-SIXTH REGIMENT INFANTRY (SEVENTH RESERVES)

COLONEL ELISHA B. HARVEY to July 4th, 1862.
COLONEL H. C. BOLINGER to August 19th, 1864.
Philadelphia Companies, E, G, and K.
Total Enrollment, 284 Officers and Men.

PHILADELPHIA was represented in this regiment by the Ridgway Guards, Co. E., Capt. Charles S. Peall, Second Philadelphia Guards; Co. G, Capt. John C. Chapman, and Douglass Guards, Co. K, Capt. Casper Martino. The balance of the regiment was recruited from the interior counties in the Eastern sections of the State. At Camp Wayne, near West Chester, Pa., the regiment was drilled and uniformed. Upon July 21st, 1861, under Col. Elisha B. Harvey, the "36th" left via Baltimore for Washington, where it was mustered into the United States service upon July 27th. A week later the regiment

1802   1868

GENERAL GEO. A. M^cCALL

FIRST COMMANDER OF PENNSYLVANIA
RESERVE VOLUNTEER CORPS
ARMY OF THE POTOMAC

PRESENTED BY PENNA. RESERVE POST N^O 191
GRAND ARMY OF THE REPUBLIC
1911

TABLET PRESENTED BY PENNSYLVANIA RESERVE POST 191, G. A. R.,
TO GENERAL GEO. A. McCALL SCHOOL, at Seventh and Delancey Streets.

CAMP WASHINGTON, FAIR GROUNDS AT EASTON, PA. RENDEZVOUS FOR PHILADELPHIA COMPANIES OF THE PENNSYLVANIA RESERVE CORPS IN 1861.

(From a contemporary lithograph.)

marched to Tenallytown, there joining the Reserve Division, being assigned to the Second Brigade, commanded by Brigadier-General George G. Meade. Late in August the regiment was sent to Gen. Banks for guard duty at Great Falls, on the Potomac river. The autumn and winter were spent in camp upon Virginia soil, near Washington. With the opening of the active season in April, 1862, the "36th" was stationed at Fairfax, Va. With part of the First Corps, the regiment shared in the advance of the Reserves upon Richmond, which resulted in the battles of Mechanicsville and Gaines' Mill. At the latter affair the "36th" fought like veterans to save Butterfield's battery and lost, in killed and wounded and captured, half of its force. Assisting in guarding Gen. Hunt's artillery column in the retreat, and in desultory fighting through Savage Station, White Oak Swamp and Charles City Cross Roads, the Reserves reached Malvern Hill, and after that victory moved on to Harrison's Landing. In that week of battles the "36th" had lost three hundred and one men. In August the Reserves were on the firing line along the Rappahannock river with the Army of Northern Virginia. At the close of Pope's campaign, after further heavy losses, the regiment went back to its old camp of the year before, but was at once ordered northward. On September 14th, 1862, the command helped to drive the enemy out of the passes of South Mountain and hurried on to Antietam. Upon this field the "36th" again suffered heavily and added greatly to its laurels. At Fredericksburg the regiment made, with other First Corps troops, the glorious but fruitless charge upon the Confederate right, capturing many prisoners and a battle flag. The worn remnant of the "36th" was relieved, together with the Reserve Corps generally, from further hard fighting until April 18th, 1864. It then marched away from its camp at Alexandria to have a share in the campaign which began with the battle of the Wilderness. This proved the Waterloo of the "Seventh Reserves." While driving the retreating enemy the regiment was ambuscaded, with the exception of Co. B, and two hundred and seventy-two officers and men were captured.

The few officers and men who were not captured at the Wilderness continued to rally around their colors and to fight. They numbered, together with recruits, one hundred and ten officers and men. This battle-scarred contingent was mustered out, at Philadelphia, upon June 16th, 1864.

TOTAL LOSSES (Philadelphia Companies).

Killed or died from wounds, or from disease ....officers, 1; men, 32
Died in prison at Andersonville................................ " 21

BATTLES AND ENGAGEMENTS.

Mechanicsville, Gaines' Mill, Savage Station, White Oak Swamp, Charles City Cross Roads, South Mountain, Antietam, Wilderness,

FORTY-FIRST REGIMENT INFANTRY (TWELFTH RESERVES)

COLONEL JOHN H. TAGGART.

Philadelphia Company A, 124 Officers and Men.

Re-enlisted (in 190th Regt.) 34 Men.*

ALTHOUGH formed and commanded by a Philadelphian, this regiment contained but one local company. This became Co. A, of which the Captains were Henry B. Whisner and Franklin Daniels. The "41st" served throughout its term of enlistment with the Army of the Potomac, taking part in the several campaigns and many battles in which the Pennsylvania Reserve Division so distinguished itself. At the end of its enlistment thirty-four members of Company A re-enlisted as veterans.* Many others were discharged for disability and, at muster out, upon June 11th, 1864, at Harrisburg, the company had present but seventeen officers and men.

LOSSES (Company A).

Killed or died from wounds..men, 10.
Died from disease .... " 3.

BATTLES AND ENGAGEMENTS

Dranesville, Mechanicsville, Gaines' Mill, Glendale, Malvern Hill, Groveton, Bull Run (second), South Mountain, Antietam, Fredericksburg, Gettysburg, Bristoe Station, Rappahannock Station, Mine Run, Wilderness, Spotsylvania, North Anna, Totopotomoy, Bethesda Church.

THE RESERVE BATTERIES.

Twenty-one Philadelphians held commissions in the Pennsylvania Reserve regiments not herein recorded. One of the most distinguished was the second Colonel of the 13th Reserves (Bucktails).†

The records of the four Philadelphia batteries originally recruited as a part of the 1st Artillery Reserves (43d Regiment) will be found in the artillery group of the three years' commands, inasmuch as the batteries never served with the Reserve Corps, but were assigned, as occasion required, to co-operate with numerous other bodies of troops.

---

*These veterans participated, as part of the Third Brigade, Third Division, Fifth Corps, in the battles of Charles City Court House, Petersburg, Weldon Railroad and Hatcher's Run, Five Forks and Appomattox.

†Gen. Thomas Leiper Kane was born in Philadelphia, January 27th, 1822. He founded the town of Kane, Pa., and in 1861 recruited the 1st Bucktail Regiment (42d Pennsylvania Volunteers). He was promoted to brigadier-general June 7th, 1862, and to brevet major-general March 13th, 1865. At Gettysburg, although on sick leave, he led his brigade. Gen. Kane was wounded in two battles and was captured at Harrisonburg. He died December 26th, 1883.

FIFTY-SIXTH REGIMENT INFANTRY

Colonel Sullivan A. Meredith to November 29th, 1862.
Colonel J. William Hofmann to March 7th, 1865.
Colonel Henry A. Laycock to July 1st, 1865.

Total Enrollment, About 1,600 Officers and Men.

THIS regiment was formed from companies raised chiefly in the northern counties of the State. Two of its three colonels were citizens of Philadelphia, as were also twelve of its field and company officers and many of its rank and file. The "56th" was mustered in at Camp Curtin, upon September 1st, 1861, and remained at Harrisburg until March 8th, 1862. Its early active service was in the vicinity of Washington and along the lower Potomac River. Upon August 9th, 1862, near Fredericksburg, the command was assigned to Doubleday's Brigade, King's Division, McDowell's First Corps. At Rappahannock Station the "56th" had its first encounter with the enemy, Col. Meredith being among those wounded. A second engagement fell to the "56th" in the same vicinity the following day. At South Mountain Lieut.-Col. Hofmann commanded the brigade, the regiment being in command of Capt. Fred. Williams. In the difficult but successful charge up the mountain many of the men were killed or wounded. At Antietam the regiment lost comparatively few. Two weeks later, on the way south, the enemy was routed out of the way at Union, Va. In this affair the regiment lost fifteen. Lieut.-Col. Hofmann resumed command upon November 11th. In the Fredericksburg advance of December the regiment escaped casualties, although under artillery fire. A period of inactivity followed the never-to-be-forgotten "mud march," ending with the opening of the Chancellorsville campaign planned by Gen. Hooker. This long interval in its comfortable camp of log huts at the mouth of the Potomac Creek was always regarded by the men of the "56th" as the most enjoyable of their experiences, with just enough of drilling to keep the men in good shape.

Lieut.-Col. Hofmann was promoted to the colonelcy, and the "56th" took the field in 1863 with twenty-one officers and two hundred and eighty-nine enlisted men. At Pollock's Mills, Chancellorsville and Brandy Station the regiment repeatedly proved its effectiveness under fire. The march to Pennsylvania began upon June 25th. The "56th" was only second to the "76th" New York in the column of the First Corps, but was first in position upon the morning of July 1st, 1863,

75

and secured the honor of opening the battle of Gettysburg.* With-
the heroic First Corps the regiment made the splendid first day's fight,
sharing the glory and vicissitudes of that fateful day with the Eleventh
Corps, holding the swarming lines of the enemy in check until reinforced.
The morning of the 2d found the "56th" with Wadsworth's depleted
division, holding the crest of Culp's Hill, repelling the desperate assaults of the Confederate left wing, including that made, late in the
day, near the cemetery. The regiment was called upon, late in
the afternoon of the 3d, to support the artillery at the cemetery, but
the battle had ended. The losses of the "56th" were one officer and
sixteen men killed or mortally wounded; five officers and fifty-three men
wounded; one officer and fifty-four men captured or missing, out of
seventeen officers and two hundred and thirty-five men in action. Nearly
all of the casualties occurred upon July 1st. In the course of the following month Col. Hofmann brought from Philadelphia a considerable
accession of recruits. Without further important fighting the "56th"
entered upon camp routine through the following winter. In March
the veterans re-enlisted with the usual joyful holiday period at home.
The command returned to camp upon April 20th, 1864. Two weeks
later began the series of fierce conflicts in the Wilderness, a deadly
month of constant sorties, assaults and marches, with almost daily losses
of comrades by bullet, shell or capture. Upon June 16th the army crossed
the James River and coiled about Petersburg. In September the old
First Corps was consolidated into a division and assigned to the Fifth
Corps. Col. Hofmann, having been breveted brigadier-general, Lieut.-
Col. George B. Osborn was promoted as colonel, but soon afterward retired from the service. The next commander of the "56th" was Lieut.-
Col. John T. Jack. Its last commander was Lieut.-Col. Henry A. Laycock, under whom the regiment shared the trials and triumphs of the
closing months of a struggle so needlessly prolonged.

The muster out took place July 10th, 1865, at Philadelphia.

TOTAL LOSSES.

Killed ....officers, 5; men, 73
Wounded ....   "   26; "   329
Captured or missing ....   "   2; "   178

BATTLES AND ENGAGEMENTS.

Rappahannock Station, Sulphur Springs, Gainesville, Groveton, Second Bull
Run, South Mountain, Antietam, Union, Upperville, Fredericksburg, Pollock's Mills,
Chancellorsville, Brandy Station, Gettysburg, Mine Run, Wilderness, Spotsylvania,
North Anna, Totopotomoy, Bethesda Church, Cold Harbor, Petersburg, Weldon
Road, Poplar Spring Church, Hatcher's Run, Dabney's Mill, Boydton Road, White
Oak Road, Five Forks, Appomattox Court House.

---

*An exception must be made in favor of Buford's Cavalry regiments, which
were engaged in skirmishing with the Confederate advance before the arrival of
any of the First Corps.

FIFTY-EIGHTH REGIMENT INFANTRY

COLONEL J. RICHTER JONES to May 23d, 1863.
COLONEL CARLTON B. CURTIS to July 2d, 1863.
LIEUT.-COLONEL CECIL CLAY to January 24th, 1866.
(Philadelphia Companies A, B, C, D and K.)
Total Enrollment, 850 Officers and Men.

THIS regiment was formed on February 13th, 1862, by the union of two partially organized regiments, one of which was being raised in Philadelphia and the other at Camp Curtin, Harrisburg. The Philadelphia companies, which had been encamped at Roxboro, proceeded by steamer to Fortress Monroe, the left wing joining them, by rail and steamer, at that point. The command arrived at Camp Hamilton, on Hampton Roadstead, on the day of the naval battle between the Monitor and the Merrimac.

The "58th" formed part of the column, under Gen. Wool, which occupied Norfolk and Portsmouth. Through the balance of the year the regiment was employed in guard duty, reconnoissances and work upon the forts in that section. On January 5th, 1863, the regiment embarked with the expedition under Major-Gen. J. G. Foster (18th Army Corps) to New Berne, N. C. The troops entrenched eight miles westward, between the Neuse and Trent Rivers. From this base frequent advances were made, with attendant skirmishing. In one of these, undertaken on May 22d, at Batchelor's Creek Station, Col. Jones was killed.* Under command of Col. Curtis the "58th" was ordered to Washington, N. C., and, with other troops, held the post, in the face of frequent attacks, until withdrawn, late in April, 1864. The "58th" was now assigned to the Eighteenth Corps, which operated south of the James River with the army of Major-Gen. Benjamin F. Butler. In May the Eighteenth Corps, under Gen. W. F. Smith, joined the Army of the Potomac. A portion of the regiment, including Companies B, D and K, of Philadelphia, took part in a gallant charge at Cold Harbor on June 1st. During the severe battle at this place, on the 3d, the "58th" drove the enemy from his rifle pits, holding the position, under deadly fire until re-enforced. The Eighteenth Corps was now returned, by transports, to Bermuda Hundred, on the James River, and the investment of Petersburg began. The veterans of the regiment who had re-enlisted were sent upon furlough to Philadelphia on June 24th. They returned to camp with numerous recruits on August 25th. The arms of the regiment were, at this time, exchanged

---

*Writing from Camp Curtin, Harrisburg, on January 13th, 1862, Col. Jones urged an official friend at Washington to induce the Secretary of War to send the 58th Regiment on this expedition, as the command wanted active service.

for new Springfield rifles. On the night of September 28th portions of the Tenth and Eighteenth Corps, under Major-Gen. E. O. C. Ord, crossed to the north side of the James River and, in the morning, advanced toward Richmond. The "58th," under Major Charles A. Winn, and the 188th Pennsylvania Regiment, Major F. H. Reichard, were formed for the assault upon Fort Harrison, one of the most formidable of the defensive works around the Confederate capital. The charge across open, rising ground and the capture of the works is recorded as one of the most brilliant episodes of the war. Six of the nine officers of the "58th" and one hundred and twenty-eight, out of the two hundred and twenty-eight men in line, were killed or wounded. The loss of the "188th" was also very heavy. After the arrival of additional troops the survivors of the two regiments were sent into another fight, at the left, close to the James River, where the field was in range of the enemy's gunboats. This movement, which failed, again cost the assailants large loss. Repeated assaults upon Fort Harrison were made by the Confederates the next day, but the citadel was held. The "58th" participated in further affairs, in the autumn, eastward of Richmond. On November 19th Capt. Cecil Clay, of Company K, promoted to the rank of lieutenant-colonel, was placed in command. The regiment was active in the final campaign which resulted in the fall of Petersburg and Richmond. The regiment was retained in service, under the direction of the Freedman's Bureau, for provost duty in tidewater Virginia.* It was finally mustered out at City Point on January 24th, 1866, the last of the fighting infantry regiments of the Keystone State to stack arms, fold its colors and return to civilian life.

TOTAL LOSSES.

Killed or died from wounds...................................officers, 6; men, 68
Died from disease.. "   6; "   139

BATTLES AND CAMPAIGNS.

Occupation of Norfolk, Suffolk, New Berne, Cove Creek, Sandy Ridge, Kinston, Wise's Cross Roads, Dover Road, Kinston (April 28th, 1863), Gum Swamp, Batchelor's Creek. On duty at Washington. Advance on Neuse River road, Blounts' Creek, Butler's Campaign, James River, Fort Darling, Drewry's Bluff, Bermuda Hundred, Cold Harbor. Siege of Petersburg and Richmond, including Hare's Hill, Chapin's Farm, New Market Heights, Fair Oaks. Expedition to Fredericksburg (March, 1865). Signal Hill, near Richmond. Occupation of Richmond.

---

*Service of this character was peculiarly distasteful to the Union regiments, being devoid of the excitements and ardor of campaigning. The men were scattered in detachments over large sections, the inhabitants of which naturally regarded them as oppressors and enemies, this requiring great self-control upon the part of the rank and file. The "58th" is credited, however, in having made many friends while on provost duty, and they certainly enforced order where it was sorely needed.

SIXTY-FIRST REGIMENT INFANTRY

COLONEL OLIVER H. RIPPEY to May 31st, 1862.*
COLONEL GEORGE C. SPEAR to May 3d, 1863.
COLONEL GEORGE F. SMITH to September 7th, 1864.
COLONEL ROBERT L. ORR to June 28th, 1865.
Philadelphia Companies G, H and I.
Total Enrollment, 500 Officers and Men.

THIS regiment was formed at Pittsburgh, being hastened to Washington, when not fully recruited, on March 1st, 1862. Companies M, O, P and R of the 23d (Pennsylvania) Regiment, enlisted between August 12th and September 4th, 1861, were transferred to the 61st, thus filling the command to maximum strength.† The regiment was assigned to the First Brigade, First Division, Fourth Corps, then commanded by Major-Gen. Erasmus D. Keyes. The "61st" participated in the Peninsular movement upon Yorktown, Williamsburg and Richmond. In its first important encounter with the enemy, at Fair Oaks, May 31st, 1862, the regiment suffered almost unprecedented losses. Eleven officers and two hundred and ninety-nine enlisted men were killed or wounded or were missing. Col. Rippey* was among the dead, Lieut.-Col. Spear (wounded) and Major Smith were among the captured. The command now devolved on Capt. Robert L. Orr, of Company H, who posted the regiment on the new line, occupying the field of the battle. Almost daily here and near Seven Pines the regiment skirmished to the 28th, then moving in the "change of base" to Malvern Hill and Harrison's Landing. The Fourth Corps was withdrawn from the James River late in August, moving to Centreville, Washington and the Maryland shore of the Potomac River. The "61st" reached Antietam upon the evening of September 17th, assisting in the running fights with the retreating Confederates. Lieut.-Col. Spear had been exchanged, and, upon return, was promoted to command. In October the division was transferred to the Sixth Corps, with which the regiment was engaged at the first (Burnside)

---

*Col. Rippey, a veteran of the Mexican War, had served in the three-months' campaign as Lieut.-Col. of the 7th Regiment. George C. Spear was promoted as Lieut.-Col. from the rank of junior major of the 23d. The Continental Guard, which had been raised by Capt. Spear prior to his promotion, was the first company which left Philadelphia for the South. George F. Smith, commissioned major, was promoted from the rank of captain in the 49th Regiment.

†The companies thus transferred became G, H and I in the "61st." They were commanded as follows: Company G, Capts. John W. Crosby, William M. Dawson, Vincent P. Donnelly, John Barrett and Charles H. Bewley; Company H, Capt. Robert L. Orr; Company I, Capts. George W. Mindil and Charles S. Greene.

79

assault at Fredericksburg, December 13th, 1862. In February, 1863, the "61st" was placed in a light brigade of the Sixth Corps.

At the second battle of Fredericksburg, on May 3d, 1863, the "61st" was selected as the "forlorn hope" to open the fight for the possession of the hills. The regiment made the desperate charge, gaining Marye's Heights and captured two guns from the Washington Artillery of New Orleans, the first ever lost by that famous battery. The command now devolved, in the absence of other field officers, upon Major George W. Dawson. Following this charge the "61st" was immediately sent to again meet the enemy at Salem Heights, with further severe punishment. Under the third Colonel (Smith) the "61st" made, with the Sixth Corps, the famous forced march to Gettysburg. The light brigade to which the "61st" was attached (Neill's) was sent to reinforce the Twelfth Corps at the extreme right of the line. The regiment was not, therefore, seriously engaged. The regiment wintered at Brandy Station. In the spring (1864) the command was recruited to five hundred men. From the opening of the Wilderness Campaign, upon May 5th, to its close, less than six weeks later, the regimental loss was (according to Bates' History) in killed, wounded and missing, about thirty officers and four hundred men. In early July the Sixth Corps was suddenly hurried from the front of Petersburg to Washington, once more imperiled by the restless enemy. In the resulting clash at Fort Stevens and the pursuit, further loss of officers and men reduced the thin line of survivors. The term of service expired on September 3d, 1864. Under Col. Smith the regiment returned to Pittsburgh. The veterans and recruits were formed into five companies as the "Sixty-first Battalion." Subsequently, Col. Smith returned to the command. Of the original Philadelphia enlisted men, seventeen re-enlisted. In its last fight Lieut.-Col. John W. Crosby, formerly captain of Company G, lost his life.

The records of the Adjutant-General, War Department (as shown by a report of April 4th, 1888) indicate a total regimental loss, from all causes, of nine hundred and thirty-two officers and men. The "61st" lost more officers, killed, than any other regiment in the Union Army.*

TOTAL LOSSES.

Killed ....officers, 2; men, 27
Wounded .... " 2; " 36
Died of disease... " 12
Captured .... " 5

BATTLES AND ENGAGEMENTS.

Fair Oaks, Malvern Hill, Antietam, Fredericksburg, Marye's Heights, Salem Heights, Gettysburg, Rappahannock Station, Wilderness, Spotsylvania, Cold Harbor, Petersburg, Fort Stevens, Opequon, Fisher's Hill, Cedar Creek, Petersburg, Sailor's Creek, Appomattox C. H. (surrender).

---

*"Regimental Losses," Fox,

UNION VOLUNTEER HOSPITAL.
Adjoining the old Navy Yard.

COOPER SHOP SOLDIERS' HOME, Race and Crown Streets.

STATE ARSENAL, S. E. COR. OF SIXTEENTH AND FILBERT STREETS.

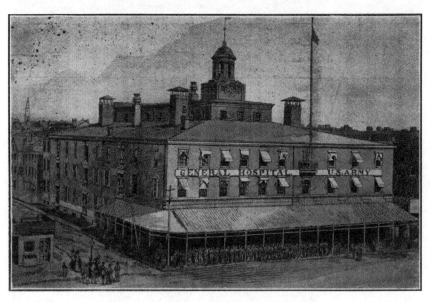

BROAD STREET U. S. GENERAL HOSPITAL.
On the site of present Parkway Building, Broad and Cherry Streets.

SIXTY-SIXTH REGIMENT INFANTRY

COLONEI ALFRED W. CHANTRY to January 18th, 1862.
COLONEL JOHN PATRICK to February 6th, 1862.

THIS organization, which was recruited in May and June, 1861, was declined by the State authorities upon the ground that the city's quota had been filled. Its officers received authority from the Secretary of War to proceed with their work, and upon June 13th were notified that if the regiment was fully recruited *and uniformed* within ten days it would be mustered in. In order that the command might comply with this condition a patriotic citizen, Benjamin L. Berry, guaranteed the cost of the uniforms. The repeated delays and discouragements, however, resulted in the withdrawal of many of the men. The recruits were barracked at the Girard House, and later, at the building adjoining the Custom House. In August the command was mustered in at its camp in Camac's Woods.

The urgent need of more troops in the vicinity of Washington prompted the Government to call for many organizations still in the course of formation. When, on August 24th, Col. Chantry's command left for the front it consisted of a battalion of five companies. At Washington these companies were assigned to the first of three brigades constituting a provisional division under the command of Gen. Fitz John Porter. Additional recruits were sent on from Philadelphia, and the adjutant's report of October 10th showed a total strength of six hundred and twenty officers and men.* The regiment was known, up to this period, as the "30th."

In September it was sent to the command of Gen. Banks, at which time it was finally recognized as a part of the Pennsylvania contingent and numbered as the "66th." Upon January 18th, 1862, Col. Chantry was relieved and Lieut.-Col. Patrick was commissioned to succeed him. Three weeks later this officer and a number of the company officers resigned. Upon March 1st, by order of Governor Curtin, the regiment was disbanded. Companies A and G were assigned to the 99th Regiment. Companies B, C and D were transferred to the 73d Regiment. Companies E, F and K were distributed among the companies of the "73d." The subsequent records of the companies and men thus disposed of prove that the "66th" was composed of good fighting material which had been badly handled, through no fault of its men in the process of becoming soldiers of the Union.

---

*Bates' History, Vol. 2.

SIXTY-SEVENTH REGIMENT INFANTRY

COLONEL JOHN F. STAUNTON to September 4th, 1864.
COLONEL JOHN C. CARPENTER to July 14th, 1865.

Philadelphia Companies, B, E and I.

Total Enrollment, 360 Officers and Men.

THE "67th" was one of the semi-Philadelphia regiments, the greater part of its recruits coming from nine of the northern and western counties. Authority for its formation was issued upon July 24th, 1861, by the Secretary of War. Col. Staunton, three of his field officers and twelve company officers were Philadelphians. The regiment was soon located in camp at Camac's Woods, where it remained until April 3d, 1862, when it was ordered to guard duty at Annapolis, Md., and at Camp Parole, near that point.

In February, 1863, the "67th" was moved to Harper's Ferry, and later was stationed, under Gen. Robert H. Milroy, at Berryville, Va., to patrol the lower Shenandoah Valley and its gaps. Upon June 15th, 1863, the regiment was cut off from the main column by a large Confederate force, near Winchester, and was captured, with the exception of about seventy-five men. The officers were detained in prison a year, but the enlisted men were exchanged in October.

While in camp at Brandy Station a large proportion of the men re-enlisted. Three hundred and fifty rank and file, with their officers, were sent home on furlough. Upon return to duty the veterans were stationed at Port Royal and White House, Va.

In June the recruits, who had been with the 135th Regiment (Pennsylvania), rejoined the "67th" in front of Petersburg, taking part in an affair at Reams' Station. The third Confederate advance into Maryland caused the transfer of the Third Division of the Sixth Corps by transports to Baltimore, and by rail, to checkmate Early. This movement ended, the Sixth Corps became a part of Sheridan's force, meeting the enemy again at Winchester on September 19th, 1864 (Opequon), and subsequently driving Early out of the defences at Fisher's Hill (September 22d, 1864), and far to the southward.

Near Strasburg, Va., a month later, the "67th" was identified with the battle of Cedar Creek, which was made famous by the stirring war poem (T. Buchanan Reid), "Sheridan's Ride."

At the end of the year the Sixth Corps was returned to the army in front of Petersburg, the "67th" participating in the siege and forward movement which ended at Appomattox, after which it marched with the column sent on to Danville, a precautionary measure, which was ended by Johnston's surrender upon April 26th. The last commander of the regimental remnant was Captain John C. Carpenter, of Company E. One Philadelphia officer, Capt. William E. Tucker, died from wounds while in the field.

TOTAL LOSSES. (Philadelphia Companies.)

From wounds and disease ....officers, 1; men, 55

BATTLES.

Winchester, pursuit of Lee's army after Gettysburg, Wapping Heights, Rappahannock, Bristoe Campaign, Kelly's Ford, Brandy Station, Mine Run, Payne's Farm, Rapidan, White House, Wilderness, Spotsylvania Court House, assault on the Salient, North Anna, Totopotomoy, Cold Harbor, Petersburg, Reams' Station, Monocacy, Charlestown, Opequon, Winchester, Fisher's Hill, Cedar Creek, siege of Petersburg, Appomattox Campaign.

SIXTY-EIGHTH REGIMENT INFANTRY

COLONEL ANDREW H. TIPPEN.

Philadelphia Companies A, B, C, D, E, F, G and K.

Total Enrollment, 1,049 Officers and Men.

WHEN Col. Tippen undertook the organization of this regiment it attracted many of the officers and enlisted men of the 20th Regiment, of the three months' service, in which Col. Tippen had ranked as major. This experienced officer had seen service in Mexico as a lieutenant in the regular infantry. Lieut.-Col. Anthony H. Reynolds, Major Thomas Hawksworth, Major Robert E. Winslow and Capt. Michael Fulmer were also veterans of the Mexican campaign. The "68th" was, with good reason, known as the "Scott Legion Regiment." The regimental camp was located in Frankford, Philadelphia. Company H was raised at Pottstown and Company I in Chester County.

The urgent need of more troops resulted in the muster of the regiment upon September 2d, 1862, and its immediate departure for Washington, where it was encamped upon Arlington Heights. Early in October the "68th" was sent to guard Conrad's Ferry, on the upper Potomac River. Soon afterward a detachment of about forty men, guarding the regimental baggage, was captured. Under the Burnside regime the "68th" was assigned to Robinson's Brigade, Birney's Division, Third Corps. At Fredericksburg, December 13th, 1862, the regiment experienced its first battle in support of artillery. Major Hawksworth was mortally wounded and Lieut. Joseph E. Davis was killed. About forty of the enlisted men were killed or wounded. At Chancellorsville the regiment met with severe fighting and additional losses, capturing a stand of colors and a number of prisoners. In this battle Captains

James Shields and John D. Paulding were mortally wounded. Sickles' Third Corps reached Gettysburg from Emmittsburg upon the evening of July 1st, the "68th" taking position just east of the Peach Orchard. Here, upon the 2d, it was exposed to continuous artillery fire, and, at sunset, was involved in the terrific fighting on Sickles' front, resulting in a retreat of the survivors to the new line near Little Round Top. Here the regiment was held in reserve upon the 3d, with some additional losses. The regimental casualties in this battle were four officers killed or mortally wounded, thirty-four men killed or mortally wounded, nine officers and one hundred and seventeen men wounded, thirteen men captured. The officers who lost their lives were Capt. George W. McLearn and Lieutenants Andrew Black, John Reynolds and Lewis W. Ealer. Upon the return to Virginia the "68th" was engaged at Wapping Heights and, on October 14th, at Auburn. Col. Tippen was taken prisoner at the latter affair and was absent, at Libby Prison, nine months, during which time Lieut.-Col. Robert E. Winslow commanded. Hard fighting and heavy marching signalized the closing weeks of 1863. Capt. Milton S. Young was killed at Locust Grove on November 27th. With the opening of the campaign of 1864 the "68th" went with that portion of the Third Corps which was consolidated with the Second Corps, then commanded by Gen. Hancock. In April the "68th" was selected as provost guard at the headquarters of Gen. Meade, under the immediate command of the Provost General of the Army, an honor which did not, however, absolve it from reserve duty upon the battle line. Col. Tippen was exchanged and resumed command upon June 26th. Headquarters duty occupied the regiment during the balance of its stay in Virginia, a detachment being stationed at City Point. In the last charge upon the enemy's lines at Petersburg the "68th" was with the storming party, losing Major John C. Gallagher, mortally wounded, and a number of officers and men. At Sailor's Creek, upon April 6th, 1865, the Confederate General Ewell and his force were captured. The "68th" was detailed to guard the officers, about six hundred in all, to City Point. While en route the prisoners were informed, much to their dismay, that Gen. Lee had surrendered. The regiment returned to the headquarters in charge of six thousand recruits, being then sent, in company with the 143d Pennsylvania Regiment, to Hart's Island prison camp, near New York, for guard duty. Here the regiment remained until mustered out June 9th, 1865.

TOTAL LOSSES.

Killed or died from wounds..............................officers, 10; men, 58
Died of disease or other causes................................	"	51
Wounded, not mortally	"	15;	"	190
Captured or missing	"	3;	"	100

BATTLES AND ENGAGEMENTS.

Fredericksburg, Chancellorsville, Gettysburg, Wapping Heights, Auburn, Kelly's Ford, Mine Run, Wilderness, Guinea's Station, Petersburg.

THE "CALIFORNIA" REGIMENTS, LATER KNOWN AS THE PHILADELPHIA BRIGADE

SELDOM, among the records of American soldiery, have the uncertainties of official procedure been more strikingly illustrated than in the case of the four so-called "California" regiments of 1861, which were destined to win fame and glory as the "Philadelphia Brigade."*

Early in May, 1861, a number of citizens of the Pacific coast, who were in Washington, decided that California ought to be represented in the Army of the Union upon the Atlantic slope, and to that end urged Edward D. Baker, then United States Senator from Oregon, to form a regiment in the East to the credit of that distant State. Senator Baker decided to undertake the task provided that he be allowed to enlist men for three years. At the instance of the President, the Secretary of War addressed Senator Baker as follows: "You are authorized to raise for the service of the United States a regiment of troops (infantry), with yourself as colonel, to be taken as a portion of any troops that may be called from the State of California by the United States, and to be known as the 'California Regiment.' Orders will be issued to the mustering officer in New York to muster the same into service as presented."†

Senator Edward D. Baker was, at this time, a striking figure among the great men of the nation. He was fifty years old, and of commanding appearance and great eloquence. Born in London, England, he had emigrated in 1815, with his father's family, to Philadelphia, where his father taught school, and the future United States Senator found, when old enough, work as a weaver in a mill near Eleventh and Christian streets. When he was nineteen years old the Baker family moved to Illinois, where his career ran parallel with that of his friend and sometime opponent, Abraham Lincoln. Thus, in time, Baker became a Congressman, forsaking this honor to lead a regiment in the war with Mexico. Upon his return he was again sent to Congress from Illinois, after which he became associated with Isaac J. Wistar, of Philadelphia, in a law firm at San Francisco. It was largely due to his influence that California was held against secession intrigue. In December, 1860, Col. Baker found himself once more in Washington, as the first Senator

---

*On April 21st, 1861, a meeting of citizens of California was held at the Metropolitan Hotel in New York City, Senator Edward D. Baker being one of the vice-presidents. Resolutions were adopted "to raise a regiment composed of men from the Pacific coast and others who might choose to join."

†The Union force of actual Californians comprised eight regiments of infantry, two regiments and one battalion of cavalry and a battalion of mountaineers, all of which were engaged throughout the war in maintaining order in the Department of the Pacific.

85

from the new State of Oregon. When, a few months later, the opportunity came to him to again assume the sword, he looked to New York city for the material of his projected regiment. Mr. Wistar, an old Indian fighter, advised him, however, to depend upon Philadelphia, and the latter, who became one of his officers, began recruiting here. As a result, of the ten companies raised, nine were from Philadelphia and one from New York city. As fast as companies were formed they were sent to New York city for muster and to camp at Fort Schuyler. They were regarded as a part of the regular army. They were uniformed in gray suits, which had been confiscated in New York when just ready to be shipped to a Confederate artillery regiment. The "First California Regiment" paraded in Philadelphia upon June 29th, 1861, many people supposing the men to be actual California soldiers. After a brief stay at Suffolk Park they were sent south. While in camp at Washington the regiment was increased to fifteen companies, the accessions coming from Philadelphia. Senator John C. Breckenridge tried to induce a revolt in the camp during the absence of Col. Baker, but the eloquence of their leader, upon his return, prevailed.

In October, 1861, by authority of the President, Col. Baker increased his command to a brigade. The additional regiments thus credited to California were those of Colonels Owen, Baxter and Morehead, all from Philadelphia, respectively designated the 2d, 3d and 5th California Regiments. The 4th California Regiment, as planned, was composed of artillery and cavalry. These troops were soon detached. After the unfortunate affair at Ball's Bluff, in which Col. Baker was killed, the State of Pennsylvania claimed these four splendid infantry regiments as a part of its quota, and they became known as "the Philadelphia Brigade," Pennsylvania Volunteers. The gray uniforms of the initial regiment, then designated the 71st Regiment, Pennsylvania Volunteers, had been discarded for the Union blue, and the men were no longer in danger of being mistaken by their comrades for Confederates. Under the command of Brig.-Gen. W. W. Burns, they were now identified with Gen. Sedgwick's Division of the Second Corps.

The Philadelphia Brigade was unique in the history of the Civil War as the only organization of its kind coming from a single city of the North. The story of its achievements and losses forms one of the most brilliant pages in the annals of our citizen soldiery of the patriotic Quaker City.

On July 1st, 2d and 3d, 1887, the veteran Confederates of Pickett's Division were the guests of the Philadelphia Brigade at Gettysburg, where these former enemies met in the first assemblage of the kind on record.

Again, on July 3d, 1913, a stirring incident of the semi-centennial week at Gettysburg, the few survivors of these historic combatants met at "the stonewall." In token of this final meeting each participant was given a medal provided at the instance of Hon. John Wanamaker.

SIXTY-NINTH REGIMENT INFANTRY

COLONEL JOSHUA T. OWEN to November 29th, 1862
COLONEL DENNIS O'KANE to July 3rd, 1863.
LIEUT.-COL. WILLIAM DAVIS to July 1st, 1865.
Total Enrollment, 1,715 Officers and Men.

THE basis of this regiment was a body of Irish-American militia known as the Second Regiment, Second Brigade, First Division Pennsylvania Militia, out of which the 24th Regiment was formed for the three months enlistment, under Col. Joshua T. Owen.* At the conclusion of this service Col. Owen speedily organized a new regiment of ten companies which was accepted by the Government and mustered in by Col. Edward D. Baker as the "Second California" Regiment, August 19th, 1861. Subsequently, two companies of Zouaves known as the "Baker Guards" were added to the command.

The regiment was located at Camp Owen, Haddington, until September 17th, when it proceeded to Washington, where the men were promptly placed at work upon construction of defences on Virginia soil.

The "69th," now with Sumner's Second Corps, placed its first battle upon its flag at Yorktown, and to that "Fair Oaks" was added a few weeks later.

In the McClellan movement around Richmond, following the battle of Gaines' Mill, the "69th" won fame by a spirited onslaught upon the Confederate line at Glendale, in support of the Pennsylvania Reserve Corps, an action pronounced by Gen. Hooker, who directed it, to have been "the first successful bayonet charge of the war." Ofttimes, on other fields, the "69th" demonstrated its Celtic superiority in the use of the bayonet. At Antietam the regiment lost heavily. In November, 1862, Col. Owen became brigade commander and Lieut.-Col. Dennis O'Kane was promoted to the colonelcy. At Fredericksburg, in December, the "69th" was in the thick of the fight, losing fifty-one officers and men killed, wounded or captured. At Chancellorsville the "69th" assisted in covering the retreat. The Philadelphia Brigade marched with the Second Corps from Uniontown, Maryland, to Gettysburg, a distance of twenty miles, arriving upon the field late on July 1st.

---

*Joshua Thomas Owen was a native of Wales. He graduated in and practiced law in Philadelphia and established with his brother the Chestnut Hill School for Boys. He served as a private of the First Troop, P. C. C., in the three months' campaign, following which he helped to organize the 69th Regiment Infantry. He was promoted as brigadier-general for gallant conduct at the battle of Glendale, June 30th, 1862. After the war he became a legal publisher. Died November 7th, 1887.

88

Here the brigade was placed in the Union center upon Cemetery Ridge. At this point, on the evening of July 2d, a charge of the Confederate line, following Sickles' fight, was handsomely repulsed. The assault upon Rickett's guns at the right, occurring at about the same hour, resulting in the bloody repulse of the "Louisiana Tigers," has attracted far more historic attention. All day, July 3d, the "69th" with the "71st" and "72d" Regiments and two companies of the "106th" lay upon the battle line while the artillery fought its Titantic duel. Here, at the "copse of trees" was the center of the storm. At three o'clock the long, gray line of Pickett's men was seen advancing across the valley. The "flying wedge" of this heroic force headed straight for the stone wall. From the awful melee around the guns of Wheeler and Cushing the Philadelphia Brigade wrested victory.

Out of two hundred and fifty-eight officers and men in this scene of carnage the "69th" lost six officers and thirty-six men killed, seven officers and seventy-six men wounded, two officers and sixteen men taken prisoners. Among the slain were Col. Dennis O'Kane and Lieut.-Col. Martin Tschudy.

The remnant of the "69th" under Capt. William Davis, of Company K, was returned to Virginia, where there was more work to do.

In March, 1864, the survivors re-enlisted, and after a splendid reception at Philadelphia, returned, with Lieut.-Col. William Webb in command, to the old fighting ground, battling, in Hancock's Corps, through the Wilderness, at Spotsylvania, Cold Harbor and Petersburg. Here the "106th" (originally the "Fifth California") was merged as a separate battalion with the "69th." At Reams Station Lieut.-Col. Davis was wounded and Major Patrick S. Tinen took command.

In February, March and April, 1865, the regiment shared in the battles of the final campaign, and in its last fight, at High Bridge, Virginia, witnessed the death of Gen. Thomas A. Smyth of Philadelphia, the last brigade commander to fall in the course of the war. This gallant officer began his military career as captain of Company H of the old "24th." Soon afterward the men who had re-enlisted and the recruits were transferred to the 183d Regiment.

The balance of the regiment was mustered out on July 1st, 1865.

TOTAL LOSSES.
Killed or died from wounds.............................officers, 12; men 166
Died from disease... "   3; " 110
Wounded .... " 31; " 315
Captured or missing...................................... "   4; " 181

BATTLES.
Yorktown, Fair Oaks, Peach Orchard, Savage Station, Glendale, Malvern Hill, Chantilly, Antietam, Fredericksburg, Chancellorsville, Gettysburg, Kelly's Ford, Mine Run, Wilderness, Spotsylvania, North Anna, Totopotomoy, Cold Harbor, Petersburg, Strawberry Plain, Deep Bottom, Reams' Station, Boydton Road, Dabney's Mill, Hatcher's Run, Appomattox Court House.

SEVENTY-FIRST REGIMENT INFANTRY

Colonel Edward D. Baker to October 21st, 1861.
Colonel Isaac J. Wistar to November 29th, 1862.
Colonel R. Penn Smith to July 2d, 1864.
Total Enrollment, 1,665 Officers and Men.*

THE story of the formation of this command as the "1st California" Regiment has been outlined upon preceding pages. Soon after the death of Col. Edward D. Baker at Ball's Bluff, a lamentable affair in which the regiment lost heavily, the brigade was claimed as a part of its quota by the State of Pennsylvania and was so credited. The four commands were designated the "69th," the "71st," "72d" and "106th" Regiments, and became the "Philadelphia Brigade," Pennsylvania Infantry. Upon recovery from his wounds, inflicted at Ball's Bluff, Lieut.-Col. Isaac J. Wistar became colonel of the "71st." Brig.-Gen.

The neglected little military cemetery at Ball's Bluff.

W. W. Burns commanded the brigade, which was attached to Sedgwick's Division of the Second Corps. Early in 1862 the "71st" was engaged under Gen. N. P. Banks in West Virginia. The Philadelphia Brigade was soon transferred to the Virginia peninsula, where Gen. McClellan was operating against the enemy at Yorktown and Williamsburg. The Union advance was pushed to within sight of Richmond. At Fair Oaks the "71st" was engaged in constant fighting and skirmishing for four weeks. After the battle of Gaines Mills the "change of base" from the

*A portion of this regiment was recruited at Odd Fellows' Hall, Frankford.

89

Chickahominy River to the James River developed several attacks upon the army's endless wagon trains, in the course of which the regiment participated in four battles, making repeated charges and losing many officers and men before resting at Malvern Hill. At Harrison's Landing, upon the James River, five companies, L, M, N, P and R, were disbanded, the men being assigned to the depleted original ten companies. The scene of action was now transferred to the region in front of Washington, resulting in the battles of Chantilly and the Second Bull Run, where the "71st" assisted in covering the rear of Pope's retreat. In the northward movement which checked the Confederates at Antietam, Brig.-Gen. O. O. Howard commanded the Philadelphia Brigade. The "71st" left upon the field of Antietam one-third of its strength. In the Fredericksburg campaign, nearly three months later, the regiment, led to fruitless sacrifice by Lieut.-Col. John Markoe, was again a heavy loser. The survivors fought again, under Hooker, at Fredericksburg, after which they wintered in camp at Falmouth. The Second Corps, under Maj.-Gen. Hancock was sent, in June, 1863, to Pennsylvania. The "71st" was now under command of Col. Richard Penn Smith. Arriving at Gettysburg the regiment was placed in the center of the battle-line. Upon the afternoon of July 2d the brigade became involved in a charge during the attack upon Gen. Sickles' position, but the supreme test of its endurance was reserved for the final scene. It was just at this point that the "high-water line" of the great Rebellion is now fittingly marked. Here the gray billow broke against the solid wall of the Army of the Potomac, never to return. At Gettysburg the regiment lost ninety-eight officers and men. Following the retreating enemy back to the soil of Virginia, the Second Corps fought, through the autumn, over long-familiar ground. The "71st" wintered at Stevensburg. When the army resumed operations in May, 1864, Lieut.-Col. C. Kochersperger was in command. He was wounded at the battle of the Wilderness. Capt. Mitchell Smith, who succeeded him, was killed at Spotsylvania. At Cold Harbor the regiment made its last stand. It was now entitled to discharge. The veterans and recruits were transferred to the "69th" Regiment. One hundred and fifty-three men returned to Philadelphia and were mustered out on July 2d, 1864.

TOTAL LOSSES.

Killed or died from wounds.....................officers, 14; men, 147
Died from disease or other causes......................... " 1; " 98
Wounded .... " 24; " 372
Captured or missing....................................... " 10; " 320

BATTLES.

Falls Church, Poolesville, Ball's Bluff, Fair Oaks, Peach Orchard, Savage Station, Glendale, Antietam, Fredericksburg (1862), Fredericksburg (1863), Gettysburg, Mine Run, Wilderness, Spotsylvania, North Anna, Bethesda Church, Cold Harbor. **Present also at Yorktown, Malvern Hill, Bristoe Station and Totopotomoy.**

SEVENTY-SECOND REGIMENT INFANTRY

(Baxter's Philadelphia Fire Zouaves)

COLONEL DE WITT CLINTON BAXTER.

Total Enrollment, 1,600 Officers and Men.

———

THE volunteer firemen of Philadelphia were patriotic, intelligent and brave, and were prompt in their response to the call of President Lincoln in April, 1861, enlisting in large numbers in the three months' regiments soon afterward in the field. At the end of this term of service they were equally ready to volunteer "for three years or the war." The regiment of Fire Zouaves, which Col. De Witt Clinton Baxter formed, was composed of this fine, hardy material, nearly every fire company in the city being represented in its ranks. Camp was established at Haddington, near the old Bull's Head tavern. The regiment was mustered in August 10th, 1861, and left for Washington on September 16th. The command was assigned to Baker's Brigade, Sedgwick's Division, Sumner's Corps.

This brigade, having its origin as the "California Brigade" under direct authority of the President, was rated, at that time, as a body of regular troops. It was only after the death of Col. E. D. Baker that the several Philadelphia regiments of which it was composed were claimed by the State of Pennsylvania and given numerical designations accordingly.

While at Camp Observation, Maryland, the Fire Zouaves were increased to fifteen companies, having a muster roll of about 1,600 officers and men. The uniform then worn, of the showy French Zouave pattern, and the picturesque drill of the regiment attracted great popular admiration.*

Col. Baker fell at Ball's Bluff, Va., October 22d, 1861. He was succeeded in command of the brigade by Gen. W. W. Burns. The four regiments were rechristened as the "Philadelphia Brigade," and as such became a part, throughout their entire term of service, of the Second Corps.

After six months of comparatively peaceful guard duty and marches along the upper Potomac River and in the Shenandoah Valley the brigade entered upon the Peninsular Campaign, covering the interval from April 4th, when the march began from Fortress Monroe, to the return to that point on August 22d, and including the movements and battles outlined in the experiences of the 69th and 71st Regiments.

---

*The greater part of the regiment eventually discarded this conspicuous uniform in the course of the Peninsular Campaign. At Gettysburg the 72d was garbed in the plain blue uniforms of the regulation pattern, the figure of the Zouave in bronze being but a type of the regimental synonym.

The "72d" reached Alexandria, Va., on August 28th, hastening thence with the Corps to the support of Pope's force, arriving near Manassas in time to assist in covering his retreat. At Antietam the "72d" met with severe and prolonged fighting and heavy loss. The campaign ended with further losses in the occupation of Fredericksburg and operations at Chancellorsville. The regiment was encamped at Falmouth, Va., to the opening of the Gettysburg campaign. The command reached the field on the evening of July 1st and went into position near the center of the battle line, and there, at the "bloody angle," stands today the Zouave, in bronze, typifying, with clubbed musket, the heroic hand-to-hand battle the regiment made on July 3d, 1863. When the advance of the Confederate column across the valley began the "72d" was posted in support and to the rear of the batteries upon Hancock's front. As the enemy drove in the brigade pickets from the Emmitsburg road, the regiment was rushed to the front line, striking the assailants at the famous stone wall and the "clump of trees." Upon the morning of that eventful day the Fire Zouaves numbered four hundred and fifty-eight officers and men. After the fury of the conflict was past there were but two hundred and sixty-six of the "72d" left for further duty. Soon afterward Col. Baxter succeeded Gen. Webb in command of the brigade. Lieut.-Col. Theodore Hesser now commanded the Fire Zouaves, only to fall, a few months later, at Mine Run. In the campaign of 1864 the regiment fought in the Wilderness, at Spotsylvania, and again, with heavy loss, at Cold Harbor. At Petersburg the Philadelphia Brigade, all four regiments in line, stormed the Confederate defences and held them. This was the "72d's" last battle. A few days later the survivors were sent home and were mustered out.*

TOTAL LOSSES.

Killed or mortally wounded	officers, 12;	men,	198
Died from disease or other cause	" 1;	"	119
Wounded in action, not mortally	" 25;	"	533
Captured or missing	" 2;	"	163

BATTLES.

Yorktown, Fair Oaks, Peach Orchard, Savage Station, Glendale, Malvern Hill, Chantilly, Antietam, Fredericksburg, Chancellorsville, Gettysburg, Mine Run, Wilderness, Spotsylvania, North Anna, Totopotomoy, Cold Harbor, Petersburg.

---

*The semi-centennial anniversary of the muster in of the 72d Regiment, Baxter's Zouaves, was celebrated by the survivors and their families at Belmont Mansion on October 12th, 1911. Of the one hundred and fifteen living at that date, sixty-five attended. Among them were Major John Lockhart and Capt. Thomas F. Longaker, the only surviving officers.

ONE HUNDRED AND SIXTH REGIMENT INFANTRY

Colonel Turner G. Morehead to April 5th, 1864.
Lieut.-Col. William L. Curry to May 11th, 1864.
Total Enrollment, 1,020 Officers and Men.

A FTER the return of the 22d Regiment, of the three-months' enlistments, its Colonel, Turner G. Morehead, a veteran of the Mexican War, and some of his officers commenced to recruit a new regiment for the three-year service. It was mustered in during August, September and October, 1861. Many members of the Philadelphia Light Guards and a large number of the enlisted men of the "22d" joined this command, which was first known as the "Fifth California" Regiment, being part of Colonel Baker's California Brigade, but later as one of the four regiments composing the Philadelphia Brigade.

The "106th" joined Colonel Baker's Brigade just prior to the battle of Ball's Bluff, Va., in which part of his force was trapped.

Under Brigadier-General William W. Burns, and as a unit to the Second Army Corps in the Second Brigade, Second Division, Second Corps of the Army of the Potomac, the "106th" shared in all of the marches and battles of the Philadelphia Brigade through the Virignia Peninsula up to the gates of Richmond, and from Savage Station to Harrison Landing, fighting desperately at Savage Station, at Glendale and Malvern Hill, then in the succeeding Pope Campaign, where, at Flint Hill, acting as rear guard of the army in the retreat from the Second Bull Run, they led the enemy into a trap, inflicted great loss upon him and checked his advance in that direction, thence along the road that led to Antietam.

Here, with Gen. Oliver O. Howard as Brigade Commander, on that beautiful September morning, in what is known as the "West Wood," the brigade fought heroically against fearful odds when all the other troops had left, holding their ground until the enemy, in overwhelming numbers, swept around their flank, compelled them to retire, leaving upon that part of Antietam's bloody field five hundred and forty-five of their members killed and wounded.

The Second Corps now returned to Virginia and to Fredericksburg's fatal field where, for the first time, the Philadelphia Brigade was commanded by one of Philadelphia's sons, Brigadier-General Joshua T. Owen, who led his brigade in that fearful charge upon Marye's Heights, until he got within ninety yards of the famous stone wall, and, unwilling to give up one foot of the ground he had gained with such heavy loss, directed his men to lie down, and all that long, cold December day they lay there, subjected to both infantry and artillery fire, until relieved after dark.

The regiment had been so depleted by the storm of battle at Antietam and Fredericksburg that, after a winter in camp and accession of recruits, it reported to Gettysburg, along with the equally reduced 69th, 71st and 72d Regiments, with but three hundred and thirty-five officers and men. The brigade was now commanded by Brigadier-General Alexander S. Webb. Arriving upon the field on the morning of the second, Companies A and B were at once advanced as skirmishers to the Emmitsburg road, and during the morning made a gallant attack upon the Bliss House, between the lines, and with the help of four companies of the 12th New Jersey Regiment, dislodged the enemy, burned the house and barn and captured one hundred prisoners.

Near the conclusion of the heavy fighting on the left of our line, on the afternoon of July 2d, when Wright, with his Georgia brigade, had swept around the right of Sickles' command and had captured the guns of Brown's Rhode Island Battery and was forcing his way to the position of the Philadelphia Brigade, Gen. Hancock ordered the 106th Regiment to charge upon the advancing enemy, upon whom the brigade was pouring a withering fire. Dashing over the low stone wall the regiment rushed the then discomfited enemy and drove him back to and beyond the Emmitsburg road, recapturing the guns of Brown's Battery and two hundred and fifty prisoners, principally of the 48th Georgia Regiment, including its colonel and twenty officers. The regiment returned to its position with the brigade and was immediately hurried to the right, upon request of Gen. Howard, leaving a detail of fifty men and two full companies, A and B, with the brigade, upon the front of Gibbon's Division of the Second Corps.

In the gathering shadows of evening a gray column of Early's men, among them the vaunted "Louisiana Tigers" was sent swarming up the slope of Cemetery Hill east of the Baltimore pike, where Rickett's and Weiderick's batteries needed instant help, and the "106th" arrived in time to join with the decimated regiments of Howard's Eleventh Corps, saved the guns of those batteries, and hurled back the few survivors of that gallant and deadly sortie.

On the morning of the fourth, the regiment was ordered to advance and reconnoitre towards the town. Finding their way but feebly contested, they pushed forward and found that the enemy had evacuated. Thus the "106th" Regiment was among the first to enter Gettysburg since the retreat through it on the night of July 1st. Its outpost line and the two companies that remained with the brigade shared the glory of the repulse of Pickett at the "clump of trees."

After Gettysburg, the Philadelphia Brigade, less than a regiment in numbers, returned to Virginia, and went into camp near Brandy Station for the winter, during which time many of the regiment re-enlisted. In April, 1864, Col. Morehead resigned.

During the summer campaign of 1864, battle followed battle with terrible regularity, as the waning fortunes of the Confederacy made its brave soldiery more desperate, and our men more determined to bring the war to an end, beginning with the three-days' battle of the Wilderness and continuing through Spotsylvania Court House, North Anna, Totopotomoy, Cold Harbor and Petersburg, in all of which the regiment was in the thickest of the fighting and suffered the heavy loss of five officers and one hundred and ten men from its already reduced numbers. Among the many lost at Spotsylvania was Lieut.-Col. William L. Curry, who died, a month later, of his wound.

Before Petersburg, the "106th" was given surcease of fighting, when its term of enlistment expired, but, unfortunately, before that event, on June 22d, 1864, three officers and ninety-one men were taken prisoners.

On July 27th the veterans and recruits were consolidated into three companies, F, H and K, and united with the 69th Regiment for field service, but retained its identity as a separate battalion. The remainder of the regiment was sent to Washington, and after a period of guard duty at Arlington Heights, for about thirty days, was ordered to Philadelphia and was mustered out on September 10th, 1864.

The 106th Battalion, left in the field, served through Deep Bottom, Reams Station, Boydton Plank Road, Hatcher's Run and Dabney Mills to the scene of the surrender of Appomattox, participated in the Grand Review at Washington, and was mustered out on June 30th, 1865.*

TOTAL LOSSES.

	officers,		men,	
Killed or died from wounds	9;		90	
Died of disease or other causes	"	1;	"	94
Wounded, not mortally	"	24;	"	373
Captured or missing	"	5;	"	152

BATTLES.

(Including those of the 106th Battalion.)

Yorktown, Fair Oaks. Peach Orchard, Savage Station, Glendale, Malvern Hill, Flint Hill, Antietam, Fredericksburg, Chancellorsville, Haymarket, Gettysburg, Kelly's Ford, Mine Run, Wilderness. Spotsylvania, North Anna. Totopotomoy, Cold Harbor, Petersburg, Strawberry Plains, Deep Bottom, Ream's Station, Boydton Plank Road, Hatcher's Run (February 6 and 7, 1865), Hatcher's Run (March 25, 1865), Dabney's Mill, Appomattox Court House.

---

*On October 18th, 1911, fifteen of the thirty survivors of the regiment met at 1108 Sansom street to celebrate the semi-centennial anniversary of organization. Those present were Col. R. W. P. Allen, the only surviving original officer; Thomas Thompson, Dr. G. J. R. Miller, Col. Joseph R. C. Ward, J. E. Heller, W. H. Huddell, George Waldron, Joseph Weber, George Hellem, William H. Abrams, Daniel E. Ridge, Maurice Finn and Sergt.-Major William H. Neiler.

SEVENTY-THIRD REGIMENT INFANTRY

COLONEL JOHN A. KOLTES to August 30th, 1862.
COLONEL GUSTAVUS A. MUEHLECK to January 27th, 1863.
LIEUT.-COL. WILLIAM MOORE to February 8th, 1864.
LIEUT.-COL. CHARLES C. CRESSON to August 24th, 1865.*
Total Enrollment, 1,260 Officers and Men.

T HIS regiment, largely recruited from the local German rifle companies, was originally known as the "Pennsylvania Legion." It was encamped, during the summer of 1861, at Engle & Wolf's farm, upon the east side of the Schuylkill River. The regiment, under Col. John A. Koltes, left for Washington upon September 24th, where it was assigned to Blenker's German Division. The autumn and winter were devoted to camp and picket duty in Virginia. Upon March 3d, 1862, three hundred and fifty men from the disbanded 66th Regiment were added to its ranks. In May the division joined Fremont's Mountain Department in West Virginia, the 73d scoring its first battle at Cross Keys. Under Gen. Sigel, the German regiments formed a staunch rear guard for Pope's retreat, incident to which were the battles of Freeman's Ford and Groveton. At the hard-fought battle of the second Bull Run, August 30th, the "73d" was the target for deadly artillery fire, losing two hundred and sixteen killed and wounded, including Colonel Koltes, acting brigade commander, and Capt. Augustus Breuckner, acting major. Without further engagements the "73d" wintered at Falmouth, Va. At this time Lieut.-Col. William Moore succeeded Col. G. A. Muehleck, resigned. Under Hooker's reorganization the regiment formed part of Col. A. Buschbeck's First Brigade, Second Division of the Eleventh Corps. At Chancellorsville the regiment lost one hundred and six officers and men, killed, wounded and missing. Among the killed was Capt. Henry J. Giltinan. Capt. Jacob Liebfried was mortally wounded.

After a week of hurried marching, from Edward's Ferry, the Eleventh Corps reached Gettysburg upon July 1st. At two o'clock P. M. the "73d" was in position and charged into the town, assisting effectively in halting the Confederates. The regiment's second position fronted upon the Taneytown road, west of the Junction of the Emmitsburg road, being exposed to continuous artillery fire. An assault was made at this point by a Confederate column, which was repulsed with great loss. Upon the second the "73d" occupied the same position upon the scene of the

---

*Lieut.-Colonel William Moore was commissioned colonel January 27th, 1863. Lieut.-Colonel Charles C. Cresson was commissioned colonel May 1st, 1865. Neither of these officers was mustered with the above rank.

CITIZENS' VOLUNTEER HOSPITAL, AT BROAD STREET AND WASHINGTON AVENUE. Maintained by private subscriptions. This hospital received sick and wounded men of the army and navy passing through the City or arriving at the railroad station opposite. Fire ambulances carried them thence to the various military hospitals.

MOYAMENSING HALL (Christian Street Hospital, U. S. Army).

OLD CARRIAGE FACTORY AT FIFTH AND BUTTONWOOD STREETS, used as a
hospital, military prison and provost barracks.

final Confederate assault in the afternoon. When the enemy withdrew the regiment, with its brigade, occupied the town. The regimental losses were seven killed and twenty-seven wounded out of fourteen officers and three hundred and eighteen men present.*

At Alexandria, Va., during the remainder of the summer, the "73d" was occupied, under Colonel Moore, who had returned, in convoying drafted men. In September the Eleventh Corps was transferred, under Gen. Hooker, to the West. Late in October the brigade marched from Bridgeport, Tenn., toward Chattanooga, having a skirmish en route at Wauhatchie. Upon arrival at Chattanooga Col. Moore retired from command, being invalided, and as the regiment had no field officers, Lieut.-Col. Joseph B. Taft, of the 143d New York Regiment, was placed in command.

The "73d" was in the storming line at Missionary Ridge upon November 25th. In the terrific fighting which ensued, Colonel Taft was killed, and nearly all of the survivors of the "73d" were made prisoners. The regimental flag was secreted about his person by Capt. John Kennedy, of Company H, and after his exchange, six months later, was brought safely home. The remnant of the "73d" wintered at Chattanooga. In January, 1864, those who re-enlisted were given a veteran's furlough. The old Eleventh Corps, being merged into the Twentieth Corps, the veterans and recruits of the "73d" marched and fought with Sherman to Atlanta, on to Savannah and northward through the Carolinas. The last commander of the regiment was Lieut.-Col. Charles C. Cresson. At Bentonville, N. C., it fought in the last important battle of the war. After the surrender of Johnston, at Raleigh, N. C., the "73d" marched to Alexandria, Va., where it was mustered out on July 14th, 1865.

TOTAL LOSSES.

	officers		men
Killed, or died from wounds	5;	"	96
Died of disease	" 0;	"	114
Wounded, not mortally	" 18;	"	303
Captured or missing	" 18;	"	160

BATTLES AND ENGAGEMENTS.

Cross Keys, Rappahannock River, Groveton, Bull Run (second), Chancellorsville, Gettysburg, Wauhatchie, Missionary Ridge, Rocky Face Ridge, Resaca, New Hope Church, Pine Knob, Kenesaw Mountain, Peach Tree Creek, Atlanta, March to the Sea, Savannah, Bentonville, Durham Station (Johnston's Surrender).

---

*Having no field officers the regiment was commanded in this battle by Capt. D. F. Kelly. The "73d" was among the first troops to occupy the town of Gettysburg as the Confederates withdrew on the morning of July 4th. Skirmishing with the rear guard of the enemy from street to street, they were hailed with joy by the inhabitants, who had remained concealed in their homes awaiting, with intense anxiety, the issue of the battle.

SEVENTY-FOURTH REGIMENT INFANTRY

COLONEL ALEXANDER VON SCHIMMELFENNIG to November 9th, 1862.
COLONEL A. VON HARTUNG to July 11th, 1864.
COLONEL GOTTLIEB HOBURG to August 29th, 1865.
Philadelphia Companies A and K.
Total Enrollment, 197 Officers and Men.

THE "74th" was largely composed of men of German birth or parentage. Originating at Pittsburgh, the majority of its recruits were from the western counties. It was mustered into the United State service, as the 35th Regiment, upon September 14th, 1861, and was then sent to camp at Engle & Wolf's farm, near the Columbia Bridge, upon the Schuylkill River, Philadelphia.

Col. Schimmelfennig was an experienced officer of the Prussian Army, and this fact attracted many German veterans to the regiment. While at Philadelphia a detachment, locally recruited by Capt. Alexander Von Mitzel, was added to Company K. Later, while in winter quarters at Hunter's Chapel, Virginia, a Philadelphia company joined the command, under Capt. Von Hartung. This company had been on duty at Fort Delaware and became Company A. The number of the regiment was changed to "74th" and it was attached to Blenker's German Division.

In March, 1862, the "74th" marched to the Shenandoah Valley to reinforce Fremont's Mountain Department, assisting in driving Stonewall Jackson's force southward after the battle of Cross Keys. Under Major-Gen. Franz Sigel a forced march was made to Cedar Mountain. In Pope's movement of August, 1862, the regiment met the enemy at Freeman's Ford. Here Brig.-Gen. Henry Bohlen, commanding the brigade, was killed, Col. Schimmelfennig taking his place. Battles followed at Groveton and Bull Run (second). During the Antietam campaign the "74th" was posted in the defences of Washington. Col. Schimmelfennig having been promoted, the command fell upon Major Von Hartung, who subsequently became colonel.

Under Hooker, in 1863, Sigel's troops were in the disaster at Chancellorsville, where the "74th" lost heavily while protecting the retreat. The First Brigade, Third Division of the Eleventh Corps, arrived at Gettysburg early in the afternoon of July 1st. The "74th" was first advanced to the west of the Carlisle Road in support of artillery. In this position the regiment lost one hundred and three officers and men out of one hundred and thirty-four present (at the site of its monument).* The

---

*(Quoted from dedication address by Capt. Paul Rohrbacker, Gettysburg, July 2d, 1888.) The official records, as well as the monumental inscription at Gettysburg, testify that the "74th" numbered, at that battle, three hundred and eighty-one officers and men, losing a total in killed, 10; wounded, 40; captured or missing, 60.

99

remnant retreated to the new line at Cemetery Hill, where those of the command who had been on picket duty rejoined. This position was held to the end of the battle.

Upon August 7th the Third Division, now under Brig.-Gen. George H. Gordon, was transported to South Carolina, serving upon the coast islands near Charleston until August 17th, 1864. In September the majority of the veterans were mustered out. The regiment was recruited and reorganized and assigned to guard the Baltimore and Ohio Railway. In March, 1865, seven new companies were added. The regiment was finally mustered out at Clarksburg, Va., upon August 29th, 1865.

Forty of the commissioned officers serving at various periods with the regiment were from Philadelphia.

TOTAL LOSSES (Regimental).

Killed in action ....officers, 2; men, 39
Died of wounds .... " " 19
Died of disease and other causes........................... " 1; " 71
Wounded, not mortally .... " 9; " 129
Captured or missing...................................... " 4; " 128

BATTLES AND ENGAGEMENTS.

Cross Keys, Freeman's Ford, Groveton, Second Bull Run, Chancellorsville, Gettysburg, John's Island, James Island.

SEVENTY-FIFTH REGIMENT INFANTRY

COLONEL W. HENRY C. BOHLEN to April 28th, 1862.
COLONEL FRANCIS MAHLER to July 1st, 1863.
MAJOR AUGUST LEDIG to March 8th, 1864.
LIEUT.-COL. ALVIN VON MATZDORFF to September 1st, 1865.
Total Enrollment, 1,293 Officers and Men.

THIS fine regiment was recruited in 1861 almost entirely from among the patriotic German citizens of Philadelphia. Numbers of its officers had been schooled in foreign armies. Col. Bohlen had served as aide to Gen. Worth, in Mexico. In recognition of this fact the regiment's first rendezvous, at Hestonville, was named "Camp Worth." The "75th" was mustered in by companies during August and in September, prior to its departure for Washington, on the 26th. Joining Gen. Louis Blenker's German division the regiment established its camp at Hunter's Chapel, Va. Aside from minor detours the command remained here until the following spring. On

April 6th, 1862, the "75th" was sent, in inclement weather, to the Mountain Department at Winchester. At Berry's Ferry, on the Shenandoah river, while Companies I and K were being taken across, the craft utilized sank, drowning two commissioned officers, Capt. Christian Wyck and Lieut. Adolph Winter, and fifty-one men, who were engulfed by the weight of their accoutrements. First Sergeant Joseph Tiedemann, of Company K, lost his life in an effort to save his captain. This tragic affair cast a long-felt gloom over the regiment.

Reporting to Major-Gen. Fremont at Winchester, on April 18th, Col. Bohlen was commissioned brigadier-general, and with Fremont's First Corps the regiment, under Lieut.-Col. Mahler, joined the other German regiments from Philadelphia in an advance in pursuit of the retreating Confederates up the Shenandoah Valley. At Cross Keys and Port Republic the "75th" was engaged on the left flank, losing heavily. At this time the regiment became a part of the Second Brigade, Third Division, First Corps, of which Major-Gen. Franz Sigel, who had succeeded Fremont, was in command. This energetic German officer now led his troops eastward, across the Blue Ridge, in order to effect a junction with Gen. Pope's army. Lieut.-Col. Mahler received his commission as colonel on July 20th. At the battle of Freeman's Ford, on August 22d, Gen. Bohlen was killed.* In close and desperate fighting at the second battle of Bull Run the regiment lost one hundred and thirty-three, killed and wounded. Among those killed were Lieutenants William Froelich and William Bowen. Five officers were wounded. More than a score of non-commissioned officers and men were honored with special mention in reports for bravery on this field. Sigel's corps was designated the "Eleventh" in November. When the army undertook its abortive winter sorties upon Fredericksburg, the "75th" experienced its full share of mud marching. At Chancellorsville, May 2d, 1863, the regiment, upon the exposed right flank of the battle line, was overcome by an avalanche of Stonewall Jackson's men, losing in the confusion its Lieut-Colonel and forty men captured. The regiment rallied near United States Ford and remained there until assigned a position in the second line of battle.

The movement preceding the Gettysburg campaign began on June 12th. Nineteen days later the Eleventh Corps, approaching Gettysburg after a trying fourteen-mile march from Taneytown, on the morning of July 1st, heard the guns of the First Corps. Hurrying through the village, to the great joy of the residents, the Eleventh Corps formed its line of battle to the right of the Carlisle road, advancing to the attack at one o'clock. The two Corps here held back the determined and confident Confederates until late in the day, then retreating to a new position upon Cemetery Hill, providentially fortified by Gen. Steinwehr.

---

*The body of Gen. W. Henry C. Bohlen rests in the family vault in front of St. John's Evangelical Lutheran Church, Race Street below Sixth Street.

In its part of the conflict of that momentous day the "75th" was arrayed against a portion of Dole's Brigade, Rode's Division, Ewell's Corps, which inflicted upon it a loss of seventy-two per cent. in killed and wounded, of the fifteen officers and one hundred and seventy-nine men actually on the firing line.* Two officers and twenty-nine men were killed, six officers and ninety-seven men were wounded and three men were captured or missing. This percentage of loss was exceeded at Gettysburg by but one other regiment, the 1st Minnesota, which recorded casualties of eighty-two per cent. The losses of the "75th" all occurred within the deadly half hour during which the command was under fire. Among the killed were Lieuts. Henry Hauschild and Louis Mahler; of the wounded Col. Francis Mahler and Lieut. William J. Sill died in consequence. After Col. Mahler had been wounded the command devolved upon Major August Ledig, an experienced and courageous officer.†

The Eleventh Corps was transferred to the Army of the Cumberland in the autumn of 1863. At the end of its journey westward the "75th" was stationed at Bridgeport, Alabama, to guard the railroad bridge spanning the Tennessee River at that point. In the subsequent movement to Wauhatchie the regiment was engaged in support of Gen. Geary's Pennsylvanians in the night battle of October 28th and 29th, taking some prisoners. The "75th" was present at the several closing battles around Chattanooga, after which it was sent in the direction of Knoxville with a column moved for the re-enforcement of Burnside. On January 2d, 1864, the regiment was re-mustered as a veteran organization, and returned upon furlough to Philadelphia. Two months later, with many recruits, it rejoined the Army of the Tennessee near Nashville. At the battle of Franklin, Tenn., on November 30th, Company E, then on outpost duty, was captured. A large mounted detachment was organized in the fall of 1864 for duty at headquarters, being thus engaged for several months in provost and scout service. Without further battles the "75th" was retained in the army to September 1st, 1865, when it was mustered out, and arrived on the 12th

---

*While in bivouac at Taneytown on the evening of June 30th fifty men were detached from the regiment to assist in guarding the reserve ammunition train. This contingent, absent on this duty from the encounter of July 1st, has not been duly allowed for by military writers generally in estimating the percentage loss on that day by the 75th Regiment.

†Col. Mahler was crippled in the thick of the fight by the fall of his horse, which had been shot, but he remained a conspicuous figure in the encouragement of his line, receiving a mortal wound at the moment when the "75th," outflanked, began to fall back. At this instant Lieut. T. Albert Steiger, in command of Companies I and K, ran to his assistance and, despite the imminent danger of death or capture, brought him, with great difficulty from the field. Col. Mahler died on the morning of July 4th at the field hospital of the Eleventh Corps.

in Philadelphia, having served more than four years. Two hundred and thirty-six officers and men were present at the discharge.

TOTAL LOSSES.

Killed, or died from wounds.................................officers, 6; men, 57
Died from disease .... " 57
Drowned (on the Shenandoah) ....—....... " 2; " 51
Wounded, not mortally .... " 11; " 219
Captured, or missing ....—.............. " 4; " 95

BATTLES.

Cross Keys, Freeman's Ford, Groveton, Second Bull Run, Fredericksburg, Chancellorsville, Gettysburg, Wauhatchie, Lookout Mountain, Missionary Ridge, Franklin, Nashville.

EIGHTY-FIRST REGIMENT INFANTRY

COLONEL JAMES MILLER to May 31st, 1862.
COLONEL CHARLES F. JOHNSON to November 24th, 1862.
COLONEL H. BOYD McKEEN to June 3d, 1864.
COLONEL WILLIAM WILSON to June 29th, 1865.

Philadelphia Companies A, B, C, D, E and F.

Total Enrollment, 1,100 Officers and Men.

THE "81st," recruited in Philadelphia and the counties of Carbon and Luzerne by James Miller, a soldier of the Mexican War, was assembled at the camp near Easton, Pa., the officers and men being mustered in during August, 1861. The regiment proceeded to Washington October 10th, there being attached to Casey's First Brigade, First Division, Second Corps. Routine duty occupied the winter and spring to the opening of the peninsular campaign.

At Fair Oaks the regiment experienced its first important battle, Col. Miller being among the slain. Lieut. Horace M. Lee, of Company F, was mortally wounded. Capt. Samuel Sherlock, of Company D, was killed on picket June 15th. During the "change of base" the regiment fought at White Oak Swamp, Peach Orchard, Savage Station, Glendale and Malvern Hill, losing Col. Johnson, Captains Connor and Harkness wounded, and Lieut.-Col. Eli T. Connor killed. Late in August the "81st" was hurried to the field of the Second Bull Run, arriving at the end of the fighting. On the way to Antietam, in September, the regiment assisted in clearing the pass at South Mountain. The regimental losses at Antietam, chiefly incurred in a gallant charge by Richardson's Division, included Capt. Philip R. Schuyler and Lieut. William H. Vandyke, killed.

In the Burnside campaign against Fredericksburg the "81st" was under fire at Falmouth. In November Col. Johnson resigned because of wounds and Major H. Boyd McKeen was promoted to colonel.

At the battle of Fredericksburg, December 11th-15th, 1862, the "81st" charged through the town with the division, losing Lieut. Clinton Swain, of Company C, killed. In this assault, also, Col. McKeen and five captains were wounded and a large number of the rank and file were killed or wounded. In the Chancellorsville campaign of April, 1863, further losses were incurred. Guarding the northward roads and clearing the passes en route, the Second Corps was occupied in June on its way to Gettysburg, arriving on the field on the evening of July 1st. Taking its place in the line of battle, the "81st" was posted, at first, near the cemetery, but later moved in support of Sickles' position in front of Little Round Top, here participating in the terrific fighting, in the afternoon, upon that portion of the field. From one hundred and seventy-five officers and men present the regiment lost, killed, nine men; wounded, five officers and forty men; captured, eight men.

In the Mine Run campaign Capt. David J. Phillips was killed. Early in January, 1864, the "81st" re-enlisted, and, with the opening of the campaign, Col. McKeen was advanced to command of the brigade and Major William Wilson assumed command of the regiment. This officer was commissioned colonel on October 30th, 1864. After Spotsylvania the Second Corps essayed, without success, to dislodge the enemy at Cold Harbor. Col. McKeen here fell, at the head of his troops, a dauntless leader, bearing the scars of three former wounds.

In front of Petersburg Capt. David H. Ginder was killed, during the assault of June 17th. At Strawberry Plains, in July; Ream's Station and Deep Bottom, in August, the "81st" won further laurels. The winter was spent in the trenches before Petersburg. In the final campaign the regiment escaped material losses to April 7th, when, almost within sight of Appomattox, the "81st" was one of three regiments sent, under Brig.-Gen. Nelson A. Miles, into a charge on the entrenched Confederates, and was nearly destroyed. Captains Charles Wilson and John Bond, both Philadelphians, were killed. At the end of this disastrous affair there remained only Col. William Wilson, two line officers, thirty-six enlisted men and the colors.*

The "thin short line" left in the field was returned to Washington and mustered out on June 29th, 1865.

The "81st" lost more officers and men in the four years of service than any other command largely composed of Philadelphia volunteers. Of the field and staff, four were killed in battle and two died from disease; of the line officers, fourteen were killed outright, and of the wounded, some afterward died in consequence.

---

*Oration of Capt. Harry Wilson, September 12th, 1889, at dedication of monument, Gettysburg, page 409, "Pennsylvania at Gettysburg," Vol. I.

TOTAL LOSSES.

Killed, or died from wounds..............................officers, 18; men, 190
Died from disease, etc. .... " 2; " 89
Wounded, not mortally .... " 44; " 518
Captured or missing .... " 3; " 190

BATTLES.

Yorktown, Fair Oaks, Peach Orchard, Savage's Station, White Oak Swamp, Glendale, Malvern Hill, Antietam, Fredericksburg, Chancellorsville, Gettysburg, Bristoe Station, Kelly's Ford, Mine Run, Wilderness, Spotsylvania, North Anna, Totopotomoy, Cold Harbor, Petersburg, Strawberry Plains, Deep Bottom, Ream's Station, Petersburg (Squirrel Level Road), White Oak Road, Sutherland Station, Amelia Court House, Farmville (Cumberland Church), Appomattox.

EIGHTY-SECOND REGIMENT INFANTRY

COLONEL DAVID H. WILLIAMS to February 14th, 1863.
COLONEL ISAAC C. BASSETT to July 13th, 1865.
Total Enrollment (about) 2,300 Officers and Men.

THIS regiment was organized at Washington, July 27th, 1861, nine companies being from Philadelphia and one (B) from Pittsburgh. It was attached to Graham's Brigade, First Division, Fourth Corps. In the course of its history it was consecutively identified with the First Brigade, Third Division, Sixth Corps; the Fourth Brigade, First Division, Sixth Corps, and the Third Brigade, First Division, Sixth Corps. The division remained on duty in the defences of Washington to March 10th, 1862, then advancing on Manassas, and a few days later embarked to Fortress Monroe and marched up the Peninsula against Yorktown and Williamsburg. At Fair Oaks, in its first severe battle, the "82d" lost thirty-two men killed and wounded. During June the regiment was engaged in the "change of base," being engaged at White Oak Swamp and Glendale. At Malvern Hill, July 1st, Lieuts. James B. Grier and Mark H. Roberts were killed. In September the division moved from Harrison's Landing, by transports, to re-enforce Gen. Pope. Following the battle of Chantilly the Maryland Campaign resulted in the battle of Antietam, the 82d being under fire at Sharpsburg. Couch's Division was now transferred to the Sixth Corps, with which the regiment fought at Williamsport and in the December attack upon Fredericksburg. While in winter quarters Col. Williams was succeeded in command by Lieut.-Col. Bassett.

The campaign of 1863 opened with the Chancellorsville struggle. At the second attempt on Fredericksburg the "82d" formed part of the assaulting column at Marye's Heights (May 3d), and also fought on the same day at Salem Church, losing heavily. Among the fatally wounded was Capt. John H. Delap.

The evening of July 1st, 1863, found the regiment encamped on Pipe Creek, near Manchester, Maryland, thirty-seven miles southeast from Gettysburg. Here the Sixth Corps began its forced march of seventeen hours. In the battles of the 2d and 3d of July the "82d" had few casualties. The pursuit of Lee ended with an action near Funkstown, July 12th. In the Bristoe Campaign the regiment supported the cavalry at Brandy Station, and in November was engaged at Rappahannock Station and Robertson's Tavern. Part of the regiment re-enlisted as a veteran organization while at Brandy Station on January 1st, 1864, being accorded a furlough home. Those who had not re-enlisted were sent with Shaler's Brigade to guard duty at the Johnson's Island Prison Camp in Lake Erie. This detachment returned to the front in May and participated in the battle of Spotsylvania. The 82d Veterans met with its greatest ordeal at Cold Harbor on June 3d, 1864, losing there, in killed, wounded and missing, one hundred and seventy-three officers and men. Among the killed was Lieut. Robert G. Creighton. Crossing the James River on June 16th the brigade was involved in the operations in the vicinity of Petersburg until hurried, with the Sixth Corps, to the defence of Washington, then threatened by Early. The pursuit now led into West Virginia, with actions at Charlestown and Halltown. At Halltown the non-veterans completed their term of service and were ordered home. The veterans and recruits were organized into a battalion of five companies, retaining the regimental number. This contingent served under Gen. Sheridan in the final Valley campaign and through the winter and spring siege of Petersburg. In its last battle, at Sailor's Creek, three days before the surrender at Appomattox, Lieut. William H. Myers was killed. Following the dispersal of the Confederates in Virginia the "82d" marched to Danville and three weeks later turned homeward. After the Sixth Corps review at Washington on June 8th the battalion was returned to Philadelphia, and on July 13th, 1865, was mustered out.

TOTAL LOSSES.

Killed or died from wounds	officers,	5;	men, 107
Died from disease or other causes		"	61
Wounded, not fatally		21; "	378
Captured or missing		"	52

BATTLES, ETC.

Warwick River, Yorktown, Williamsburg, Fair Oaks, White Oak Swamp, Glendale, Malvern Hill, Chantilly, Antietam, Williamsport, Fredericksburg, Franklin's Crossing, Marye's Heights (Fredericksburg), Salem Church, Banks' Ford, Gettysburg, Funkstown, Culpeper Court House, Rappahannock Station, Mine Run, Robertson's Tavern, Spotsylvania (non-veterans), North Anna, Totopotomoy, Hawe's Shop, Hanover Court House, Cold Harbor, Weldon Railroad, Fort Stevens, Snicker's Gap, Charlestown, Halltown, Winchester, Siege of Petersburg, including Dabney's Mills, Hatcher's Run, Fort Steadman, Fall of Petersburg, Sailor's Creek, Appomattox Court House.

EIGHTY-EIGHTH REGIMENT INFANTRY

(Cameron Light Guards)

COLONEL GEORGE P. MCLEAN to December 14th, 1862.
COLONEL GEORGE W. GILE to March 2d, 1863.
COLONEL LOUIS WAGNER to June 6th, 1865.
Philadelphia Companies, C, D, E, F, G, I and K.
Total Enrollment, 1,400 Officers and Men.

———————

THIS regiment was recruited under the title of the "Cameron Light Guards," three of its ten companies, A, B and H, coming from Reading and vicinity. The first camp (Stokley) was located near the Schuylkill river, just below the Wissahickon creek, the site, now appropriately marked, being within the present limits of Fairmount Park. The companies were mustered in during August and September, 1861. The regiment received marching orders and left the city October 5th. Muskets and the regimental number in the Pennsylvania line were provided at Alexandria, Va., where the command was posted through the fall and part of the winter. Upon February 18th, 1862, five companies were sent to guard the forts upon the Maryland side of the Potomac. Two months later the entire regiment was ordered to rendezvous at Cloud's Mills, Md., where it was assigned to Brigadier-General A. Duryea's Brigade, First Corps, in company with the 107th Pennsylvania Infantry. On April 15th, 1862, the "88th" was sent to picket the railroad west of Bull Run. Early in May the regiment embarked at Alexandria for Aquia Creek, advancing, on the 11th, to the Rappahannock river. The tactics of the Confederates here defeated the Federal plans. After a return over the same route the "88th" was entrained at Alexandria for Manassas. From this point, under Maj.-Gen. E. O. C. Ord, the Division started upon a march to the Shenandoah Valley, a trying and fruitless expedition, entailing a loss of about one hundred men upon the regiment, due to exposure and exhaustion. At Cedar Mountain, Rickett's Division, of which the "88th" was a part, was placed in support of artillery. Pope's arduous campaign ended with the second battle of Bull Run. In this terrific contest the "88th" lost twenty-eight officers and men killed (including Lieut.-Col. Joseph A. McLean and Capt. Belsterling of Company C), eighty-five wounded and forty-eight missing. Under Major Gile the "88th" marched through Washington on the night of September 5th. With brief respite the regiment was hurried to South Mountain and Antietam, and reached this historic field with three hundred and fifty men. Here the loss was eighteen killed and sixty wounded. During the battle, Major Gile being wounded, Capt. H. R. Myers assumed command. A few days later the remnant of the "88th" was led by Capt. Griffith, of Company H, who commanded until, on October 30th, Col. George P. McLean returned to the camp. Soon afterward this officer resigned because of ill health. Major George W. Gile was commissioned Colonel and Capt. Louis Wagner Lieut.-Col. Burnside's winter campaign against the stronghold of Fredericksburg involved the "88th" in the costly assault upon the Confederate right at Franklin's Crossing, the regimental loss being seven killed (including Acting Adjutant Charles H. Kartsher and Lieut. George H. Fulton), and thirty-four wounded. After the famous "mud-march" of January, 1863, the regiment, now commanded by Lieut.-Col. Louis Wagner, who had been wounded at Bull Run, August 30, 1862, occupied winter quarters at Fletcher's Chapel, Va. The campaign of 1863 began with a brief advance, late in April, across the Rappahannock, and a forced march by the brigade to the Union right at Chancellorsville. *The march of eighteen days to Gettysburg, under Major B. F. Foust, ended upon that field on July 1st.

Hurrying from its bivouac of the night before, the First Corps was the first body of infantry to reach the scene. Gen. Reynolds, with Wadsworth's Division, hastened to the support of Buford's Cavalry, northwest of the town. On arrival of Gen. Henry Baxter's Brigade it was placed in the line of battle from which, led by the "88th," a charge was made, resulting in the capture of many prisoners and three battle flags, of which the "88th" brought back two.† Baxter's brigade checked the left advance of the Confederates until the Union artillery was withdrawn. In the re-alignment of the army, after the arrival of Gen. Hancock, at 3 P. M., Baxter's Brigade was placed at Cemetery Hill. During the afternoon of the 2d the brigade was sent to the left to assist the Third Corps, but returned after dark to Cemetery Hill. On the third day Baxter's Brigade served with the Eleventh, Twelfth and Second Corps in turn, and that night was advanced, as the Confederates retreated, on picket duty. The loss of the "88th" was ten killed, fifty-four wounded and forty-two missing, out of two hundred and ninety-six officers and men engaged.

Through rain and mud the "88th" now returned to the long desolated wilds of Virginia. Its subsequent service included almost constant movement, hardships and fighting. The regiment re-enlisted on Feb-

---

*On returning from this arduous duty, Lieut.-Col. Wagner was compelled to apply for leave of absence by reason of his wounds breaking out anew. Later he was assigned to duty at Camp William Penn, Chelten Hills, Pa., for the organization of colored troops, and at the conclusion of this duty returned to the regiment and was mustered out as Colonel, his commission dating from March 3, 1863.

†The colors captured by the "88th" were those of the 23d North Carolina and 12th Alabama Regiments. The prisoners captured exceeded in numbers the officers and men of the "88th" present in the charge.

ruary 6th, 1864, and enjoyed a furlough of two months. The old First Corps had been consolidated with the Fifth Corps. Many recruits were added. In the Wilderness, at Spotsylvania, Cold Harbor, Petersburg, and Weldon Railroad and through the waning struggle, down to Appomattox, the regiment added glory to its colors. In the final campaign, at Five Forks, the "88th's" last battle, several of the original members, including Capt. Thos. J. Koch and Lieut. Daniel J. Lehman, were killed or fatally wounded.

The Fifth Corps remained at Appomattox until April 15th. After the surrender the "88th" received an accession of several hundred conscripts. The original members who participated in the Grand Review at Washington numbered less than one hundred. The regiment was finally mustered out upon June 30th, 1865.

TOTAL LOSSES.

Killed or died from wounds...............................officers, 7; men, 98
Died of disease.. " " 72
Wounded, not mortally.. " 28; " 336
Captured or missing.. " 5; " 164

BATTLES.

Cedar Mountain, Rappahannock Station, Thoroughfare Gap, Second Bull Run, Chantilly, Antietam, Fredericksburg, Chancellorsville, Gettysburg, Mine Run, Wilderness, Spotsylvania, North Anna, Totopotomoy, Bethesda Church, Cold Harbor, Petersburg, Weldon Railroad, Dabney's Mills, Boydton Road, Five Forks, Appomattox.

NINETIETH REGIMENT INFANTRY

COLONEL PETER LYLE.
Total Enrollment, 1,600 Officers and Men.

THE 90th Regiment was a re-organization of the 19th Regiment of the three months service, and the parent command of both was the National Guard Regiment, 2d Regiment, First Brigade, First Division Pennsylvania Militia. On August 29th, 1861, at a meeting held at the National Guards' Armory, it was resolved to tender the services of the regiment to the Government. The War Department accepted the offer and recruiting was commenced at once. The "90th" established Camp McClellan, at Nicetown, and remained there through the winter, leaving for Baltimore upon March 31st, 1862, where arms were received. Three weeks later the regiment moved to Washington, from which six companies were sent to Aquia Creek and four companies to Belle Plain. Later the command was brigaded at Falmouth, Va., as part of the Second Brigade, Second Division, Third Corps. Near the end of May the Second Division was sent in haste to the Shenandoah Valley, but Jackson's "foot cavalry" had vanished and the troops returned to join Pope's army in time to move on Cedar Mountain, where the "90th" was first under fire. For two weeks, beginning upon August 15th, the Second Brigade marched and skirmished up to the battles of Gainesville and the Second Bull Run, where the "90th" was depleted by about two hundred officers and men in killed, wounded and prisoners. The "90th" was in line at Chantilly, but not actively engaged. On the way to Antietam the Second Brigade met and repulsed the Confederate force at South Mountain. At Antietam the "90th" lost ninety-eight killed and wounded. Among the latter was Col. Lyle, Acting Brigade Commander. In September the regiment was transferred to the First Corps, with which it was identified through the ensuing eighteen months. At Fredericksburg the command lost, among those killed, Lieut. Charles W. Duke, of Company K, the first officer of the "90th" to perish. In the Chancellorsville Campaign the regiment was in the battle line upon May 3d, sustaining some loss. Upon the night of June 30th, 1863, the "90th" camped gladly upon Pennsylvania soil at Marsh Creek, arriving in position at Gettysburg to the left of the Cashtown Road when the battle was already raging, holding this position until the line was forced back through the town to Cemetery Hill, there entrenching. Chaplain Horatio S. Howell was killed in front of the Lutheran Church during the retreat.* The "90th" numbered that morning two hundred and eight. All of its loss, a total of ninety-four killed, wounded or captured, was suffered in that heroic contest of the "first day" of Gettysburg. Among the officers wounded were Capt. John T. Durang and Adj. David P. Weaver. The First Corps was nearly destroyed.† In the great drama of the second and third days the "90th" had but a minor part. Returning to the old Virginia battle region, the opposing armies surged to and fro through the autumn and early winter, the devoted regiments marching, countermarching, responsive to every alarm. The "90th" added Mine Run to its battle list. In the course of the winter the First Corps was consolidated with the Fifth Corps, the "90th" being united with Maine, Massachusetts and New York troops to form the First Brigade, Second Division.

At intervals the regiment received accessions of recruits, mainly in drafted men, most of whom deserted whenever possible to do so. With the opening of the Wilderness campaign the regiment met with disaster through a confusion of orders, upon May 5th, losing half of its effective

*A bronze tablet marks the spot where Chaplain Howell, refusing to surrender, was slain.

†The First Corps brought to Gettysburg 8,200 officers and men. Its total casualties, in killed, wounded and prisoners, amounted to 5,683, leaving less than twenty per cent. to answer roll call upon the morning of the 2d of July.

---

strength of two hundred and fifty-one men in an unsupported charge. At Laurel Hill (Spotsylvania), upon the 10th, it again lost heavily, including Lieut. Jesse W. Super killed. The small contingent of the "90th" yet remaining shared in the fortunes of the brigade (now in the Third Division) at Cold Harbor, North Anna and in the vicinity of Petersburg. The regiment was now under the command of Capt. William P. Davis. Its last important fight was incident to the destruction of the Weldon Railroad, south of Petersburg, where Lieut. James S. Bonsall was killed and a number of officers and men captured. Upon November 26th, while in garrison at Fort Dushane (Weldon Railroad), the regiment's term of service ended. Those entitled to discharge were mustered out, and upon arrival at Philadelphia were received with great enthusiasm. The veterans and recruits were attached to the 11th Pennsylvania Infantry. Of the original officers at the time of the discharge, Lieut.-Col. William A. Leech and Maj. Jacob M. Davis were in captivity. Eighteen field and company officers were mustered out with the regiment or were transferred to other commands. Col. Peter Lyle was one of the few Philadelphia officers of his rank who were mustered out with their regiments.

TOTAL LOSSES.

Killed or mortally wounded .... officers 5; men, 98.
Died of disease .... " 1; " 126.
Wounded, not mortally .... See. Regt. Hist.
Captured or missing .... " " "

BATTLES AND ENGAGEMENTS.

Cedar Mountain, Rappahannock Station, Sulphur Springs, Thoroughfare Gap, Bull Run, Chantilly, South Mountain, Antietam, Fredericksburg, Fitzhugh House, Chancellorsville, Gettysburg, Mine Run, Wilderness, Todd's Tavern, Spotsylvania, Laurel Hill, Guinea Station, North and South Anna, Bethesda Church, Cold Harbor, White Oak Swamp, Petersburg, Jerusalem Plank Road, Weldon Railroad, Poplar Springs, Ream's Station, Hatcher's Run.

NINETY-FIRST REGIMENT INFANTRY

COLONEL EDGAR M. GREGORY.
Total Enrollment, 2,100 Officers and Men.

T HE 91st Regiment was recruited in Philadelphia during the fall of 1861, and was mustered in on December 4th at Camp Chase, located east of Darby Road at Fifty-first Street.* On January 21st, 1862, the command moved to Washington, being there employed in camp routine and provost duty. From April 22d to August 23d the "91st" was stationed at Alexandria, Va., of which city Colonel Gregory was Military Governor. On the latter date the regiment was assigned to the First Brigade, Third Division, Fifth Corps. The active field service of the regiment began with the hurried march of the Fifth Corps to Antietam, the First Brigade arriving after the battle had ended. The "91st" was destined, however, to share in the severe fighting at Fredericksburg three months later, where the loss in officers and men was one of the heaviest inflictions experienced in the course of its service. While in line of battle upon the Fredericksburg road the regiment was subjected to heavy artillery fire, losing Lieut. George Murphy killed and Major Geo. W. Todd mortally wounded. In the desperate charge upon the heights later in the day the "91st" lost two officers and eighty-seven men killed and wounded. In the battle of Chancellorsville, at the opening of the campaign of 1863, Col. Gregory was severely wounded.† Capt. Theo. H. Parsons and Lieut. George Black were mortally wounded.

The Fifth Corps reached Gettysburg on the morning of July 2d, and the "91st" was posted upon Little Round Top, a position which it occupied, despite the repeated assaults upon the left of the Union Line throughout the day, and which it held to the end of the battle. The "91st" now marched and camped alternately, with occasional skirmishes, through forty-five days, traversing old battle scenes to the banks of the Rappahannock River.

On December 26th, 1863, nearly all of the regiment re-enlisted, arriving home on furlough January 3d, 1864, the event being signalized by

---

*Prior to this date a partially organized regiment being formed by Col. Edward E. Wallace, and which had been in camp upon Ridge road, was merged into the "91st," of which the latter officer became lieutenant-colonel.

†Colonel Gregory remained with the regiment and in the field to the close of the war, and afterward, as an officer of the Freedman's Bureau, he served to November 30th, 1867. Eventually, he died from the effect of the wound he received in this battle.

parade in front of Independence Hall.* Six weeks later the command, with numerous recruits, rendezvoused at Chester, Pa., leaving for Washington, under command of Lieut.-Col. Joseph H. Sinex, and rejoined the Fifth Corps, which was soon afterward engaged in the series of sanguinary battles between the Wilderness and the James River. Colonel Gregory returned to the regiment at Cold Harbor. The "91st" effected a crossing of the James River on June 13th, fighting its way to a junction with the forces in front of Petersburg, losing eighty-two men killed and wounded. Lieut. John Stewart died from wounds received in this movement. At this time the veterans and recruits of the 62d Regiment, Pennsylvania Infantry, not entitled to discharge, were assigned to the "91st." All of the subsequent service of the regiment, covering a period of ten months, was experienced south of the James River, the command taking part in nearly all of the engagements around Petersburg, including the destruction of the Weldon Railroad and the battle of Five Forks. In two affairs at Hatcher's Run the regiment lost, respectively, Capt. James H. Closson and Lieut. John Edgar, Jr., both of whom died from wounds. At Appomattox the regiment was among those detailed to receive the arms of the captured Confederates. Turning northward the regiment marched through Petersburg and Richmond to Washington. Following the Grand Review the "91st" was encamped at Alexandria to July 10th, where it was mustered out, reaching Philadelphia on July 12th, 1865. In the course of its career the regiment experienced frequent brigade and division changes, but it fought, throughout, under the Maltese cross of the Fifth Corps.†

TOTAL LOSSES.

Killed, or died from wounds...............................officers, 6; men, 102
Died from disease or other causes..........................   "   2; "   84
Wounded, not mortally ....   "   20; "   321
Captured or missing ....   "   0; "   69

BATTLES.

Fredericksburg, Chancellorsville, Gettysburg, Rappahannock Station, Mine Run, Wilderness, Spotsylvania, North Anna, Totopotomoy, Bethesda Church, Cold Harbor, Petersburg, Weldon Railroad, Poplar Spring Church (Peeble's Farm), Raid on Weldon Railroad, Hatcher's Run, Dabney's Mill, Second Hatcher's Run, Boydton Plank Road, Five Forks, Appomattox Court House.

---

*The men who did not re-enlist were transferred to the 155th Pennsylvania Infantry.

†Badges, distinctive of the several army corps, were issued by general order from headquarters of the Army of the Potomac on March 21st, 1863.
The form of the badge designated the corps. The divisions of the respective corps were distinguished by the color of the badge. The First Division, red; Second Division, white; Third Division, blue, etc. Sheridan's Cavalry Corps wore a white badge in the pattern of a sun-burst with a blue centre showing crossed sabres in gold. Wilson's Cavalry Corps badge was a red banner suspended from a rifle and emblazoned with crossed sabres. All of the army corps adopted distinctive badges excepting the Thirteenth and Twenty-first Corps.

CAMP MEIGS, SIXTH CAVALRY (RUSH LANCERS), OLD SECOND STREET AND NICETOWN LANE, August to December, 1861.

CAMP N. P. BANKS, 114TH REGIMENT, COLLIS' ZOUAVES, NICETOWN. July and August, 1862.

CAMP BALLIER, 98TH REGIMENT, RIDGE AVENUE. August and September, 1861.

NINETY-FIFTH REGIMENT INFANTRY

(Gosline's Pennsylvania Zouaves)

COLONEL JOHN M. GOSLINE to June 29th, 1862.
COLONEL GUSTAVUS W. TOWN to May 3d, 1863.
COLONEL THOMAS J. TOWN to August 6th, 1863.
COLONEL JOHN HARPER to July 17th, 1865.

Total Enrollment, 1,962 Officers and Men.

COMPANY A of the 18th Regiment, in the three-months' service, originated in the Washington Blues, a time-honored militia organization dating from 1817, of which John M. Gosline was captain. After its term of service had ended Capt. Gosline with his Lieutenants, Gustavus W. Town, and Thomas J. Town, secured authority to recruit a regiment of infantry under the synonym "Pennsylvania Zouaves." Seven weeks later the command was ready for the field. All of the companies excepting a part of Company B (which contained a contingent from Burlington County, N. J.) were recruited in Philadelphia. "Camp Gibson" was established in Jones' Woods near Hestonville. The regiment was known, numerically, as the "45th."* The uniform, of a modified Zouave pattern, was neat and picturesque. The regiment paraded through the city on October 12th, dined at the Union Volunteer Refreshment Saloon and at 7 P. M. entrained for Washington, where it established camp. On the 24th it paraded as escort at the funeral of Col. Edward D. Baker, late commander of the "California Brigade." The regiment was attached to Gen. Oliver O. Howard's Brigade, but a few days later was ordered to Gen. John Newton's Third Brigade of Franklin's Division in the vicinity of Alexandria. The "95th" wintered here, and with the opening of the campaign of 1862, after a preliminary advance toward Richmond, Franklin's Division was sent to the Peninsula and first met the enemy at West Point at the head of York River. At Gaines' Mills, on June 27th, the Pennsylvania Zouaves met with fearful loss. One hundred and sixty-nine of its officers and men were killed or wounded. Among those who fell mortally wounded were Col. John M. Gosline and Major William B. Hubbs. Lieut. Hamilton Donahue was killed. The "95th" shared in the subsequent battles and hardships incident to the "change of base," and in August returned by transport to Washington, being rushed at once to the assistance of Gen. Pope at Manassas. At Crampton's Gap, incident to the Antietam Campaign, the "95th" had a little battle of its own, capturing many prisoners and gun from a Georgia battery. At

---

*It was also numbered the "54th," but when, in the following November, the regiment was credited to the State of Pennsylvania it became the "95th."

Antietam Franklin's Division broke the Confederate line and held the field at the "Dunker Church." Here the "95th" lost two killed and twenty wounded. After the futile demonstration under direction of Burnside at Fredericksburg the "95th" built its winter quarters at White Oak Church. On April 28th, 1863, two Philadelphia regiments, the "119th" and the "95th," were detailed to cross the Rappahannock River below Fredericksburg and protect the operation of building a pontoon bridge at the point which was afterward known as Franklin's Crossing, and which resulted in the storming of Marye's Heights and the coincidental battle at Salem Church. In this stubborn and sanguinary fight the "95th" lost five officers killed, eight wounded, one hundred and sixty-nine enlisted men killed and wounded, and thirty-seven men captured.* The dead included Col. Gustavus W. Town, Lieut.-Col. Elisha Hall and Adjutant Eugene D. Dunton. Major Thomas J. Town was wounded. The "95th" shared in the great march of the Sixth Corps to Gettysburg, being then under the command of Capt. Theodore H. McCalla, and numbering three hundred and fifty-six men. The regimental casualties at this field were small.

The campaign through the balance of the year added to the regimental colors the names of Rappahannock Station and Mine Run. The "95th" wintered in a fine camp on the Hazel River. While here two hundred and forty-five of the original members re-enlisted, this being the first regiment in the Army of the Potomac to veteranize. The campaign of 1864, under Gen. Grant, began on May 4th with an advance which continued through forty days of almost constant battling, which included the Wilderness, Spotsylvania, North Anna, Totopotomoy and Cold Harbor.

The regiment's first experience in this trying period was the loss of Lieut.-Col. Edward Carroll, killed, in the Wilderness, on May 5th, and a week later, at the "Bloody Angle" near Spotsylvania, where the regiment rushed to the support of the right flank of the army and saved the day, it was once more terribly depleted of officers and men.

In this hard-fought, but triumphant, campaign the regiment lost one officer and forty-two men killed, five officers and one hundred and twenty-three men wounded, of whom eleven afterward died.

The menace of Early against Washington sent the Sixth Corps hurrying to the defence of the capital. After the affair at Fort Stevens the pursuit of the Confederates led into the Shenandoah Valley and resulted in the battle of Fisher's Hill. At Middletown, on October 15th, the term of service of the non-veteran, original members expired. These men were detained and were engaged, on October 20th, in a fight at

---

*Major-Gen. St. Clair A. Mulholland cites this disaster to the "95th" in his book, "Heroism of the American Volunteer," in these words: "This splendid Philadelphia regiment held an advanced position where the fighting was desperate and severe. * * The "95th" ranks with the 20th Massachusetts in having the largest number of field and staff officers killed in a battle, each losing six."

Fisher's Hill, in which several were killed. They were mustered out on November 2d.

The veterans and recruits were organized into a battalion of four companies to which were joined a battalion of the 96th Pennsylvania Infantry, both under the designation of the 95th Regiment. This re-organized command participated in the battle of Cedar Creek, which cleared the region of the enemy. It cost the "95th" nine killed and fifty-seven wounded and missing. In December the Sixth Corps joined the army in front of Petersburg. The "95th" had a share in the active work which led up to the end of hostilities in Virginia. At its final battle, Sailor's Creek, three days before the surrender, Capt. James J. Carroll of Company A, a veteran officer of the original regiment, was killed.

After a brief period of duty at Danville the regiment proceeded, by leisurely marches, to Washington, was mustered out on July 17th, 1865, and reached Philadelphia on July 19th, being finally discharged five days later.*

TOTAL LOSSES.

Killed or died from wounds..............................officers, 11; men, 172
Died of disease or other causes........................... " 1; " 72
Wounded, not mortally..................................... " 20; " 410
Captured or missing .... " —; " 76

BATTLES.

West Point, Gaines' Mills, Seven Days' Battles, Crampton's Gap, Antietam, Fredericksburg, Franklin's Crossing, Marye's Heights, Salem Church, Gettysburg, Rappahannock Station, Mine Run, Wilderness, Spotsylvania, North Anna, Totopotomoy, Cold Harbor, Fort Stevens, Summit Point, Opequon, Fisher's Hill, New Market, Cedar Creek, Dabney's Mill, Petersburg (Fort Fisher), Petersburg (assault), Sailor's Creek, Appomattox Court House.

---

*On the evening of October 12th, 1911, survivors of the command held a re-union banquet in Philadelphia in celebration of the fiftieth anniversary of their departure to the war. A majority of the one hundred and thirty-three then known to be living were present.

NINETY-EIGHTH REGIMENT INFANTRY

COLONEL JOHN F. BALLIER to November 26th, 1862.
COLONEL ADOLPH MEHLER to March 12th, 1863.
COLONEL JOHN F. BALLIER (re-mustered) to July 13th, 1864.
LIEUT.-COLONEL CHARLES REEN to June 29th, 1865.

Total Enrollment, 2,025 Officers and Men.

U PON the return of the 21st Regiment of the three months' service, at the end of July, 1861, Col. Ballier formed, from its ranks and with new recruits, the 98th Regiment, which was gathered at Camp Ballier. The men were chiefly of German origin.* Eight companies left Philadelphia for Washington on September 30th. Two companies, G and H, joined the command in December. The regiment encamped through the winter at Tenallytown, Maryland. On March 26th, 1862, the regiment was embarked to Hampton, Va., soon advancing as part of the Third Brigade, First Division, Fourth Corps, up the Peninsula, first coming under fire at Williamsburg, May 5th, 1862. As a part of the advance guard of the army the "98th" marched to Mechanicsville, near Richmond, arriving there on May 26th. It thus missed the battles of Fair Oaks and Seven Pines, fought four days later. In the "change of base" the regiment skirmished near Fair Oaks, and, on July 1st, fought at Malvern Hill, losing about fifty killed, wounded and missing. Suffering much from malarial sickness, the regiment marched back to Yorktown and proceeded, on transports, to Alexandria, in time to assist in covering the retreat from Bull Run. In September, the march was made to Antietam, the division arriving after the close of the battle. After establishing winter quarters near Falmouth the respite was broken by the Burnside movement on Fredericksburg and the subsequent "mud march," in January, 1864.

When Major-Gen. Hooker took command of the Army of the Potomac the "98th" was transferred to the Third Brigade, Third Division, Sixth Corps. With this historic corps the regiment fought at Marye's Heights and Salem Heights (both on May 3d). Here Col. Ballier was wounded and the command reverted to Lieut.-Col. George Wynkoop. Upon the 4th the regiment was again in action near Bank's Ford, losing twenty-nine officers and men killed and wounded.

At Gettysburg the Third Brigade was posted near Little Round Top in the rear of Sickles' position and near the Trostle house. Here, being out of direct gun fire, it was subject to few losses. After the close of the campaign of 1863, at Mine Run, on December 2d, the regiment established winter quarters at Brandy Station. At this time the com-

---

*Company A was the exception, most of its members being Irishmen.

mand numbered but three hundred and twenty-nine; of these, all but one hundred re-enlisted on December 23d. In January the "98th" was removed to Charlestown, West Virginia. Soon afterward, leaving the contingent not re-enlisted at Harper's Ferry, the regiment went to Philadelphia, on furlough. Again in the field, under Col. John F. Ballier, at the opening of the Wilderness Campaign, the regiment suffered repeated losses at Wilderness, Spotsylvania, North Anna, Totopotomoy and Cold Harbor. In five weeks the casualties were three officers and twenty-four men killed, six officers and one hundred and two men wounded.

At Petersburg the regiment assisted in the first Weldon Railroad movement, after which the Sixth Corps was hurried upon transports to Washington, joining the Nineteenth Corps, just arrived from New Orleans, in defending the Capital and its forts from threatened capture by Early. At Fort Stevens, a few miles north of Washington, Early's column was repulsed on July 12th and the crisis was averted. In this affair the "98th" lost thirty-six officers and men killed and wounded. Among the latter was Col. Ballier. In the Shenandoah campaign which followed, at Opequon, Fisher's Hill and Cedar Creek (Sheridan's Ride) two officers and nineteen men were killed, six officers and fifty-six men wounded. In January, 1865, the remnant of the "98th" left its camp, near Winchester, to again join in the siege of Petersburg. The regiment was now commanded by Lieut.-Col. Charles Reen. This officer was severely wounded on April 2d in a skirmish which cost the regiment still further losses. After the surrender at Appomattox seven hundred drafted men and substitutes were assigned to the regiment, and it was sent forward to Danville.* Following Johnston's surrender to Sherman, the "98th" marched to Washington, where it was mustered out on June 29th. The veterans were received at Philadelphia with great rejoicing among the Germans and the citizens generally.

TOTAL LOSSES.

Killed or died from wounds	officers, 9;	men,	112
Died of disease	" 1;	"	72
Wounded, not mortally	" 29;	"	329
Captured or missing		"	54

BATTLES.

Yorktown, Williamsburg, Malvern Hill, Fredericksburg, Marye's Heights, Salem Heights, Gettysburg, Rappahannock Station, Mine Run, Wilderness, Spotsylvania, North Anna, Totopotomoy, Cold Harbor, Petersburg, Fort Stevens, Opequon, Fisher's Hill, Cedar Creek, Petersburg (Fort Fisher), Petersburg (assault), Sailor's Creek, Appomattox.

---

*The conscripts and substitutes were without weapons upon this march, but nevertheless added greatly to the work of the veterans, who were obliged to watch both these unwilling warriors and the scattered parties of now irresponsible Confederates.

NINETY-NINTH REGIMENT INFANTRY

COLONEL ROMAINE LUJEANE to November 7th, 1861.
COLONEL THOMAS W. SWEENEY to January 24th, 1862.
COLONEL PETER FRITZ to June 10th, 1862.
COLONEL ASHER S. LEIDY to April 9th, 1864.
COLONEL EDWIN R. BILES to July 1st, 1865.
Total Enrollment, 2,140 Officers and Men.

RECRUITING for this regiment was authorized in July, 1861, and three companies, A, B and C, were ordered to Washington, as a part of the 32d Regiment, on August 8th, under command of Romaine Lujeane, an Italian officer, who soon afterward resigned. The balance of the command was mustered in at various dates to January 18th, 1862, being forwarded in detachments. A large proportion of the men had served in the three months' campaign. By the addition of two companies of the 66th Regiment, which became H and K of the "99th," the regiment was fully organized. Col. Thomas W. Sweeney and Lieut.-Col. William P. Seymour, the accredited organizers, resigned in January, and Peter Fritz was commissioned colonel. Colonel Fritz was placed in command of a chain of forts forming the southern defences of Washington, among which the companies were distributed. Colonel Fritz resigned June 10th, 1862, and Lieut.-Col. Asher S. Leidy was commissioned to succeed. The "99th" joined the Army of the Potomac at Harrison's Landing, on July 4th, 1862, being attached to the Second Brigade, First Division, Third Corps. Following a series of movements, the Third Corps participated in the battles of the second Bull Run and Chantilly.

At the first advance on Fredericksburg, December 13th, the "99th" crossed the river on the left under Franklin, and amid desperate fighting lost sixty officers and men killed and wounded. In the Chancellorsville campaign Birney's Division, Third Corps, executed a notable charge by moonlight, and later covered the retreat of the army.

The "99th," under command of Major John W. Moore,* made the forced march to the field of Gettysburg from Emmitsburg, making its bivouac on the night of July 1st in the Peach Orchard. In the formation of the troops in front of Little Round Top on the 2d, the position of the "99th" was near the Devils' Den. Here the "99th" defended its position gallantly until relieved by a division of the Fifth Army Corps, then pushing forward, in support of Webb's Brigade of the Second Corps, to the Emmitsburg Pike, where it remained until the morning of July

*In September, 1864, Major John W. Moore was commissioned colonel of the 203d Regiment, and was killed on January 15th, 1865, in the final assault on Fort Fisher, N. C.

4th.* The official report indicates that the "99th" reached Gettysburg with three hundred and thirty-nine officers and men, losing in killed, wounded and missing one hundred and ten.

In the southward march the "99th" took part in the battle of Wapping Heights. For nearly three months the regiment rested in camp among the foot-hills of the Blue Ridge, and then, on October 10th, it was put in motion and was engaged in the Kelly's Ford and Mine Run campaign.

In February, 1864, the majority of the men re-enlisted. Upon return from furlough, on April 7th, 1864, the old Third Corps having been consolidated with the Second Army Corps, the "99th" became a part of Birney's Division.

On April 9th, Colonel Leidy resigned and was succeeded by Lieut.-Col. Edwin R. Biles. Now the army under Grant, its new commander, made its last crossing of the Rapidan. The great forward march, which was to know no retreat, was commenced. The "99th" started, in this campaign, with three hundred and twenty-five officers and men. At Spotsylvania it captured two cannons, two battle-flags and many prisoners, but it reached Cold Harbor with but four officers and sixty men. Here the thin line was strengthened by the accession of the veterans and recruits of the 26th Regiment. Thus reinforced, with the brigade, the "99th" crossed the James River and was merged in the host of besiegers around Petersburg. Late in July the Second Corps was sent to check a Confederate movement at Deep Bottom, a second tour to this troublesome point being necessary in August. Thereafter the fighting was all south of the James River. In the two weeks preceding the surrender of the rebel forces, as far as General Lee's army was concerned, the regiment lost, near Appomattox, seventy-six men killed and wounded. Many of these were from a contingent of drafted men received on March 26th.

Marching to Washington, the "99th" participated in the Grand Review, and upon July 1st, 1865, was mustered out at Philadelphia.

TOTAL LOSSES.
Killed or died from wounds..............................officers, 9; men, 124
Died from disease or other causes........................ "   1; "   117
Wounded, not mortally.................................... "   29; "   412
Captured or missing..................................... "   2; "   155

BATTLES.
Bull Run (second), Chantilly, White's Ford, Fredericksburg, Chancellorsville, Gettysburg, Wapping Heights, Auburn, Kelly's Ford, Mine Run, Wilderness, Spotsylvania, North Anna, Totopotomoy, Cold Harbor, Petersburg, Strawberry Plains, Deep Bottom, Poplar Springs Church, Boydton Plank Road, Hatcher's Run, Petersburg (Watkin's House), Amelia Springs, Appomattox Court House.

---

*When the regiment reached the pike it was deployed as skirmishers and videttes sent forward in charge of Lieut. S. Bonnaffon, Jr. During the night of the 3d or the early morning of the 4th they discovered evidence that the enemy was retreating or preparing to retreat, and so reported.

ONE HUNDRED AND NINTH REGIMENT INFANTRY
(Curtin Light Guards)

COLONEL HENRY J. STAINROOK to May 3d, 1863.
LIEUT.-COL. LEWIS W. RALSTON to April 12th, 1864.
Total Enrollment, 1,055 Officers and Men.

U PON the return from service of the 22d Regiment in the three months' enlistment, Capt. Henry J. Stainrook, of Company C, was commissioned as colonel of volunteers, and began the formation of a new regiment for the three years' term. Eight of the ten companies were raised in Philadelphia.

Headquarters were established in the Globe Hotel, on Sixth street, below Chestnut street, and later a camp was formed at Nicetown. Reporting at Washington, upon May 10th, 1862, the regiment was assigned to Cooper's Brigade, Second Division, Bank's Corps, and encamped at Bolivar Heights, Virginia, then threatened by Jackson's column of Confederates. Here the regiment first encountered the enemy. Upon June 2d the brigade was sent to the Army of the Shenandoah, being assigned to Prince's Brigade, Auger's Division, Banks' Corps, Army of Northern Virginia. With this force the "109th" fought at Cedar Mountain, August 9th, 1862. Col. Stainrook was wounded here, but remained in the field, later acting as commander of the brigade at Antietam, where, however, the "109th" was not actively engaged.

In September, following the last named battle, the regiment was assigned to the Second Brigade, Second Division, Twelfth Corps, and again stationed at Bolivar Heights. In November it was joined to the Third Brigade of the same division and corps. The only special event of the winter in the experience of the regiment was the ever remembered "mud march." In April, 1863, the "109th" was returned to the Second Brigade, which was composed of the 109th, 111th, 124th and 125th Pennsylvania Regiments. At the series of battles of May 1st to 4th, 1863, known as "Chancellorsville," the "109th" lost heavily, including its brave and efficient Colonel (Stainrook), who was killed upon May 3d by a sharpshooter.

Upon the night of June 30th, 1863, the Twelfth Corps camped at Littlestown, Pa., about twelve miles east from Gettysburg, resuming its march upon the morning of July 1st. At Two Taverns, a point two miles from Gettysburg, upon the Baltimore Pike, the Second Brigade was halted to rest. Resuming the march, it filed to the left, halting on Little Round Top for the night. The "109th," mustering one hundred and forty-nine officers and men, was marched early the following morning with the brigade to a position at the extreme right upon the Rock Creek slope of Culp's Hill, where it fortified and awaited the enemy.

The fighting here began in the evening, continued all night and well into the morning of the third. The crash of cannon-fire, rattle of musketry and the burning woodlands through the hours of darkness gave no rest to the Union army. The final charge of the Confederates, at this point, ended at 11.30 A. M. on the third, with their repulse. The "109th" was then stationed along Baltimore Pike to the end of the battle. At Williamsport, Maryland, on July 12th, the retreating enemy was just in front, but the opportunity to then and there wage a final battle and probably hasten peace was lost.

At the end of September the Twelfth Corps was ordered, under Major-Gen. Hooker, to the Army of the Cumberland, being combined with the Eleventh Corps to form the Twentieth Corps. During October the "109th" was engaged in the movements of approach to Chattanooga. Upon the night of October 28th, six regiments of infantry and a section of Knap's battery, including the 29th, 109th and 111th Pennsylvania Regiments, were attacked at Wauhatchie, a railroad junction five miles west of Chattanooga, by a superior force of the enemy. In a fierce battle of three hours, at 3 A. M., October 29th, the assailants were defeated with heavy loss. The casualties of the "109th" were four (one officer and three enlisted men) killed and thirty wounded. The command also fought at Lookout Mountain and Missionary Ridge. In January, 1864, the regiment re-enlisted and was sent on furlough to Philadelphia. The "109th" rejoined the division on May 5th as a part of the First Brigade.

Gen. Sherman's Georgia campaign now began. Marching southward one hundred miles, the army fought its "one hundred days of battles." The "109th" lost most heavily at Resaca and Pine Knob. The heavy fighting ended with the fall of Atlanta. Then ensued the great march to Savannah and, with the beginning of 1865, northward through the Carolinas. At Goldsboro, N. C., upon March 31st, the depleted "109th" was consolidated with the 111th Regiment.

With the surrender of the last armed force of the enemy the "111th" was marched to Washington, and mustered out on July 19th, the veterans of the old "109th" reaching home upon the following day.

TOTAL LOSSES.

Killed or died from wounds...................................officers, 3; men, 62
Died of disease or other causes..............................officers, 0; men, 58
Wounded, not mortally.......................................officers, 12; men, 180
Captured or missing...officers, 3; men, 42

BATTLES, ETC.

Harper's Ferry, Cedar Mountain, Chancellorsville, Antietam, Gettysburg, Wauhatchie, Lookout Mountain, Missionary Ridge, Resaca, New Hope Church, Pine Knob, Kennesaw Mountain, Peach Tree Creek, Atlanta, the Savannah Campaign, and the Campaign of the Carolinas.

ONE HUNDRED AND TENTH REGIMENT INFANTRY

COLONEL WILLIAM D. LEWIS, JR., to December 20th, 1862.
COLONEL JAMES CROWTHER to May 3d, 1863.
LIEUT.-COL. DAVID M. JONES to October 9th, 1863.
LIEUT.-COL. ISAAC ROGERS to May 28th, 1864.
LIEUT.-COL. ENOCH E. LEWIS to June 16th, 1864.
LIEUT.-COL. FRANK B. STEWART to June 8th, 1865.
Total Enrollment, 1,475 Officers and Men.

———————

THIS regiment was organized from six companies recruited west of the Susquehanna and four companies, E, F, G and I, from Philadelphia. It was mustered in on October 24th, 1861, and rendezvoused at Camp Curtin. Col. William D. Lewis, of Philadelphia, had held the same rank in the 18th Regiment of the three months' service. On January 4th, 1862, the regiment reported to Brig.-Gen. Frederick West Lander, then at Hancock, Maryland, where the Baltimore and Ohio Railroad was threatened. The regiment was assigned to Tyler's Third Brigade, Second Division, Fifth Corps (Banks). Early in March the "110th" moved to Winchester, near which, on the 23d, the division, now commanded by Brig.-Gen. James Shields (Gen. Lander having died), fought the battle of Kernstown, in which the regiment won great praise, in special orders, for gallantry. Out of three hundred present the loss was fifty-two killed and wounded. Near Fredericksburg, in June, the regiment was assigned to the Fourth Brigade, Second Division, Third Corps, and with this corps was sent to the Shenandoah Valley, disputing the Confederate advance at Port Republic and Front Royal. The Fourth Brigade was on duty near Alexandria and at Warrenton, W. Va. The "110th" was now assigned to the Fourth Brigade, Second Division, and, under Gen. Pope, fought at Cedar Mountain, Thoroughfare Gap and Manassas. During the Antietam campaign the regiment was stationed in the defences of Washington, and was present, under Gen. Franklin, in the battle of December 13th, at Fredericksburg, losing heavily. Upon the 23d Col. Lewis resigned because of disability, and Lieut.-Col. Crowther succeeded him. During the winter the regiment was reorganized as a battalion of six companies. In the Chancellorsville campaign of May, 1863, Col. Crowther was killed and nearly half of the regiment were killed, wounded or captured. The heavy losses of the Third Corps resulted in a readjustment, in which the "110th" was assigned to the Third Brigade, First Division, commanded by Major-Gen. David B. Birney. In the great movement to head off Gen. Lee from the invasion of Pennsylvania the Third Corps was already lined up along Pipe Creek, fifteen miles south of Gettysburg (a point proposed by Gen. Meade for the expected battle), when information impelled Gen. Sickles to hurry to the support of the First and Eleventh Corps. The Third Brigade was, however, left at Emmitsburg. It was nearly noon upon the 2d of July when the "110th" got into the battle line, its position being at the Peach Orchard, the storm center of the Confederate assault of the afternoon. Here Col. Jones was wounded and Major Isaac Rodgers took command. When the regiment was relieved and fell back to the main line it had lost fifty-three killed and wounded out of one hundred and fifty-two officers and men present.

The "110th," now numbering but little more than the strength of a single company, was subjected to much active work during the fall in the Rapidan and Mine Run movements. In January, 1864, the regiment re-enlisted, and, after the usual furlough, was recruited and drilled in preparation for the coming campaign. The brigade was transferred to the 2d Corps (Hancock's), and Lieut.-Col. Isaac Rodgers was commissioned colonel. Six days of battles in the Wilderness now ensued, during which the regiment again lost heavily. Col. Rodgers was mortally wounded on May 12th. The way to Petersburg was attended with constant skirmishes and battles, but the Second Corps crossed the James River on June 14th, appearing in front of Petersburg, and was at once sent into the cauldron of battle. Here the "110th" was reinforced by the veterans and recruits of the 115th Regiment. With this welcome accession the "110th" remained among the trenches and forts at Petersburg for the ensuing eleven months. In that long period of watching and waiting the Second Corps crossed the James River upon two occasions, in both of which the enemy was met and beaten at Deep Bottom. In an attack upon Fort Steadman, made by the Confederates, upon March 25th, 1865, Lieut.-Col. Isaac C. Hamilton was severely wounded, and the command devolved upon Major Frank B. Stewart, who was later commissioned colonel, the last of the regiment's leaders. At Amelia Springs, on April 5th, the enemy was once more encountered. This was the regiment's twenty-sixth and last battle. The "110th" participated in the Grand Review and was mustered out upon June 28th, 1865.

TOTAL LOSSES. (Philadelphia Companies.)*

Killed or died from wounds..................................officers, 3; men, 16
Died from disease or other causes............................ " 18
Wounded, not mortally.. " 1; " 13
Captured or missing.. " 9

BATTLES.

Hancock, Kernstown, Front Royal, Port Republic, Cedar Mountain, Thoroughfare Gap, Second Bull Run, Fredericksburg, Chancellorsville, Gettysburg, Auburn, Kelly's Ford, Mine Run, Wilderness, Spotsylvania, North Anna, Totopotomoy, Cold Harbor, Petersburg, Strawberry Plains, Deep Bottom, Poplar Spring Church, Boydton Road, Hatcher's Run, Petersburg (Watkins' House), Amelia Springs, Appomattox Court House (surrender).

*Not including Company G, of which muster rolls are not on file.

INDEPENDENT CORPS, ZOUAVES D'AFRIQUE, INFANTRY

CAPTAIN CHARLES H. T. COLLIS.

THIS company included many French soldiers who had served as Zouaves in the campaigns of France and who had been identified with the 18th Regiment, in the three months' service. It was recruited at Philadelphia by Charles H. T. Collis, proposing to serve as a bodyguard to Major-Gen. N. P. Banks. The uniform adopted was that of the French Zouaves d'Afrique and was retained by the corps and by the 114th Regiment, to which it was later attached, throughout the war.

The corps was mustered in and sent to Fort Delaware on August 17th, 1861, where it was thoroughly drilled in zouave tactics. Late in September the Zouaves reported to Gen. Banks, at Darnestown, Md. After a period of guard duty the corps went into winter quarters. In the spring of 1862 the command served, for a short time, with Geary's Independent Brigade and then rejoined Gen. Banks in the Shenandoah Valley. In a number of battles and skirmishes, including Middletown, Cedar Mountain, second Bull Run, Chantilly and Antietam, the Zouaves had shown those qualities of dash and bravery for which this type of infantry is usually famous. After the affair at Middletown, Capt. Collis was commissioned colonel and detailed to proceed to Philadelphia and recruit his command to a full regiment. With nine fully uniformed companies he arrived at Washington upon August 31st, 1862. The original company in the field, from which many of the officers of the new regiment were selected, became Company A. (See 114th Regiment.)

ONE HUNDRED AND FOURTEENTH REGIMENT INFANTRY
(Collis Zouaves)

COLONEL CHARLES H. T. COLLIS.
Total Enrollment, 1,100 Officers and Men.

THE single company of Zouaves d'Afrique which Capt. Collis had recruited and led to war one year before, formed the basis as Company A of the Zouave regiment raised in Philadelphia in the summer of 1862, and which as the 114th Infantry left the city upon September 1st. At Washington this command was encamped at Fort Slocum, but soon afterward was assigned to the First Brigade, First Division, of the Third Corps, then commanded by

Major-Gen. David B. Birney. The Zouaves received their "baptism of fire" on December 13th, when the division was rushed across the Rappahannock river, at Franklin's Crossing, below Fredericksburg, to the assistance of the Pennsylvania Reserves. The loss of the "114th" was twelve killed and seventeen wounded.* The Third Corps appeared in front of Fredericksburg again in January, 1863 (Burnside's "Mud March"), and a third time at the end of April, at the beginning of the Chancellorsville campaign, crossing the river, however, at United States Ford, about ten miles above the city. In the battle of May 3d the Zouaves fought with heroic persistence, finally retiring with a loss of one hundred and seventy-three killed and wounded. Of the twenty-seven officers present only three escaped death or wounds. Among those killed were Maj. Joseph S. Chandler and Capt. Frank A. Elliott of Co. F. The survivors returned after this bitter experience to camp at Falmouth.

The Third Corps reached Gettysburg after the close of the fighting upon July 1st, and was ordered to the left of the new line of battle, then being extended to the Round Tops. On the morning of the 2d Gen. Sickles advanced a portion of his corps, including the "114th," to and across the Emmettsburg Pike to the right of the Peach Orchard, under the command of Lieut.-Col. Fred. F. Cavada. The Zouaves were a fair mark for the rebel pickets during the morning and for the artillery fire that preceded the infantry attack later in the day. The Confederates surged along the line like a billow sweeping a stormy beach, reaching the front of the "114th" when the Zouaves were forced backward, some, including Lieut.-Col. Cavada, in command, being captured. The regiment re-formed under Maj. Edward R. Bowen, took a new position in front of the Taneytown Road, but was not again heavily engaged in the course of the battle. The regimental losses were nine men killed, one officer and eighty-five men wounded, three officers and fifty-seven men captured or missing. Four of the wounded men subsequently died from their injuries. Those captured were near the Sherfy House.

Through the fall and winter of 1863-4 Maj. Bowen continued in command, Col. Collis being in command of the brigade. The regiment shared the fortunes of the Third Corps in its marching and fighting, including battles along the Rappahannock.

In April, 1864, the "114th" was honored by selection as the first of six regiments of infantry and one regiment of cavalry organized as an independent brigade for duty at the headquarters of Gen. Meade. Col. Collis was appointed commander of this body of troops. This duty continued until March 15th, 1865, and involved the assistance of other troops in action, while the elite brigade from headquarters was expected to exhibit a high standard of gallantry.

* An incident following the battle was the capture of the regimental band of seventeen pieces, with their instruments. The unfortunate musicians were eventually exchanged, and being provided with new instruments, remained with the regiment to the end of the war. (Bates' History, vol. 3, page 1185.)

In the final weeks of activity around Petersburg the "114th" was engaged in the storming of the Confederate works on April 2d, and, during the pursuit, at Sailor's Creek. At the affair of the 2d, three veteran officers who had originally served in the Zouaves d'Afrique of 1861 lost their lives. They were Capt. A. J. Cunningham, Company A, Maj. Henry M. Eddy,* and First-Lieut. Edward T. Marion, Company I.

After the Appomattox surrender the "114th" was transferred to the Fifth Corps, with which the Zouaves marched to Washington, where they were mustered out on May 29th, 1865.

TOTAL LOSSES.
Killed or died from wounds ....officers, 6; men, 83.
Died of disease or other causes .... " 1; " 35.
Wounded, not mortally .... " 16; " 261.
Captured or missing .... " 4; " 122.

BATTLES.
(Including those of the Zouaves d'Afrique, afterward Company A, prior to the organization of the regiment.)

Middletown, Cedar Mountain, Antietam, Fredericksburg, Chancellorville, Gettysburg, Wapping Heights, Auburn, Kelly's Ford, Mine Run, Wilderness, Guinea's Station, Petersburg.

ONE HUNDRED AND FIFTEENTH REGIMENT INFANTRY

Colonel Robert E. Patterson to December 2d, 1862.
Colonel F. A. Lancaster to May 3d, 1863.
Total Enrollment, 859 Officers and Men.

IN November, 1861, Col. Robert E. Patterson began the organization of this regiment, the earlier recruits being placed in camp at Hestonville. In March the command was encamped at Camden, N. J. On May 31st the eight Philadelphia companies, A, B, C, E, F. H, I and K moved to Harrisburg, where they were met by the "up State" companies and assigned to guard duty over prisoners. On June 25th the regiment was ordered to Fortress Monroe, and thence to Harrison's Landing, being there assigned to the Third Brigade, Second Division, Third Corps. With the exception of the "115th" the Third Brigade was composed of New Jersey troops. On August 4th the regiment advanced with Hooker's Division to Malvern Hill and there first came under fire. With the end of the McClellan movement the regiment marched to Yorktown, embarked for Alexandria and joined in Pope's campaign, during which it participated in the battles at Bristoe Station, where Jackson's raiders were defeated, at the Second Bull Run (August

---

* Maj. Eddy was commissioned but not mustered.

29th) and at Chantilly. During the Antietam campaign the regiment was stationed in the defences near Washington. In the first Burnside advance upon Fredericksburg the "115th," temporarily in command of Lieut.-Col. Olmstead of the 2d New York Infantry, was under heavy and long continued fire in the course of Hooker's attack, near Franklin Crossing. After the trying experience of the "mud march" Col. Olmstead was relieved and Lieut.-Col. Lancaster was commissioned colonel.* At the opening of the battle, May 3d, Col. Lancaster was killed at the head of his regiment. Under command of Major John P. Dunne the "115th" pushed on and assisted in the capture of two stands of colors and many prisoners. The regimental loss in killed, wounded and missing was one hundred and eleven, including five officers killed or mortally wounded, and three officers wounded, not mortally. At Gettysburg the "115th," then mustering but one hundred and eighty-two officers and men, shared the experiences of the Third Corps in the actions in front of Little Round Top, on July 2d, losing three men killed, eighteen wounded and three missing. The struggling armies now surged back to the old, blood-stained fields and wilds of Virginia, marching, skirmishing and camping by the way; to and fro across the fords of the Rapidan the Third Corps advanced and retreated. After the brief Mine Run campaign the "115th" encamped for the winter at Brandy Station. In March the Third Corps was discontinued. The old Second Division was transferred to the Second Corps. A new general from the west set the bugles calling in May and the army was put in motion. The objective point was Petersburg, and the fighting on the way was terrific. In the Wilderness, at Spotsylvania, on the North Anna and at Cold Harbor the "115th" gained glory and lost men. After five weeks of this final battling upon the old fighting ground the "115th" crossed the James River and advanced to Petersburg. Grant was there to stay. The wasted regiments were revised. Of the "115th" but seven officers and eighty-four men remained in the field. It was consolidated into three companies and attached to the 110th Regiment, the field and staff officers being mustered out on June 23d, 1863. The subsequent service of the veterans and recruits, thus transferred, is a part of the story of the "110th."

TOTAL LOSSES.

Killed, or died from wounds.................................officers, 6; men, 32
Died from disease ....   "   2; " 40

BATTLES.

Malvern Hill (2d), Bristoe Station, Groveton, Bull Run (2d), Chantilly, Fredericksburg, Chancellorsville, Gettysburg, Mine Run, Wilderness, Spotsylvania, North Anna, Totopotomoy, Cold Harbor.

---

*Colonel Patterson had been detailed to duty in charge of drafted men at Philadelphia in November. Continued disability led to his resignation soon afterward. Colonel Lancaster recovered from his wounds and rejoined the regiment in April, 1862.

ONE HUNDRED AND SIXTEENTH REGIMENT INFANTRY

Colonel Dennis Heenan to December 13th, 1862.
Colonel St. Clair A. Mulholland to June 6th, 1865.
Total Enrollment, 1,660 Officers and Men.

THIS regiment was recruited in the summer of 1862, during which time it was in camp at Jones' Woods on the Lancaster Pike. The command was mustered in on September 1st, leaving the following day for Washington, where arms, the old style musket, and camp equipage were furnished. On the 6th the regiment moved to Rockville, Md. A month later, at Harper's Ferry, the "116th" was attached to Gen. Thomas Francis Meagher's Irish Brigade, Hancock's First Division, Second Corps.*

On the way to Fredericksburg in early November the Second Corps skirmished at Snicker's Gap and Charlestown, Va. Reporting to Major-Gen. Burnside, in front of Fredericksburg, the "116th" crossed the river to the attack on the 12th, and on the following morning participated in the historic assault upon Marye's Heights, in which the sacrifice of the regiment included Lieut. Christian Foltz, killed; Lieut. Robert B. Montgomery, fatally wounded; Major George H. Bardwell, Capt. S. G. Willauer, Lieut. Robert T. Maguire, Lieut. Garrett Nowlen and Capt. John O'Neill, wounded. The losses of the rank and file were twenty-three killed and fifty-three wounded.

At the battle of Chancellorsville a detail of one hundred men of the "116th" saved five guns of the 5th Maine Battery from between the lines, a gallant act which added much to the fame of the command.

On June 14th, 1863, the Second Corps began its two-hundred-mile march, ending at Gettysburg. The marching record of June 29th to Uniontown, Pa., was thirty-three miles. The "116th" reached Gettysburg late on the evening of July 1st, now rated as a battalion, taking position on Cemetery Ridge. Following the attack upon Sickles' front on the 2d, the "116th," which had been marched with the brigade to the ground in front of Little Round Top. advancing, met the enemy at close quarters and effected the capture of a large number of prisoners. That evening the battalion returned to its first position, which it occupied during the final Confederate charge on the 3d. The battalion lost a total of thirty-seven killed, wounded and missing out of one hundred and sixty-five officers and men present.† On August 13th, 1863, the orders

*The First Division of the Second Corps lost, in the course of the war, 2,287 killed, 11,724 wounded and 4,833 captured or missing—a total of 18,844, not including fatalities from sickness.

†Address of brevet Major-Gen. St. Clair A. Mulholland, Gettysburg, September 11th, 1889.

came that regimental status of the "116th" was to be restored. Major Mulholland and other officers were ordered to Philadelphia to secure recruits. During the period of Major Mulholland's absence the command devolved upon Senior Capt. Seneca Grubb Willauer.*

Incident to the gradual southward movement subsequent to Gettysburg the Second Corps, and especially the Irish Brigade, marched and fought through the autumn and early winter, its greatest achievement being participation in a rear-guard march of seventy-six miles in fifty-six hours, in the course of which it fought two battles in one day, respectively at Auburn and Bristoe Station, guarding the reserve artillery, the army baggage and capturing two colors, five guns and four hundred and fifty prisoners. After the trying Mine Run campaign, the battalion went into winter quarters. In February Capt. Garrett Nowlen became temporary commander. The regimental formation was restored on May 3d, 1864, when Major Mulholland, having secured his recruits, resumed command with the rank of colonel. ready to follow General Grant, the new head of the Army. Then followed the historic series of battles, beginning with the Wilderness, Spotsylvania, North Anna, Cold Harbor and lesser combats, and then across the James River to the investment of Petersburg, leaving all along the trail the graves of comrades fallen in the awful carnage. Lieut.-Col. Richard C. Dale and Lieut. Henry Kiel were killed at Spotsylvania. The officers wounded included Col. Mulholland, Capts. Frank Leib, F. E. Crawford, Charles Coslett, and Lieuts. Louis Sacriste, Robert J. Alston, S. G. Vanderheyden, John C. Wright, Zadoc B. Springer and Joseph W. Yocum. Of the enlisted men fifty were killed, one hundred and twenty were wounded and thirty were missing.

In its first assault at Petersburg the "116th" carried the Confederate works at a loss of many killed, wounded and missing. At this time the regiment was detached from the Irish Brigade and became a part of the Fourth Brigade, then commanded by Gen. John R. Brooke.† The hardships and monotony of life in the trenches gave a welcome zest to the frequent battles on either side of the James River. In the course of the ten months occupied in the reduction of the Confederate citadel the regiment lost, among its numerous members slain, Capts. Garrett Nowlen, Samuel Taggart and Henry D. Price. The "116th" made its last fights in the four battles of the first week in April, 1865, and was not only witness of the scene at Appomattox, but first to receive the news of the surrender. After the Grand Review the remnant of the regiment arrived home and was mustered out on June 6th, 1865. Brevet Major-Gen. St.

---

*Acting Major Seneca Grubb Willauer commanded the 116th Battalion from August 13th, 1863, to February 5th, 1864, when he was transferred to the Veteran Reserve Corps, U. S. A.

†Major-Gen. John R. Brooke, retired from the regular service in 1903, survives at the time this book is in course of publication, an honored member of the military order of the Loyal Legion.

9

Clair A. Mulholland, riding at the head of his veterans, was the only original officer to be present in the line.

TOTAL LOSSES.*

Killed or died from wounds..............................officers, 10; men, 141
Died from disease or other causes........................   "   2;   "   86
Wounded, not mortally ....   "   31;   " 307
Captured or missing ....   "   7;   " 106†

BATTLES, ETC.

Charlestown, Snicker's Gap, Fredericksburg, Chancellorsville, Gettysburg, Falling Waters, Auburn, Bristoe Station, Mine Run, Morton's Ford, Wilderness, Todd's Tavern, Po River, Spotsylvania, Spotsylvania Court House, North Anna, Pamunky River, Totopotomoy, Cold Harbor; assaults on Petersburg, Williams' Farm; Siege of Petersburg, Deep Bottom, Strawberry Plains, Reams' Station, Hatcher's Run, Dabney's Mills, Gravelly Run, Sunderland Station, Amelia Court House, Sailors' Creek, Farmville, Appomattox.

ONE HUNDRED AND EIGHTEENTH REGIMENT INFANTRY

COLONEL CHARLES M. PREVOST to September 30th, 1863.
COLONEL JAMES GWYN to June 1st, 1865.
Total Enrollment, 1,296 Officers and Men.

THE patriotic resolution of the Corn Exchange, of Philadelphia, adopted at a meeting held upon July 24th, 1862, under which immediate action was taken for the formation of a regiment of infantry and its equipment, resulted in the rendezvous, one month later, at Camp Union, near the Falls of Schuylkill, of the historic command which, nearly one thousand strong, went forth as the 118th Regiment. To accomplish this result the Corn Exchange offered the inducement of a liberal bounty, and provided each recruit with articles of comfort not usually furnished by the Government. Many of the officers had previously seen service in earlier commands.‡

---

*The figures relating to officers are taken from the Regimental History, brevet Maj.-Gen. St. Clair A. Mulholland. The record of losses in enlisted men are from the official records of the Adjutant General of the Army.

†Of those captured forty-five died in the Southern prisons.

‡Capt. Frank A. Donaldson had formerly served as an officer in the 71st Regiment and was among those who were made prisoners of war at the action of Ball's Bluff.

The regiment left Philadelphia upon September 1st, 1862, reaching
Washington the following day, and was attached to the First Brigade,
First Division, Fifth Corps. A few days later the Fifth Corps was started
upon its trying march through Maryland, which ended at Antietam. Here
the "118th" was placed in support of artillery and was not actually involved.

Three days after the battle the regiment participated in a reconnaissance, crossing the Potomac at a ford near Shepherdstown. The enemy
having been discovered in force and the purpose of the reconnaissance
accomplished, the troops were ordered to recross to the Maryland side
of the river. Through a mistake the order was not delivered to the
"118th", and it was left unsupported to resist the attack of a Confederate
division. The men, although inexperienced, less than three weeks from
home and armed with defective muskets, made a gallant stand, but were
overpowered and compelled to retreat across the river. The losses of
the "118th" were seventy-one officers and men killed or who died from
their wounds, seventy-five wounded and sixty-seven captured, a total
of two hundred and thirteen. The Confederate loss in the engagement,
in Gen. Hill's Division, was reported to be two hundred and sixty-two
officers and men.

Burnside's experiment, which occasioned the battle of Fredericksburg,
cost the "118th", at the assault upon Marye's Heights, seven killed, forty-
three wounded and sixteen missing. After the January "mud march"
the regiment went into winter quarters. In April Col. Prevost having
recovered from his wounds again took command. A few weeks later
Col. Prevost was promoted and placed in command of the Invalid Corps,
prior to which, however, he led the regiment through the fighting around
Chancellorsville.*

The Fifth Corps started northward upon June 10th, having frequent
brushes with the Confederate cavalry en route. Arriving at Gettysburg
upon the morning of July 2d, the regiment was posted near Cemetery
Hill, but in the afternoon it was hurried to the support of Sickles, on
the left, where it became hotly engaged. The following morning the
command was sent to Round Top, which position it occupied to the end
of the battle. At Warrenton, Virginia, on August 6th, one hundred and
nine recruits arrived, and on September 15th one hundred and eighty-five
more were received. Desultory fighting kept the men moving through
the autumn. At the end of the year, at Beverly Ford, Lieut.-Col. Gwyn
received his commission as colonel. During the conflicts in the Wilderness, and in the course of the advance to Petersburg, the "118th" had
heavy fighting with numerous casualties. In front of Petersburg the
fighting was constant. Grant was remorselessly wearing out the besieged
enemy. Regiments were used unsparingly, and the "118th" was accorded

*In 1864 Col. Prevost was stationed as commandant at the military prison
located at Elmira, N. Y.

its full share of the work. Early in the following February the army began upon the final chapter of the war. At Dabney's Mills several of the regimental officers were killed or wounded. The whole region was alive, at this time, with moving troops and the deadly grinding of the mills of war. Petersburg fell upon April 2d, Richmond the next day, and then, like a cyclone, Sheridan's cavalry swept after the fugitive remnants still obedient to Lee. The Fifth Corps was at Five Forks upon the 1st and there had its last fight. The 118th Regiment was among the advanced troops at Appomattox. It was the first to receive and direct the officer bearing the flag of truce from the Confederate headquarters which resulted in the end of hostilities. It was detailed with the First Brigade to receive the rebel arms and colors. Fifteen thousand muskets and eighty-four battle flags were laid down along the brigade front. Turning homeward, the "118th" was in the line of the Grand Review at Washington upon May 23d. A week later it was mustered out. Upon arrival at Philadelphia the veterans were splendidly banqueted at Sansom Street Hall by the Corn Exchange, and upon the 10th of June marched in the review of the returned Philadelphia volunteers.

TOTAL LOSSES.

Killed or died from wounds.................................officers,   9; men, 132
Died from disease or accident..............................   "   1; "   112
Wounded, not mortally ....   "   18; "   312.
Captured or missing ....   "   5; "   285.

BATTLES.

Antietam, Shepherdstown, Fredericksburg, Chancellorsville, Upperville, Gettysburg, Rappahannock Station, Mine Run, Wilderness, Spotsylvania, North Anna, Totopotomoy, Bethesda Church, Cold Harbor, Petersburg, Weldon Road, Poplar Springs Church (Peeble's Farm), Hatcher's Run, Dabney's Mill, Boydton Plank Road, Five Forks, Appomattox (surrender).

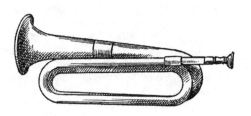

ONE HUNDRED AND NINETEENTH REGIMENT INFANTRY

(" Gray Reserves ")

COLONEL PETER C. ELLMAKER to January 12th, 1864.
COLONEL GIDEON CLARK to June 19th, 1865.
Total Enrollment, 1,216 Officers and Men.

THE "119th," composed, in a large degree, of officers and rank and file from the First Regiment Militia, of Philadelphia, was known as the "Gray Reserve" Regiment. In its enthusiastic recruitment, the officers were effectively aided by a committee of thirteen citizens. The command was mustered in between August 15th and September 17th, 1862. Responding promptly to the urgent orders of the Government, the regiment left Philadelphia on September 1st, not fully organized. From the Arsenal in Washington, with the addition of a tenth company, the command, upon receiving guns and accoutrements, was sent to Tenallytown. In October the regiment joined the First Brigade, Second Division, Sixth Corps, then at Hagerstown, Maryland. Moving to Falmouth, opposite Fredericksburg, in November, the regiment first came under fire in the effort to capture that stronghold, on December 12th and 13th. After the "mud-march" of January the "119th" remained in winter quarters. In February the regiment was assigned to the Third Brigade, First Division, with which it was identified throughout its subsequent career. Upon the opening of the Chancellorsville campaign the Sixth Corps was moved, at night, to the right bank of Rappahannock river, at Franklin's Crossing. On May 3d, 1863, in the two battles of Marye's Heights and Salem Church the regiment lost twelve killed and one hundred and twelve wounded, or about thirty-five per cent. of effective strength.

In the evening of July 1st, 1863, the Sixth Corps was at Manchester, Maryland, from which camp, at ten o'clock, began the historic forced march of thirty-seven miles to Gettysburg. Arriving at 4.30 P. M. on the 2d, the corps remained in the rear of the Fifth Corps, taking position, early on the 3d, at the extreme left, in rear of Round Top, a post of great responsibility, but, as events proved, far from the heavy fighting of the day. On the 4th the "119th" occupied Little Round Top. Pursuing and skirmishing with laggard fragments of Lee's Army, notably at Fairfield Gap and Funkstown, the Third Brigade finally rested at Warrenton, where about two hundred recruits were received by the "119th."

At Rappahannock Station, on November 7th, the Third Brigade, under command of Col. Ellmaker, led the assault upon the enemy's works, resulting in the capture of sixteen hundred prisoners and a large amount of material. In this brilliant affair the "119th" lost seven killed and forty-three wounded, three of the killed being Capt. Cyrus M. Hodgson and Lieuts. Edward Everett Coxe and Robert Reaney. After the brief Mine Run campaign, the "119th" had a respite of six months of routine. On January 12th, 1864, Col. Ellmaker resigned, and was succeeded by Lieut.-Col. Gideon Clark.

With the beginning of the forward movement of May, 1864, directed by Major-Gen. U. S. Grant, the armies met in the dark and bloody Wilderness, and, in the week following May 5th, the "119th" lost two hundred and fifteen officers and men. Then, at the North Anna, the Pamunkey, Totopotomoy and Cold Harbor, further weeks of carnage ensued, until, on the 19th of June, the "119th" found its task again in the trenches around Petersburg. In the course of the deadly six weeks following its departure from its winter quarters on Hazel river the regiment lost, among those slain in battle, Major Henry P. Truefitt, Capt. Charles R. Warner and Lieuts. George G. Lovett, Edward Ford and George C. Humes.

Soon after the return of the Third Brigade from the crippling of the Weldon Railroad it was dispatched, with the entire Sixth Corps, to Washington, meeting Early's invasion at Fort Stevens, driving his troops back to the hills and, under Sheridan, scattering them at Winchester.

At this time the "119th" was detached and detailed for duty at Philadelphia, in anticipation of election disturbances. Its absence from the front covered a period of about two weeks. The command then returned to Winchester, Va., where the Third Brigade remained until November 30th, then returning to the vicinity of Petersburg.

In the final campaign, resulting in the dislodgement of the enemy from Petersburg, and in the pursuit, ending at Appomattox Court House, the regiment had its almost constant share of danger, loss and glory. In the final assault at Petersburg Adjt. John D. Mercer was fatally wounded. After the surrender the Sixth Corps was sent, as a precautionary measure, to Danville, but with the passing of the exigency, turned homeward. The "119th" arrived in Philadelphia on June 6th and on the 19th was mustered out.

TOTAL LOSSES.

	officers,	men,
Killed or died from wounds	9;	132
Died from disease or other causes	" 1;	" 71
Wounded, not mortally	" 12;	" 279
Captured or missing	"	" 75

BATTLES, ETC.

Fredericksburg, Marye's Heights, Salem Church, Gettysburg, Rappahannock Station, Mine Run, Wilderness, Spotsylvania, North Anna, Totopotomoy, Cold Harbor, Petersburg, Fort Stevens, Winchester (Opequon), Dabney's Mill, Petersburg (Fort Fisher), Petersburg (assault), Sailor's Creek, Appomattox Court House.

ONE HUNDRED AND TWENTY-FIRST REGIMENT INFANTRY

COLONEL CHAPMAN BIDDLE to December 1st, 1863.*
LIEUT.-COLONEL ELISHA W. DAVIS to April 20th, 1863.
LIEUT.-COLONEL ALEXANDER BIDDLE to January 9th, 1864.
LIEUT.-COLONEL THOMAS M. HALL to January 9th, 1864.
Philadelphia Companies B, C, D, G, H, I, and K.
Total Enrollment, 891 Officers and Men.

I N the formation of this regiment the recruits gathered largely from Venango County for the proposed 145th Regiment by Elisha W. Davis were included.† These mountaineers were organized as Companies A, F and part of E. The balance of the regiment was raised in Philadelphia. The "121st" camped near Chestnut Hill, in August and September, 1862, and was soon afterwards sent to Arlington Heights, Va. On October 1st the command was moved to Frederick, Md., and attached to the First Brigade, Third Division of the First Corps, which was mainly composed of Pennsylvania Reserves, and commanded by Major-Gen. George Gordon Meade. With these experienced troops the "121st" entered its first battle, at Fredericksburg, December 13th, losing, in the campaign, one hundred and eighty killed and wounded. The heroic steadiness of the "121st" at Fredericksburg elicited special praise from Gen. Meade. A number of officers and men were mentioned for bravery in special orders, among them Lieut. Joseph G. Rosengarten, who saved the colors after the color bearer had fallen.‡

The routine of the winter camp was broken by the "mud march" and one or two minor expeditions. The activities of the army began upon the opening of May, 1864, with the battle of Chancellorsville, where the loss of the "121st" was small in numbers. One of the officers killed was Capt. W. D. Dorr, a gallant soldier.§ The First Corps began its northward march (ending at Gettysburg) on June 12th, reaching the field and

---

*Col. Chapman Biddle had been identified with the old militia in Philadelphia and was among the first to act, at the critical moment, in April, 1861, for the military support of the National Government. He organized Company A of the 1st Regiment Pennsylvania Artillery, which was later known as Landis' Battery. Capt. Biddle and Lieut. Alexander Biddle resigned in August to organize an infantry regiment, which was designated the "121st."

†The Venango County recruits, on arrival in Philadelphia, were placed in Camp John C. Knox near Manayunk, where they were quartered until consolidated with the "121st." They were chiefly woodsmen and good marksmen, thus adding greatly to the effectiveness of the command.

‡Lieutenant Rosengarten was soon afterward detailed upon the staff of Major-Gen. John F. Reynolds.

§Capt. William W. Dorr, of Company K, killed at Spotsylvania on May 10th, 1864, was a son of the Rev. Dr. Dorr of Christ Church, upon the walls of which his comrades placed a memorial tablet.

going into position upon the extreme left of the line at eleven o'clock A. M. on July 1st. This position was held nearly five hours.

The First Brigade, which had gone into battle with twelve hundred and eighty-seven officers and men, numbered, for further duty at the close of the day, but three hunded and ninety.* In the retreat to Cemetery Hill the regiment made a stand at the Seminary, and, from a barricade, held the advancing Confederates back until nearly all of the army had passed. Falling back through Gettysburg the "121st" called the roll. Out of seven officers and two hundred and fifty-six men in the line that morning, but two officers and eighty-two men responded.† Upon July 2d the regiment was posted on the Taneytown Road to the left of the cemetery, and on the 3d near the center of the line and in reserve.

After Gettysburg, ten months elapsed before the regiment was again engaged in battle. In the meantime it had performed a great amount of marching, guard duty and picketing. In March, 1864, the remnants of the First Corps were distributed, the "121st" going to the Third Brigade, Fourth Division, Fifth Corps. With some brigade and division changes it remained in this corps to the end of the war. Between May 4th and June 16th, 1864, or from the Rapidan to the James, the Fifth Corps fought its way almost daily, each brigade and regiment having its own hardships, losses and victories. The "121st" lost many of its veteran members and several officers. At Petersburg the regiment was engaged upon the construction of the famous "Fort Hell," near the "Mine." It participated in the first and second expeditions sent to destroy the Weldon Railroad, and was in the affairs of Boydton Plank Road and Five Forks. At Appomattox Court House the regiment was detailed to guard duty during and after the formalities of the surrender. On May 12th it was sent, with captured property, to Burkeville, and from that point began the homeward march. At Washington it participated in the Grand Review, and was mustered out on June 2d, 1865.

TOTAL LOSSES. †

Killed or died from wounds ....officers, 5; men, 104.
Died from disease or other causes........................... "   2; "   66.
Wounded, not mortally, officers and men......................   293.

BATTLES.

Fredericksburg, Chancellorsville, Gettysburg, Wilderness, Spotsylvania, North Anna, Totopotomoy, Bethesda Church, Cold Harbor, Petersburg, Weldon Railroad, Peeble's Farm, Dabney's Mill, Boydton Plank Road, Five Forks, Hatcher's Run, Appomattox Court House.

---

*The 1st Brigade was in command, at that time, of Lieut.-Col. Chapman Biddle. The regiment was in command of Major Alexander Biddle.

†The inscription upon the regimental monument indicates a loss, at Gettysburg, of twenty men killed or fatally wounded, five officers and ninety-three men wounded, and sixty captured, out of three hundred and six present.

CAMP STANTON, 19TH CAVALRY, ISLINGTON LANE. July to October, 1863.
(Redrawn from a war time wood cut.)

CAMP UNION, 118TH REGIMENT, QUEEN LANE, FALLS OF SCHUYLKILL,
August, 1862.

CAMP GALLAGHER, 13TH CAVALRY (1 BATTALION), FALLS OF SCHUYLKILL.
August and September, 1862.

ONE HUNDRED AND FORTY-SEVENTH REGIMENT INFANTRY

Lieut.-Col. Ario Pardee, Jr.
Philadelphia Companies M and P.
Total Enrollment, 150 Officers and Men.*

WHILE the 28th Regiment was in camp at Louden Heights, Virginia, in October, 1862, a regiment was organized at that point, which became the "147th" Infantry of the Pennsylvania line. Five companies of the "28th" were transferred to the new command, two of which, M and P, numbering one hundred and fifty men, were from Philadelphia.* Major Ario Pardee, Jr., of the "28th," became commander of the "147th," with the rank of lieutenant-colonel. The two regiments were sometimes styled the "28th Legion." The "147th," in the First Brigade, Second Division, Twelfth Corps, participated in the second Burnside campaign of January and February, 1863, and the Chancellorsville Campaign of May, losing about one hundred in killed, wounded and missing. In June, 1863, the regiment moved with the Twelfth Corps to Gettysburg, taking position on the evening of July 1st near Round Top, and later at Culp's Hill. On the night of the 2d and forenoon of the 3d the "147th" was engaged at the latter point, losing twenty-five killed and wounded. With the Hooker transfer, the "147th" was sent to reinforce the Army of the Cumberland, becoming a part of the Second Division of the Twentieth Corps. It was in line at the battles of Lookout Mountain, Missionary Ridge and Ringgold. On December 29th, 1863, the majority of the men re-enlisted and, after the usual furlough, returned to join Gen. Sherman's campaign through Georgia and the Carolinas, having a part, with the 28th and 29th Regiments, in all of the dangers, hardships and glory of that crowning achievement of the war. The thrilling story of the arduous campaign of the army led by Gen. William T. Sherman is equally the story of this efficient regiment. Soon after the surrender of Gen. Johnston the Pennsylvania troops were moved to Washington and there, on July 15th, 1865, the "147th" was mustered out of the service.†

BATTLES.

Chancellorsville, Gettysburg, Lookout Mountain, Mission Ridge, Ringgold, Dug Gap, Rocky Fall Ridge, New Hope Church, Pine Knob, Nose's Creek, Kenesaw Mountain, Peach Tree Creek, Atlanta (march to the sea).

---

*In addition to these two Philadelphia companies, a company of drafted men under Capt. Charles Fair, which had been on duty at the Schuylkill Arsenal, was attached to the "147th" in September, 1863.

†The casualties of the two Philadelphia companies are not obtainable.

ONE HUNDRED AND FIFTIETH REGIMENT INFANTRY

(Third Bucktails)

COLONEL LANGHORNE WISTER to February 22d, 1864.*
COLONEL H. S. HUIDEKOPER to March 5th, 1864.
COLONEL GEORGE W. JONES to June 23d, 1865.

Philadelphia Companies A, B, D and F.

Total Enrollment, 420 Officers and Men.

THIS regiment was partly recruited in Philadelphia (which furnished companies A, B, E and F) and in the Counties of Crawford, Union and McKean. It rendezvoused at Camp Curtin, being mustered in on September 4th, 1862. Soon afterward the command was sent to Washington and assigned to guard duty. Companies D and K were stationed at the Soldiers' Home, where President Lincoln and his family resided in the summers. The latter company, from Crawford County, commanded by Capt. David V. Derrickson, was retained to the end of the war as the special guard of the President.†

In February the "150th" became part of the Second (Bucktail) Brigade (Brig.-Gen. Roy Stone), Third Division, First Corps. In May General Stone's brigade was present at the battle of Chancellorsville, but was not actively employed. The Third Division, under Major-Gen. Abner Doubleday, reached the scene of the opening battle at Gettysgurg at 11.30 A. M. on July 1st. The "150th," mustering three hundred and ninety-seven officers and men, was in position on the left of the Chambersburg Pike, near Willoughby Run. This position was held until near four o'clock, the regiment then retreating toward and through the town. In the retreat the regiment colors were lost.‡ The remnant of the regiment re-formed on Cemetery Hill, but two officers remaining. Three officers had been slain. Col. Wistar and twelve of his officers, the majority wounded, had been captured. On the morning of July 2d one hundred and nine (including the two officers) were present for duty.

---

*Col. Langhorne Wister, of Philadelphia. had served as captain of Company B, 42d Regiment, the original "Bucktails," which was designated the 13th Regiment, Reserve Corps.

†President Lincoln wrote a "request" on November 1st, 1862, that this company should be allowed to remain as his personal guard. He honored Capt. Derrickson as a companion and friend. When the latter was transferred to duty in Pennsylvania he was succeeded by Lieut. Thomas Getchell.

‡The colors were captured from a wounded color-bearer by North Carolina troops, and were sent to Jefferson Davis. They were found among his effects when he was captured, at the close of the war, and are now preserved at the Capitol at Harrisburg.

138

During the day the regiment was active at various points of danger, and after nightfall advanced and recaptured two guns of a regular battery, lost during the afternoon. Retiring from picket duty early on the 3d, and while on the battle line in the afternoon, some further casualties occurred. The total regimental loss (as officially stated) was fifty-seven killed, one hundred and thirty-nine wounded and seventy-seven captured or missing; a few of the latter, however, were accounted for the morning of the 2d.

With an accession of recruits, the "150th" participated in the movements of the army upon the Rappahannock, finally forming its winter camp at Culpeper. Col. Wister, who had been exchanged, resigned on February 22d. The regiment was transferred, in March, to the Third Brigade, Fourth Division, Fifth Corps, and was now commanded by Major George W. Jones,* promoted from captain.†

With the Fifth Corps the "150th" was engaged in the heavy fighting which began on May 5th in the Wilderness, and which ended at Bethesda Church, on June 1st. Crossing the James River the deadly struggle was renewed around Petersburg. The "150th" was among the troops at the Mine Explosion, the first move on Weldon Railroad (where it built Fort Dushane), at Hatcher's Run, and, in December, in the destruction of the Weldon Railroad. As a great number of prisoners had been captured the war-worn "150," with the "149th," was sent, as guards, to the prison camp at Elmira, N. Y., and remained there on duty until mustered out, on June 24th, 1865. Company K (President's Guard) was mustered out at Harrisburg on June 15th, 1865.

TOTAL LOSSES.‡

Killed or died from wounds..........................officers, 4; men, 108
Died from disease or other causes......................... "   1; "   94

BATTLES.

Chancellorsville, Gettysburg, Wilderness (two days), North Anna, Spotsylvania (three days), Totopotomoy, Hatcher's Run, Bethesda Church, Petersburg, Weldon Railroad, Dabney's Mill.

---

*Both Lieut.-Col. Huidekoper and Major Thomas Chamberlin had resigned on account of wounds.

†Capt. Cornelius A. Widdis (subsequently commissioned lieutenant-colonel) became a prisoner July 1st, 1863, at Gettysburg, and was not released until the end of the war.

‡Col. Thomas Chamberlin, the regimental historian, states that the exact number of wounded, captured and missing cannot be enumerated. The regimental history (Edition of 1905) includes a list of forty-nine men captured, of whom twenty-three died at Richmond and Andersonville.

As a graphic and entertaining presentation of experiences in a soldier's life, few books of the Civil War equal the "Recollections of a Drummer Boy," a work written by Harry M. Kiefer, of the 150th Regiment.

ONE HUNDRED AND FIFTY-SEVENTH REGIMENT INFANTRY

Lieut.-Col. Edmund T. Tiers.

Total Enrollment, about 350 Officers and Men.

W HEN partially recruited in December, 1862, this command was ordered to guard duty at Fort Delaware. Upon February 27th, 1863, the recruits of a tentative regiment, designated the "156th," "Board of Trade Rifles," were enlisted with the "157th," the whole being organized as a battalion of four companies. The battalion was assigned to duty in the defences around Washington as a part of Tyler's Division, Twenty-second Corps.

In May, 1864, the battalion was attached to the Second Brigade, Fourth Division, Fifth Corps. In this position and with the Second Division later, the "157th" experienced a considerable period of fighting.

The battalion was transferred to the 191st Regiment* in front of Petersburg on March 21st, 1865, and with that regiment shared in the engagements and pursuit of the enemy immediately preceding the surrender of Lee's army at Appomattox. Soon after this great event the "191st" marched to Washington, took part in the Grand Review upon May 23d, and was mustered out June 28th, 1865.

TOTAL LOSSES.

Killed or died from wounds .... 31 men.
Died from disease .... 34 "

BATTLES.

Bethesda Church, Petersburg, Mine Explosion, Weldon Railroad, Poplar Springs Church, Yellow House, Boydton Plank Road, Hatcher's Run, Warren's raid, Dabney's Mills, Hatcher's Run, Appomattox campaign.

---

* The 190th and 191st Regiments were formed from veterans and recruits of the several Pennsylvania Reserve regiments at the end of their respective terms of service. The greater part of these regiments suffered capture and long imprisonment at Andersonville and other southern prison pens, where a large percentage died. For an impressive narration of their experiences the reader is referred to pages 281-287, Volume V, Bates' History of the Pennsylvania Volunteers. The men of the "191st" still in the field, together with the "157th," were armed with Spencer repeating rifles, with which they did effective work in the running fights between Hatcher's Run and Appomattox.

ONE HUNDRED AND EIGHTY-THIRD REGIMENT INFANTRY

(Fourth Union League Regiment)

COLONEL GEORGE P. McLEAN to May 3d, 1864.
COLONEL J. F. McCULLOUGH to May 31st, 1864.
COLONEL JAMES C. LYNCH to March 13th, 1865.
COLONEL GEORGE T. EGBERT to July 13th, 1865.
Total Enrollment, 1,200 Officers and Men.

OF the nine infantry regiments of Philadelphia organized under the direction of the Union League, the "183d" served longest and experienced, by far, the most vicissitudes. It was recruited during the fall of 1863 and through the following winter. Camp was established in Frankford, but was subsequently located in barracks upon the lot now covered by the buildings of the Union League. The command left Philadelphia upon February 23d, 1864. The "183d" was the last distinctively local regiment sent to the front. Upon reporting it was assigned to the First Brigade, First Division, Second Corps, then upon the Rapidan river.

The newcomers were led without delay into the very heart of war. In the month dating from May 5th the brigade participated in seven battles, a record for raw troops probably unequalled in the annals of the Pennsylvania line.* In the course of the campaign, during May, Col. George P. McLean, Lieut.-Col. William Powell, Major John Reynolds and Adj. Theodore F. Mann resigned, the last named because of ill health. Capt. John F. McCullough, a veteran officer of Company A, 140th Regiment, was commissioned colonel. This officer was killed upon May 31st, at Totopotomoy Creek. Two weeks later Capt. James C. Lynch, of the 106th Regiment, Acting Inspector General of the Second Division, Second Corps, was commissioned third colonel of the "183d." The regiment was moved to the front at Petersburg, being actively engaged in assaults and skirmishes. While here the re-enlisted men and recruits of the 72d Regiment (Baxter's Zouaves) were added to the "183d." Maj. George T. Egbert became lieutenant-colonel and Capt. Augustine T. Lynch major. The Second Corps was twice sent across the James river, meeting the enemy on both occasions. At Deep Bottom the regiment assisted in the capture of four guns. At Ream's Station, upon the Weldon Railroad, south of Petersburg, the "183d" was again engaged, on August 25th. During the fall and winter the regiment was engaged in guard and outpost duty incident to the siege. Upon October 6th Col. Lynch was mustered out. He was succeeded by Lieut.-Col.

---

*At Spotsylvania, on May 14th, a party of volunteers from the brigade, led by Captain Augustine T. Lynch, of this regiment, captured two Confederate guns from between the lines.

George T. Egbert. Maj. Augustine T. Lynch became lieutenant-colonel and Capt. Horace P. Egbert major.

In the constant fighting marking the final struggles of the besieged Confederates, the regiment was repeatedly under fire, losing some officers and men killed, wounded or captured. In these movements the First Division was detached and, under Gen. Nelson A. Miles,* joined Gen. Sheridan's force at Five Forks, and while returning met the enemy in an engagement, on April 2d, at Sutherland's Station, a point on the South Side Railroad. The "183d" shared, also, in the final combats at Farmville and Appomattox. After the surrender the march to Washington and the Review of May 23d, the "183d" was returned to Philadelphia, where it was mustered out on July 13th, 1865.

TOTAL LOSSES.

Killed or died from wounds ....officers, 5; men, 92.
Died of disease or other causes .... "   3; "   89,

BATTLES.

Wilderness, Spotsylvania, Corbin's Bridge, Po River, North Anna, Totopotomoy, Cold Harbor, Petersburg, Strawberry Plains, Deep Bottom, Ream's Station, Five Forks, Sutherland Station, Farmville, Appomattox Court House.

---

*This detour is mentioned by Gen. Nelson A. Miles in his "Recollections." *Cosmopolitan Magazine,* March, 1911, in these words:

"The hardest fighting and greatest loss of life occurred in the First Division, Second Corps, in which more men were killed and wounded than in any other division, East or West. This division broke through the enemy's lines and routed a division of the enemy at Sutherland Station, made most important captures at Sailor's Creek, and led the pursuit so vigorously and tenaciously that Gen. Lee rode up to our very lines on the morning of April 9th to surrender the Army of Northern Virginia.

ONE HUNDRED AND EIGHTY-SIXTH REGIMENT INFANTRY

COLONEL HENRY FRINK.
Total Enrollment, 1,079 Officers and Men.

THIS regiment was recruited in Philadelphia in the spring of 1864 for provost duty. Many of its officers had served in other commands. The regiment was stationed at Philadelphia throughout its term of service, which ended August 15th, 1865.

FIRST BATTALION INFANTRY (SIX MONTHS' SERVICE)

LIEUTENANT-COLONEL JOSEPH F. RAMSEY.
Total Enrollment (Philadelphia Companies), about 200 Officers and Men.

TWO companies of this regiment, C, Capt. John R. Miles, and E, Capt. W. F. Robinson, were raised in Philadelphia. The regiment was mustered in on June 23d, 1863, and was engaged in various parts of the State on duty in provost and draft riot emergencies. Co. C was stationed at the provost barracks, Fifth and Buttonwood streets, Philadelphia. At the end of its period of service the battalion was re-enlisted and recruited, forming the 187th Regiment, three years' service.

ONE HUNDRED AND EIGHTY-SEVENTH REGIMENT INFANTRY

COLONEL JOSEPH F. RAMSEY to September 29th, 1864.
COLONEL JOHN E. PARSONS to August 3d, 1865.
Total Enrollment (Philadelphia Companies), about 150 Officers and Men.

THIS regiment was formed from the First Battalion Infantry, in service six months, on provost duty from July, 1863, to the end of the year, and which contained two companies, E and F, from Philadelphia. Although all of the field officers were from other communities of the State, at least seventeen of the company officers were Philadelphians.

143

The regiment was organized at Camp Curtin in March, 1864. The command reached Washington on May 19th. Marching to the front it joined the army during the battle of Cold Harbor and was assigned to the First Brigade, First Division, Fifth Corps. With this corps the "187th" fought its way to join the lines then investing Petersburg, and shared in the movements and sorties, involving continuous skirmishing, through the summer, during which the regiment lost many officers and men. On September 22d, 1864, the regiment was detached and ordered to Philadelphia. With headquarters at Camp Cadwalader,* the "187th" was employed on provost duty in Philadelphia and at disturbed points in the State.† Col. Ramsey having resigned and Major George W. Merrick being disabled from wounds, Capt. John E. Parsons (then assistant adjutant-general of the brigade) was commissioned lieutenant-colonel. The regiment acted as a guard of honor upon the arrival and departure of the remains of President Lincoln in April, 1865. The "187th" was assembled at Harrisburg and mustered out on August 3d, 1865.

TOTAL LOSSES (Philadelphia Companies).

Killed or died from wounds. ....men, 8
Died from disease and other causes....................................... " 9

BATTLES.

Cold Harbor, before Petersburg, Jerusalem Plank Road, Weldon Railroad (June 21st-23d, 1864), Mine Explosion, Weldon Railroad, August 18th-21st, 1864).

*"No military rendezvous of any kind established in this city since the breaking out of the war has been the cause of so much complaint or the source of as many communications of a disparaging character as Camp Cadwalader. These complaints consist mainly of suffering endured by the men stationed there and injustice done them by a certain set of unprincipled officials who have charge of matters and things generally within the enclosure. Filthy quarters, miserable diet, embezzlement of money belonging to soldiers, an utter disregard for the welfare and comfort of the men, constitute a portion of the evils complained of and which have caused so many desertions that would otherwise not have taken place." Quoted from a Philadelphia newspaper (History of the 187th Regiment).

†At all times, dating from the first draft, a considerable element of the Pennsylvania population dwelling in remote sections were strongly opposed to military service. In this respect they held the same attitude as that of the loyal mountaineers of the South, who only became soldiers of the Confederacy upon compulsion. The tasks of the military detachments sent out under the orders of the provost marshals to enforce conscriptions, capture deserters and break up disloyal gatherings were full of incident and danger. The "Army of Fishing Creek" is not mentioned in Official Reports, but that it deserves a place in Civil War history is vouched for by a correspondent of the *Philadelphia Inquirer,* who was witness of its "invasion of Columbia County," in September, 1864, a narration of which may be found in "The American Bastile," John A. Marshall, page 310.

ONE HUNDRED AND EIGHTY-EIGHTH REGIMENT INFANTRY

COLONEL GEORGE K. BOWEN to March 27th, 1865.
COLONEL JOHN G. GREGG to July 1st, 1865.
COLONEL JAMES C. BRISCOE to November 26th, 1865.
COLONEL SAMUEL IRVIN GIVIN to December 14th, 1865.
Total Enrollment, 1,200 Officers and Men.

TWENTY months after the 152d Regiment (3d Heavy Artillery) had entered the service, a regiment of infantry was formed from its surplus men, of whom about six hundred volunteered for the purpose, and, with additional recruits, the command took the field as the "188th," under command of Lieut.-Col. George K. Bowen, formerly captain of Company C, 152d Regiment. A large proportion of the officers and many of the enlisted men were Philadelphians. At Yorktown in April, 1864, it was assigned to the Third Brigade, First Division, Eighteenth Corps. Early in May the corps was embarked to Bermuda Hundred and advanced to invest Fort Darling, a strong work at Drury's Bluff, six miles below Richmond. During an assault on May 16th the right wing of the regiment was driven back from an advanced position and in course of the movement was fired upon by the supporting troops by mistake, the loss partly from this error being eleven men killed and sixty wounded. In the terrific fighting of June 1st and 3d at Cold Harbor the "188th" again lost a large percentage. The corps was now moved to the lines at Petersburg, occupying an exposed position on the extreme right. Here, in two month's time, the "188th" lost about half of its effective force from powder and sickness.

At the capture of Fort Harrison the skilled artillerymen of the "188th" manned the fortress guns and materially expedited the flight of the enemy, who returned, however, to suffer still worse punishment at the hands of the captors, on the following morning. In holding Fort Harrison against the persistent efforts of the Confederates to recover it, the "188th" lost, in killed and wounded, about one hundred and sixty officers and men.

At the end of the campaign the Eighteenth Corps was reorganized as the Twenty-fourth Corps. Four hundred recruits now joined the regiment and winter quarters was constructed. On March 4th, 1865, the brigade (now the "Third" of the Third Division) was sent on an expedition by transports to Fredericksburg, to destroy Confederate supplies. As soon as it was discovered at Fort Harrison, on April 3d, that Richmond was being deserted by the enemy the Union troops were rushed to the city, the "188th" assisting in subduing the fires and in restoring public order. The Third Brigade was encamped at Manchester. Some weeks after the surrender at Appomattox the members

10   145

of the 199th Regiment, whose enlistments had not expired, were merged with the "188th," Col. James C. Briscoe, of the former, taking command, and the regiment moved to Lynchburg. Upon the promotion of Col. Briscoe as brigadier-general in command of the post, Lieut.-Col. S. Irvin Given was advanced to the colonelcy. The several companies were stationed at Danville and other points in Virginia to enforce good order, and remained in this trying service until December 14th, when the regiment was assembled at City Point and mustered out.

TOTAL LOSSES.

Killed or died from wounds ....officers, 10; men, 114
Died from disease ....officers, 2; men, 66

BATTLES, ETC.

Drewry's Bluff, Cold Harbor, Petersburg, Chaffin's Farm, Fair Oaks (second), occupation of Richmond.

INDEPENDENT COMPANY ACTING ENGINEERS

CAPTAIN HENRY E. WRIGLEY to November 8th, 1862.
CAPTAIN ALBERT S. WHITE to March 29th, 1863.
CAPTAIN WILLIAM P. GASKILL to July 5th, 1864.
CAPTAIN SAMUEL C. SMITH to June 20th, 1865.

170 Officers and Men.

THIS was a special command of civil engineers, draughtsmen, artisans, mechanics and sailors. The expense of organization and equipment was met by William Struthers, a distinguished Philadelphian. The outfit included tools, forges and material required in field work. The men carried short carbines. The company was mustered upon August 9th, 1862, and encamped at Camp Struthers, Philadelphia. Soon afterward the company was employed upon the defences in front of Washington. After the battle of Antietam the headquarters of the command was established at Harper's Ferry, and from that point the force operated in detachments, in the work of construction or destruction, for the assistance of the Army of the Potomac, as circumstances required. A portion of the company accompanied the Eleventh and Twelfth Corps when they were transferred to the Army of the Cumberland, and laid a pontoon bridge across the Ohio river at Belleair for the passage of the troops.

In November, 1862, Capt. Wrigley was transferred to the Corps of Topographical Engineers, and was succeeded by First Lieut. Albert S. White. This officer died upon March 29th, 1863, and First Lieut. Willian Penn Gaskill commanded the company until July 5th, 1864. The last captain was Samuel C. Smith, who was out just prior to the discharge of the company upon June 20th, 1865.

FORTY-THIRD REGIMENT LIGHT ARTILLERY
(First Light Artillery Reserves)

COLONEL CHARLES T. CAMPBELL to December 9th, 1861.
COLONEL ROBERT M. WEST to May 29th, 1864.
LIEUT.-COL. JAMES BRADY to July 19th, 1865.
Philadelphia Batteries C, D, G, and H.
Total Enrollment, Philadelphia Batteries, 912 Officers and Men.

OUT of a large body of recruits gathered at Philadelphia by James Brady, in April, 1864, four batteries of light artillery were finally organized, and with four companies from the interior of the State, and, subsequently, one from Washington, D. C., a regiment of field artillery was accepted by the State as the fourteenth of the Reserve Corps regiments, and when taken over by the National Government it was enrolled as the "Forty-third" of the Pennsylvania line.

The Philadelphia batteries were armed and accoutred by the city, and the regiment, as a whole, was made ready for war by the State. The four local batteries, C, D, G and H, were commanded, in the course of the war, by fifteen captains, and the practice of designating artillery organizations, in accounts of battles, by the names of their *pro tem.* commanding officers leads to great confusion of identity.

Battery C—Captains, J. G. Simpson, Jeremiah McCarthy and Sharp L. Williams. 166 officers and men.

Battery D (partly from Blair County)—Captains Edward H. Flood, Michael Hall, Andrew Rosney and William Munk. (Estimated) 148 officers and men from Philadelphia.

Battery G—Captains, Robert M. West, Mark Kern, Frank P. Amsden, Belden Spence and L. Eugene C. Moore. 330 officers and men.

Battery H—Captain, James Brady, Andrew Fagan and Lord B. Richards. 268 officers and men.

The new artillery regiment thus provided by Pennsylvania under the law creating the reserve force was sent to the Government early in August, 1861, and located at Camp Barry, near the Capitol. As rapidly as the companies were supplied with horses and ammunition they were sent out to different divisions of the army, and each battery or group wrought its own history. The regiment was never thereafter gathered together.

Battery C was assigned to Smith's Division, D and H to Buell's

147

Division, engaged in constructing forts near Washington, and G was sent to McCall's Reserve Division. Subsequently C was united with D and H under Buell, but during the Peninsular campaign against Yorktown the three batteries were identified with Gen. Couch's Division, Fourth Corps. The history of these batteries is so nearly parallel that it is here presented (as in Bates' History) in group form.

After the siege of Yorktown and battle of Williamsburg followed the deadly battles of Fair Oaks and Seven Pines upon May 31st, 1862, where the batteries won the praise of Gen. Keyes in his official report. After the battle of Gaines' Mill the artillery of the Fourth Corps covered McClellan's retreat through White Oak Swamp and at Charles City Cross Roads. At Malvern Hill the batteries were in reserve, and covered the rear of the column on the way to Harrison's Landing. In July several changes occurred among the officers through promotion. E and H were now constituted reserve batteries of the Fourth Corps, and garrisoned at Yorktown, on the Peninsula. C and D were still attached to Couch's Division and were incorporated in the Sixth Corps. The next great battle was at Antietam, upon September 16th, 1862, where the artillerymen defended the Burnside bridge. In December the three batteries were kept busy for a week in front of Fredericksburg, shelling the enemy across the Rappahannock. About this time C and D batteries were consolidated as Battery D. The campaign of 1863 opened with Chancellorsville, during which the batteries took part in the attack on Marye's Heights, and fought, the same day, at Salem Church. Battery D did not share in the glory of Gettysburg. Battery H made the march from Washington, but arrived after the close of the battle. Soon afterwards Battery D was transferred to the Army of the Shenandoah, with which it was in line at the battle of Cedar Creek, Va., October 18th, 1864, where the timely arrival of the Sixth Corps resulted in the recapture of their lost guns and turned defeat into victory. The artillery survivors of this fierce hand-to-hand battle were now reinforced from Washington by a party of recruits. Battery C was revived, and the two commands posted along the upper Potomac during the balance of the war. They were mustered out at Harrisburg upon the 29th and 30th of June, 1865.

Battery G, together with A, B and E, shared in the campaigns of the Pennsylvania Reserve Division. Thus the Philadelphia artillery arm is represented in the enduring records of that splendid body of troops. The brief resumé of the deeds done by the infantry regiments is equally the story of its artillery. Battery G was the only one of the four Philadelphia companies which lost an officer in battle. Capt. Mark Kern was killed at Bull Run upon August 30th, 1861. At Gettysburg, Battery G. was attached to the Third Volunteer Brigade, Artillery Reserve, and temporarily commanded by Capt. R. B. Ricketts. Battery H was also present at this battle. During the latter part of its term of service Battery G was garrisoned at Fort Foote, a massive defensive work upon the Potomac river, below Washington. The battery was finally mustered out, at Philadelphia, upon July 29th, 1865.

The four Philadelphia batteries of the "43d" lost, by death, eighty-one men. Very few were lost by capture. Taking into account the long list of engagements in which these troops participated, the relatively small number of fatalities, especially among the officers, as well as the fact of immunity from capture, are most remarkable.

BATTLES AND ENGAGEMENTS.*

Battery C—Yorktown, Williamsburg, Fair Oaks, Seven Days' Battles, James River Road, Savage Station, Charles City Cross Roads, Glendale, Malvern Hill, Antietam, Fredericksburg, Chancellorsville, Mayre's Heights, Salem Heights, Bank's Ford, (after consolidation with Battery D) Berryville, Opequon, Winchester, Fisher's Hill, Cedar Creek.

Battery D— Yorktown, Williamsburg, Fair Oaks, Seven Days' Battles, James River Road, Charles City Cross Roads, Malvern Hill, Sulphur Springs, Antietam, Fredericksburg, Chancellorsville, Mayre's Heights, Salem Heights, Bank's Ford, Berryville, Opequon, Winchester, Fisher's Hill, Cedar Creek.

Battery G—Mechanicsville, Gaines' Mill, Charles City Cross Roads, Glendale, Malvern Hill, Fredericksburg, Chancellorsville, Pollock's Mill Creek, Fitzhugh's Crossing, Chancellorsville, Gettysburg, Mine Run, Morton's Ford.

Battery H—Yorktown, Williamsburg, Fair Oaks, Seven Days' Battles, Bottom's Bridge, Glendale, Malvern Hill, Gettysburg.

---

*Dyer's Compendium.

ONE HUNDRED AND TWELFTH REGIMENT ARTILLERY
(SECOND HEAVY ARTILLERY)

COLONEL CHARLES ANGEROTH, SR., to June 21st, 1862.
COLONEL AUGUSTUS A. GIBSON to August 3d, 1864.
COLONEL JAMES L. ANDERSON to September 29th, 1864.
COLONEL WILLIAM M. McCLURE to March 8th, 1865.
COLONEL S. D. STRAWBRIDGE to January 29th, 1865.
Total Enrollment, 5,315 Officers and Men.

THE attractions of garrison service made the formation of heavy artillery regiments for the national forces an easy task. In the autumn of 1861 the 112th Regiment (Second Pennsylvania Heavy Artillery) was organized by Charles Angeroth, who had been identified as colonel with the 2d Regiment, "Washington Brigade," and as lieutenant-colonel with the 27th Regiment, Pennsylvania Volunteer Infantry. This command was intended to be a siege or field regiment to conform to the regulations of the United States Army. Ten companies were raised in Philadelphia and in the counties of Franklin, Allegheny and Monroe. Three companies were sent, upon January 9th, 1862, to Fort Delaware, and upon February 25th the remaining companies left camp, in Camden, N. J., for Washington, where they were garrisoned in the defences north of the city. Here, in March, the three companies from Fort Delaware rejoined the regiment, to which, later, were added two independent companies which had been recruited in Luzerne County and had also been stationed at Fort Delaware. These were designated Companies L and M. The "112th" rebuilt and remained in the forts in the vicinity of Washington until May 27th, 1864. In the meanwhile Col. Augustus A. Gibson, a captain of the regular artillery service, who had suceeded Col. Angeroth (resigned June 21st) upon June 25th, 1862, had drilled his command into a condition of great efficiency, and it had increased in numbers to the astonishing figure of 3,300 men. The Government finally issued an order, upon April 18th, 1864, organizing, from the surplus men, the "Second Provisional Heavy Artillery." Two days later this provisional regiment, officered from the old command, was sent to the Ninth Corps, joining it at Brandy Station May 4th, participating in all of its fighting at Mine Run, Spotsylvania, Wilderness, Cold Harbor, Petersburg, Weldon Railroad, Hatcher's Run, Mine Explosion and Dinwiddie. With the single exception of the First Maine Heavy

Artillery, this regiment lost more men killed than any other in the course of the war.

Upon May 27th the "112th" joined the Second Brigade, Second Division, Eighteenth Corps, at Cold Harbor. Here the regiment was divided into three battalions and handled as infantry. The Second Battalion, under Capt. Paul T. Jones, participated in a charge in front of Petersburg, losing ten killed and sixty-five wounded. Upon August 3d, 1864, Col. Gibson was returned to service with the regulars, and Major James L. Anderson assumed the command.

In the constant fighting around Petersburg and Richmond the regiment had lost more than half of its effective strength. The nine hundred were joined, upon September 5th, by the remnant of four hundred and thirty-seven men of the "Provisionals." This contingent had been a part of the assaulting column at the disastrous Petersburg Mine Explosion, losing there over four hundred men. In the assault at Chaffin's Farm (Fort Harrison) the "112th" charged Fort Gilmer, losing four hundred and sixty-five officers and men killed, wounded and captured. In this battle Major Anderson was killed. His commission as colonel reached camp two days later. He was succeeded by Captain William M. McClure, of Battery F, who was promoted colonel October 30th, 1864.

The original term of service ended in January, 1865; the men, however, very generally re-enlisted. While upon the James River the regiment was recruited to a strength of over two thousand men. Col. McClure was honorably discharged upon March 8th, 1865. The colonelcy reverted, upon April 16th, to Lieut.-Col. S. D. Strawbridge. Battery A participated in the capture of Fort Fisher, N. C. Part of Battery M manned the guns at Fort Stevens and Fort De Russe when Early made his attack on Washington. Two detachments of the regiment served in Light Batteries B and D, United States Horse Batteries. Those in Battery B fired the last guns at Appomattox.

After the surrender the regiment was retained at Petersburg and in the lower counties of Virginia upon provost duty until its final discharge at Philadelphia, February 16th, 1866, being the last Philadelphia regiment, with one exception, in the service. It was the largest regiment in the Union Army.*

TOTAL LOSSES.

Killed or died from wounds...................................officers and men, 163
Died from disease or other causes......................... " " " 585
Captured... " " " 863

---

*A full roster of the officers and men of the regiment and of the Provisional regiment formed in 1864 from the surplus men is on file at the War Department, Washington, but is not among the records of the Adjutant General's office at Harrisburg. All obtainable names are included in the very adequate history of the regiment prepared by Geeorge W. Ward, Secretary of the Survivors' Association.

INDEPENDENT BATTALION (MARINE ARTILLERY)

Major Hermann Segebarth.
About 300 Men.

MUSTERED January, 1862. Companies A and B of this command were assigned to duty at Fort Delaware, and were recruited, in August, 1862, to four batteries, which became, upon February 17th, 1863, a part of the Third Heavy Artillery. (152d Regiment.)

ONE HUNDRED AND FIFTY-SECOND REGIMENT (THIRD HEAVY ARTILLERY)

Colonel Joseph Roberts to November 9th, 1865.
Total Enrollment, 4,978 Officers and Men.

IN August, 1862, Col. Herman Segebarth received authority from the War Department to increase the two companies, forming a battalion of marine artillery (which had served at Fort Delaware in the preceding year), to a regiment of heavy artillery. A month later Major Joseph Roberts, of the Fourth United States Artillery, was engaged in the formation of a battalion of heavy artillery. The recruits were gathered from various parts of the State of Pennsylvania but were rendezvoused at Philadelphia and Camden, N. J. Early in 1863 these commands were consolidated as the 152d Regiment, Heavy Artillery. The original and recruited companies of marine artillery became Companies A, B, G, H, K and L. Roberts' battalion became C, D and F. Major Roberts was commissioned colonel and Hermann Segebarth became major. The regimental headquarters was established at Fortress Monroe. Company H was stationed at Baltimore.* De-

---

*Company H was sent to Fort Delaware from Camp Ruff, in Camden, under arrest for insubordination, due to a fraud practiced upon the men in connection with their bounties, an offence finally resulting in the discharge of Major Segebarth from the service. (Pennsylvania at Gettysburg, Vol. II, page 900.) The company was stationed at Baltimore during its entire term of service. At various times it served as a naval detachment, heavy and light artillery and as cavalry. It was present at Gettysburg as a light battery attached to the cavalry corps, one section taking part in the battle. It was recruited chiefly in Lebanon County, but contained a number of Philadelphians.

tachments served in the Naval Brigade, upon the James River and its tributaries, and at the capture of Fort Fisher. In an engagement at Smithfield, Virginia, the gunboat containing Company A was attacked and Capt. John Krause, with many of his company, were captured. Twenty-one of these prisoners perished at Andersonville and Salisbury from starvation. Company I was detailed as guard at headquarters, Army of the James, and in that capacity witnessed the scene of the surrender at Appomattox Court House. Upon April 1st, 1864, six hundred men from the regiment volunteered to enlist in a new regiment which was designated the "188th" Pennsylvania Infantry. The several companies of the 152d were constantly sent out upon special service with the Army of the James and Army of the Potomac, acting, as occasion demanded, as light and heavy artillery and infantry. One of the detachments, a part of Company F, was returning from Wilmington, N. C., upon the steamer "General Lyon." This vessel was burned off Cape Hatteras and twenty-one of the men were lost.

At Fortress Monroe a portion of the regiment guarded Camp Hamilton, a prison and distribution camp, and after the close of hostilities in the field it was the lot of the "152d" to guard the late President of the Confederacy. Few regiments in the service were called upon to perform such varied service and none performed it more effectively. Companies A and B were mustered out at Fortress Monroe July 11th, 1865. Company H was mustered out at Baltimore upon July 25th, 1865. The balance of the regiment was retained at Fortress Monroe until November 9th, when it was mustered out at that point.

TOTAL LOSSES.

Killed or mortally wounded...men 19
Died from disease and in prison...........................officers, 1; men, 214

SERVICE AND BATTLES.

Detachments of all the companies excepting H served at times in Graham's Naval Brigade upon the Virginia rivers. Companies A, B, F and G, defence of Suffolk, April and May, 1863. Detachment of Company A at Smithfield, N. C., February 1st, 1864, and at siege of Plymouth, N. C., April, 1864. Companies D, E and G serving in forts around Richmond and Petersburg, from May, 1864, to end of the war. Company F on guard duty at prison camp, near Fortress Monroe, from September, 1863, to end of the war. Company I at Headquarters, Army of the James, and present at the surrender at Appomattox. Company M acting as siege artillery with Army of the James to end of the war. Detachments of Companies F and G fought at Fort Fisher, January 15th, 1865. Company H stationed at Baltimore, was on duty at Gettysburg.*

---

*The nature of the varied forms of service performed in the course of its line of duty by heavy artillery cannot be expressed in any enumeration of the skirmishes, engagements or battles its component parts may have experienced. The chief value of this arm is the guarding of forts and fortified camps, but its batteries were often found also upon the battle line and acting not infrequently with the navy.

INDEPENDENT BATTERY E (KNAP'S)

Philadelphia Men, 40.

U NDER the direction of Brig.-Gen. John W. Geary, by authority of the War Department, a number of men from the ranks of the 28th Regiment Infantry were detached, at Point of Rocks, Maryland, to fill a Pittsburgh company in the formation of an independent battery of light artillery. Forty of these men were taken from the two Philadelphia companies of the "28th." First Lieut. Joseph M. Knap, Company L of the "28th," was commissioned captain. This battery, mustered in upon October 1st, 1861, was thus intimately related to the "28th" and served with the latter, under Gen. Geary, in the Army of the Potomac, Army of the Cumberland and in the campaign, under Gen. Sherman, from Chattanooga to Atlanta, Savannah and Goldsboro, N. C. In this campaign it fought in one of the late battles of the war, at Bentonville, N. C., on March 19th, 1865, being the only Pennsylvania battery present. Capt. Knap resigned upon May 18th, 1863, and was succeeded by First Lieut. Charles A. Atwell (killed at Wauhatchie, Tenn., October 29th, 1863). The third captain was James D. McGill, who resigned in July, 1864, and the fourth, Thomas S. Sloan. First Lieut. Edward R. Geary, son of Gen. Geary, was killed in the action at Wauhatchie, Tenn., October 29th, 1863.*

Capt. Knap commanded an emergency battery from Pittsburgh during the summer of 1863, and in 1864 organized a "90-day" militia battalion of independent artillery.

INDEPENDENT BATTERY A (HEAVY ARTILLERY)

Captain Frank Schaffer to February 28th, 1862.
Captain Stanislaus Mlotkowski to June 30th, 1865.
150 Officers and Men.

R ECRUITED in the fall of 1861, this battery was stationed at Fort Delaware through the three years of its service. A detachment of non-re-enlisted men was mustered out September 19th, 1864. Those who re-enlisted as veteran volunteers remained at the fort up to the period of their discharge, June 30th, 1865.

---

*In addition to the two commissioned officers of the battery killed at Wauhatchie, the command lost twenty-four men killed and wounded out of forty-eight present. The enemy left upon the field more men than were in the entire Union force opposed to them.

CAVALRY VOLUNTEERS. THREE YEAR ENLISTMENTS

PHILADELPHIA furnished to the Union armies more cavalrymen than any other city with the possible exception of New York. The only body of volunteer cavalry in the field during the three months' campaign, and the first volunteer regiment of cavalry mustered into the three-year service were of Philadelphia origin. This arm attracted a large element from youth of position and wealth. The officers were generally worthy of the men they led.

FIFTY-NINTH REGIMENT (SECOND CAVALRY)

COLONEL R. BUTLER PRICE to January 31st, 1865.
LIEUT.-COL. JOS. P. BRINTON to February 28th, 1865.
MAJOR JOSEPH STEELE to June 17th, 1865.
COLONEL WILLIAM W. SANDERS to July 13th, 1865.
Total Enrollment, 1,970 Officers and Men.

OF the twelve companies composing this regiment seven, A, B, C, E, G, H and K, were recruited in Philadelphia, the balance coming from the interior counties. The command was formed between September, 1861, and April, 1862. The Philadelphia companies were rendezvoused at Camp Patterson, Point Breeze.

Upon April 14th, 1862, the regiment was assembled at Baltimore, and upon the 25th proceeded to Washington, and, being furnished with mounts, was encamped at Cloud's Mills, Va., where the command was assigned to Cooke's Brigade, 1st Reserve Army Corps. Early in August the regiment moved to the Rapidan River and there joined Gen. N. B. Buford's Brigade of the Second Corps. In the course of Pope's campaign at Cedar Mountain, the second Bull Run and Chantilly the regiment performed important services and sustained considerable loss. On September 10th Col. Price succeeded Gen. Buford in command of the brigade. Lieut.-Col. Joseph P. Brinton assumed command of the regiment. On October 1st Price's Brigade became the First Brigade, Bayard's Division. In the autumn movements on the Occoquan River, a tributary of the Potomac, a portion of the regiment was overwhelmed, losing about one hundred killed, wounded and missing. Wintering in this section, the 2d Cavalry joined the Second Brigade of Stahel's Division, at Fairfax Court House, on April 4th, 1863. In the Gettysburg campaign this division was commanded by Major-General Alfred Pleasonton. The duties of the regiment at Gettysburg, as it was attached to the provost guard at headquarters, being the patrol of the rear, to escort the body of Gen. Reynolds and guard three thousand prisoners to Westminster, Maryland, and, later, to perform provost duty after the battle; its losses were few. After the pursuit of the enemy and a series of forays, the regiment was attached, on October 19th, to the Second Brigade, Second Division, Cavalry Corps. The cavalry was actively engaged in the various clashes of the Mine Run campaign and in a raid into the Shenandoah Valley. While in winter quarters at Warrenton a large proportion of the regiment re-enlisted. When the veterans returned, with many recruits, the 2d Cavalry participated in the battle at Todd's Tavern, on May 7th, 1864, and in Sheridan's raid toward Richmond, destroying the railroad and supplies, defeating Stuart's Cavalry at Yellow Tavern and attacking the works within sight of the Confederate capital. Crossing the Chickahominy River, the raid was continued to the James River, after which the cavalry finally rejoined the army. A second equally daring raid, for the destruction of the railroads, formed a part of the cavalry duties in the general advance commanded by Gen. Grant. In July the Second Brigade was employed in front of Petersburg. Subsequently it accompanied the expedition to Deep Bottom, north of the James River, and was engaged in the affairs of August 14th and 16th at Malvern Hill and Charles City Cross Roads. In February, 1865, Lieut.-Col. Brinton was honorably discharged. He was succeeded by Junior Major Joseph Steele. Under this officer the regiment participated in the campaign incident to the reduction of Petersburg and the event of Appomattox.

After a brief connection with the 1st Pennsylvania Provisional Cavalry the regiment was mustered out at Cloud's Mills, Va., July 13th, 1865.

TOTAL LOSSES.

Killed or died from wounds.................................officers, 6; men, 52
Died from disease or other causes.......................... " 2; " 183
Wounded, not mortally .... " 9; " 108
Captured or missing .... " 1; " 90

BATTLES.

Wolftown, Cedar Mountain, Rappahannock Station, Catlett's Station, Second Bull Run, Chantilly, Occoquan, Gettysburg, Bristoe Station, Mine Run, Wilderness, Todd's Tavern, Beaver Dam Station, Yellow Tavern, Ground Squirrel Bridge, Richmond Fortifications, Meadow Bridge, Brook Church, Hawes' Shop, Hanover Court House, Cold Harbor, Trevilian Station, White House Landing, Baltimore Cross Roads, St. Mary's Church, Jerusalem Plank Road, Lee's Mills, Malvern Hill, Deep Bottom, White Oak Swamp, Ream's Station, Poplar Spring Church, Wyatt's Farm, Stony Creek Station, Boydton Road, Hatcher's Run, Appomattox Campaign.

SIXTIETH REGIMENT (THIRD CAVALRY)

(Young's Kentucky Cavalry)

COLONEL WILLIAM H. YOUNG to October 31st, 1861.
COLONEL WILLIAM W. AVERILL to September 26th, 1862.
COLONEL JOHN B. MCINTOSH to July 21st, 1864.
LIEUT.-COLONEL EDWARD S. JONES to August 24th, 1864.
Total Enrollment, 1,856 Officers and Men.

WILLIAM H. YOUNG, of Kentucky, undertook the organization of this regiment in Philadelphia in the summer of 1861. The several companies were recruited in various sections. Companies A (the Merchant Troop), B, C, F, I, K and M were raised in Philadelphia, D came from Washington (being known as the "President's Mounted Guard"), E was recruited in Lycoming, Clinton and Tioga Counties, G was of Pittsburgh origin. H (the old "Adamantine Guards," dating from 1801) was from Cumberland County, L came from Schuylkill County. A few of the men in Company I were from Delaware County. The first company (A) was sent to Washington on July 18th and other companies speedily followed, although without uniforms or equipments. The regiment was assembled and equipped in Washington Park, Washington, D. C. It was, as official records prove, the first volunteer cavalry regiment of the Union Army to take the field.*

The unfortunate and unaccountable synonym of the regiment resulted in its failure to secure its proper numerical designation and it thus became known to fame as the "3d" Cavalry.

Soon after organization the command of the regiment was given to William W. Averill, a graduate of West Point and an accomplished officer of the regular army, under whom the men were thoroughly drilled through the winter at Camp Marcy, upon the site of which the important army post of Camp Meyer is now located. With the opening of an active campaign on March 10th, 1862, the 3d Cavalry was the extreme advance of the Army of the Potomac, and the first Union troops to enter Centreville and to traverse the battlefield of Bull Run since the

---

*HEADQUARTERS CAVALRY BRIGADE.

WASHINGTON, D. C., September 11, 1861.

COLONEL W. H. YOUNG, Commanding Kentucky Cavalry.

Colonel, allow me to congratulate you upon having put the first regiment of cavalry in the field. * * * *

GEORGE STONEMAN, *Brig.-Gen. and Chief of Cavalry.*

(Extract)

157

disastrous rout of the summer of 1861. A few days after this episode the regiment was embarked from Alexandria via Fortress Monroe to the Virginia Peninsula. Here the 3d Cavalry was attached to Heintzelman's Third Corps. Following the reduction of Yorktown and Williamsburg the cavalry swept in advance of the army toward its goal at Richmond. Then followed the month of battles and marches, beginning with Fair Oaks and ending at Malvern Hill and Harrison's Landing, the cavalry constantly defending the army trains from the inroads of the enemy. At Harrison's Landing the cavalry arm was reorganized, the "3d" being assigned to the First Brigade, which was in command of Col. Averill, who was active in forays upon both sides of the James River. When McClellan's army again moved the 3d Cavalry proceeded down the Peninsula, embarked at Yorktown, and on September 6th reached Washington and was at once hurried through Maryland, and on the evening of September 16th Companies C and H were the advance troops to first develop the enemy's position at Antietam. Upon Col. Averill's promotion to the rank of brigade commander, another cavalry officer of the regular service, Lieut. John B. McIntosh, a graduate of the Naval Academy, was commissioned colonel. After a period of frequent brushes with the enemy the "3d" went into winter quarters on Potomac Creek, remaining there until the following March. At this time the Cavalry Corps was organized under Gen. Stoneman. The cavalry signalized the beginning of the campaign of 1863 at Kelly's Ford, "the first cavalry battle of the Civil War." Then followed Chancellorsville and Stoneman's raid and the prelude to Gettysburg. Upon that field the Second Cavalry Division, far out upon the right flank, had its own battle, of momentous importance to the army and the Nation, but obscured by the dramatic events nearer the town. It was here that the "3d" was the point of the flying wedge that broke Stuart's advance and saved the lines on Cemetery Ridge and the reserves from attack in the rear. The tactical importance of this action as a factor in the general result of the battle cannot be overestimated.

The autumn movements included actions at Culpeper, Rapidan Station and Occoquan. At the latter affair Lieut. Ellwood Davis, of Company H, was killed. In the trying Mine Run experience the "3d" was engaged at New Hope Church and Parker's Store, losing fifty-three men, killed, wounded and captured. At the end of the year the regiment was "veteranized." Those who re-enlisted, at a time when the conditions were most depressing, numbered seventy-five. This contingent, together with men whose terms of enlistment had not expired and five newly recruited companies, carried the colors of the "3d" through to Appomattox and for several months later. A tragic event, occurring at this period, was the death of Capt. Walter S. Newhall, drowned, on December 18th, 1863.* (Note on following page.)

Under a new commander, coming from his western triumphs, the Army of the Potomac renewed, in the spring of 1864, its determined efforts to carry the flag of the Union further south. The Cavalry Corps was now led by Major-Gen. Philip H. Sheridan. The 3d Cavalry was honored by selection for duty at Headquarters of the army, under the command of the Provost Marshal General, and as the escort of Gen. U. S. Grant once more led the army toward the James River. The 3d Cavalry was the first to reach Butler's "bottled up" command. An order was issued on July 17th which resulted in the formation of the veterans and recruits into an independent veteran battalion.

The non-veterans when entitled to discharge were sent to Washington and thence to further duty in the Shenandoah Valley. This contingent was finally mustered out at Philadelphia, August 24th, 1864. The Philadelphians who remained with the colors reached home, as part of the 5th Cavalry, one year later.

The 3d Battalion escorted Gens. Grant and Meade into the fallen City of Petersburg and a few days later led the army, as escort of Gen. Meade, to Appomattox Court House, and was witness of the formal surrender agreed upon at the McLean house.

While engaged upon provost duty at Richmond the 3d Battalion was consolidated into four companies and under Lieut.-Col. James W. Walsh the command was transferred to the 5th Cavalry. Here the identity of the "3d" was lost. These troops were mustered out at Richmond on August 7th, 1865, and returned by sea to Philadelphia. A number of the officers afterward entered the regular army, one, Col. John B. McIntosh, reaching the rank of brevet major-general.

TOTAL LOSSES.

Killed or died from wounds.................................officers, 1; men, 44
Died from disease or other causes......................... "   2; " 125
Wounded, not mortally..................................... "   7; "   59
Captured or missing....................................... "   7; " 161

BATTLES.

Magruder's Ferry, Springfield Station, Vienna, Yorktown, Williamsburg, Savage Station, Jordan's Ford, Charles City Cross Roads, Malvern Hill, Sycamore Church, Antietam, Harper's Ferry, Four Locks, Unionville, Piedmont, Ashby's Gap, Amissville, Newby's Cross Roads, Kelly's Ford, Hartwood Church, Stoneman's raid, Brandy Station, Aldie, Gettysburg, Old Antietam Forge, Shepherdstown, Culpeper, Rapidan Station, Occoquan, Mine Run, Ellis' Ford, Warrenton, Wilderness, Spotsylvania, North Anna, Totopotomoy, Cold Harbor, Petersburg, Boydton Plank Road, Weldon Railroad, Hatcher's Run, Appomattox Court House.

*Fearless, enterprising and efficient, Capt. Walter Symonds Newhall, of the Germantown family of the name, was the admiration of every cavalryman. In the opening months of the war he had served as an officer under the intrepid Major Zagonyi in the western army. At the date of his death he was Acting Assistant Adjutant General on the brigade staff. Upon starting to join his brother, Capt. Frederick C. Newhall, of Gen. Pleasonton's staff, upon a visit home, he was drowned by his horse falling upon him at a ford of an effluent stream of the Rappahannock River. Ever afterward the Newhall memorial flag was carried with the regimental colors at the head of the regiment.

SIXTY-FIFTH REGIMENT (FIFTH CAVALRY)

("Cameron Dragoons")

COLONEL MAX FRIEDMAN to March 9th, 1862.
LIEUT.-COL. STEPHEN E. SMITH to September 29th, 1862.
COLONEL DAVID CAMPBELL to October 13th, 1862.
LIEUT.-COL. WILLIAM LEWIS to April 29th, 1864.
COLONEL ROBERT M. WEST to August 7th, 1865.

Total Enrollment, about 3,000 Officers and Men.

THIS regiment was composed of twelve companies, of which ten were recruited in Philadelphia, and two, L and M, in Pittsburgh. Under the synonym of the "Cameron Dragoons" the command was regarded as an independent organization, being formed by direct orders of the Secretary of War. In October, 1861, it was credited by the Government to the quota of the State of Pennsylvania, and was designated by Governor Curtin as the 65th Regiment of the line. In its formative period it was encamped upon Ridge road, near Girard College, leaving for Washington on August 22d, where the Pittsburgh companies reported later. The urgent need of cavalry at that time resulted in the immediate use of these untried troopers who began, by detachments, their active service as scouts under Brig.-Generals Louis Blenker and William F. Smith, in the Army of the Potomac, and later as part of the advance brigade commanded by Col. Robert M. West. In May, under the command of Col. David Campbell, the regiment was transferred to the vicinity of Yorktown and Williamsburg, Va., (with the exception of Companies I and K) operating in the rear of the army then moving toward Richmond. The regiment remained in this section of Virginia about sixteen months, and although liberally recruited, was greatly reduced from malarial sickness, which filled the hospitals and caused many deaths.* In this interval Col. Campbell had been captured, exchanged and had resigned, the command devolving on Lieut.-Col. William Lewis. On September 8th, 1863, the regiment was ordered to Norfolk, and thence sent into the Dismal Swamp and Currituck regions of Virginia and North Carolina. The warfare in this truly dismal section of the South, against guerillas and bushwhackers, was difficult and trying. At Great Bridge, in Norfolk Co., Va., in October, 1864, about one-half

---

* The records of this regiment reveal the interesting fact that, although in active service through a period of four years, but one of more than one hundred officers was killed, this solitary exception being Lieut. Samuel M. Williamson, of Company H, who refused to surrender after being twice wounded. The relatively large mortality list of officers and men who succumbed to disease was the inevitable result of almost constant campaigning in the malarial tidewater lowlands of Virginia and North Carolina.

of the regiment re-enlisted. Soon afterward the regiment was assigned to a brigade of cavalry commanded by Col. Samuel P. Spear, of the 11th Pennsylvania Cavalry, then near Norfolk, and participated in an expedition intended to liberate the prisoners held at Richmond. This movement failed, and the 5th Cavalry returned to its winter camp at Great Bridge, Va. In March, 1864, the regiment received two hundred and thirty-one recruits. Lieut.-Col. Lewis was mustered out on April 29th, and Maj. Christopher Kleinz was appointed to succeed him.

With the beginning of the active campaign of 1864, in May, the Fifth Cavalry distinguished itself in Kautz's effective raid into Sussex County to cripple the Weldon Railroad. This finally brought the regiment into touch with Gen. Butler's force at Bermuda Hundred, from which base another raid was made upon the Richmond & Danville Railroad, and after much skirmishing the command returned to the James river. On May 22d Col. Robert M. West, of the 43d (Pennsylvania) Regiment (First Artillery Reserve Corps) was commissioned colonel of the 5th Cavalry, which was now employed in the early demonstrations which began the long siege of Petersburg, and in June participated in Wilson's raid, resulting in the further destruction of the Weldon Railroad. In the cavalry battle at Ream's Station the regiment lost in killed, wounded and captured, about three hundred men.

In the series of swift actions, north and south of the James river, the cavalry was invariably at the front, and when the 5th Cavalry established winter quarters at Charles City Road it was but a shadow of a regiment. It remained here, on the picket line, to March 25th, 1865, when, under Lieut.-Col. Christopher Kleinz, it joined the cavalry led by Major-Gen. Philip H. Sheridan, thus having a spirited share in the fighting which led to the surrender of Appomattox. After this event the cavalry division was sent to Lynchburg, but, a few days later, began its march toward Richmond and Washington. On May 19th three hundred and thirty-one officers and men were mustered out, and on June 6th the remainder was consolidated with the 3d Cavalry, which, in turn, was mustered out on August 7th, at Richmond, Va.

TOTAL LOSSES.

Killed or died from wounds ....officers, 1; men, 76.
Died from disease or in southern prisons*................... " 6; " 210.

BATTLES, ACTIONS, ETC.

Pohick Church; Flint Hill and Hunter's Mill; scout to Gloucester Point (detachment); scout about Williamsburg; Mechanicsville (skirmish); seven days before Richmond (Companies I and K); Savage Station; White Oak Swamp Bridge; Malvern Hill; reconnaissance to Gloucester, etc. (detachment), Williamsburg and Fort Magruder; scout from Yorktown; Burnt Ordinary; Olive Creek Church (detachment); Williamsburg; Whittaker's Mills; Chowan River; Nine

*Of those captured from the 5th Cavalry, seventy-six died in the Southern prison pens.

Mile Ordinary; Diascund Bridge; Dix's Peninsular campaign; Barnesville; Baltimore Crossroads; Bottom's Bridge (July 2d); Bottom's Bridge (Aug. 26-29); New Kent Court House; Dismal Swamp region, N. C.; Kempsville, Indiantown, Drummond Lake (Companies F and H); advance to Raleigh (detachment); Currituck Court House; Back Bay; scout from Great Bridge (detachment); Bingo Landing (detachment); Camden Court House; expedition to South Mills and Camden; Wistar's expedition toward Richmond; Deep Creek; Ballahock Station; expedition to the Blackwater (detachment); Kautz's raid on the Petersburg and Weldon R. R.; Kautz's raid on Richmond and Danville R. R.; before Petersburg; siege operations against Petersburg and Richmond, including Roanoke Station; Wilson's raid; Staunton River Bridge; Stony Creek; Ream's Station; demonstration to Deep Bottom and Malvern Hill; New Market Heights; Darbytown Road; Charles City Crossroads; Fair Oaks; Appomattox campaign, including Dinwiddie Court House, Five Forks, Hatcher's Run, near Amelia Court House; Burkesville, Sailor's Creek, Prince Edwards Court House, Appomattox Court House; duty at Richmond and other points to Aug. 16th, 1865.

SEVENTIETH REGIMENT (SIXTH CAVALRY)

COLONEL RICHARD H. RUSH to September 29th, 1863.*
COLONEL CHARLES L. LEIPER to June 17th, 1865.
Total Enrollment, 1,800 Officers and Men.

O F the ten original companies of this regiment, known as the "Philadelphia Light Cavalry," nine were of local origin and one, Company G, came from Reading. Col. Rush, who had an enviable reputation as a cavalry officer of the regular service, was authorized to select his officers, and they were chosen with reference to their social standing, soldierly qualities and experience in the three-months' regiments then returning from the field. Recruiting began at headquarters, 883 Market street, on July 27th, 1861. As rapidly as companies were formed they were sent to Camp Meigs, on the Logan Estate at Old Second street and Nicetown lane. Major-Gen. George B. McClellan expressed the wish that the command should be armed with lances, a weapon not before used by American troops. This suggestion was adopted by the officers.† The lances were provided at the end of

---

*Col. Richard Henry Rush was born in England January 14th, 1825, his father being at the time United States Minister to the Court of St. James. He graduated from the United States Military Academy in 1846 and served with the army in Mexico. After his discharge from the colonelcy of the 6th Cavalry he became commander of the Veteran Reserve Corps. He died October 17th, 1893.

†This weapon was nine feet long, with an eleven inch, three-edged blade. The staff was of Norway fir, with a ferrule and counter-poise at the heel. Each lance bore a scarlet swallow-tailed pennant. They were made under the supervision of the titled European officers attached to the staff of Major. Gen. McClellan who probably suggested the innovation to him. The lance was discarded eventually, being unsuited to use in the South.

November and were carried by the 6th Cavalry at the presentation of State flags on December 4th (in which five infantry regiments participated) and in a street parade on December 6th, long remembered as one of the most imposing military displays ever seen in Philadelphia. Thereafter the regiment was called "Rush's Lancers." It was completely uniformed, equipped and mounted by the Government before being ordered into active service.

On December 10th Companies A, B, C and F proceeded to Washington, and the balance of the command followed within a few days. The regiment was encamped at Camp Barclay, north of the city. On January 1st, 1862, to the music of their splendid mounted band, the Lancers, nearly 1,000 strong, paraded through the Capital City.

The 6th Cavalry entered Virginia on March 10th, 1862. On May 3d it was embarked upon a fleet of schooners and tug boats to Fortress Monroe, being attached to Emory's Second Brigade, Cavalry Reserve. During the month the regiment as a whole, or in detachments, fought its way up the peninsula, sharing the fortunes of McClellan's army, then near Richmond, picketing the roads and covering the retirement of the artillery and wagon trains through the "change of base." With the exception of three detached companies the regiment acted as headquarters guard from Harrison's Landing, and in early September moved from Washington, with Pleasanton's Cavalry Division, upon the Antietam Campaign. In the battle of the 17th (Antietam) the regimental loss was slight. In October the Confederate raider, Gen. J. E. B. Stuart, occupied the attention of the cavalry in Maryland.

Two additional companies were recruited in Philadelphia and, as L and M, joined the regiment in November. Part of the regiment was detailed as headquarters guard in December in Franklin's Grand Division, during the Fredericksburg campaign. After the "mud march" substantial winter quarters were built at Belle Plain Landing, on the Potomac River. Illness, due to exposure in the early campaign of 1862, compelled Col. Rush to resign, Major Robert Morris, Jr., taking temporary command. During the Chancellorsville campaign the regiment raided with Stoneman's Cavalry in the rear of the Confederates, destroying the railroads and canals. At Beverly Ford, on May 9th, the 6th Cavalry charged the Confederate artillery, and sustained its greatest loss, many of the officers and men being killed, wounded or captured. With the Cavalry Reserve Brigade the regiment reached Gettysburg on the night of July 2d, occupying a position at the extreme left near Round Top, fighting dismounted, on the 3d, losing twelve officers and men killed and wounded. Merritt's Cavalry was immediately sent to Williamsport, Maryland, and there fought the retreating Confederates, at heavy cost, meeting them again in the passes of the Blue Ridge, with further casualties. After a period of recuperation at Washington the 6th Cavalry entered upon the Mine Run campaign, later going into winter quarters near Culpeper. On December 31, 1863, one hundred and forty men re-enlisted. In the two months of constant battling, from Spotsylvania through to Petersburg, the 6th Cavalry followed Sheridan in two effective raids. At Petersburg, on July 3d, Major James Starr, who had been wounded in the Wilderness, resumed command. In August the cavalry were hastened to the Shenandoah Valley, there encountering the usual summer raiders. While in this section a large proportion of the men were mustered out. The veterans and recruits were sent to the re-mount camp in Maryland, and in November the regiment was quartered at Hagerstown. At Winchester, Va., in January, eight hundred recruits were added to the regiment and Major Leiper was mustered as lieutenant-colonel.

On February 27th Merritt's First Cavalry Division moved as a part of Sheridan's force upon the last chapter in their long and varied record of warfare. After four weeks of destructive energy the cavalry reached Petersburg. In the exciting final running fight to Appomattox the regiment waged its last battle, dismounted, on the White Oak Road. After the dispersal of Lee's brave fragment of an army the regiment was sent to Danville, Va.* On June 17th, 1865, at Washington the men of the old "6th" were merged with the 2d† and 17th Provisional Cavalry and were subsequently sent to Louisville, Kentucky, there being mustered out on August 7th.

TOTAL LOSSES.

Killed or died from wounds ....officers, 7; men, 72
Died from disease or other cause .... "   3; " 86
Wounded, not mortally .... " 11; " 222
Captured or missing .... "   6; " 204

BATTLES, ETC.

Hanover Court House, Beaver Dam Station, Gaines' Mill, Glendale, White Oak Swamp, Malvern Hill, Jefferson, Crampton's Gap, Antietam, Fredericksburg, Occoquan, Stoneman's Raid, Beverly Ford, Aldie, Gettysburg, Greencastle, Williamsport, Boonsboro, Beaver Creek, Funkstown, Falling Waters, Manassas Gap, Brandy Station, Bristoe Station, Mine Run, Charlottesville, Wilderness, Spotsylvania, Beaver Dam Station, Yellow Tavern, Meadow Bridge, Old Church, Cold Harbor, Trevilian Station, Petersburg, Deep Bottom, Berryville, Smithfield, Waynesboro, Dinwiddie Court Hose, Five Forks, Appomattox Court House.

---

*"No organization in either the regular or volunteer service enjoyed a more enviable reputation in every respect, and its service was of so valuable a character to the Government that every endeavor was made by me, after its muster out, to have an organization formed, the nucleus of which should be such officers and men of the original regiment as were desirous of again entering the service."

PHILIP H. SHERIDAN,
Major-Gen., U. S. A.

†The 2d Provisional Cavalry was commanded by Col. Hampton S. Thomas, late major of the 1st Cavalry.

EIGHTY-NINTH REGIMENT (EIGHTH CAVALRY)

COLONEL ERNEST G. CHORMAN to January, 1862.
COLONEL DAVID McM. GREGG to January 17th, 1863.
LIEUT.-COL. SAMUEL WILSON to October 17th, 1864.
COLONEL PENNOCK HUEY to January 13th, 1865.
COLONEL WILLIAM A. CORRIE to August 3d, 1865.
Total Enrollment, 1,816 Officers and Men.

THIS regiment was recruited in July, August and September, 1861, being originally planned as a command of mounted rifles. The Philadelphia companies were C, D, E, F, G, H, I, K, L and M; the latter company, however, was partly raised in Bucks and Montgomery counties. Companies A and B came from Chester and Lycoming counties respectively. The organization camp was at Nicetown. Leaving Philadelphia on October 4th, the regiment was soon afterward stationed upon Arlington Heights, Va., being attached to Gen. Fitz John Porter's Division. In January, 1862, Capt. David McM. Gregg, of the 6th (Regular) Cavalry, was commissioned as colonel, and under this officer the command became thoroughly efficient. In April the 8th Cavalry was ordered to Hampton, Va. After the capture of Yorktown the regiment was sent up the Peninsula, meeting with parties of the enemy at New Kent Court House and Bottom's Bridge. In the campaign against Richmond the 8th Cavalry was alternately advance and rear guard of the army, and was involved in constant skirmishes between Seven Pines and Fair Oaks, through to Malvern Hill and Harrison's Landing. Late in August the regiment was transported to Alexandria and attached to the Second Brigade, Brig.-Gen. Alfred Pleasonton, Cavalry Division. In the campaign which included the battle of Antietam the 8th Cavalry rode through Maryland and on to Gettysburg, then endangered by raiders. The regiment reached Antietam the day after the battle. Upon its southward march, in eighteen days, beginning with November 1st, the command fought thirteen actions and skirmishes. One squadron was present with Franklin's Grand Division at the battle of Fredericksburg on December 12th-14th. With its camp at Falmouth and at Aquia Landing the 8th Cavalry picketed the lower Rappahannock River through the winter. In January Col. Gregg was promoted to the rank of brigadier-general, Major Pennock Huey being commissioned colonel. The regiment was now attached to Pleasonton's Cavalry Division. On April 21st, 1863, the cavalry held the fords of the Rappahannock, the "8th" leading the extreme advance to Chancellorsville. On the evening of May 2d, at the left of the Union line, the 8th Cavalry unexpectedly encountered the leading column of Jackson's Confederates. Col. Huey ordered and led a charge into the mass of infantry, in which about one hundred and fifty of the regiment were killed and wounded. Among the officers who died here was Major Peter Keenan, second in command.* It was near this scene, and as a result of the charge, that Major-Gen. Thomas Jonathan Jackson ("Stonewall") was wounded by his own troops, in the darkness, from the effects of which he died eight days later.

After an affair near Bank's Ford and several weeks of patrol duty in King George County the regiment, leaving Falmouth, moved northward toward Maryland. The Second Brigade, under Col. Huey, joined in Gen. Kilpatrick's raid upon the Confederate rear, which included a midnight battle at Monterey Pass, and severe engagements at Hagerstown, Williamsport, Boonsboro, St. James College and Jones' Cross Roads, all incident to the Confederate retreat from Gettysburg. At Williamsport, Md., on July 14th, the regiment waged the last fight of the campaign north of the Potomac River.

Throughout the balance of the summer and the autumn the activities of the 8th Cavalry included a succession of engagements, skirmishes and raids which ended with the dash of December into the Luray Valley, and a second raid across the Blue Ridge at Chester Gap in early January, 1864, which was attended with great suffering from the intense cold. At Warrenton winter quarters were established and here the regiment re-enlisted, being given the usual furlough. The campaign of 1864 began with the cavalry raid, led by Gen. Philip H. Sheridan, through the Wilderness up to the fortifications of Richmond. In the course of this, and a subsequent raid to Gordonsville, the 8th Cavalry sustained heavy losses constantly. Through July and August the "8th" rode and fought alternately through the region south of Petersburg and the old battle grounds north of the James River. Finally, on August 20th, it crossed the James for the last time in the course of the war. Through the fall, winter and spring there was no such thing as "cease firing" for the cavalry. Few kept count of the forays, the skirmishes, the battles. It was one constant Titanic struggle up to that disastrous cavalry duel at Farmville, two days before the surrender, when the expiring prey turned and left its heavy mark upon the 8th Cavalry. Those who escaped this punishment made the final charge of the war in Virginia at Appomattox.

With the disappearance of an armed opponent force in Virginia the cavalry was hurried toward the scene of Sherman's operations, but was not needed. The 8th Cavalry was then sent to Lynchburg, its several squadrons being stationed for the restoration of order in various towns. On July 24th the 8th and 16th Cavalry Regiments were consolidated. At Richmond, on August 11th, the men were mustered out of the service.

The regimental historian states that the 8th Cavalry participated in

---

*The official report of Brig.-Gen. Alfred Pleasonton with regard to this affair and the publication of a poem entitled "Keenan's Ride" led to a controversy which was long and bitter. For details see "A True History of the Charge of the 8th Cavalry at Chancellorsville," Pennock Huey (Colonel), second edition, 1885.

one hundred and thirty-five battles, engagements and skirmishes, a record equalled by but one other command.

TOTAL LOSSES.

Killed or died from wounds	officers, 5;	men,	57.
Died from disease or other causes	" 2;	"	126.
Wounded, not mortally	" 8;	"	185.
Captured or missing	" 6;	"	308.

BATTLES, ETC.

Yorktown, New Kent Court House, Bottom's Bridge, the Chimneys, White Oak Swamp (May 24th, 1862), Savage's Station (May 24th, 1862), Seven Pines (May 24th, 1862), Fair Oaks (May 25th, 1862), Garnett's Farm, Fair Oaks (May 31st, June 1st, 1862), White Oak Swamp (June 28th, 1862), Malvern Hill (July 1st, 1862), Haxall's Landing, Carter's Farm, Malvern Hill (August 5th, 1862), Harrison's Landing, Falls Church, Sugar Loaf Mountain, Frederick City, Middletown, Antietam or Sharpsburg (September 18th, 1862), Blackford's Ford, Martinsburg, Shepherdstown, Monocacy (mouth of the), Philomont, Union, Upperville (November 3d, 1862), Ashby's Gap, Markham, Barbee's Cross Roads, Hazel River, Corbin's Cross Roads or Amissville, Leedstown, Fredericksburg, Richard's Ford, Ely's Ford, Ely's Ford Road, Tabernacle Church, Chancellorsville, United States Ford, Bank's Ford, Gainesville, Thoroughfare Gap, Emmitsburg, Monterey Gap, Smithsburg, Hagerstown, Williamsport, Boonsboro, Jones' Cross Roads, St. James' College, Shepherdstown, Culpeper Court House, Rapidan Station, Sulphur Springs, Auburn, Bristoe Station, Wilderness or Todd's Tavern, Spotsylvania, Beaver Dam Ford, Ground Squirrel Church, Hungary Station, Brook Church or Fortifications of Richmond, Gaines' Mill, Cold Harbor, Trevilian Station, St. Mary's Church, Petersburg, Strawberry Plains, Deep Bottom, Reams' Station, Jerusalem Plank Road, Stony Creek Road, Wyatt's House, Vaughan Road, Boydton Plank Road, Belfield, Rowanty Creek, Hatcher's Run, Dinwiddie Court House, Five Forks, Amelia Springs, Sailor's Creek, Farmville, Appomattox Court House.

NINETY-SECOND REGIMENT (NINTH CAVALRY)

(Lochiel Cavalry)

COLONEL EDWARD E. WILLIAMS to October 9th, 1862.
COLONEL THOMAS C. JAMES to January 13th, 1863.
COLONEL THOMAS J. JORDAN to July 18th, 1865.
Total Enrollment, 2,400 Officers and Men.

THIS regiment was organized at Harrisburg on August 29th, 1861. It was recruited chiefly in the interior counties, but also contained a considerable number of Philadelphians. On November 20th the command moved to Kentucky, there serving in detached battalions in the Department of the Cumberland, and later in Tennessee. In September, 1862, the regiment was attached to the

Cavalry Division, Army of the Ohio. The command continued to serve in Kentucky and Tennessee, under Gen. Don Carlos Buell, engaged almost constantly in defending those States from occupation by the Confederates, and in raids, often far into wild and desolate regions. Col. Williams resigned on October 9th, 1862, Lieut.-Col. Thomas C. James being promoted to the colonelcy. This officer died at Philadelphia on January 13th, 1863.* Major Thomas J. Jordan, who had been absent as a prisoner of war for several months, became the third colonel, dating from Col. James' death. The "9th" participated in the Rosecrans campaign, losing heavily at the battle of Chickamauga. After an arduous campaign in East Tennessee the regiment was re-enlisted and recruited to a strength of twelve hundred officers and men.

In September, 1864, Col. Jordan was assigned to command of the entire cavalry force in Tennessee, then opposing the Confederate force of Gen. Wheeler. The regiment joined Gen. Sherman's army at Marietta, Ga., in November, being assigned to the First Brigade, Third Division of Cavalry, and participated, after the fall of Atlanta, in the march to Savannah and thence through the Carolinas, fighting its last battle near Raleigh, and performing important service in connection with the negotiations which finally led to the surrender of Gen. Joseph E. Johnston. Throughout this campaign, Col. Jordan having been promoted to command of the brigade, the "9th" was commanded by Major John M. Porter, under whom the command was finally mustered out at Lexington, N. C., on July 18th, 1865.

TOTAL LOSSES.

Killed, or mortally wounded.................................officers, 6; men, 66
Died from disease... " 2; " 155

BATTLES, ETC.

Lebanon, Ky., Spring Creek, Tompkinsville, Glasgow, Crab Orchard, Frankfort, Perryville, Raid to East Tennessee and Kentucky, Watauga Bridge, Jonesville, Union, reconnaissance from Franlkin, Spring Hill, Thompson's Station, Rutherford Creek, near Franklin, Davis' Mills, Triune, Eaglesville, Middleton, Guy's Gap, Shelbyville, Elk River, Jonesboro, Chickamauga, Sparta, Mossy Creek, Dandridge, Fair Garden, McNutt's Bridge, Frankfort, Lawrenceburg, Readyville, Woodbury, Camp Creek, Sweetwater, Lafayette, Ga., March to the Sea, Siege of Savannah, Campaign of the Carolinas, Bennett's House.

---

*Col. Thomas C. James commanded the First Troop Philadelphia City Cavalry in the three months' campaign of 1861.

ONE HUNDRED AND EIGHTH REGIMENT (ELEVENTH CAVALRY)

(Harlan's Light Cavalry)

COLONEL JOSIAH HARLAN to August 19th, 1862.
COLONEL SAMUEL P. SPEAR to May 9th, 1865.
COLONEL FRANK A. STRATTON to August 13th, 1865.

Philadelphia Companies C and E.

Total Enrollment, 390 Officers and Men.

———————

U NDER authority of the Secretary of War, Josiah Harlan, of Philadelphia, was engaged in August and September, 1861, in raising a regiment to be known as "Harlan's Light Cavalry." One company was recruited in Iowa, two in New York State, one in Ohio and a part of another in New Jersey. Of the Pennsylvania companies, "C" and "E"" were composed of recruits enlisted in Philadelphia. Organization was effected at Philadelphia on October 5th. While in camp of instruction in Virginia, this command, in common with others of its independent status, was rated as irregular and was, as Congress required, added to the Pennsylvania line as the "108th." The several companies of the regiment served, in the course of their enlistment, upon the Virginia Peninsula, in the Dismal Swamp and Blackwater regions, in tide-water North Carolina, along the Weldon Railroad, on the James River, in front of Richmond and in the Shenandoah Valley. The "108th" achieved a high reputation as an active and efficient scouting regiment. It was re-enlisted in November, 1864. The regiment was conspicuous among the cavalry which, under Gen. Sheridan, pursued the Confederates to Appomattox, at which time it captured and delivered to the proper officials one hundred and ten field pieces, forty-one mortars, six heavy guns and an immense amount of other military stores.

Among the officers of non-Philadelphia companies, and upon the staff, in addition to Col. Harlan, twenty were Philadelphians.

Company C was commanded successively by Captains John H. Struthers, John Cassells and Randolph T. Stoops. This company enrolled a total of one hundred and ninety-three officers and men. Of these one officer, First Lieut. Henry B. Neilson, was killed (at Ream's Station, August 25th, 1864). Of the rank and file, eight men were killed or died from wounds, disease, or while prisoners of war. A number were wounded and captured.

The several captains of Company E were John Hartman, Jr., Amintor Davidson, William Bailey (killed at Ream's Station, Va., June 29th, 1864), Robert S. Monroe (killed at Five Forks, Va., April 1st, 1865, while serving as major) and Charles Kirkham. Lieut. William Lancaster was killed at Five Forks, Va., April 1st, 1865. Of the rank and file fifteen men were killed or died from wounds, twelve died from disease, and a number died while in Southern prisons.*

BATTLES AND ENGAGEMENTS.

Beaver Dam, Franklin, Va., Siege of Suffolk, South Anna River, Ashland, Stony Creek, Weldon Railroad, Jerusalem Plank Road, Petersburg, Staunton River, Reams Station, Front of Richmond, Five Forks, White Oak Road, Deep Creek, Amelia Court House, Burkeville Junction, Prince Edward Court House, Appomattox, and many minor affairs.

ONE HUNDRED AND THIRTEENTH REGIMENT (TWELFTH CAVALRY)

(Curtin Hussars)

COLONEL WILLIAM FRISHMUTH to April 20th, 1862.
COLONEL LEWIS D. PIERCE to December 13th, 1864.
CAPTAIN MARCUS A. RENO to July 20th, 1865.
Total Enrollment, 2,236 Officers and Men.

THIS regiment was composed, in the course of its term of service, of recruits from all sections of Pennsylvania. Having its rendezvous in Philadelphia, it naturally attracted a large number of local members. Of the officers its first colonel, William Frishmuth, and at least twenty-seven others, were Philadelphians. The regiment was encamped at Camp McReynolds, near the junction of Ridge road and Columbia avenue, from January to April, 1862. Before being ordered to the front Col. Frishmuth resigned.

Having performed guard duty near Washington, dismounted, the regiment finally received mounts late in July. There was brief time for cavalry drill before orders came directing the "12th" to reinforce Gen. Pope. In this effort the regiment, led at the time by Major Darius Titus, encountered, unexpectedly, a large force of Jackson's Confederates near Manassas, and, choosing the alternative of a charge, lost, in killed wounded and captured, two hundred and sixty. Major Titus was one of those captured. Major James A. Congdon then withdrew the regiment to Centreville and gave to Gen. McClellan, in person, important information concerning the location of the enemy. The "12th" was then sent to patrol the Maryland side of the Potomac River.

*A tabulated list of casualties in Companies C and E has not been obtainable.

Joining Pleasonton's Cavalry Division the regiment was active, under Lieut.-Col. Jacob Kohler, in the Antietam campaign, and after the battle was assigned, with the 1st New York Cavalry, to guard the Baltimore and Ohio Railroad. The regiment was attached to the First Brigade, Second Division of the Eighth Corps, Department of the Susquehanna, operating in the Shenandoah Valley through the spring of 1863, being then in command of Lieut.-Col. Joseph L. Moss. In June the regiment, leading a reconnoissance upon the Front Royal road, discovered the approach of Lee's Army, and formed part of a force engaged in disputing his advance, an incident of which was a night battle and a retreat to Hancock on the Potomac. During the battle of Gettysburg the "12th" operated in the vicinity of McConnellsburg, Pa., and following up the Confederate retreat, captured a large number of prisoners with wagon trains and artillery. At this time Col. Pierce had resumed command.

The regiment wintered at Martinsburg, West Virginia, and after re-enlistment and the usual furlough, reassembled at that point in April, 1864, with many recruits.

The summer of 1864 was marked by a determined attempt to prevent Early's Confederates from attacking Washington. The "12th" fought his cavalry at Solomon's Gap, Pleasant Valley and Crampton's Gap. Failing in his demonstration upon the capital Early turned northward, which resulted in the second battle of Kernstown, where the "12th" lost heavily and won special mention in the reports.

With Gen. Sheridan's Army of the Shenandoah, the "12th" formed a part of Torbert's Division, with headquarters at Charlestown, Va. Col. Pierce was succeeded, December 15th, by Capt. Marcus A. Reno, an officer of the regular army. In the spring of 1865 the command was sent across the Blue Ridge, with other troops, to clear that region of guerillas, participating in a battle at Hamilton. Upon rejoining the Cavalry Division at Winchester, a movement was started toward Lynchburg. This was halted by news of the surrender of Gen. Lee's Army, after which the "12th," having assisted in the parole of all the Confederates in that section, was stationed at Winchester until mustered out on July 20th, 1865.

TOTAL LOSSES.

Killed or died of wounds ....officers, 2; men, 32.
Died from disease .... " 1; " 107.

BATTLES, ETC.

Maryland Campaign, Antietam, Martinsburg, Moorefield, Newtown, Kearnysville, Bunker Hill, Charlestown, near Winchester, reconnaissance to Wardensville and Strasburg, Fishers' Hill, Cedarville, Winchester, McConnellsburg, Pa., Cunninghams' Cross Roads, Greencastle, Pa., Clear Springs, Martinsburg, Jeffersonton, near Winchester, Middletown, Winchester, Charlestown, Bolivar Heights, near Hillsboro, Snicker's Ferry, Ashby's Gap, near Kernstown, Winchester, Bunker Hill, Cherry Run, Winchester, Charlestown, Halltown, Mt. Zion Church, Newtown, Harper's Ferry, near Hamilton, Goose Creek, Duty at Winchester in the Shenandoah Valley.

ONE HUNDRED AND SEVENTEENTH REGIMENT (THIRTEENTH CAVALRY)

(Irish Dragoons)

COLONEL JAMES A. GALLAGHER to October 6th, 1863.
COLONEL MICHAEL KIRWIN to July 14th, 1865.
Total Enrollment, 2,275 Officers and Men.

UNDER authority of the Secretary of War, James A. Gallagher, of Philadelphia, undertook the formation of a squadron of cavalry, to be known as the "Irish Dragoons," which was to have been attached to the Irish Brigade, then being recruited in New York city by Gen. Thomas Francis Meagher. Further authority was given to increase this command to a regiment. Eventually these troops were included in the Pennsylvania quota. Eight companies, A, B, C, D, H, I, K and M, originated in Philadelphia.

In August, 1862, Companies A, B, C and D were encamped at Frankford; Companies H, I and K were at Camp Gallagher, on the site of the former camp of the 88th Regiment, Falls of the Schuylkill. A detail of one hundred men was sent to Perryville and Elkton, Maryland, on September 8th, 1862, returning to Camp Gallagher one week later. Companies H, I and K were ordered to Baltimore September 17th, where, at Camp Fairgrounds, they were joined by the companies from the Frankford camp. Subsequently the remaining companies, E, F and G, arrived, and at Camp Carroll the regiment was mounted. The regiment was ordered to the Point of Rocks on December 13th for scouting duty on both side of the Potomac River, having a skirmish with White's Cavalry at Leesburg, Va., on January 8th, 1863. The regiment was assigned February 1st to Elliott's brigade, under Gen. Milroy.

Its first important battle, at Winchester, June 13-15th, 1863, was opened by the "13th," and after performing notable services the regiment covered the retreat of the army to Harper's Ferry. The regimental loss in the four days, in killed, wounded and missing, was three hundred and twenty-two.

Gen. Lee's pontoon bridge at Falling Waters was destroyed by a detail from Company H on July 2d. The regiment joined the Second Brigade of Gregg's Cavalry Division on July 8th. At Culpeper, on September 14th, the "13th" captured a large amount of stores.

At Jefferson, Va., in October, Col. Gallagher resigned as a result of injuries and the command was assumed by Major Michael Kirwin.

At Sulphur Springs, on the Rappahannock River, October 12th, the regiment lost one hundred and sixty-three officers and men, nearly all being made prisoners. On the 24th the regiment relieved the 2d Penn-

172

173

sylvania Cavalry, on duty at army headquarters. Company G was detailed to the headquarters of the Second Corps. Three extra companies, which had been sent to the regiment (not indicated on the official records), were merged into the original companies in February, 1864. With Gregg's cavalry, the "13th" participated in the Wilderness Campaign of May 5th-11th, 1864, and accompanied Sheridan's raid, losing ten killed and thirty-five wounded and missing, at Hawe's Shop. Here Capt. John Kline was killed and Capt. Patrick Kane was mortally wounded. A second raid was made toward Lynchburg, incident to which was a cavalry fight at Trevilian Station. During the general advance to and across the James River, initiated by Gen. U. S. Grant, Sheridan's cavalry, engaged in convoy of the wagon trains, was in constant conflict with the enemy. Gregg's Division fought a losing battle at St. Mary's Church, a point ten miles north of Harrison's Landing. Here, the "13th" again met with depletions. The regiment crossed the James River on June 30th, had a share in the advance to the Jerusalem Plank Road, and recrossed the James, skirmishing at Malvern Hill and Lee's Mills. At Coggin's Point, on September 16th, a detachment of one hundred and fifty from the "13th" were overpowered and captured. The regiment's closing operations of 1864, in the vicinity of the James River and Petersburg, included battles at Wyatt's Farm, Boydton Plank Road and Hatcher's Run. At the latter affair Capt. Nathaniel S. Sneyd was among the killed. With a cavalry expedition to Stony Creek Station, on the Weldon Railroad, December 1st, the "13th" made its final battle, although subsequently engaged in a number of minor affairs. In February the regiment was transported to Wilmington, N. C., reporting to Gen. Schofield. From that city it was sent southward to meet the head of Gen. Sherman's Army. On March 13th a detachment of the regiment had the honor of being the first of the eastern army to greet the veterans of the great march "from Atlanta to the sea." A month later the flag of the "13th" was raised by Sergeant Daniel Caldwell, of Company H, upon the dome of the Capitol of the State of North Carolina, at Raleigh. Following the surrender of Johnston's force, the "13th" was employed in the restoration of order. On July 14th, 1865, the command was sent to Philadelphia, being mustered out at Camp Cadwalader on the 27th.

TOTAL LOSSES.

Killed or died from wounds...........................officers, 3; men, 67
Died from disease.. " 220

BATTLES.

Strasburg, Fisher's Hill, Winchester, Falling Waters, Culpeper, Sulphur Springs, Auburn, Bristoe Station, Spotsylvania, Hawes' Shop, Cold Harbor, Deep Bottom, Trevilian Station, Gaines' Mill, White House Landing, St. Mary's Church, Lees' Mills, Malvern Hill, Wyatts' Farm, Boydton Plank Road, Stony Creek, Hatcher's Run, Gravelly Run, Second Hatcher's Run, siege of Petersburg, advance on Raleigh, surrender of Johnston.

*The fact should be noted that the "13th" fought three times at Hatcher's Run.

ONE HUNDRED AND FIFTY-NINTH REGIMENT (FOURTEENTH CAVALRY)

(Stanton Cavalry)

COLONEL JAMES N. SCHOONMAKER to July 31st, 1865.
CAPTAIN JOSEPH W. HALL to November 6th, 1864.
CAPTAIN HENRY N. HARRISON to November 2d, 1865.
Philadelphia Company A.
Total (Company) Enrollment, 233 Officers and Men.

O NE Philadelphia Company (A) was identified with the 14th Cavalry. The balance of the regiment was raised in the western counties of the State. Company A was recruited chiefly in the rural upper section of the City by Capt. Joseph W. Hall, and was known as the "Washington Cavalry." The regiment rendezvoused at Hagerstown, Md., on November 24th, 1862, under Col. James M. Schoonmaker of Pittsburgh, and after a month of drill was assigned to picket duty along the lower Shenandoah River, and after May, 1863, was attached to Averill's Fourth Separate Brigade, Department of West Virginia. The regiment was active in this mountain region during the greater part of its enlistment, performing a great amount of arduous and effective service. In April, 1864, the "14th" was moved into the Shenandoah Valley under Gen. Hunter, participating in the numerous battles and skirmishes incident to the struggle for the possession of that rich source of supplies. After the surrender of the Confederates at Appomattox the regiment was encamped at Washington, from where, on June 11th, 1865, it was ordered to Fort Leavenworth, Kansas, where it was consolidated into a battalion of six companies. Company A, then under command of Capt. Henry N. Harrison, was detailed as headquarters' escort to Gen. G. M. Dodge, department commander. The Company (A) was retained in the service to November 2d, 1865, when it was mustered out and sent home.

TOTAL LOSSES (COMPANY A).

Killed or died from wounds, or while prisoners of war..................men, 17.
Died from disease .... " 8.
Total regimental loss, killed, died from wounds, disease or in
prison ....officers, 2; men, 393.

BATTLES AND ENGAGEMENTS.

Beverly, Huttonsville, Falling Waters (detachment), Moorefield (detachment), Warm Springs, Greenbrier, White Sulphur Springs, Droop Mountain, raid on Salem, raid on Saltville, Cove Gap, Lynchburg campaign, including New Market, Piedmont, Lexington, Buchanan, near Lynchburg; Liberty, Salem, Winchester, Moorefield, Sheridan Valley campaign, including Fisher's Hill, Weir's Cave, Cedar Creek, Front Royal, Millwood, Ashby's Gap.

ONE HUNDRED AND SIXTIETH REGIMENT (FIFTEENTH CAVALRY)

Colonel Wm. J. Palmer.
Total Enrollment, 1,700 Officers and Men.

THE regiment was formed of an independent company known as the Anderson Troop, which was organized in October and November, 1861, by Wm. J. Palmer, private secretary to John Edgar Thomson, President of the Pennsylvania Railroad Company. It was intended as the headquarter guard to Brigadier-General Robert Anderson, briefly in command of the Army of the Cumberland. Its members, one hundred in number, were carefully selected from over the State. The troop was accepted by Gen. Don Carlos Buell, Second Commander of the Army, as his body guard. The troop maintained its identity as a separate organization until after the battle of Stone River, by which time it had become so depleted in numbers that the company, then under the command of Lieut. Thos. S. Maple was, in March, 1863, honorably mustered out of service.

In the summer of 1862 Capt. Palmer secured authority from the War Department to raise a full regiment, and it became known as "The Anderson Cavalry." All of the officers were selected from the Anderson Troop. The care exercised in recruiting the men induced many to seek an enlistment, and within two weeks the ranks were full, the men coming from over thirty counties of the State. About thirty-five per cent. were raised in Philadelphia, the enlistment being made in one of the offices of the Pennsylvania Railroad Company, at Third street and Willings Alley. All of the enrolled men were assembled at Carlisle, Pa., and on August 22d, 1862, were sworn into the United States service.

In September, 1862, the enemy invaded Maryland. The regiment was not yet fully organized, armed or uniformed, but Col. Palmer took two hundred men on cars to Greencastle and, impressing horses, proceeded to place his outposts around Gen. Longstreet's forces at Hagerstown, Md. So well was this done that the report in the Confederate army was that ten thousand of the Anderson Cavalry were in their front. Col. Palmer went repeatedly within the enemy's lines and obtained much information, which, with the assistance of William Bender Wilson, of the telegraphic service, he was able to send to Governor Curtin, and for several days this was all the information that Gen. McClellan had of his enemy. After the battle of Antietam, Col. Palmer crossed the Potomac in an endeavor to discover the movements of the Confederates, but their troops captured him, although he had changed his uniform for a civilian suit and assumed the character of a student in minerology. He was suspected as being a spy, but no evidence could be had to sustain it. He was held in Castle

Thunder until the following January, when he was exchanged. Col. Palmer returned to his regiment in February, 1863, and at a most critical period in its career, and under his superb management made it one of the best in the army.

In November, 1862, the regiment took the cars for Louisville, where the command received horses and soon started for Nashville. The capture of Col. Palmer had prevented the regiment from completing its organization. When it moved with the army to Stone's River only two hundred and seventy-two men, under Majors Adolph G. Rosengarten and Frank B. Ward, marched with them. In the engagements which followed it suffered severely. Major Rosengarten was killed and Major Ward was mortally wounded. Fourteen of the men were killed, ten wounded and fifty-six captured.

Fully reorganized into twelve companies, the regiment served through the Chickamauga Campaign, on duty at the headquarters of Major-General Rosecrans, and engaged in scouting, courier and escort duties. After the battle of Missionary Ridge, which resulted in the expulsion of Bragg's army from this section, the command marched to the relief of Gen. Burnside at Knoxville, being the first to arrive. The winter campaign was unusually severe, but eminently successful. The regiment took part in six important engagements and captured numerous prisoners and a large amount of Confederate equipment. They recaptured twenty-three Union soldiers and nineteen army wagons. Their losses, among officers, were one killed, two wounded and one captured; nineteen enlisted men were wounded or captured.

Three companies, B, H and K, of the 15th Cavalry were detailed to act as the escort at Gen. Thomas' headquarters in the Atlanta Campaign, and when Atlanta was captured they returned to the regiment. One of the men, Arthur O. Granger, of Company C, acted as private secretary to General Sherman and was with him to the end. At the surrender of Gen. Johnston it was he who wrote out the articles of capitulation.

Private A. D. Frankenberry, of Company K, was attached to the Signal Corps, and when the Confederates swung around to the rear and attacked Allatoona Pass, was stationed on Kenesaw Mountain. From this place he signalled to Gen. Corse over the heads of the enemy the message which inspired the once popular hymn (written by P. P. Bliss) "Hold the Fort."

The regiment followed Sherman's army as far as Calhoun, Ga., and from there was sent to help Gen. Gillam in an effort to capture Saltville. At the same time Gen. Burbridge was coming down from the North to co-operate, but Burbridge was driven back and badly defeated. It was necessary for Gillam to send a despatch to Burbridge, and Col. Palmer, with seventy-five men, delivered it, after an adventurous ride over the mountains into Kentucky.

When Sherman started on his march to the sea, Atlanta was abandoned and Gen. Thomas fell back to the line of the Tennessee River, and eventually to Nashville. After the battle here, in which Gen. Hood suffered a disastrous defeat, the regiment followed in pursuit for two hundred and fifty miles into the State of Mississippi, and succeeded in capturing and destroying Hood's pontoon train of seventy-eight boats, three hundred and ten wagons and capturing two pieces of artillery. This pursuit and capture was highly commended.

In Gen. Grant's last official report of the move of the armies embracing the years 1864 and 1865, and embodying the movements of all the troops in the field of over a million men, he only commends two regiments—one of infantry for the defence of Paducah, Ky., and the "15th" for the destruction of Gen. Hood's train. When Gen. Sherman received the dispatch of this capture he read it to his staff, and said, "The '15th' is the best regiment in my department. They can ride faster, do more hard work and capture more trains than any regiment I have."

In January, 1865, Col. Palmer, with less than one hundred and fifty men, crossed the Tennessee and at Red Hill, Ala., surprised and routed the Confederate brigade commanded by Gen. Lyon and returned to Huntsville, Ala., with one captured cannon and more prisoners than men in the command.

In March, 1865, the command left Chattanooga, and at Knoxville joined the Cavalry Division commanded by Gen. Geo. Stoneman. Col. Palmer was, at this time, appointed a brigadier-general, and later, commanded the whole cavalry division. The "15th" was now commanded by Lieut.-Col. Chas. M. Betts.

The railroads of western North Carolina were pretty thoroughly destroyed. Four companies, under Major Wagner, raided to Lynchburg, Va., and gave the impression to Gen. Lee, who was then retreating before Gen. Grant, that his command was the advance of the Army of the Cumberland. Wagner rejoined the regiment at Salisbury, N. C., and soon after the whole division started in pursuit of the fugitive Confederate President and his cabinet, but the glory of his capture fell to another command.

At this time Gen. Stoneman was making preparation to attack Salisbury, and demonstrations were ordered along the line of railroad at prominent places to divert the attention of the enemy. Col. Betts, with about a hundred men, marched towards Greensboro, N. C. Early in the morning, after being in the saddle all night, he learned that the 3d South Carolina Cavalry were in camp only half a mile distant. While they were in much superior numbers he attacked vigorously at once, surprised them while getting their breakfast and captured their commander, Col. Johnston, and a large number of his men—in fact, about twice as many as Col. Betts had in his command.

Another battalion, under Capt. Kramer, got to Jamestown early in the morning, burned a train of commissary stores for Lee's army, destroyed an arms factory and captured more prisoners than he cared to handle, one man, George Alexander, taking twelve.

The other battalion burned the bridge over Reedy Fork. Jefferson Davis and the fleeing Confederate officials had crossed it not an hour before. It was during this pursuit that Lieut.-Col. Betts captured seven wagons containing the baggage and official papers of Gens. Beauregard and Pillow and also about $2,000,000 in coin and securities belonging to the Central Railroad and Banking Company of Georgia and of the banks in Macon; also over five million of Confederate money. This money was sent, under guard, to headquarters, and after the rebellion ended was returned, intact, to the owners.

The regiment marched to Nashville, completing the longest raid by any cavalry force during the war, about 2,000 miles. June 21st, 1865, it was mustered out of service. The "15th" was the only independent scouting regiment in the Union service.*

TOTAL LOSSES.

Killed or mortally wounded..................................officers, 3; men 22
Died of disease .... " 103

BATTLES AND ENGAGEMENTS.

Antietam, Hillsborough Pike, Stone's River, Lavergne, The Barrens, Rover, Tullahoma, Chickamauga, Mission Ridge, Gatlinsburg, Dandridge, Mossy Creek, capture of Vance's Raiders, Fair Garden and Indian Creek, Resaca, Cassville, Dallas, Peach Tree Creek, Jonesboro, Devault Ford, Carter's Station, Kingsport, McKinney's Mills, Decatur, capture of Hood's pontoon and supply trains, Moulton, Red Hill, Wickesboro, Wytheville, Greensboro, capture of Salisbury, capture of 3d S. C. Cavalry, capture of part of Jefferson Davis' train, capture of Gen. Bragg. In addition numerous skirmishes not officially recorded.

---

*In reviewing the results accomplished by the "15th," one cannot but credit them to the splendid soldierly qualities of Gen. Palmer, a Philadelphian, and to the high character of its enlisted men. The General was, after the war, the pioneer railroad builder of the West, and not only laid the rails, but peopled the country, and was instrumental in opening up mines, factories and farms, through which many millions are now in lucrative occupations. In 1907, while suffering from a broken neck, occasioned by an accident, he called to his beautiful home in Colorado Springs' all of the men of his old regiment, from every part of the country, wherever they were located, and kept them in entertainment for a week, paying every attendant expense.

ONE HUNDRED AND SIXTY-FIRST REGIMENT (SIXTEENTH CAVALRY)

COLONEL J. IRVIN GREGG to August 1st, 1864.*
LIEUT.-COL. JOHN R. ROBISON to August 11th, 1865.
Total Enrollment, 1,266 Officers and Men.

THIS regiment, composed of men gathered from all portions of Pennsylvania, had a considerable Philadelphia contingent, chiefly in Company I, Capt. William H. Fry (afterward major). The regiment was formed at Harrisburg in the fall of 1862, and was sent to Washington November 23d. Early in January, 1863, the "16th" was assigned to Averill's Cavalry Brigade, which it joined near Falmouth, Va. At Kelley's Ford, March 17th, the regiment achieved a victory, on the right flank, in this, its first important battle.

In the Gettysburg campaign, Col. Gregg being in command of the brigade, the "16th" was led by Captain John K. Robison, who, as lieutenant-colonel, continued in command throughout the enlistment. The regiment participated in all of the great cavalry movements connected with the campaigns of the Army of the Potomac, including Sheridan's raid on Richmond, and was in at the death at Hatcher's Run, Dinwiddie Courthouse, Five Forks, Amelia Springs and Sailor's Creek. In this final group of battles many of the regiment were wounded. At Farmville, on the 7th of April, Lieut.-Col. Robison received his third wound. After a tour of duty at Lynchburg, subsequent to the Appomattox surrender, the "16th" was mustered out August 7th at Richmond, Va.

TOTAL LOSSES.

Killed or mortally wounded ....officers, 5; men, 100.
Died of disease .... "   3; "   194

BATTLES, SKIRMISHES, ETC.

Rappahannack Bridge, Grove Church, Hartwood Church, Kelly's Ford, Elk Run, Chancellorsville Campaign, Stoneman's Raid, Brandy Station, Aldie, Middleburg, Gettysburg, Shepherdstown, Culpeper C. H., Crooked Run, Bristoe Campaign, Mine Run Campaign, Expedition to Luray, Kilpatrick's Raid, Rapidan Campaign, Siege operations against Petersburg, including movements to Deep Bottom; Malvern Hill, Strawberry Plains, Ream's Station, Poplar Springs Church, Dinwiddie C. H., Boydton Plank Road, Hatcher's Run, Stony Creek, Disputantia Station, Dabney's Mills, Hatcher's Run, Appomattox Campaign, Expedition to Danville.

---

* Colonel John Irvin Gregg began his military career as a private soldier in the war with Mexico, from which he emerged a captain of regular infantry. For services in the Civil War he was brevetted major-general of volunteers.

ONE HUNDRED AND SIXTY-THIRD REGIMENT (EIGHTEENTH CAVALRY)

COLONEL TIMOTHY M. BRYAN, JR., to December 29th, 1864.
COLONEL T. F. RODENBOUGH to October 31st, 1865.
Total Enrollment (Philadelphia Companies) about 450 Officers and Men.

A LTHOUGH Col. Bryan and a number of his officers were Philadelphians, this command, as organized and placed in the field, contained no Philadelphia companies, but early in 1863 two companies which had been partly recruited in this city were added to the regiment, as L and M, at Washington.*

The 18th Cavalry served throughout its enlistment in the Army of the Potomac and the Army of the Shenandoah. Both of its colonels were West Point graduates and officers of the cavalry in the regular service. With the exception of one company, the regiment was consolidated on June 24th, 1865, with the 22d Cavalry to form the "Third Pennsylvania Provisional Cavalry." This command was stationed at various points in West Virginia for the suppression of guerillas, after the close of the war being mustered out at Cumberland, Maryland, on October 31st, 1865.

TOTAL LOSSES (COMPANIES L AND M).

Killed or died from wounds ....officers, 1; men, 12.
Died of disease and while prisoners of war .... "   0; " 19.
Wounded, not mortally .... "   1; " 21.

BATTLES, ETC.

Chantilly, Aldie, Hanover, Hunterstown, Gettysburg, Monterey Pass, Smithsburg, Hagerstown, Boonsboro, Funkstown, Hagerstown, Falling Waters, Port Conway, Rapidan Station, Robertson's Ford, James City, Culpeper, Brandy Station, Groveton, Buckland Mills, Hay Market, Stevensburg, Raccoon Ford, Kilpatrick's raid, Wilderness, Spotsylvania, Yellow Tavern, Meadow Bridge, Hanover Court House, Ashland Station, Bethesda Church, Cold Harbor, St. Mary's Church, Yellow House (Weldon Railroad), Winchester, Summit Point, Charlestown, Kearnysville, The Opequon, Front Royal, Milford, Waynesboro, Brock's Gap, Columbia Furnace, Tom's Brook, Hupp's Hill, Cedar Creek, Lebanon Church, Mount Jackson.

---

* In the autumn of 1862 an enthusiastic citizen of Haddonfield, N. J., was active in securing recruits for the "Continental Cavalry." Two companies, intended as A and B, were camped at Haddonfield. Adverse circumstances led many of the recruits to leave camp and to enlist elsewhere. Their names were, however, carried upon the company records as "deserters." Those who remained were, with their officers, mustered into the service and attached to the 18th Cavalry.

ONE HUNDRED AND EIGHTIETH REGIMENT (NINETEENTH CAVALRY)

COLONEL ALEXANDER CUMMINGS.
LIEUT.-COL. JOSEPH C. HESS.
LIEUT.-COL. FRANK REEDER.
Total Enrollment, 1,762 Officers and Men.

THIS regiment was recruited, with the exception of Companies L and M, at Philadelphia, from June to October, 1863, its camp being located (Camp Stanton) opposite Odd Fellows' Cemetery. All of the officers, with one exception, and a majority of the enlisted men had seen previous service. Early in November the regiment reported at Washington, from which it started, on November 13th, for Mississippi, but enroute received orders to proceed to Columbus, Kentucky, where it was assigned by Major-Gen. A. J. Smith, in command Department of the Tennessee, to Waring's Brigade, Brig.-Gen. B. H. Grierson's Cavalry Division, Sixteenth Corps, Col. Cummings having been detached on recruiting duty without further service to the regiment.* The "19th" was now commanded by Lieut.-Col. Joseph C. Hess. In February the regiment marched with Griersons' column upon a raid into West Tennessee, there destroying large supply depots and much railroad property. With headquarters at Memphis, the cavalry engaged in a series of expeditions in Tennessee and Mississippi with varying fortunes. At Guntown, Miss., on June 10th, the "19th" shared in a defeat at the hands of Forrest. Early in July a detachment of the regiment accompanied Col. Klarge's expedition from Memphis to Grand Gulf, Miss. In August, after further conflicts with Forrest, the "19th" was moved rapidly to Little Rock and thence into Missouri, against the force under Sterling Price. Returning to Memphis on October 20th, the command was moved by transports to Nashville, where, as a part of the brigade of Brig.-Gen. J. H. Hammond, it was engaged in the battle of Nashville (December 15-16th, 1864), which resulted in the defeat of Hood's Confederates. This result entailed a hot pursuit by the Union cavalry and a second notable battle on January 2d, 1865, at Franklin, Miss. This campaign of pursuit continued through the month, with constant losses of officers and men.

Upon February 4th, 1865, at Gravelly Springs, Alabama, the regiment was reorganized as a battalion of six companies (the supernumerary

---

* Col. Cummings was the originator of *Cummings' Evening Telegraphic Bulletin,* the initial issue of which appeared in Philadelphia on April 12th, 1847. This paper made a specialty of telegraphic news, and is perpetuated in the present *Evening Bulletin.*

officers being mustered out), and, under the command of Lieut.-Col. Frank Reeder, embarked, with some detentions at Cairo and Vicksburg, for New Orleans. From the Crescent City, a few days later, the command proceeded to Baton Rogue, operating from this point on scout and picket duty through the following six months. On June 13th the battalion was reduced to four companies, these companies, A, B, C and D, occupying a region within which the embers of rebellion still smouldered. On July 25th, at Clinton, La., the battalion defeated a Confederate detachment of Gen. Wirt Adams' command. In December, Companies A and C were ordered into Texas, and in January, 1866, near Marshall, Company A had a fight with guerillas, losing five men killed.*

In April, 1866, the battalion was assembled at New Orleans, where, after several weeks of provost duty, it was mustered out on May 14th, the last of the Pennsylvania troops to turn homeward and resume the occupations of peace.

TOTAL LOSSES.

Killed or died from wounds ....officers, 0; men, 15.
Died from disease.. "   3; " 109

BATTLES, SKIRMISHES AND EXPEDITIONS.

Movements to Union City, Trenton, Colliersville, Tenn., and Okalona, Miss. (including Egypt Station, West Point, Ivy Farm, Okolona, Tallahatchie River); operations against Forrest in West Tennessee (including Cypress Creek and near Raleigh, April 3d and 9th); expedition to Guntown, Miss. (including Tishamingo Creek, Waldron Bridge and Davis Mills); Grand Gulf expedition; Oxford, Miss., expedition (including Hurricane Creek); detachment to Little Rock and Missouri (including Noconah Creek, Co. F); Owens' Cross Roads, battle of Nashville, Hollow Tree Gap, Franklin, West Harpeth River, King's Hill, Sugar Creek, Gravelly Springs, service in Louisiana and Texas to end of enlistment.

---

*Bates' History, vol. 5, page 4. The affair above mentioned, at Clinton, and that at Marshall, are not found in the official lists of battles, engagements, etc.

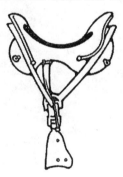

ONE HUNDRED AND EIGHTY-FIRST REGIMENT (TWENTIETH CAVALRY). SIX MONTHS' SERVICE

COLONEL JOHN E. WYNKOOP to January 7th, 1864.
Total Enrollment, 1,266 Officers and Men.

PURSUANT to an order of the War Department, dated June 9th, 1863, three cavalry regiments were organized in Pennsylvania to serve six months. These troops were composed, in part, of existing independent companies and militia of the emergency class and of new recruits. They were the 181st, 182d and 185th Regiments of the line, designated respectively the 20th, 21st and 22d Cavalry. The first of these commands contained many men recruited in Philadelphia. This regiment was organized in July, 1863, from five companies of Emergency Militia and seven of six-months' men, at Camp Curtin, and sent from that point upon scout duty, with other troops, into Maryland, crowding upon and skirmishing with the rear-guard of the retreating Confederate Army. Later, a battalion was stationed along the line of the Baltimore and Ohio Railroad in West Virginia. Five companies were detailed, in the draft riot period, to Philadelphia, Reading and Pottsville. The companies upon the loyal border performed several effective raids and met with some casualties. Brigaded with Federal cavalry and artillery from Pennsylvania and Virginia, the 20th Cavalry helped to clear a large section of country of disloyal elements. On muster out, January 7th, 1864, the regiment was reorganized on a three years' basis, with camps at Philadelphia and Harrisburg.

ONE HUNDRED AND EIGHTY-FIRST REGIMENT (TWENTIETH CAVALRY). THREE YEARS' SERVICE

COLONEL JOHN E. WYNKOOP to January 15th, 1865.
COLONEL GABRIEL MIDDLETON to June 20th, 1865.
Total Enrollment, 1,500 Officers and Men.

ON the completion of the term of service of the original regiment, enlisted for six months, the command was re-organized on a three-year basis. Twelve of the Philadelphia officers were retained. The regiment was mustered in at Harrisburg and Philadelphia and assigned to the First Brigade, Second Division, Eighth Corps. Later the "20th" was attached to Gen. Franz Sigel's force in the Shenandoah Valley as part of the Second Brigade,

First Cavalry Division, with which it shared in the battle of New Market. With the column of Major-Gen. David Hunter, who succeeded Sigel, the regiment won fame by capturing nearly 800 prisoners at the battle of Piedmont. Gen. Hunter then led his column, reinforced by divisions under Gens. Crook and Averill, upon a demonstration against Lynchburg. The subsequent retreat into the fastnesses of West Virginia was attended by great suffering, due to want of food for the men and forage for the horses. Major-Gen. George Crook now assumed command. The augmented force in this department was reorganized under Major-Gen. Philip H. Sheridan. The 20th Cavalry was attached to the Second Brigade, First Division Cavalry, Army of the Shenandoah, and actively participated in the raid upon Gordonsville near the end of December, 1864, capturing two pieces of artillery and the fortifications in the engagements at Magruder's Farm and Jack's Shop.

During this raid many of the men were severely frost-bitten. In January the regiment was sent to Lovettsville, Va., and thence a few weeks later to Duffield Station to protect the railroad against Moseby's raiders. On February 26th the command moved to rejoin the brigade at Winchester. During Hunter's raid the "20th" was always in the advance, being the first to reach Staunton and Lynchburg. In July, 1864, the regiment, now with Sheridan's force opposing Early, fortified at Hall Town, and for doing so was rewarded, soon afterward, at Cumberland, with new mounts. Through the autumn and winter the regiment was continually moving and had no rest in winter quarters. It was considerably re-enforced at this time. The Army of the Shenandoah resumed active operations on February 27th, 1865. The "20th" was now in command of Col. Gabriel Middleton. It was active in a destructive raid upon the communications and stores of the enemy, which ended in a junction with Gen. Grant's army in front of Petersburg. The regiment participated in the cavalry movements and the severe fighting which ended with the surrender of the remnant of the Confederate Army at Appomattox with many casualties to officers and men. After the surrender the "20th" was ordered forward to Danville and later to Washington, where it was consolidated with the 2d Cavalry as the 1st Provisional Cavalry. This organization was mustered out at Cloud's Mills on July 13th, 1865.

TOTAL LOSSES.

Killed or died from wounds ....officers, 3; men, 22
Died from disease .... " 3; " 100

BATTLES AND ENGAGEMENTS.

New Market, Harisonburg, Piedmont, Staunton, Midway, Cedar Creek, Piney River, Near Glasgow, Lynchburg, Salem, Martinsburg, Snicker's Ferry, Ashby's Gap, Kernstown, Bunker Hill, Martinsburg, Madison Court House, Liberty Mills, Gordonsville, Swope's Depot, Staunton, Waynesboro, Goochland Court House, Dinwiddie Court House, Five Forks, Scott's Cross Roads, Tabernacle Church, Sailors' Creek, Appomattox Court House, in addition numerous skirmishes and minor actions.

CAMP WILLIAM PENN, TRAINING CAMP FOR COLORED TROOPS ENLISTED INTO THE UNITED STATES ARMY, located in Cheltenham Township, Montgomery County, Pa.

(From a contemporary lithograph.)

SCHOOL FOR THE SELECTION OF OFFICERS OF COLORED REGIMENTS,
1210 Chestnut Street.

ARMY BANDS

THE formation of the several Philadelphia regiments of the three-months' service included the enlistment of many of the best military musicians in the city. In some cases the pay for extra musicians was borne by the regimental officers. Associations of patriotic citizens subscribed to enable favorite regiments to keep numerically strong bands in the field.* When the short term regiments came home and recruiting became active for the three years' regiments nearly all of the best bandsmen re-enlisted. For a time Birgfield's excellent band enjoyed almost a monopoly of local engagements, and was, in fact, in much demand for all home parades and other demonstrations through the war.

General Order No. 91, October 26th, 1861, provided that no more bands for volunteer regiments were to be mustered in, and that vacancies occurring in the bands should not be filled. All enlisted bands in the army were discharged by General Order dated July 29th, 1862, to take effect within thirty days. It was provided, however, that a band of sixteen pieces should be allowed to each brigade.

The following list comprises the best known of the military bands attached to local regiments:

Band of 17th Regiment. Leader, J. Moosbruger.
Band of 21st Regiment. Leader, Conrad Hoffman.
Band of 23d Regiment. Leader, Theo. Herman.
Band of 27th Regiment. Leader, Theo. Artelt.
Band of 28th Regiment. Leader, William F. Simpson.†
Band of 29th Regiment. Leader, Daniel Repass.
Band of 31st Regiment. Leader, Josiah Wagner.
Band of 65th Regiment (mounted). Leader, William Ziegler.
Band of 70th Regiment (mounted). Leader, Philip Ehrmann.
Band of 71st Regiment. Leader, Edward Schemser.
Band of 75th Regiment. Leader, Rudolph Wittig.
Band of 82d Regiment. Leader, Alex. Anderson.
Band of 88th Regiment. Leader, E. Ermentrout.
Band of 90th Regiment. Leader, Jacob L. Bricker.
Band of 95th Regiment. Leader, Joseph Whittington.
Band of 98th Regiment. Leader, Christopher Storz.
Band of 106th Regiment. Leader, Fridoline Stopper.
Band of 114th Regiment. Leader, Frank Rauscher.

---

*By General Order No. 15, May 4, 1861, regimental bands were limited to sixteen musicians; additional men were at the expense of private subscription.

†It has been stated that this band was organized by Antrim C. Beck, one of the eight brothers of the famous Beck's Band, four of whom were enlisted in the band of the "28th."

185

COLORED TROOPS—CAMP WILLIAM PENN

SEVEN years prior to the commencement of the Civil War the *Washington Union,* organ of the administration of President Franklin Pierce, asserted that "if the Union of the States is dissolved and war ensues upon the question of a revival of the slave trade, while the slave holders cannot hope to battle with success against the Northern States, allied with England, they can and will place a great army of negroes in the field and defy their enemies."* A lively commentary upon that assumption is presented in the feat of a negro pilot of Charleston Harbor, Robert Smalls,** who, early in 1862, with eight other colored men, seized the armed steamer *Planter* and, running her safely past the forts, delivered her to Admiral DuPont of the blockade fleet. This incident strengthened the position of those who advocated the enlistment of negroes in the Union army and navy.† Upon July 17th, 1862, Congress enacted a bill authorizing the President "to employ as many persons of African descent as he may deem necessary and proper for the suppression of the rebellion, and for this purpose he may organize and use them in such manner as he may judge best for the public welfare."‡

The President made no haste to avail himself of this authority. He first signed, as a war measure, the Emancipation Proclamation relating to the slaves held in the disloyal States. This became effective upon January 1st, 1863, and it was not until then that the question of enrolling colored troops was actively considered.§ Upon February 13th, 1863, Hon.

---

*Out of the entire Southern white population but three in one hundred held a property interest in slaves. Of the slave-holding class but twenty per cent. owned more than one slave. A large proportion of the political and military leaders of the South were non-slave holders. Among them were Robert E. Lee, Joseph E. Johnston and A. P. Hill. "Slavery and Abolition," Hart.

**Robert Smalls subsequently became a colonel of colored troops and after the close of the war was elected to Congress from South Carolina.

†The first recorded suggestion for the employment of colored troops in the Northern armies is found in a letter written to Hon. Simon Cameron, Secretary of War, on April 16th, 1861, by Burr Porter, late major in the Ottoman Army. (Official documents.)

‡Soon after the occupation of New Orleans, in 1862, Major-Gen. Benjamin F. Butler, recruited colored troops and in South Carolina Major-Gen. David Hunter had formed negro regiments about the same time, this procedure being made the subject of Congressional inquiry.

§President Lincoln, writing to Horace Greeley, date of August 22d, 1861, said: "If there be those who would not save the Union unless at the same time they could save slavery, I do not agree with them. If there be those who would not save the Union unless they could at the same time destroy slavery, I do not agree with them."

Charles Sumner presented a bill providing for the enlistment of 300,000 colored troops. It was reported upon negatively. The State of Massachusetts, however, proceeded to enlist the colored organization famous as the "54th Regiment Massachusetts Volunteer Infantry, Colored." One company of this regiment (B) was raised in Philadelphia by James Morris Walton, Esq., who became major of the "54th." Lieutenants Frank M. Welsh and E. N. Hallowell were also active in securing Philadelphia recruits. Nearly every company of the "54th" contained Philadelphia and Pennsylvania men. This was true, also, of the 55th Massachusetts Colored Regiment, of which Norwood Penrose Hallowell, of Philadelphia, became colonel. So deeply rooted was the old prejudice in Philadelphia against the blacks, that recruits raised here for the two above designated regiments were sent away at night in small squads by rail. Referring to these colored recruits the Philadelphia *Inquirer* said, June 26th, 1863, that "Pennsylvania has already lost fully 1,500 men who have enlisted in Massachusetts."

At a meeting held in Philadelphia upon March 25th, 1863, for the promotion of a colored brigade to be commanded by Col. William Angeroth, a committee, including Messrs. F. C. Philpot, James Logan, Jacob Keefer, Charles Angeroth, Jr., W. Henry Moore and William Frishmuth, reported that the Secretary of War had promised immediate authority to proceed.*

At another gathering of citizens held in Sansom Street Hall on the evening of June 19th, 1863, the following persons were named to constitute a general committee for raising black regiments: Thomas Webster, Chairman; J. Miller McKim, William H. Ashurst, Evan Randolph, N. B. Brown, Adolph E. Borie, William D. Kelley, George H. Boker, Caleb H. Needles, William Rotch Wister, Thomas J. Megear, Henry Samuel, Henry C. Howell, B. F. Reimer, George T. Thorn, Enoch R. Hutchinson, William M. Tilghman, A. H. Franciscus, Cadwalader Biddle, Samuel S. White, William P. Stotesbury, George M. Connarroe, George Truman, Jr., Charles Wise, John McAllister, Abraham Barker and A. G. Cattell.

On the same date Lieut.-Col. Charles C. Ruff, U. S. A., notified the Citizens' Bounty Fund Committee that, as mustering officer at this post, he had "orders to authorize the formation of one regiment of ten companies, colored troops, each company to be eighty strong, to be mustered into the United States service and provided for, in all respects, the same as white troops." A week later, as a rendezvous for this class of troops, Camp William Penn was established outside of the city limit, in Cheltenham township, Montgomery County. Lieut.-Col. Louis Wagner

---

*General Order No. 143, May 22d, 1863, provided for a bureau to be attached to the office of the Adjutant-General at Washington to record all matters relating to the organization of colored troops. Non-commissioned officers of colored regiments were selected from the ranks.

(of the 88th Regiment, Pennsylvania Infantry), who had been badly wounded at Bull Run, was appointed to command the camp.

Upon June 17th, 1863, during the emergency excitement preceding the battle of Gettysburg, a company of colored men, under Capt. A. M. Babe, appeared at the City Arsenal and applied for uniforms and guns. They were fitted out without question and sent to Harrisburg, but were promptly returned to Philadelphia. This company was accepted by the Government and mustered upon June 26th, 1863, and was said to have been the first company of colored troops of Philadelphia enrolled in the United States service.

When the opportunity came to the free blacks of the north to enlist under the flag of the Union their leading men were prompt in appeal to their manhood. In Philadelphia thousands of copies of a circular were distributed reading in part as follows:

"This is our golden moment. The Government of the United States calls for every able-bodied colored man to enter the army for the three years' service, and join in fighting the battles of Liberty and the Union. A new era is open to us. For generations we have suffered under the horrors of slavery outrage and wrong! Our manhood has been denied, our citizenship blotted out, our souls seared and burned, our spirits cowed and crushed, and the hopes of the future of our race involved in doubt and darkness. But now the whole aspect of our relations with the white race is changed. * * * * If we love our country, if we love our families, our children, our homes, we must strike *now* while the country calls. More than a million of white men have left comfortable homes and joined the armies of the Union to save their country. Cannot we leave ours and swell the hosts of the Union, save our liberties, vindicate our manhood and deserve well of our country? * * * * Men of color! Brothers and fathers! We appeal to you! By all your concern for yourselves and your liberties, by all your regard for God and humanity, by all your desire for citizenship and equality before the law, by all your love of country, to stop at no subterfuges, listen to nothing that shall deter you from rallying for the army. Strike now and you are henceforth and forever Freemen!"

SIGNERS:—E. D. Bassett, William D. Forten, Frederick Douglass, William Whipper, D. M. Turner, James McCrummell, A. S. Cassey, A. M. Green, J. W. Page, L. R. Seymour, Rev. J. Underdue, John W. Price, Augustus Dorsey, Rev. Stephen Smith, N. W. Depee, Dr. J. H. Wilson, J. W. Cassey, P. J. Armstrong, J. W. Simpson, Rev. J. B. Trusty, S. Morgan Smith, William E. Gipson, Rev. J. Boulden, Rev. J. Asher, Rev. J. C. Gibbs, Daniel George, Robert M. Adger, Henry M. Cropper, Rev. J. B. Reeve, Rev. J. A. Williams, Rev. A. L. Stanford, Thomas J. Bowers, Elijah J. Davis, John P. Burr, Robert Jones, O. V. Catto, Thomas J. Dorsey, I. D. Cliff, Jacob C. White, Morris Hall, James Needham, Rev. Elisha Weaver, Ebenezer Black, Rev. William T. Catto, James R. Gordon, Samuel Stewart, David B. Bowser, Henry Minton, Daniel Colley, J. C. White, Jr., Rev. J. P. Campbell, Rev. W. J. Alston, J. P. Johnson, Franklin Turner and Jesse E. Glasgow.

White officers for the colored troops were selected with great care, generally from regiments of white troops in the field. The committee for the supervision of recruiting of colored regiments opened a school of instruction at 1210 Chestnut street, where, under the direction of Maj. George A. Hearns, U. S. A. Commissioner, Col. John H. Taggart (late an officer of the 12th Regiment, Veteran Reserve Corps), instructed applicants for commissions. Upon October 3d, 1863, the 6th

Regiment and four companies of the 8th Regiment, colored troops, were paraded in the city under the command of Col. John W. Ames, and escorted by Lieut.-Col. Louis Wagner and staff. These regiments were reviewed at the Union League Club and provided with a dinner at the Union Volunteer Refreshment Saloon. The soldierly bearing of these troops won for them and their officers great praise from the newspapers and the public.*

The colored regiments mustered at Camp William Penn were numbered the 3d, 6th, 8th, 22d, 24th, 25th, 32d, 41st, 43d, 45th and 127th, and as they were rated as part of the regular force of the United States Army, they were not credited upon the quota of Philadelphia or of the State of Pennsylvania.

The records for bravery under fire and efficiency in the campaigns in which they were employed, to the credit of the colored soldiers in the Union Army, were shared by the ten thousand nine hundred and forty rank and file, and nearly four hundred white officers commanding them, all of whom were originally assembled at Camp William Penn.

Upon a pillar of the Court of Honor erected in honor of the 33d Annual National Encampment of the Grand Army of the Republic, September 4th to 9th, 1899, was inscribed the name, for distinguished heroism, of Serg. Arthur Harold of Company A, 8th Regiment, United States Colored Troops, who was killed at Petersburg.

In a general order of October 11th, 1864, Maj.-Gen. Benjamin F. Butler, referring to a charge made by these troops at New Market, wrote: "Better men were never better led, better officers never led better men. A few more such charges and to command colored troops will be the post of honor in the American armies."

Ever since the Civil War colored regiments have been a part of the military arm of the nation.

THIRD REGIMENT INFANTRY (U. S. COLORED TROOPS)

Colonel Benjamin G. Tilghman.

Organized at Camp William Penn in August, 1863, this regiment was attached to the Fourth Brigade, Tenth Corps, and was stationed at Morris Island, Charleston Harbor, S. C., at Hilton Head, S. C., and in February, 1864, transferred to Vogdes' Division, District of Florida. With this and other commands its subsequent service was confined to the State of Florida. The "3d" participated in the assaults on Forts Wagner and

---

*For the assistance of these volunteers the Colored Women's Sanitary Commission was formed, with headquarters at 404 Walnut street. The officers were Mrs. Caroline Johnson, President; Mrs. Arena Ruffin, Vice-President; Rev. Stephen Smith, Treasurer; Rev. J. Asher, Secretary.

Gregg, and in operations at Charleston, S. C.; also in a series of expeditions and actions in Florida. For a considerable period the regiment served as heavy artillery. The command was retained in the service for garrison duty at Jacksonville, Fernandina and other points to October 21st, 1865, when it was mustered out.

BATTLES, ETC.

Operations on Morris' Island, S. C., including Forts Wagner and Gregg, expedition to Florida, expedition to Lake City, Fla., expedition to Camp Milton, Fla., expedition to Bryant's plantation.

SIXTH REGIMENT INFANTRY (U. S. COLORED TROOPS)

COLONEL JOHN W. AMES.

Leaving Camp William Penn on October 14th, 1863, the "6th" joined the army at Fortress Monroe, and was, in the course of its history, attached to the Eighteenth, Tenth and Twenty-fifth Corps. In its two years of service the regiment had a more active part in a field of operations covering a large portion of two States than any other colored regiment originating in Pennsylvania. With its camp at Yorktown, Va., the regiment accompanied expeditions into North Carolina and to various points on the peninsula, joining the colored division under Gen. B. F. Butler on the James River in May, 1864, and participating in battles and operations incident to the siege of Petersburg and Richmond. Its most notable record was gained at the battle of Chaffin's Farm (New Market Heights), where it lost most heavily. Here a company, led by Capt. John McMurray, went into the charge with thirty-two men and returned with but three. This was the greatest average company loss recorded of any troops in the course of the war. It was in this charge that Capt. Robert B. Beath, subsequently commissioned lieutenant-colonel, lost his leg.

With the Twenty-fifth Corps in the operations on the North Carolina coast at the beginning of 1865, the "6th" was in the advance upon and capture of Fort Fisher, and in the following campaign, which cleared eastern North Carolina of the enemy and finally led to a junction with Gen. Sherman's army at Raleigh and the capitulation of Gen. Johnston, after which the "6th" performed garrison duty at Wilmington, N. C., to its muster out on September 20th, 1865.

The chaplain, Rev. Jeremiah W. Asher, lost his life at Wilmington through attendance on men suffering from malignant fever.

TOTAL LOSSES.

Killed or mortally wounded...................................officers, 8; men, 79
Died of disease.. " 5; " 132
Wounded, not mortally, and missing (officers and men)........ 168

BATTLES.

Expedition against Richmond, skirmish near Williamsburg, expedition from Yorktown to New Kent Court House, City Point, Petersburg (June 9th, 1864), Butler's operations against Petersburg and Richmond, Petersburg (assault June 15th, 1864), Petersburg (June 16th, 18th, 1864), Dutch Gap, Chaffin's Farm (Fort Harrison), Fort Fisher (December, 1864), Fort Fisher (January, 1865), Sugar Loaf Battery, N. C., occupation of Wilmington. N. C., skirmish, Phillips Cross Roads, N. C.

EIGHTH REGIMENT INFANTRY (U. S. COLORED TROOPS)

COLONEL JOHN W. FULLER.

This regiment was ready for the field in December, 1863, and left Philadelphia for Hilton Head, S. C., on January 16th, 1864, from which point it was ordered to Jacksonville, Fla. At the battle of Olustee, a point about fifty miles westward from that city, on February 20th, the "8th" met with disastrous losses. Among the wounded was Capt. (afterward Lieut.-Col.) George E. Wagner, brother of Gen. Louis Wagner. After several months of further campaigning in Florida the regiment was sent to the Tenth Corps, operating in front of Richmond and Petersburg. The "8th" was engaged in the battles of Chaffin's Farm (Fort Harrison), Darbytown Road and the second Fair Oaks. After wintering in the trenches before Richmond the regiment participated in the final struggle around Petersburg, and was present at the scene of the surrender at Appomattox. After several weeks of duty at Petersburg the "8th" was sent by transport to Texas, serving there until November. The regiment was mustered out on the 10th, and finally discharged at Philadelphia December 12th, 1865.

TOTAL LOSSES.

Killed or mortally wounded..............................officers, 4; men, 115
Died of disease .... " 132
Wounded, not mortally... " 245
Captured or missing... " 72

BATTLES.

Olustee, Bermuda Hundred, Chaffin's Farm, Darbytown Road, siege of Petersburg, Hatcher's Run, fall of Petersburg, pursuit of Lee, Appomattox Court House.

NOTE.—This regiment is included in the well-known and oft quoted list of "Three Hundred Fighting Regiments." Fox.

TWENTY-SECOND REGIMENT INFANTRY (U. S. COLORED TROOPS)

COLONEL JOSEPH B. KIDDOO.

This regiment proceeded from Camp William Penn to Yorktown, Va., at the end of January, 1864, and as a part of Hinck's Division, Eighteenth Corps, participated in Butler's demonstrations against Petersburg and Richmond, and was engaged in the attack on Fort Powhattan incident to Grant's advance to and across the James River. The "22d" was active in the heavy siege operations beginning in June, 1864, and ending with the fall of Petersburg and Richmond, fighting in many notable battles incident to that period of the war. It was honored by selection as one of the first Union regiments sent into Richmond. It was detailed as part of the escort at the funeral obsequies of President Lincoln at Washington, after which it was sent to the Eastern Shore of Maryland in pursuit of the assassins. The "22d" was now transported to Texas as part of the Twenty-fifth Corps, where it was kept on patrol duty along the Rio Grande River for four months. The regiment was mustered out October 16th, 1865.

TOTAL LOSSES.

Killed or died from wounds................................officers, 2; men, 70
Died of disease, etc............................,............. "   1; " 144

BATTLES, ETC.

Engaged on duty near Yorktown, Butler's operations, Bermuda Hundred, Fort Powhattan, Dutch Gap, assault at Petersburg, Chaffin's Farm (New Market), Fair Oaks (October 27th, 28th, 1864), Chaffin's Farm (November 4th), in trenches before Richmond, occupation of Richmond, duty in Texas to end of enlistment.

TWENTY-FOURTH REGIMENT INFANTRY (U. S. COLORED TROOPS)

COLONEL ORLANDO BROWN.

This regiment was moved from Camp William Penn to Washington May 5th, 1865. After a brief stay at Camp Casey it was assigned to guard prisoners at Point Lookout, Md., and subsequently to patrol and provost duty at Richmond, Va., and points in Virginia, with headquarters at Burkeville. It was mustered out at Richmond October 1st, 1865.

TWENTY-FIFTH REGIMENT INFANTRY (U. S. COLORED TROOPS)

COLONEL OCTAVIUS A. SCROGGS.

The right wing of this regiment left Philadelphia March 15th, 1864, and was assigned to garrison duty at Beaufort, N. C., later joining the left wing at New Orleans. In October the command was sent to Pensacola, Fla., in which State it was garrisoned at Forts Pickens and Barrancas to the conclusion of its service, December 6th, 1865.

CONFEDERATE PRISONERS AT FORT DELAWARE.

FORT MIFFLIN, A PRISON FOR DESERTERS.
(Redrawn from a sketch by T. H. Wilkinson.)

THIRTY-SECOND REGIMENT INFANTRY (U. S. COLORED TROOPS)

Colonel George W. Baird.

Organized at Camp William Penn in the spring of 1864, the "32d" was ordered to Hilton Head, S. C., arriving there on April 27th. A few weeks later the command was sent to Morris Island, joining the troops then operating against Charleston. Here and at points along the South Carolina coast the regiment was on duty throughout its term of service. It was mustered out August 22d, 1865.

TOTAL LOSSES.

Killed or died of wounds...................................officers, 2; men, 35
Died of disease.. " 113

BATTLES, ETC.

Duty at Hilton Head, Morris' Island, siege operations, expedition to Boyd's Neck, Honey Hill, raid on Savannah Railroad, Devaux Neck, James' Island, occupation of Charleston, Potter expedition, Dingle's Mills, Statesboro, Camden, Boydkin's Mills, Beach Creek, Denken's Mills.

FORTY-FIRST REGIMENT INFANTRY (U. S. COLORED TROOPS)

Colonel Llewellyn F. Haskell.

This regiment left Camp William Penn October 18th, 1864, proceeding to the vicinity of Richmond, there being attached to Hinck's Division, Tenth Corps. The regiment remained with the Army of the Potomac until May 25th, 1865, being then sent by sea to join the Twenty-fifth Corps in Texas,* where it was engaged on guard and patrol duty. In September, 1865, the "41st" was reduced to a battalion of four companies. It was mustered out at Brownsville November 10th, and disbanded at Philadelphia on December 14th, 1865.

BATTLES AND SERVICES.

Deep Bottom, before Richmond. Fair Oaks (October 27th, 28th, 1864), picket duty at Chaffin's Farm, Hatcher's Run, Fall of Petersburg, pursuit of Lee, Appomattox Court House, on duty at Edenburg, Texas.

---

*The Twenty-fifth Corps was composed of colored troops of the Tenth and Eighteenth Corps. It was created December 3d, 1864, and the entire corps was transferred to Texas in May and June, 1865. It was commanded by Major-Gen. Godfrey Weitzel.

FORTY-THIRD REGIMENT INFANTRY (U. S. COLORED TROOPS)

Colonel Stephen B. Yeoman.

Organized at Camp William Penn, this regiment was stationed at Annapolis April 18th, 1864. It was attached to the Ninth Corps from September to November, being then transferred to the Twenty-fifth Corps, and participated in the active campaigns incident to the siege of Petersburg and Richmond, being often engaged. After the conclusion of hostilities in Virginia the regiment was dispatched to Texas. It was mustered out October 20th, and discharged at Philadelphia November 30th, 1865.

TOTAL LOSSES.

Killed or died of wounds.....................................officers. 3; men, 48
Died of disease.. " 188

BATTLES AND SERVICES.

Campaign from the Rapidan to the James River, before Petersburg, operations against Richmond, mine explosion, Weldon Railroad, Poplar Grove Church, Boydton Plank Road, Hatcher's Run, before Richmond through the winter, Hatcher's Run, fall of Petersburg, pursuit of Lee, Appomattox Court House, duty at Petersburg and City Point, duty on the Rio Grande River to end of enlistment.

FORTY-FIFTH REGIMENT INFANTRY (U. S. COLORED TROOPS)

Colonel Ulysses Doubleday.

This regiment was recruited during the summer of 1864. Four companies were ordered from Camp William Penn in July for garrison duty at Arlington Heights. Six companies left Philadelphia late in September and were assigned to the Tenth Corps. These companies experienced the fighting with which the command is credited, being engaged in several of the battles incident to the investment of Petersburg and Richmond. The battalion from Arlington joined the later companies in camp at Chaffin's Farm and shared with them in the Appomattox campaign, after which the regiment was ordered to Texas along with other colored regiments and employed there on guard and provost duty. The "45th" was mustered out at Brownsville November 4th, 1865.

BATTLES AND SERVICES.

Guard duty at Arlington (four companies), movements around Richmond, Chaffin's Farm, Fort Harrison, Fair Oaks (October 27th, 28th, 1864), winter in the trenches before Richmond, Hatcher's Run, fall of Petersburg, pursuit of Lee, Appomattox Court House, guard duty at City Point, duty on the Rio Grande to end of enlistment.

ONE HUNDRED AND TWENTY-SEVENTH REGIMENT INFANTRY (U. S. COLORED TROOPS)

COLONEL BENJAMIN F. TRACY.

This regiment was the last to leave Camp William Penn. It was ordered to City Point, Va., in September, 1864, and there attached to the Tenth Corps. Its movements and engagements were identical with those of the left wing of the "45th" Regiment, including the transfer after Lee's surrender to further duty in Texas. It was mustered out upon the Rio Grande river October 20th, 1865.

SOME OF THE FIGHTING REGIMENTS

A N oft-quoted list of three hundred regiments, selected from the entire Union force for superior fighting records, by Col. William F. Fox* includes the following commands identified with Philadelphia: Cavalry—11th Regiment. Infantry—26th, 28th, 61st, 69th, 71st, 72d, 81st, 95th, 116th, 118th, 119th, 121st, 150th Regiments, 6th and 8th U. S. (Colored) Regiments. In qualifying his selections, Col. Fox says: "It is not claimed that these are *the* three hundred fighting regiments of the army, but that they are the three hundred fighting regiments which evidently did considerable fighting during the war."

An impartial study of the records made by a number of Philadelphia regiments not included in the above list must awaken a sense of regret that their achievements as effective fighters were not duly considered in the compilation thus set forth.

PHILADELPHIA REGIMENTS WHICH SUSTAINED A LOSS IN KILLED AND MORTALLY WOUNDED EXCEEDING TEN PER CENT. OF TOTAL ENROLMENT IN ACTIVE SERVICE.*

	Total		
61st Regiment	237	11.9	per cent.
69th "	178	10.3	" "
72d "	193	12.9	" "
81st "	208	12.9	" "
106th "	104	10.3	" "
118th "	141	11.0	" "
119th "	141	11.5	" "
121st "	109	12.5	" "
188th "	103	10.3	" "
150th "	112	10.3	" "

*"Regimental Losses in the American Civil War."

FORT DELAWARE AND FORT MIFFLIN

FORT DELAWARE, the chief defensive work for the Port of Philadelphia, was building, according to the original plan, in 1850.* At this time historic Fort Mifflin, within sight of the present Navy Yard at League Island, was the only point of protection afforded Philadelphia. During the Civil War a garrison was maintained at Fort Mifflin, where large supplies of ammunition were stored. Here, also, was the execution ground for deserters and "bounty jumpers."† Fort Delaware, located in mid-stream, upon an island of one hundred and twenty-five acres, is a massive structure, its ground plan forming an irregular pentagon. In 1861 its armament consisted of nineteen columbiads, fourteen eight-inch guns and a large number of smaller cannon. The range of gun-fire was three miles. This place was admirably adapted for a military prison camp. The post was placed in the command of Brig.-Gen. A. Shoepf, U. S. A. In April, 1861, a single company of seventy regular artillerymen guarded the fort.‡ On April 24th the Commonwealth Artillery, volunteers from Philadelphia, reinforced the garrison. A guard-boat, the Hero, was employed as a patrol. The space outside of the fort was gradually covered with barracks for the prisoners of war who were guarded here at a later time.

The weakness of the forts of the Delaware River and Bay was a cause of much anxiety to the civil and military authorities of Philadelphia and to the State Government, and while, in the course of the war, much was done to strengthen the armaments of old Fort Mifflin and Fort

---

*In 1851 the construction work on Fort Delaware was in charge of Capt. George B. McClellan, of the Corps of Engineers, U. S. A. He was subsequently sent by Jefferson Davis, Secretary of War, to study military science in the Crimea. He resigned from the army in 1857 to enter the field of railroad construction and operation. In 1859, when a member of the *Inquirer* staff visited the fort, it was far from completion, and no guns had been sent for emplacement. The work at that period was under charge of Captain John Newton, U. S. A.

† in the winter of 1863-64 the crew of the bark A. I. were imprisoned at Fort Mifflin. This vessel, laden with heavy cannon from the Navy Yard, shells from ordnance stores and powder from the Dupont Mills, was, it has always been thought, destined to voluntary capture by the Confederates. The ship was finally released by orders from Washington, but the mystery of the disloyalty in high places revealed in this strange transaction was never cleared up. The case of the owners against Provost Marshal Gen. George Cadwalader was only settled by a verdict for the defendant five years later. The story has been recorded in "A True Romance of the Rebellion," by A. A. Gen. Cyrus S. Haldeman.

‡It is stated in Sharf & Westcott's history that, on April 19th, 175 men proceeded to garrison Fort Delaware. The Commonwealth Artillery and Pennsylvania Guards left for Fort Delaware on the night of April 24th.
Fort Mifflin was garrisoned by the Richmond (Philadelphia) Artillery and the Kensington Rifles with a detachment of police on the morning of April 23d, 1861.

Delaware, these works were not made secure against the danger of reduction, especially by "foreign" fleets, of which there was, much of the time, good reason to be afraid. This reasonable apprehension was reflected in repeated representations from the Pennsylvania Legislature to the United States Government.*

Among the Philadelphia troops stationed at Fort Delaware, following those of the Commonwealth Artillery, were Segebarth's Marine Artillery, two companies, and also Independent Battery A, Heavy Artillery, Capt. Frank Schaffer. From March 1st, 1862, the battery was commanded by Capt. Stanislaus Mlotkowski. This command, enlisted for three years, was stationed here from September 19th, 1861, to the conclusion of the war, having been reorganized at the end of its enlistment, in September, 1864. It was finally discharged from service June 30th, 1865.

A battalion of four companies of the 157th Regiment, Lieut.-Col. Edmund T. Tiers, was stationed at the fort in December, 1862. Companies D, G and H, 3d Heavy Artillery, were stationed here in the early part of 1862.

Companies L and M, of the 2d Heavy Artillery (112th Regiment), were on duty at the fort two months, in the summer of 1863. The 196th Regiment, Penna. Vols. (5th Union League Regiment), was located here in November, 1864.

The 215th Regiment (9th Union League Regiment), Col. Francis Wister, served at the fort from June to August, 1865.

The prisoners were generally, if not altogether, conveyed to Fort Delaware through Philadelphia. The largest single party of Confederates arrived upon June 9th, 1863, and came from Vicksburg.† They numbered twenty-four hundred. As a rule, the prisoners, as well as their

---

* Joint Resolution approved February 26th, 1862 (Pamphlet Laws, 1862, page 550), relative to the defences of Delaware River and Bay.

WHEREAS, New exigencies have arisen to force upon the attention of Pennsylvania the unprotected condition of the eastern coast of the State. * * * * *

Be it Enacted, etc., That, moved by the deepest solicitude in view of the continued delay of the United States Government, we urge upon our Senators and Representatives in Congress the exertion of the most strenuous and immediate efforts to secure a system of adequate defence for the Delaware River and Bay. The Governor of this Commonwealth is requested to confer with the Governors of New Jersey and Delaware to secure co-operation of these States in the furtherance of this important object, alike indispensable to the interests of these States.

Again, by Joint Resolution of May 26th, 1862, the Pennsylvania Legislature urged insistently and impressively that the Government should provide such defensive works "as shall remove all apprehension from sudden invasion of either domestic or foreign foes." The State authorities offered to pledge the credit of the Commonwealth, if necessary, to the extent of one million dollars for this purpose.

† The siege of Vicksburg began upon May 18th. The surrender occurred on July 4th. These prisoners were captured during the intervening assaults conducted by Gen. U. S. Grant.

guards, were given a hearty meal at the refreshment saloons before taking steamers at the foot of Washington avenue. This kindly treatment was a surprise to the captives.

It was reported that on July 1st, 1863, the prisoners at the fort numbered three thousand five hundred and seventy-six. Prior to and during the battle of Gettysburg these prisoners confidently expected speedy release at the hands of the advancing Confederate army. Much anxiety existed, with regard to them, in Philadelphia, and the guards were greatly increased. During July and August, following the battle, in excess of nine thousand additional prisoners arrived at the fort. This accession necessitated more extensive hospital facilities. In September, 1863, a new hospital, containing six hundred beds, and in every way sanitary and comfortable, was opened for the use of both the prisoners and their guards, without distinction. As a story had been spread abroad that the prisoners were being ill-treated, a number of Confederate surgeons, confined at the fort, united in a communication to the Philadelphia newspapers denying the report and testifying to the very low death rate among the prisoners. At this time there were many among the prisoners who realized that the Confederacy was destined to fail and were glad to avail themselves of an opportunity to enlist in the Union army.*

One detachment of two hundred recruits from among the prisoners was taken to Baltimore and attached to a Federal cavalry regiment.

At a time when many thousand of our ill-fated Union volunteers were being starved to death at Salisbury, N. C.; Florence, S. C., and at Andersonville, Ga., the bill of fare served in the hospital, to Confederates, in the prison camp at Fort Delaware, was as follows:

Sunday:
> Breakfast—bread and butter, cold meat, coffee. Dinner—beef soup, potatoes, bread pudding. Supper—bread and butter, tea, stewed fruit.

Monday:
> Breakfast—bread and butter, hash, coffee. Dinner—Irish stew, bread. Supper—mush and milk, coffee.

Tuesday:
> Breakfast—fried mush and molasses, coffee. Dinner—soup, roast beef, vegetables, bread. Supper—cold beef, bread and butter, tea.

Wednesday:
> Breakfast—two eggs, bread and butter, coffee. Dinner—pork and beans, potatoes, bread pudding. Supper—mush and milk, bread and butter, tea.

Thursday:
> Breakfast—bread and butter, mush and molasses, coffee. Dinner—chicken soup, potatoes, bread and rice. Supper—cold beef, bread and butter, stewed fruit, tea.

---

* To the West Philadelphia police is due the credit of capturing the only lone invader, of the four dreaded northward forays of the Confederate hosts, who succeeded in entering this City save as a prisoner of war. On July 22d, 1864, George Bane, of Moseby's Cavalry, was picked up at Grays Ferry. Clad in his dusty uniform, he disclaimed any credit as a deserter. Having been left in the rear of Early's raiders, he "just thought he would like to see what Philadelphia looked like," so he toured northward. He was registered at Fort Delaware.

Friday:
> Breakfast—two eggs, bread and butter, coffee. Dinner—mutton stew, vegetables, bread. Supper—mush and milk, coffee.

Saturday:
> Breakfast—fried mush and molasses. Dinner—roast beef, potatoes, bread and butter, coffee. Supper—cold beef, bread and butter, coffee.

Two books, written by Confederate civilians, furnish interesting side-lights upon experiences of prisoners of war held in northern military prisons during the Rebellion period. The first of these, John A. Marshall, author, entitled "The American Bastile," was printed in Philadelphia in 1869, and purports to set forth the sufferings of about one hundred northern men arrested and immured upon various charges of treasonable conduct. Of the list five persons, Charles and Edward Ingersoll, William H. Winder, John Apple and John E. Robinson, were Philadelphians. The pages of this work are strongly tinctured with the wrath of the "unreconstructed" and cannot be regarded as impartial testimony. The other, entitled "United States Bonds, or Duress by Federal Authority," was penned by the Rev. Isaac W. K. Handy (father of the late Moses P. Handy, journalist), a minister of Portsmouth, Virginia. Dr. Handy's book deals entirely with prison life at Fort Delaware, where he was detained over a period of fifteen months, beginning July 21st, 1863. This volume* is a valuable and temperate journal of "inside" experiences at the great prison camp, dealing, as it does, with all fairness, concerning the routine of the prison and the incidents of which he was a witness, and testifying, in a modest way, to the religious influence he was able to exert over a large proportion of his fellow prisoners. The book contains the names of six hundred Confederates who were removed from Fort Delaware on August 20th, 1864, by transport to Morris Island, S. C., as a measure of reprisal.

Dr. Handy's estimate of the commandant at Fort Delaware is suggested in the following quotation (Page 272):

> "I was passing a sally-port when I heard my name called by the Commandant, and before I could cross over he said, 'You will be released in a few days.' As I was approaching General Schoepf (who was walking with General Jeff. Thompson) the Commandant said, pointing to me, 'He is a Rebel, too.' I inquired of General Thompson how he happened to be at Fort Delaware. 'He came here,' said General Schoepf, 'to be well treated. We know how to treat the soldier here, don't you think so?' I very cordially assented to this remark. The General continued, 'You must not abuse me when you leave here.' 'I shall not be disposed to do so,' I replied. 'You have always treated me with great kindness. I think you have the good feeling of all the prisoners.' "

It is further related that the famous guerilla chief had been invited to dine with the commanding officer and was visited, a little later, by his reverend acquaintance, who found him comfortably roomed and "seated in front of a good coal fire."

---

* A copy of Dr. Handy's book may be seen at the Philadelphia Library.

THE NAVY

PENNSYLVANIA was well represented in the navy register of the Civil War period. The most notable figure, native of Philadelphia, in the service was Capt. Charles Stewart. This fine old sea fighter was born when the British occupied Philadelphia in 1778. In 1862 he was promoted to the rank of rear admiral. For a long term he was the senior retired officer of the navy, and was only retired after seventy-one years of service. He died, at the age of ninety-one, in 1869. Other distinguished naval officers, natives of the State and all Philadelphians by birth or residence, were:

Rear Admirals James L. Lardner, David Dixon Porter, Sylvanus W. Godon, John A. Dahlgren, John C. Howell, Elie A. F. Lavalette, Clark H. Wells, James McQueen Forsyth, Lewis Wood Robinson, Henry Kuhn Hoff, Edward York McCauley, George Wallace Melville, John Marston, George Campbell Read.

Commodores William McKean, Joseph Beale, Edward Rees Thompson, Garrett J. Pendergrast, John C. Febiger, William Talbot Truxton, James H. Watmough, William J. McCluney, William Ronckendorf.

Captains Benjamin Franklin Garvin, George Cochran, Albert Carpenter Gorgas, William Rawle Brown, Henry S. Steelwagen, H. A. Adams.

Commander Abner Reed.

Lieut. Commanders A. Boyd Cummings, John Livingston, D. Borthwick, James Patterson Robertson, Clarke Merchant, Henry Douglas McEwan, George H. White.

Lieutenants Frank M. Ashton, Harrison Allen, Henry Clay McIlvaine.

U. S. MARINE CORPS.

Brig-Gen. Jacob Zeilin, Col. Charles Grymes McCawley, Col. James Forney, Major John C. Cash, Lieut. James Black Young.

Surgeons Edward F. Carson, Samuel H. Peltz and William Whelan.

NECROLOGY.

Of the above officers those who were killed or died during the war included:

George Campbell Read, U. S. N., Rear Admiral. Died August 22d, 1862.

Garrett J. Pendergrast, U. S. N., Commandant, U. S. Navy Yard at Philadelphia. Died November 7th, 1862.

Abner Reed, Commander. Died July 12th, 1863, from wounds received in action.

Edward F. Carson, Surgeon. Died July 22d, 1864.

Samuel H. Peltz, Surgeon. Died January 15th, 1865.

William Whelan, Surgeon, Chief of the Naval Medical Bureau. Died June, 1865.

UNITED STATES NAVY YARD, FOOT OF FEDERAL STREET, DELAWARE RIVER.
(Redrawn from a war time print.)

U. S. S. NEW IRONSIDES.

U. S. S. TUSCARORA.

WORK AT THE OLD PHILADELPHIA NAVY YARD AND IN PRIVATE SHIPYARDS

THE first United States Navy Yard at Philadelphia was located in the First Ward, just south of Washington avenue, and fronting upon the Delaware River. The entrance was on Federal street. It included, in an irregular quadrangle, eighteen acres, which were enclosed upon the land sides by a high brick wall. The principal buildings were two great ship-houses, moulding lofts, machine shops and barracks. A sectional floating dry-dock was also a part of the equipment. In the ante-bellum days the average number of men employed was eight hundred. These civilian employees very generally lived, with their families, in the neighborhood.

The Navy Yard occupied the site of the pre-Revolutionary Association Battery, where, at a later period, Joshua Humphries had a shipyard. This leading naval architect built the frigate United States here, in 1797, and in 1799, launched the famous frigate Philadelphia, which was presented to the Government by the State of Pennsylvania, a ship forever associated with the brilliant exploit of Stephen Decatur in the harbor of Tripoli.* The Government established the Navy Yard in the year 1800, and it became the chief building and outfitting plant of the Navy. The ship of the line North Carolina was launched here in 1820, and in 1837 the frigate Pennsylvania, the largest ship ever constructed, up to that date, was completed. The Vandalia, Dale, Germantown, Wyoming, Raritan, Wabash, Lancaster, Mississippi and Susquehanna were all built at this yard by Philadelphia workmen. The Princeton, fastest ship of her time, famous in the annals of the Kane Arctic Expedition, was turned out here. Of these Philadelphia ships the Pennsylvania, Germantown and Raritan were burned April 20th, 1861, at the Portsmouth, Va., Navy Yard.

The Civil War gave employment, at this Navy Yard, to a force of mechanics numbering, at times, 2,500 to 3,000 men. A remarkable achievement was the building of the sloop of war Tuscarora, which was constructed in fifty-eight days and launched on August 24th, 1861. This

---

*Joshua Humphries was appointed First Chief Naval Constructor, and was succeeded by his son, Samuel Humphries, who held the position to 1846.

feat had never been equalled in naval history. Upon December 7th this fine ship was taken to New York for her armament, and in a few months was busy hunting down Confederate privateers in European waters. Constant repair and outfitting work throughout the war left scant time for new construction. In February, 1861, the workmen were busy outfitting "Water Witch," Jamestown, Pawnee and St. Lawrence. In the course of the war, however, a number of notable sea fighters were built "of good Delaware white oak" at this historic yard. Of the forty United States warships upon the seas at the beginning at 1861 the Brooklyn, Crusader, Falmouth, Mohawk, Macedonian, Pawnee, Pocahontas, Powhattan, Sabine, St. Louis, Wyandotte and Supply were enrolled in the home squadron. The balance were in distant parts of the world, and as they gradually reported upon the coast they were assigned to the various navy yards for refitting and recruiting. The Philadelphia Navy Yard had, of these, its full quota.

Upon June 18th, 1862, the City Councils had undertaken a movement to induce the Government to establish a new navy yard at League Island. Eventually the city presented the site to the Navy Department, and the Government began the preparatory work. After removal to that location the old Navy Yard was sold at auction upon December 2d, 1875.*

The New Ironsides.

By far the most important vessel built at this port for war purposes and the most formidable ship of the navy was the New Ironsides, the contract for which was awarded to William Cramp & Sons. This fighting monster was launched, armed and in service eleven months after the work was commenced. She was a distinctly new type, having a displacement of 5,080 tons, ship-rigged, 1,800 horsepower, and carried sixteen 2,200 pounder Dahlgren guns and two Parrott rifled guns on pivots. The broadside weight was 1,100 pounds. Her wooden framing was the heaviest ever placed in a ship. She was sheathed with four-inch iron plates backed with fourteen inches of oak. The plating covered the ship from the spar deck to a line four feet below the water level. Length, 232 feet; beam, 57 feet 6 inches; draught, 15 feet. The New Ironsides, being intended for coastwise service, was barque rigged. The plates for the ship were made by Bailey, Brown & Co., of Pittsburgh, and at the Bristol (Pa.) Iron Works. The engines were built by S. V. Merrick & Sons, Philadelphia. This new type of sea fighter was launched upon May 10th, 1862, being christened by the venerable Com-

*Report of 1862, Gideon Welles, Secretary of the Navy:
In March, 1861, the navy had only 42 vessels in commission. Only 207 men were available as recruits at all of the naval stations. The entire number of seamen was 7,600. Upon December 1st, 1862, the navy had 427 vessels in commission and building, the average strength of the naval force for the year being about 20,000.

modore Charles Stewart, and soon afterward became the flagship of Admiral S. F. Du Pont.

In the course of the war the New Ironsides participated in twenty battles, including that of Fort Fisher, where she engaged the heavy Confederate batteries at short range, and through it all sustained but slight injuries. While laid up at League Island in 1866 she was destroyed by fire.

In other private shipyards hundreds of skilled mechanics were busy upon Government ship construction and repair throughout the war, and at the Neafie & Levy plant many of the engines were built for naval use. This firm built the boilers for the ponderous iron submarine battery which was constructed at Bordentown, N. J., by E. A. Stevens. A gunboat was also launched at Bordentown on March 15th, 1862, which is said to have been the first warship ever built in New Jersey. In the summer of 1862 two monitors, the Sangamon and Lehigh, were completed at Chester, Pa., by the firm of Reaney, Son & Archbold. This firm also built the steamer Wateree. Several gunboats were also built at Wilmington, Delaware.

SHIPS OF WAR BUILT AT THE PORT OF PHILADELPHIA DURING THE WAR.

AT THE U. S. NAVY YARD:

Sloop-of-War "Tuscarora." Launched August 24th, 1861. Machinery, S. V. Merrick & Sons.
Sloop-of-War "Juniata." Launched March 20th, 1862. Machinery, Pusey, Jones & Co., Wilmington.
Sloop-of-War "Swatara." 1862. Machinery, Washington.
Steamer "Miami." Launched Nov. 17th, 1861. Machinery, S. V. Merrick & Sons.
Sloop-of-War "Yantic." 1864. Machinery, S. V. Merrick & Sons.
Sloop-of-War "Monongahela." Launched July 10th, 1862. Machinery, S. V. Merrick & Sons.
Sloop-of-War "Shenandoah." Launched Dec. 8th, 1862. Machinery, S. V. Merrick & Sons.
Gunboat "Kansas." 1863.
Steam Frigate "Neshaminy." Launched Oct. 5th, 1865.
Steamer "Tacony." 1863. Machinery, Morris Towne & Co.
Ironclad double turret Monitor "Tonawanda." 1864. Machinery, S. V. Merrick & Sons.

IN PRIVATE SHIP YARDS:

Gunboat "Kittanning." Launched Oct. 1st, 1861. Simpson & Neill.
Gunboat "Itasca." Launched Oct. 1st, 1861. Hillman & Streaker. Machinery, J. P. Morris & Co.
Gunboat "Wissahickon." Launched Oct. 2d, 1861. John W. Lynn.
Gunboat "Sciota." Launched Oct. 15th, 1861. Jacob Birely. Machinery, J. P. Morris & Co.
Ironclad Frigate "New Ironsides." Launched May 10th, 1862. Wm. Cramp & Sons. Machinery, S. V. Merrick & Sons.
Transport "Wyalusing." Launched May 12th, 1863. Wm. Cramp & Sons. Machinery, Pusey, Jones & Co., Wilmington.
Gunboat "Pontiac." Launched May 16th, 1863. Birley, Hillman & Co.
Sloop-of-War "Chattanooga." Launched Oct. 13th, 1864. Wm. Cramp & Sons.

The downtown river wards furnished a large percentage of the men who formed the crews of the Philadelphia-built warships, and later, when drafts impended in some of these wards, this fact and the employment of thousands of men in the shipyards and machine shops along or near the Delaware River was urged as a valid reason for the deficiency found in filling their quotas of volunteers for the army.*

Numerous prize ships were brought to this port, and our ship owners lost many merchant vessels at the hands of Confederate privateers. The packet ship "Tonawanda," of the Cope Line, Capt. Theodore Julius, was captured upon October 9th, 1862, by the famous "Alabama" and bonded for $80,000. This bond was never enforced.†

WAR SERVICE OF OUR SHIPS

RECORDS of the war service of some of the Philadelphia-built vessels of the Civil War have been furnished for this book by the Navy Department. They are as follows:

"Itasca," gunboat, 507 tons. Served during Civil War with West Gulf Squadron; engaged in operations against Forts Jackson and St. Philip, April 20th-24th, 1862; actively engaged on Mississippi River, sharing in a number of captures; took prominent part in Battle of Mobile Bay, Aug. 5th, 1864. Sold in New York, November 30th, 1865.

"Juniata," sloop-of-war, 1240 tons. Commissioned December 4th, 1862; served with the North Atlantic Squadron, cruising on coast, and taking a number of prizes; took part in attacks on Fort Fisher, December 24th, 1864, and in January, 1865; cruised on coast of Brazil and west coast of Africa, 1866; out of commission, 1867-68. Sold, March 25th, 1891.

"Sciota," gunboat, 507 tons. Served with West Gulf Squadron; took part in engagement with Forts Jackson and St. Philip, April 24th, 1862; made the passage of Vicksburg batteries, June 28th, 1862; engaged Ram "Arkansas" as she passed the fleet; engaged batteries at Donaldsonville, October 4th, 1862; captured and destroyed a number of schooners in the Rio Grande; sunk in a collision in Mississippi River with

*At the close of the war the United States navy had in service 51,500 seamen and 7,500 officers. The total number killed during the war was 4,647 officers and men. The value of the captures made by the navy was estimated for ships and cargoes at $31,000,000. The sailors and marines enlisted from Pennsylvania during the war numbered 14,307.

†While the English-built Confederate privateers, largely manned by British crews, were capturing and burning American merchant ships, Philadelphia filled

"Antonia," July 14th, 1863; floated and repaired; co-operated with troops in Matagorda Bay, December 29th, 1863; engaged batteries in St. Bernard River, February 8th and 9th, 1864, capturing several schooners; sunk by torpedo in Mobile Bay, April 14th, 1865; raised and repaired. Sold at New York, October 25th, 1865.

"Shenandoah," sloop-of-war, 1375 tons. Served with North Atlantic Blockading Squadron; captured several blockade runners; took part in attacks on Fort Fisher, December 24th, 1864, January 13-15, 1865; cruised in search of the Confederate vessel "Florida," July, 1864; 1865, in South Atlantic Squadron; 1866-69, in Asiatic Squadron; 1870-71, at Boston Navy Yard; 1872-73, on the European Station; 1874-75, laid up in ordinary at New London; 1876-77, laid up in ordinary at New York; 1878-79, repairing at New York; 1880-82, flagship, South Atlantic Squadron; 1883, repairing at Boston; 1884-86, on Pacific Station. Sold July 30th, 1887.

"Wissahickon," gunboat, 507 tons. Commissioned November 25th, 1861; served with West Gulf and South Atlantic Blockading Squadrons; on active duty in Mississippi river, below Forts Jackson and St. Philip, passing forts with fleet, April 24th, 1862; engaged batteries at Grand Gulf, June 8th to 10th, 1862; passed batteries at Vicksburg, June 28th, 1862; engaged Ram "Arkansas," July 15th, 1862; engaged Genesis Point Battery, November 19th, 1862; engaged Fort McAllister, January 27th, 1863, and February 1st, 1863; assisted in the destruction of the Confederate Steamship "Nashville," February 28th, 1863; again attacked Fort McAllister, March 3d, 1863; engaged batteries on Cumming's Point, July 1st, 1863; engaged Fort Morgan, July 12th, 1863, and Fort Sumter, August 17th and 18th, 1863; took part in operations against Savannah, in December, 1864. Sold at auction in New York, October 25th, 1865.

"Miami," double-ender, 730 tons. Commissioned January 29th, 1862; took part in operations against Forts Jackson and St. Philip, April, 1862; actively employed in operations on Mississippi river in June and July, 1862; actively engaged with North Atlantic Blockading Squadron in 1863, at Plymouth, N. C., and in the Sounds of North Carolina, and engaged enemies' batteries in James river. Sold at auction in Philadelphia, August 10th, 1865.

"Monongahela," sloop-of-war, 1378 tons. Commissioned January 15th, 1863; served with West Gulf and North Atlantic Squadrons; actively engaged with Admiral Farragut's fleet at passage of Port Hudson, March 14th-15th and 20th, 1863; was Farragut's flagship from May 23d to June 22d, 1863; active operations against Port Hudson and Vicksburg, June 8th-23d, 1863; took part in Battle of Mobile Bay, August 5th, 1864; rammed the Ram "Tennessee;" 1865, with West Gulf Squadron and undergoing repairs; North Atlantic Squadron, 1866-67; carried by tidal wave on St. Croix Island, November 18th, 1867; repaired and placed in service again; used as a training ship for midshipmen, and for several years as a storeship; while serving as station ship at Guatanamo Bay, Cuba, this ship was totally destroyed by fire on the night of March 17th, 1908.

"Pontiac," double-ender. Put in commission July 7th, 1864; cruised in search of Confederate Steamship "Florida;" took part in joint expedition in Broad river, S. C., November 29th, 1864, and in operations against Savannah, December, 1864-January, 1865. Sold October 15th, 1867.

"Wyalusing," double-ender. Commissioned February 8th, 1864; took active part in action with Ram "Albemarle" and two steamers in Albemarle Sound, May 5th, 1864, running into and taking one of the steamers, the "Bombshell;" took part in bombardment and capture of Plymouth, N. C., October 30th, 1864; captured several blockade runners. Sold at Philadelphia, October 15th, 1867.

---

a ship—the barque *Achilles*—with food to the value of $30,000 for the relief of the starving operatives of British mills. New York City sent the ship *George Griswold* with supplies to the same sufferers. Soon afterward this ship was captured by the privateer *Georgia* and bonded for $100,000.

THE NAVAL HOSPITAL AND HOME

THE Naval Home and Hospital, maintained at Philadelphia by the United States Government, at Gray's Ferry avenue and Bainbridge street, was established in 1826. It occupies ground once the homestead of a noted Tory of the Revolution, James Pemberton. For seven years, dating from 1838, the United States Naval Academy was located here. The property was paid for by an assessment of twenty cents per capita upon the sailors of the American Navy and Merchant Marine. The beautiful grounds include twenty-five acres. The main building, constructed in 1831, is of marble, three stories high and three hundred and eighty feet long. It is flanked by the Governor's and Surgeon's residences and a number of lesser structures. This attractive "snug harbor" was crowded throughout the Civil War with wounded, sick and retired officers and sailors from the war fleets of the National Navy.

Fifty years after the opening of the Civil War veterans who fought under Farragut, Porter, Du Pont and other great Admirals of that period were still living at the Naval Home. The present average number of occupied rooms in the Naval Home is eighty-six.

THE REFRESHMENT SALOON MOVEMENT IN SOUTHWARK

WHEN, in the spring of 1861, the troops from New England, New York State and New Jersey began to move southward, the one available rail route brought them to Tacony or Camden, N. J., from which steamboats conveyed them to the foot of Washington avenue, Philadelphia, where trains of the Philadelphia, Wilmington and Baltimore Railroad awaited them. From the beginning of this movement of hurrying soldiery, the patriotic families living in the vicinity of the navy yard offered refreshments to the extent of their limited abilities. The evident need of systematic handling of food and coffee led Barzilai S. Brown, a grocer and fruit dealer, to act as a medium of distribution, and this presently resulted in the lease of a small boat-shop owned by James Crim, upon Swanson street, below Washington avenue, as a "free refreshment saloon for soldiers." This was at first referred to as "Brown's," being so called in letters written to their home newspapers by some grateful volunteers. The enterprise was organized, however, upon May 27th, 1861, as the "Union Volunteer Refreshment Saloon," and under that title was maintained until December 1st, 1865.

The Committee was composed of the following persons:

Arad Barrows, Chairman; J. B. Wade, Secretary; B. S. Brown, Treasurer; J. T. Williams, Steward; Dr. E. Ward, Surgeon; Isaac B. Smith, Sr., Erasmus W. Cooper, John W. Hicks, George Flomerfelt, John Krider, Sr., Isaac B. Smith, Jr., Charles B. Grieves, James McGlathery, John B. Smith, D. L. Flanagan, Chris. Powell, Capt. W. S. Mason, Curtis Myers, Chas. M. Clampitt, Richard Sharp, James Carroll, Robert R. Corson, Samuel B. Fales, John T. Wilson, Charles N. Young, John Savery, L. M. J. Lemmens, Chas. H. Kingston, Mrs. Mary Grover, Mrs. Hannah P. Smith, Mrs. Priscilla Grover, Mrs. Margaret Boyer, Mrs. Eliza J. Smith, Mrs. Mary A. Cassedy, Mrs. Elizabeth Horton, Miss Annie B. Grover, Miss Mary D. Grover, Mrs. Helen B. Barrows, Mrs. Mary L. Field, Mrs. Annie A. Elkinton, Mrs. Martha V. R. Ward, Mrs. Eliza A. Helmbold, Mrs. Mary Green, Mrs. Emily Mason, Miss Martha B. Krider, Mrs. Mary Davis Wade, Miss Sarah L. Holland, Miss Amanda M. Lee, Miss Catharine Baily, Miss Annie L. Field, Mrs. Eleanor J. Lowry, Mrs. Sarah J. Flemington, Mrs. Kate B. Anderson, Mrs. Eliza G. Plummer, Mrs. Hannah F. Baily, Mrs. Mary Lee.

Buildings were gradually added, as funds permitted, until full regiments were promptly provided with washing facilities and bountiful meals at the hands of the hospitable men, women and maids of old Southwark. The meals usually served consisted of beef, ham, bread and butter, sweet and white potatoes, pickles, tea and coffee and sometimes cake or pie. Seven barrels of coffee and 15,000 cooked rations were often made in one day. The hungry soldiers of well-filled regiments from the northeastern states had a way of swarming from the transfer boats at Washington street wharf at most inconvenient hours, but the good people of Southwark were always ready for them. The Second Maine Infantry, for instance, arrived at one o'clock upon the morning of May 31st, and found the hot coffee, beef and bread all ready for them, much to their surprise and delight, as had the 8th and 9th New York Regiments and Garibaldi Legion, which had preceded them.

Facilities were provided in the shape of writing paper and envelopes, enabling soldiers to write home. All letters were stamped, free of cost to the writers, and mailed by their entertainers. Some of these old envelopes bear the "frank" of Congressman Leonard Myers. The gratitude of volunteers for the splendid treatment thus given them was expressed in thousands of these hurried missives, many of which were printed in distant newspapers, and the fame of patriotic Philadelphia soon spread all over the East. In September, 1861, the needs of sick and wounded soldiers left by their commands, many of them being cared for in private homes, led to the establishment of a small hospital upon the east side of Swanson street, close to the north wall of the navy yard. This modest hospital was placed by the Committee in charge of Dr. Elias Ward. It contained, at first, but fifteen beds, and was the first military hospital opened in the city. Later, more roomy quarters were occupied upon the opposite or west side of Swanson street. Dr. Ward continued at the post of duty throughout the war, and it was due to his efforts that this hospital, which ministered to thousands of sick and wounded soldiers, was recognized as a regular Government establishment. He was also actively interested with others in the purchase of a burial lot for such soldiers as died here and were not claimed by relatives.

A "Soldiers' Guide," published by Robert R. Corson, State Military Agent, was distributed freely by the Committee of the Union Volunteer Refreshment Saloon. In contained local addresses of army officials of the several departments, places of interest, railroad stations and time-tables and similar information.

Out upon Washington avenue, at the foot of a lofty flagstaff a small cannon was placed, covered when not in use, by a box embellished with patriotic devices. When a troop train left Jersey City a telegram was sent to the "Union" and the gun was fired to notify the house-wives, often busy at their own domestic cooking, to hurry to the big sheds and make ready. It was the business of the small boys, full of the ardor of the time, to watch up river for the coming of the boats. When they were seen, thronging with hungry men, every youngster rushed headlong up the tracks and the second gun was fired. This lusty little cannon was credited by contemporary newspapers with a remarkable record. Cast at the Springfield Armory, it went with the American Army to Mexico, was captured by the Mexicans at Vera Cruz, remounted at the ancient fortress of San Juan d'Ulloa, recaptured from a Mexican gunboat, sent to Philadelphia, sunk upon the receiving ship *Union* in the Delaware River, recovered and placed among the curios of the navy yard. When the war began it was used for the defence of the railroad bridge at Perryville, and was finally loaned to the Committee of the Union Volunteer Refreshment Saloon. It was popularly dubbed, at this period of its service, "Fort Brown." It was the first, it is claimed, to thunder out the news of the surrender of Gen. Lee, upon the night of April 9th, 1865. It is now preserved among the priceless trophies of Capt. Philip R. Schuyler Post, No. 51, G. A. R., in this city.

"Fort Brown"

PASSING REGIMENTS FROM THE NORTH AND EAST CONSTANTLY ARRIVED AT THE FOOT OF WASHINGTON AVENUE.
(From a war time lithograph.)

UNION VOLUNTEER REFRESHMENT SALOON.   A DAILY SCENE.

(From a war time lithograph.)

The first of the despatches from the approaching commands came upon the morning of May 27th, 1861, followed, in due time, by the 8th New York Volunteer Infantry, Col. Blencker's sturdy German command, and the next day, along with the 2d and 9th New Yorkers, the stunning Garibaldi Regiment came, eleven hundred strong, clad in their picturesque Italian uniforms. Close behind them were the heavy, grim regiments of Maine, contrasting with Col. Cameron's 79th New York Highlanders, more than a thousand of them, their kilted legs swinging to the drone of bag-pipes. Those were gloriously inspiring days down in old Southwark, and there was plenty of work in the old navy yard and outside among the soldiers to help in saving the nation. All through June and July the troops poured through the city, infantry, cavalry and artillery, hussars, zouaves and voltigeurs; whole brigades of less showy but quite as resolute regiments in the plain blue of the citizen volunteers. In July the "Union" fed 22,000 men, but that was light work compared with later records. The newspapers at first printed glowing columns in description of favorite regiments, but as time wore along the eye and mind tired of the constant pageant. Through the hot summer days and nights the men and women in the kitchens and dining sheds of the "Union," many of them of advanced age, assisted by their aides, worked unceasingly. At this time the three-months' regiments were returning, adding greatly to the almost daily demands upon the Committee and its workers.

In the first eighteen months of its operation the "Union" supplied meals to two hundred and twenty-four regiments, having an average of nine hundred men each.

In February, 1863, a large building was added to the "Union" establishment, thus increasing the dining facilities and providing hospital space upon the second floor. The work and materials for this structure were nearly all contributed by a large number of business concerns and individuals.

In the autumn of 1863 the captured Confederate Ram Atlanta was loaned to the Union Committee and exhibited to the public at the foot of Washington avenue, the admission charge adding greatly to the funds of the saloon.*

It is not generally recorded in the many eulogies of the work performed at the "Union," that at various times its Committee sent clothing, food and hospital supplies to soldiers in distant parts of the country. For instance, ten large packing boxes were filled and shipped to sick and wounded men at Rolla, Missouri, and supplies were forwarded to Anna-

---

* The Ram Atlanta was converted into an ironclad from an English blockade runner named the Fingal. This work was done at Savannah at a reported cost of $1,500,000, the money, it was stated at the time, having been derived from the sale of jewelry by Southern ladies. The Atlanta was captured in fifteen minutes, with but five shots, by the U. S. Monitor Weehawken, in the Savannah River, upon June 17th, 1863. This craft was afterward repaired at the navy yard and sent out in the following February as a war ship of the United States.

polis, Maryland, for the relief of destitute and suffering soldiers exchanged from Belle Isle, Richmond.*

Religious services were usually held on Sunday afternoons at the refreshment saloons, being attended by large numbers of citizens and soldiers. Music was provided by regimental bands and by the choirs from downtown churches.

Perhaps the most trying period of the war to citizens generally was that immediately preceding the battle of Gettysburg. Under the stress of great anxiety the ladies of the "Union" addressed the soldiers who had returned to their homes all over the East in the following words:

"The ladies of the Union Volunteer Refreshment Committee, on many a wintry night, when they have waited to welcome, with kind words, the nation's defenders, and to serve food to revive their weary frames, have been repaid for their labor by the grateful thanks and 'God bless you!' of the noble patriots, and these soldiers have, without exception, exclaimed, 'If ever Philadelphia needs defenders she will find them in the men whom their kindness has succored!' Ever have the ladies replied, 'If the hour of danger ever threatens we will remember your promise.' Soldiers, that hour has come. Shall they not find you to have forgotten? Shall they welcome you again to our city as the defenders of their homes and fire-sides, or shall they wait in vain?"

One of the first of the regiments to whom this appeal was made to come to the defence was the famous New York "Seventh." With the retreat of Gen. Lee's shattered army from Pennsylvania soil after the battle of Gettysburg, the danger was soon forgotten in the care of the thousands of the wounded brought to the city from that scene of carnage.

THE "COOPER SHOP."

The Cooper Shop Volunteer Refreshment Saloon was established upon May 26th, 1861, its projectors having taken for the purpose buildings upon Otsego street, south of Washington avenue, previously used as a cooperage by the firm of Cooper & Pearce. Emulating its neighbor, the "Union," its Committee was actively engaged from the date of its opening in the patriotic work of the time as it came, day by day, to their hands. The stirring scenes witnessed at the one saloon were equally experienced at the other.

Those active in this enterprise were:

William M. Cooper, H. W. Pearce, A. M. Simpson, W. R. S. Cooper, Jacob Plant, Walter R. Mellon, A. S. Simpson, C. V. Fort, William Morrison, Samuel W. Nickels, Philip Fitzpatrick, T. H. Rice, William M. Maull, R. H. Ransley, L. B. M. Dolby, William H. Dennis, L. W. Thornton, T. L. Coward, C. L. Wilson, R. G. Simpson, Isaac Plant, James Toomey, H. H. Webb, William Sprowle, Henry Dubosq, G. R. Birch, Christopher Jacoby, James Tosing, E. S. Cooper, Joseph Coward, J. T. Packer, Dr. A. Nebinger, R. Nebinger, Capt. A. H. Cain,

*In 1862 much-prized certificates were given to children for picking lint. So great was the zeal of the boys and girls in the schools that the Secretary of the United States Sanitary Commission sent out word late in the year that no more lint could be accepted.

Capt. R. H. Hoffner, Joseph E. Sass, E. J. Herrity, Rev. Joseph Perry, Mrs. William M. Cooper, Mrs. Sarah Ewing, Mrs. Catharine Vansdale, Mrs. Susan Turner, Miss Catharine Alexander, Mrs. Grace Nickels, Mrs. Elizabeth Vansdale, Mrs. Jane Coward, Mrs. Sarah Mellon, Mrs. Mary Plant, Mrs. Capt. Thos. Watson, Mrs. E. Deaney, Mrs. M. Haines, Miss C. T. Cooper, Miss E. Whetstone, Mrs. Louise P. Turnbull.

The Cooper Shop Hospital was in charge of Dr. Andrew Nebinger, who with his volunteer staff continued in service throughout the war, ministering to the thousands of sick and wounded brought here in that trying period.

From the funds available the Committee purchased a burial lot at Mt. Moriah Cemetery. In its report of May 10th, 1864, are found the names of a General Committee of citizens, which includes many patriotic persons not specified in the above list of the managers.

The two saloons were in constant receipt of large quantities of supplies, coming not only from merchants and other individuals but from special relief organizations formed for the purpose in the surrounding counties of Pennsylvania and New Jersey. In the later years of the war successful fairs were held in the refreshment buildings in order to raise money.

Among those who came hungry and departed satisfied were 15,000 Southern refugees and freedmen and not a few Confederate prisoners.

There is a touch of grim humor in an announcement printed in the "Fair Record" issued by the managers of the "Union" in which the public is informed that visitors to the fair (then in progress) would see some of the large numbers of Confederates from Vicksburg, then being guarded through the city en route to Fort Delaware. These unfortunates were, however, well fed upon reaching the ever-bountiful refreshment saloons.

Among the great and constant inflow of contributed supplies for the refreshment saloons were large numbers of Bibles, prayer books and tracts from the Presbyterian Board of Publication and daily papers from the several newspaper offices of the city.

Near the close of the war Messrs. William Welsh, Frederick Fraley and J. G. Rosengarten constituted the active committee of an organization entitled "An Association to Procure Employment for Rebel Deserters who have taken the Oath of Allegiance to the United States." For this purpose the sum of $2,875.00 was raised.

Green meal tickets to be presented at the Union Volunteer Refreshment Saloon were issued to many of these refugees, but the larger part of the fund was finally turned over to the latter institution.

There was rivalry between the two refreshment saloons, but it was the kindly competition of devoted men and women actuated by the highest of motives. The stories of the two are inseparable. Neither sought nor had Government, State or City aid; each had its hospital annex; each endured to the end of the war. The money outlay of the "Union" amounted to about $100,000, and that of the "Cooper Shop" was about $70,000. The "Union" fed nearly 900,000 soldiers; the "Cooper Shop" provided meals for 400,000 men. Not less than 20,000 soldiers were cared for in the two hospitals.

Of the ladies who served faithfully several died during the war, and others never recovered from the exhaustion incident to the work.

With impressive ceremonies at the Academy of Music the two refreshment saloons were closed upon August 28th, 1865, but it is stated by Mr. Samuel B. Fales that the latter institution was reopened and supplied meals to some 30,000 more returning soldiers before finally ending its splendid work upon the following 1st of December.

Thirty-five years after the close of the war, during the memorable 33d Annual National Encampment of the Grand Army of the Republic, in Philadelphia, thirty survivors of the Refreshment Saloon workers were the honored guests of the Executive Committee. But few of them now remain to rehearse the oft-told story of how Philadelphia fed the soldiers of the Union.

A SOLDIER BOY'S LETTER.

Washington, June 1, 1863.

"DEAR PARENTS:—I will endeavor to give you a faint description of our reception in Philadelphia, but I know that my pen cannot half do justice to the subject, but I do know that the remembrance of it will live in the hearts of our brave artillery boys as long as they are able to train a gun or draw a sword in the defence of their country. As soon as we reached the city we marched to the dining saloon, about ten or fifteen rods from the ferry. As soon as we got there we entered the wash-room, a room large enough to accommodate sixty or seventy men to wash at a time. Then we were marched into a splendid hall, with room enough to feed five hundred men at a time. There were gentlemen to wait on us, and they would come around and ask if we had plenty and urge us to eat more. We had nice white bread, beautiful butter, cold boiled ham, cheese, coffee, with plenty of milk and sugar. After we had eaten our fill, which was considerable, for we had eaten nothing since morning, we returned to the streets. Our knapsacks on the sidewalk were left without a guard, but they were almost covered with little children who were watching to see that no one disturbed them. One little fellow found a tin canister and he was hunting around from rank to rank until he found the owner. We were allowed a little time to rest, during which little girls in white went all around through the ranks giving the men flowers and saying kind things to them. It seemed that the people could not do us enough honor. One little girl, about ten years old, came up to me and gave me a half-blown rose, and stayed and talked with me until we started, and then she put her little face up for a kiss with as much confidence as she would to a brother. I never saw so many handsome girls in my life. We had nearly a mile and a half to march, and of all the sights I ever saw, that march beats them all. The sidewalk on each side was lined with old men and matrons, young men and maidens, girls and boys, and every one was trying to see who could shake the most soldiers by the hand. It was the very best class of people who were out to meet us. In some places the streets were completely blocked with them. It was like so many people bidding good-bye to their own sons and brothers, Anyone who thinks there is any lack of support for the war has only to march through Philadelphia.

(Signed) FOSTER,
Company B."

THE COOPER SHOP SOLDIERS HOME AND THE SOLDIERS HOME IN THE CITY OF PHILADELPHIA

THROUGHOUT the war Philadelphia was constantly thronged with soldiers who had been discharged from the army, many of them destitute and helpless. This condition became more serious as the struggle of the Union was prolonged. Soldiers from other States were often the victims of robbery and violence. It was to remedy, in some degree, this evil that the Cooper Shop Volunteer Refreshment Committee established a retreat at Race and Crown streets, called the "Cooper Shop Soldiers Home." This was opened upon December 22d, 1863. The buildings occupied had formerly been used as a Government hospital, and were the property of the city. The principal structure was the old Pennington residence. The beneficiaries of this home were "soldiers and sailors who had been honorably discharged." This is said to have been the first institution of its kind established in the United States.

BOARD OF OFFICERS.

President, Dr. Ellerslie Wallace; Vice-President, Wm. M. Cooper; Treasurer, Wm. Struthers; Secretaries, E. S. Hall and George R. Birch.

Managers—Robert P. King, Dr. Andrew Nebinger, H. W. Pearce, H. R. Warriner, Thos. H. Rice, Caleb Cope, John F. Lewis, Philip Fitzpatrick, William M. Maull, R. H. Ransley.

---

*This boyish message home was written by Foster Dealing, of the 10th New York Heavy Artillery. It was printed in the *Jefferson County News* (N. Y.), in June, 1863. The writer was living when this book was published.

Lady Managers—Mrs. M. C. Grier, President; Miss Anna M. Ross,* Vice-President; Mrs. Wm. Struthers, Mrs. J. Horner, Mrs. R. P. King, Mrs. C. Gibbons, Mrs. J. W. Paul, Mrs. H. Brooks, Mrs. T. H. Powers, Mrs. E. A. Souder, Mrs. W. S. Boyd, Mrs. W. D. Bispham, Mrs. J. Floyd, Mrs. D. Haddock, Mrs. H. Davids, Mrs. Dr. Wallace, Mrs. J. Eckel, Mrs. C. S. Rutter, Mrs. E. S. Hall, Mrs. Dr. Knorr, Mrs. B. H. Moore, Mrs. Dr. Spooner, Mrs. T. Budd, Mrs. W. Gillespie, Miss E. Emslie.

"The Soldiers Home in the City of Philadelphia" was incorporated upon April 9th, 1864. This charter resulted in the merger of two "Soldiers' Home" movements.

In furtherance of the purpose by the incorporators to establish the "Home" upon a permanent basis, a great fair was held at the Academy of Music, opening October 23d, 1865. This resulted in a profit of $107,166.00. Many public and private donations considerably increased this amount.

In the spring of 1866 the managers secured from the Legislature the large new State Arsenal building at the southeast corner of Sixteenth and Filbert streets for their purposes. This structure had been used by the Government as a convalescents' hospital. It was three floors high and built of pressed brick. In 1866 the soldier occupants numbered an average of about two hundred. A school for the instruction of maimed inmates in avocational education and a hospital were the leading features.†

The Soldiers Home continued at this site until June 11th, 1872. Following the closing of the Soldiers Home the Board of Managers turned its attention to the care of soldiers' sons. A house at 3947 Market street was taken for this purpose. Upon December 22d, 1873, this establishment was closed and the thirty-five inmates were transferred to the Educational Home for Boys, together with the sum of $36,000 for their maintenance and education covering a period of ten years, the beneficiaries being placed in care of the Lincoln Institution upon arriving at the age of twelve years. A number of girls were also provided for through an arrangement with the West Philadelphia Home, at Forty-first and Baring streets. Upon May 12th, 1884, the managers of the Soldiers Home dedicated a Soldiers Monument at Mount Moriah Cemetery, upon the lot owned by the Association, which contains the graves of sixty soldiers. The corporation was finally dissolved in 1886. The funds

*The death of the devoted worker for the creation of this Home, Miss Anna M. Ross, due to her unremitting efforts at the Refreshment Saloon, is still a sad memory with the few survivors among her associates. Post 94, G. A. R., Department of Pennsylvania, bears the name of this martyr to duty, and a city park in the Forty-third Ward also perpetuates her memory. Her grave is in Monument Cemetery.

†Among the humbler occupations adopted by the returned soldiers after the close of the war was that of messengers. The men employed by the "Soldiers' City Messenger Company" wore red military caps. The charge was one cent per block.

and burial lot were transferred to the Pennsylvania Commandery of the Loyal Legion July 2d, 1889.

SOLDIERS HOME, SOUTHEAST CORNER SIXTEENTH AND FILBERT STREETS.

BOARD OF OFFICERS.

President—Ellerslie Wallace, M. D.;* Vice-President—Andrew Nebinger, M. D.; Recording Secretary and Treasurer—E. S. Hall; Corresponding Secretary—H. R. Warriner.

Managers—Wm. Struthers, Robert P. King, John R. Baker, James C. Hand, Daniel Haddock, Jr., Jas. G. Hardie, H. C. Howell, George Trott, A. H. Franciscus, C. L. Desauque, W. H. Kern, E. C. Knight, R. H. Ransley, E. A. Souder, S. S. White, Charles J. Stille, Henry D. Moore, E. Tracy, Jos. Jeanes, Robert M. Lewis.

Surgeon—J. A. McArthur, M. D.; Assistant Surgeon—Walter W. Wilson; Steward—Capt. S. V. Odekirk; Matron—Mrs. Catharine Sprigman.

BOARD OF LADY VISITORS.

President—Mrs. Daniel Haddock, Jr.; Vice-President—Mrs. Robert P. King; Treasurer—Mrs. James C. Hand; Recording Secretary—Mrs. H. C. Townsend; Corresponding Secretary—Miss E. P. Eakin; Mrs. Jno. Carrow, Mrs. M. M. Hallowell, Mrs. R. G. Chase, Mrs. R. R. Corson, Mrs. W. Allison, Mrs. T. McCaulay, Miss E. Elmslie, Miss M. Hardie, Miss R. Wetherill, Mrs. Jas. G. Hardie, Mrs. Chas. S. Ogden, Mrs. Elliston Perot, Mrs. S. P. Godwin, Mrs. J. Haseltine, Mrs. T. M. Perot, Mrs. E. S. Field, Mrs. A. E. Jones, Mrs. M. Kelley, Miss A. M. Peters.

BEFORE ANTIETAM

WITH the departure of the new regiments, which had been in camp at the beginning of September, 1862, the city lost much of its martial stir, but recruiting, in order to fill the quota, continued active. Several regiments were still in a formative condition. On September 8th twenty-four large Sibley tents were placed in Independence Square, extending from the rear entrance of the sacred "Cradle of Liberty" along either side of the walk to Walnut street. That

---

*From Report of the Managers, Soldiers' Home, Sixteenth and Filbert streets, Philadelphia, 1867. P. (3).

evening the scene presented was one never to be forgotten. Myriad lights were festooned from the beautiful old trees and among the tents. Birgfeld's famous band rendered inspiring patriotic music, but far louder was the roar of the drums calling for recruits. Crowds surged through this exciting, tumultuous "Midway of War" and in every tent officers were busy writing down the names of volunteers. Old men and young, inspired by the impending need of defence, hurried to enroll. Within three days 295 recruits were enlisted at this Camp Independence, 251 of them going to regiments already in the field. Never since the reading of the "Declaration" had these hallowed acres witnessed such a wonderful scene.

From day to day the crowds hung about the bulletin boards. From the fields of Cedar Mountain, Kelly's Ford, Bristoe, the second Bull Run and Chantilly the guns of the determined enemy were roaring northward, McClellan's brigades disputing the pathway, but in vain. On the 11th of September Governor Curtin telegraphed to Mayor Henry: "Stir up your population to-night, form them into companies, send us 20,000 to-morrow."* The call of the War Mayor of Philadelphia was instant. He summoned the whole citizenship to rally at the precincts of the twenty-five wards, and act for the defence of the State and city. The editorials of morning papers added to the overwhelming excitement. The 12th brought a furious drenching storm, but everywhere were little groups of those who had responded, ready and willing, but lacking in leadership. It was stated that comparatively few of those thus gathered actually left the city. In the workshops better progress was made. At Baldwin's, the alarm bell rang at nine o'clock A. M., and within an hour two companies were marching to Independence Hall, the men carrying their dinner pails. At the Whitney Car Works, at the establishments of Bement & Dougherty, Mallack & Co., Furbish & Gates and Moore & Co. companies were quickly gathered. A fully equipped company reported from the works of William Sellers & Co. Employers generally agreed to continue the wages of their men during their absence in the field.

Companies and squads gathered, from the outlying districts and from the centers of banking, around the depot of the Pennsylvania Railroad Company, some in uniforms and some in overalls, some armed and others empty-handed, some sworn to service in due form, but others free of this formality, and so the trains were filled and sent speeding to help the Government in the saving of the capital city, and while this outpouring still progressed and the city sat sleepless, the bulletins proclaimed the battles of South Mountain and Antietam. Records showed that in seventeen months the old local militia had furnished more than 2,000 men, enlisted for three years, and nearly 400 officers. A new

*An enrollment of the City of Philadelphia made on September 14th, 1862, showed a total of 106,806 persons liable to military duty, including 29,194 already in the army service and 1,744 sailors and marines. Scharff and Westcott, Vol. I.

OFFICES OF JAY COOKE & CO., adjoining the Girard Bank.

UNITED STATES MINT.

1. THE NEW POST OFFICE.   2. BANK OF PENNSYLVANIA.
Both used as barracks and headquarters of the Provost.

militia had been created, and this body stood ready to respond at any time to the call of the Governor of the Commonwealth, for service within the State or beyond the borders. The authority of the Governor to call upon these troops was based upon the following provisions of the State military law:

"SECTION 1.—The militia of this Commonwealth may be called into service by the Governor thereof in case of a rebellion or an actual or threatened invasion of this or any neighboring State, but no part thereof shall be detained in service at any time longer than three months, under the mere requisition of the Governor, without the direction of the President of the United States.
"SECTION 2.—Whenever any part of the militia of the Commonwealth shall be required for the public service by the President of the United States, if no particular description of troops shall have been required, the Governor shall detach the number of men demanded in such proportions of the several descriptions as he may think proper."

Major-Gen. A. J. Pleasonton telegraphed to Governor Curtin, in response to his urgent call for troops to defend the State borders, offering 5,000 men of the Home Guard organization. Considerable confusion resulted from the announcement from Harrisburg that troops would be accepted by companies only, these to be formed into regiments and brigades after reporting at the State Capital.

Through the active efforts of the Committee on City Defence 23 companies, numbering nearly 2,000 men, were sent to Harrisburg within forty-eight hours, and within seventy-two hours 4,000 men had been sent. The 1st Regiment (Gray Reserves) and 2d Regiment (Blue Reserves) reached Harrisburg on the 15th and were sent on to Chambersburg. The hastily formed companies, largely composed of working men, were furnished with overcoats and other items of equipment from the supply in the hands of the Committee of Defence.

From the nearly two hundred and fifty companies gathered at Harrisburg from every part of the State a number of provisional regiments were hastily formed. The Gray Reserves became the "7th Regiment;" the second Blue Reserves became the "8th Regiment," the Philadelphia companies of Captains Birney, Anderson, Binder, Price, Kemouth, Levering, Johns, Keen, Corrie, Horn and Heisler were formed as the "9th Regiment." Those of Captains Smith, James, Marshall, Hartranft, Steele and Taylor became part of the "20th Regiment." The companies of Captains Rockafellow, Flynn, Murphy and Claghorn were attached to the "21st Regiment." As rapidly as these organizations were perfected the troops were pushed southward to, and in many cases beyond, the southern boundary of the State.* A large number of companies were yet to be grouped into regiments when the occasion for their services passed, and within a few days nearly all of the militia organizations and emergency volunteers were returned to their homes. The number of

---

*In a subsequent report Governor Curtin estimated that he had 15,000 men at Harrisburg and Boonsboro, 10,000 at Greencastle and 25,000 more on the way.

men who went from Philadelphia to Harrisburg in response to the call of the Governor was placed by the newspapers at 6,197. To this enumeration should be added the 3d Regiment, Reserve Corps (militia) under Col. C. M. Eakin (five companies), which had been sent to Camp Brandywine, DuPont powder works, Delaware. This brief, but instructive, experience illustrated the inadequacy of the military machinery of the State. It also stirred up the city fathers. On September 12th, despite the protests of an opposition element, Councils had conferred upon the Mayor extraordinary powers and had voted the sum of $500,000 for the further equipment of local soldiery. Companies were then forming in all sections of the city, but these were not called upon for service at that time.*

PHILADELPHIA TROOPS, PENNSYLVANIA EMERGENCY MILITIA OF 1862

SEVENTH REGIMENT, INFANTRY.

COLONEL NAPOLEON B. KNEASS.

1,100 Officers and Men.

Formed September 12th—15th, 1862, from the 1st Regiment, Reserve Brigade, First Division, Pennsylvania Militia. 1st Regiment (Gray Reserves.) Discharged September 26th, 1862. (Company L was a Light Battery commanded by Captain Isaac Starr, Jr.)†

EIGHTH REGIMENT, INFANTRY.

COLONEL ALFRED DAY.

800 Officers and Men.

Formed September 12th, 1862, from the 4th Regiment, Reserve Brigade, First Division, Philadelphia Militia. (Second Blue Reserves.) Discharged September 26th, 1862.

NINTH REGIMENT, INFANTRY.

COLONEL JOHN NEWKUMET.

650 Officers and Men.

Organized September 12th, 1862. Discharged September 26th, 1862.

*On September 25th, 1912, a semi-centennial celebration was held at Altoona, Pa., to commemorate the conference there of the War Governors of the loyal States, upon invitation of Governor Andrew G. Curtin, for the purpose of sustaining President Lincoln with money and troops.

†Starr's Battery was recruited upon the old "Union Artillery." It became Frishmuth's Battery in 1863.

TWENTIETH REGIMENT, INFANTRY.
COLONEL WILLIAM B. THOMAS.
650 Officers and Men.

Formed the 3d Regiment, Home Guard Brigade, September 18th, 1862. Philadelphia Companies A, B, C, D, E, F and K. Discharged September 27th-30th, 1862.*

TWENTY-FIRST REGIMENT, INFANTRY.
COLONEL ALEXANDER MURPHY.
400 Officers and Men.

Philadelphia Companies, A, B, C, F and G, formed September 12th to 15th, 1862. Company A was formed by the Washington Grays. Discharged September 24th to 30th, 1862.

TWENTY-FIFTH REGIMENT, INFANTRY.
COLONEL CONSTANT M. EAKIN.
300 Officers and Men.

Formed from the 2nd Regiment, Reserve Brigade, First Division, Pennsylvania Militia (First Blue Reserves), September 15th, 1862. On duty at the DuPont Powder Works, Wilmington, Del. Discharged September 30th to October 1st, 1862.

BATTALION, INFANTRY.
MAJOR JEREMIAH W. FRITZ.

Formed from the 2nd Regiment, Reserve Brigade, First Division, Pennsylvania Militia (First Regiment Blue Reserves), September 11th, 1862. Discharged September 22d, 1862.

INDEPENDENT BATTALION, BALDWIN LIGHT INFANTRY.
Company A, CAPTAIN ROBERT S. PATTON.
Company B, CAPTAIN CHARLES STUART.
Company C, CAPTAIN OLIVER B. WILSON.

Organized September 12th, 1862. Discharged September 22d, 1862.

INDEPENDENT COMPANY, INFANTRY.
CAPTAIN AQUILA HAINES.
50 Officers and Men.

Organized September 11th, 1862. Discharged September 22d, 1862.

INDEPENDENT COMPANY, INFANTRY.
CAPTAIN JOHN L. WILSON.
70 Officers and Men.

Organized September 15th, 1862. Discharged September 23d, 1862.

---

*In a collision upon the Cumberland Valley Railroad the 20th Regiment lost four men killed and thirty injured.

INDEPENDENT COMPANY, LIGHT ARTILLERY.

CAPTAIN ARCHIBALD McI. ROBERTSON.

90 Officers and Men.

Formed from Company B, 1st Regiment Artillery, Home Guard Brigade. September 11th, 1862. Discharged September 25th, 1862.

INDEPENDENT BATTERY, LIGHT ARTILLERY.

CAPTAIN E. SPENCER MILLER.

85 Officers and Men.

Formed from Company D, 1st Regiment Artillery, Home Guard Brigade, September 13th, 1862. Discharged September 24th, 1862.

INDEPENDENT BATTERY, LIGHT ARTILLERY.

CAPTAIN HENRY D. LANDIS.

100 Officers and Men.

Formed from Company A, 1st Regiment Artillery, Home Guard Brigade, September 15th, 1862. Discharged September 26th, 1862.

THE CIVIL WAR FINANCED IN PHILADELPHIA

FROM the days of the American Revolution, when Robert Morris gave his private means and the prestige of his business reputation to Washington, our wars have been financed in Philadelphia. The money to pay the cost of the War of 1812-14 was largely raised by Stephen Girard, and that for the War with Mexico was gathered together by E. W. Clark & Co.

When the long-feared Civil War became a reality the National debt (April, 1861) amounted to about $64,000,000. At its close (August 31st, 1865) it had reached the enormous sum of $2,846,021,742.04, the Nation's creditors being, chiefly, the millions of patriotic citizens, rich and poor alike, who held the Federal bonds, the greater portion of which had been sold to them by the house of Jay Cooke & Co. This establishment had been formed January 1st, 1861, by the partnership of Jay Cooke and his brother-in-law, William G. Moorhead, and occupied modest quarters upon the west side of Third Street, adjoining, upon the north, the dignified Girard Bank.

Jay Cooke, born of New England parents, was a native of Sandusky, Ohio, and came to Philadelphia in his seventeenth year upon the promise of Mr. Moorhead of a clerkship in the office of the Washington Packet Company, of which Mr. Moorhead was an officer. A year later young

Cooke entered the service of the bankers E. W. Clark & Co. eventually becoming a junior partner.

When the financiers of the North were called upon to support the Government in its costly task of the National salvation, Jay Cooke & Co. were hardly known, even locally, but Mr. Cooke, perhaps bearing in mind the experience gained under E. W. Clark & Co. in war finance, greatly desired to obtain some part of the Government's patronage. In this the young firm was somewhat aided through the friendly relations of his brother Henry, an Ohio journalist, with the family of the Secretary of the Treasury Chase.

At that period the banking capital of Philadelphia was $11,000,000, of Boston $30,000,000 and of New York $66,000,000. Of the first national bond issue amounting to $50,000,000 but $5,000,000 was allotted to the Philadelphia banks, and of this sum Jay Cooke & Co. got but $300,000. This relatively small portion was promptly sold and accounted for. The dominant attitude of the New York financiers was, at that time, that of a group of hard-headed magnates bent upon getting all possible out of a severely-pressed applicant for money. When the issue was disposed of the bankers met the President and his Cabinet at a dinner in Washington and the New York coterie told them plainly that the Government must get along with the sum thus realized as more help could not be promised. The attitude of the Philadelphia bankers was more patriotic. At Washington and in Philadelphia Secretary Chase frequently conferred with Mr. Cooke and recognized in him a sound and capable ally. Later, in the course of the war, when offered the position of Assistant Secretary of War, Mr. Cooke wisely decided to stand by his business and push the sale of the bonds.*

News of the defeat of the Union army at Bull Run reached the city upon the arrival from the front of an *Inquirer* correspondent upon the morning of July 22d, 1861. The excitement and dismay pervading the community, as the story spread, were beyond description. Upon his own initiative Jay Cooke carried a subscription paper around the financial district and, before night had secured the pledges of thirty banks, insurance companies, firms and individuals, offering a loan of $1,737,500.00 to the Government for sixty days at the rate of six per cent interest.

Upon May 15th, 1861, the Pennsylvania Legislature voted the sum of $3,000,000 for the purpose of equipping the regiments of the State Reserve Corps then forming. Cooke & Co. sold these bonds at par, a feat which further attracted the notice of Secretary Chase, who appointed the firm, upon September 4th, 1861, financial agents for the Government. Upon the following day the bonds were placed upon sale and the office of Cooke & Co. was thronged with crowds of large and small investors, who in a short time absorbed one-fourth of the entire issue.

*From April 15th to May 31st, 1861, the subscriptions to military funds by citizens of the loyal States averaged $1,000,000 per diem.

Jay Cooke personally became subscription agent for the National loan upon March 7th, 1862, this at once giving a vastly enlarged field for the exercise of his remarkable talent and industry. A bond of $1,000,000 was required by the United States Treasurer and this was, with some difficulty, furnished. In 1861 the masses were relatively poor, the per capita share of the entire money circulation of the country was but $14.00. Gold and silver was becoming scarce, the country was flooded with counterfeits of State bank currency. Every business man kept a "detector" at hand and constantly studied its pages. Retail trade, in fact every use for small change, was carried along with "shin plasters" ranging, in face value, from two to fifty cents. These were issued by all sorts of corporations without restraint.* A limited supply of badly worn Spanish coins dubbed "fips" and "levies" eked out the public need. In the latter part of 1862 postage stamps and street-car tickets were used as currency.† Specie payments were suspended upon Monday, December 30th, 1861, but the Government waited thirteen months longer before providing fractional paper currency, of which a total of $50,000,000 was printed, and this form of exchange was in common use until 1879. Under such conditions the selling of Government or any other securities was made doubly difficult. At the beginning of 1863 the Government owed the army $60,000,000. When Secretary Chase finally decided to place the whole task of keeping the war chest filled upon the broad shoulders of Jay Cooke, the latter lost no time in perfecting an organization. He created a staff of nine managers of States, placed chiefly in the Middle West; he appointed fifteen hundred agents, kept under supervision by a small army of traveling correspondents. He began a campaign of advertising marvelous in its scope and originality. In this department he enlisted the abilities of a group of then widely-known journalists, including Samuel Wilkeson, of the New York *Tribune;* C. C. Norvell, of the New York *Times,* and John Russell Young. His plan of advertising was all-pervading. It included not only the large and constant use of display announcements, but editorial and general reading columns. He bought space in not only the daily papers but in weeklies, class and foreign publications. He reached every farm-house in the loyal States through their home papers. He bought the help, if not the good-will of the hostile Democratic journals. All over the West, especially, the name of "Cooke" was used to conjure hoards of savings from the traditional old stockings. In New York and New England the bankers accounted for sales through the Philadelphia office or that established by the Cooke's in Washington.

---

*In 1862 the City of Wilmington, Del., issued fractional currency in denominations of from five to fifty cents, and the act was pronounced legal.

†In the latter part of July, 1862, the public bought postage stamps in such quantities, for currency purposes, that the Government prohibited their sale excepting for mailing purposes. Soon afterward the situation was relieved by the appearance of the fractional currency, quickly dubbed "shin plasters."

The year 1863 was witness of a great and distressing time of speculative disturbance. Upon February 1st, 1863, gold had advanced to 160 and a month later to 172. Every time that the bonds of the Nation, bearing the promise of payment with interest in gold, were raided by the bears, Jay Cooke was there with the money to buy them, as fast as offered, at par. At the Philadelphia office thirty clerks were busy, night and day, over the immense details of this wonderful business. Cooke & Co. had opened night offices for the accommodation of the working classes, and when the Government began to send along the first "20-40's" of the $500,000,000 loan they were sold faster than the Register of the Treasury could sign them. At this time money was coming in at the rate of a million and a half dollars per diem. Code telegrams, reporting sales, fluttered down upon Mr. Cooke's desk like a never-ceasing snow-storm.

As the war developed and the certainty of the Confederate failure might be safely forecast, the desire of the fighting North to "see Lincoln through the job" made it easier work for the money agencies to collect and deliver the funds which were being so lavishly expended upon the armies and the navy. The murder of the President intensified this all-pervading wish to help. In four days of the week following the tragedy, Cooke & Co's. sales were nearly $25,000,000, and in one hundred and forty days ending July 28th, 1865, the house had sold securities upon behalf of the Government to the face value of $700,000,000.*

Mr. Cooke's biographer places the total of the business done for the Government by Jay Cooke & Co., in the course of four years, at a billion and a half dollars. The gross commissions for the sales of all but the earliest bond issue was a quarter of one per cent. Mr. Cooke stated, in a letter to the Secretary of the Treasury, at the end of the war, that his firm had realized, after deducting all expenses, a profit of $220,054.49, this being about one-sixteenth of one per cent.

Throughout the war the officials of the Treasury Department and the President not less, sought constantly the advice of this tireless Philadelphia banker. A Confederate officer is quoted by Mr. Cooke's painstaking biographer with the remark, "The Yankees did not whip us in the field. We were whipped by the United States Treasury Department." To the limited extent that this may be true, large credit belongs to the Philadelphia banker who found the "sinews of war" as they were needed.

The subsequent career of the great financier of the war for the Union, though clouded with bitter defeat in his efforts to promote the Northern Pacific Railway, ended, as such a life should, in triumph.

---

*Commenting upon the impending resignation of Secretary Chase, the Philadelphia Inquirer of July 1st, 1864, said that when he assumed the duties of Secretary of the Treasury he found that the Government was able to raise but a limited amount of money, for much of which 12 per cent. interest was paid. Up to that date he had raised $1,700,000,000, all of which was subscribed by the people of the loyal States at a cost of 4 1/10 per cent. interest.

THE MILITARY HOSPITALS AT PHILADELPHIA

UNDER CHARGE OF THE MEDICAL DEPARTMENT,
MILITARY POST OF PHILADELPHIA, 1861 to 1865.

Medical Inspector—Lieut.-Col. John L. Le Conte, U. S. A., 1103 Girard street.
Medical Director—John Campbell, Surgeon, U. S. A.
Assistant Surgeon—Wm. P. Grier, U. S. A., 1103 Girard street.
Medical Purveyor—Robert Murray, Surgeon, U. S. A., 5 and 7 N. Fifth street.
Inspector of Hospitals—J. Letterman, Surgeon, U. S. A.
U. S. Laboratory—A. K. Smith, Surgeon, U. S. A., Sixth and Master streets.
Medical Director of Transportation—R. S. Kenderdine, Surgeon, U. S. V. Citizen's
  Vol. Hospital, Broad and Prime streets.
Office for Sick and Wounded Officers—1103 Girard street.
Post Surgeon—Dr. John Neill, U. S. V.
State Military Agent—Robert R. Corson, 133 Walnut street.

PENNSYLVANIA was one of four of the loyal States among whose soldiers of the Civil War the fatalities from battle exceeded those caused by disease. The Pennsylvania troops lost from battle casualties 56 per cent. and from disease 44 per cent. of all deaths during the war.

In the course of the first year of the war, before the hospital service became efficient, the general mortality in the army was 17.2 per cent. from battle casualties and 50.4 per cent. from disease per 1,000 troops. In the Atlantic Division, Army Medical Department, the mortality from disease was 33.40 per cent., and in the Central Division 82.19 per cent. per 1,000 troops.

The percentage of deaths from sickness relative to total enlistments was lower in Pennsylvania than in any other of the Northern States. This fact was largely due to the geographical position of Philadelphia, which enabled the State to employ transports to bring the wounded men of Pennsylvania regiments from tidewater Virginia and by rail from inland points to the military hospitals at this point, and the fine record made here as a result of the patriotic labor of physicians and nurses in the first year of the war. A State military agency located at Washington assisted in caring for the sick and wounded of the Pennsylvania regiments.* The Government decided to create several great army hospital establishments at Philadelphia for the reception of sick and wounded soldiers and sailors without relation to statehood. Indeed, the first modest hospital opened in the city, that conducted by the Union Volunteer Soldiers Refreshment Saloon Committee, was intended to care

---

*The interests of the Pennsylvania soldiers in hospitals were in charge of Assistant Surgeon-General Alfred W. Green, of Philadelphia, stationed at Washington.

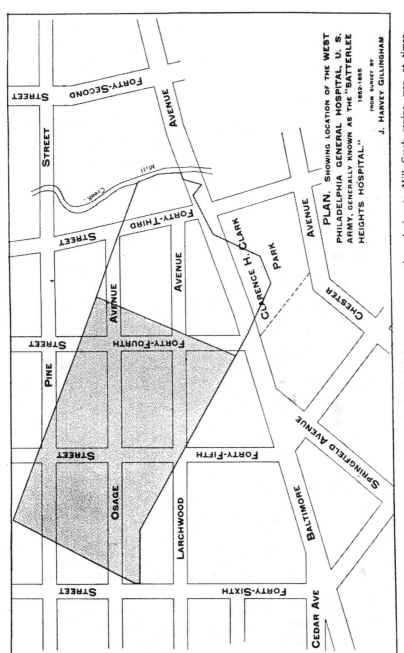

PLAN. SHOWING LOCATION OF THE WEST PHILADELPHIA GENERAL HOSPITAL, U. S. ARMY, GENERALLY KNOWN AS THE "SATTERLEE HEIGHTS HOSPITAL." 1862-1865

FROM SURVEY BY
J. HARVEY GILLINGHAM

The hospital buildings filled the shaded space. The balance of the Government reservation, sloping to Mill Creek ravine, was, at times, occupied by tents for wounded soldiers.

WEST PHILADELPHIA (SATTERLEE) U. S. GENERAL HOSPITAL, looking north from Baltimore Road.
(From a war time lithograph.)

225

for the sick and wounded men of regiments from other States passing through the city. These hospitals, the majority being located in old buildings adapted to the purpose, numbered twenty-four.* After the West Philadelphia Hospital was opened, in June, 1862, several of the smaller hospitals were closed, and in January, 1863, upon the completion of the still larger Mower or Chestnut Hill Hospital, the number was further reduced. In April, 1864, the official list contained but thirteen. In addition, there were several hospitals for soldiers maintained by citizens, and both the Pennsylvania and St. Joseph's Hospitals cared for large numbers at different periods of the war.

The earlier Government hospitals in the city in operation prior to March 1st, 1862, were located at Broad and Cherry streets, Twenty-fourth and Cherry streets, Ninth and Christian streets, Twenty-second and Wood streets and Fifth and Buttonwood streets.

By Act of the Legislature, date of February 28th, 1862, Surgeon Gen. H. H. Smith was directed to send a hospital ship to bring sick and wounded men from the scene of war, and it became expedient to do so a few weeks later. The steamer "W. Whilldin" was chartered and proceeded to Yorktown, Va. It carried Surgeons David Gilbert, R. P. Thomas, C. S. Bishop, R. J. Levis, D. S. Glenninger, H. L. Hodge, J. McBride, J. W. S. Norris, G. W. Nebinger and W. P. Moon, also several Sisters of Charity. This expedition returned with a large number of men suffering from the results of the Peninsular Campaign. It was the first of the many vessels thus laden which came up the Delaware River in the course of the war.

Under the direction of Surgeon R. S. Kenderdine, a military hospital car was maintained between Washington and Philadelphia attached to regular trains and making three trips weekly.

The "high tide" of military hospital service in Philadelphia came with the battle of Gettysburg. Upon July 5th, 1863, Assistant Surgeon Gen. James R. Smith telegraphed to Governor Curtin that the five thousand empty beds in the Philadelphia army hospitals would be filled. All through the following week the suffering, battle-torn humanity rolled in upon the city until there were more than ten thousand soldiers to be cared for by the host of surgeons and nurses awaiting them.

The friends and relatives of soldiers who were reported to be in one or another of the military hospitals of Philadelphia came to the city in large numbers from other States and often experienced much difficulty in finding the objects of their anxiety. To assist such persons the Y. M. C. A. and the United States Sanitary Commission published hospital directories, including the names of all soldiers then or previously inmates of the different hospitals, with directions for reaching them.

---

*Surgeon John Neill organized the earliest military hospitals at Philadelphia. He was appointed medical director of the forces from Pennsylvania with the rank of lieutenant-colonel. He died February 1st, 1880.

15

In the course of the Civil War the military hospitals of the North ministered to 6,454,834 cases of illness and wounds. Of these 195,657 were fatal. Although Philadelphia received a larger proportion of severely wounded men than the hospitals of the service as a whole, the average percentage of mortality was lower here than elsewhere.

The annual report of the Philadelphia Branch of the United States Sanitary Commission, January 1st, 1866, states that 157,000 soldiers and sailors were cared for in the general hospitals at Philadelphia during the war.

Out of the experience gained in the army hospitals of Philadelphia many patriotic young physicians developed the skill and knowledge which has tended to make this community famous as a center of medical and surgical education.*

THE LESSER MILITARY HOSPITALS.

LOCATION AND CAPACITY.

McClellan General Hospital	Germantown road and Cayuga street	400 beds
Summit House General Hospital	Darby road, West Philadelphia	522 beds
Hestonville General Hospital	Hestonville	172 beds
Haddington General Hospital	Haddington	200 beds
Cuyler General Hospital	Germantown	550 beds
Smallpox General Hospital	Islington lane	50 beds
Turners Lane General Hospital		275 beds
Officers' General Hospital	Camac's Woods	50 beds
Episcopal General Hospital	Front and York streets	325 beds
Broad Street Hospital	S. E. corner of Broad and Cherry streets	650 beds
St. Joseph's Hospital	Girard avenue and Seventeenth street	150 beds
Master Street Hospital	Sixth and Master streets	305 beds
George Street Hospital	Fourth and George streets	225 beds
Fifth Street Hospital	Fifth and Buttonwood streets	282 beds
Race Street Hospital	National Guards' Hall	412 beds
Twelfth Street Hospital	Twelfth and Buttonwood streets	152 beds
Filbert Street Hospital	State Armory, Sixteenth and Filbert streets	430 beds
South Street Hospital	Twenty-fourth and South streets	253 beds
Christian Street Hospital	Ninth and Christian streets	220 beds

---

*The medical records of great foreign wars from 1794 to 1850 show that the fatalities in army hospitals resulting from amputations were 58 per cent. of all cases. The surgeons of the Union Armies saved about 75 per cent. of the men operated upon.

In the course of six months, dating from July 1st, 1864, the military hospitals at Philadelphia received 46,459 sick and wounded men. Of these 974 died, 11,737 deserted and 20,178 returned to duty. The balance were still in the hospitals at the end of the year.

Catharine Street Hospital ....Eighth and Catharine streets....... 105 beds
Wood Street Hospital ....Twenty-second and Wood streets... 175 beds
Citizens' Volunteer Hospital ......Broad and Prime streets.......... 400 beds

The foregoing list is printed in the order in which it was published in official circulars issued by the Government during the Civil War period and without reference to priority of establishment. The same order is adhered to in the chapter following.

PHILADELPHIA SURGEONS WHO SERVED

THE McCLELLAN HOSPITAL, in the immediate vicinity of Wayne Junction, was in the class of general hospitals especially constructed for the purpose. While, in the case of this hospital, changes of personnel among the officers were frequent (and this also applies to the other military hospitals then in operation in Philadelphia), the officials most closely identified with the "McClellan," as far as traceable, were: Surgeon in charge, Lewis Taylor; executive officer, A. A. Surgeon J. P. Murphy; asst. executive officer, Capt. T. C. Kendall of the Invalid Corps; asst. surgeons, Isaac Morris, Jr., Levi Curtis, H. C. Primrose, W. L. Wells, H. B. Buehler and Richard A. Cleeman.*

SUMMIT HOUSE HOSPITAL was situated on the site now occupied by St. Joseph's (Catholic) Hospital, Darby road near Paschalville. Surgeon in charge, J. H. Taylor, assisted by Surgeons L. Leavitt (executive officer), James A. Buchanan, G. W. Webb and S. R. Skillern. At a later period the hospital was administered by Surgeon Winthrop Sargeant.

On August 24th, 1864, all of the white soldiers at the Summit House Hospital were removed to the Satterlee Hospital to make room for twelve hundred sick and wounded negro soldiers then being landed at Grays Ferry.

HESTONVILLE HOSPITAL, in the suburb of that name, was in charge of Surgeon D. Hayes Agnew, assisted by Surgeons R. Taylor and J. Lodge.

HADDINGTON HOSPITAL occupied the old Bull's Head Tavern at Sixty-fifth and Vine streets. This building is still standing. This hospital was opened November 2d, 1862, in charge of Surgeon R. J. Levis. It was closed about one year later.

*This hospital, the last one established at Philadelphia during the war, was arranged upon the general plan of the Mower Hospital, having an elliptic corridor from which eighteen wards radiated, the office building being in the center. It is fully described in Part I, Vol. 3, Medical and Surgical History of the Rebellion.

CUYLER HOSPITAL, Germantown, was established in the rear of the Town Hall and opened on September 19th, 1862, in charge of Surgeon James Darrach, with John Ashurst, Jr., A. A. S., as executive officer, Asst. surgeons, William R. Dunton, J. M. Leedom, T. F. Betton and R. N. Downs.

ISLINGTON LANE HOSPITAL was known locally as the "Smallpox Hospital," its function being the care of cases of this disease originating in the other hospitals. Assistant surgeon in charge, James V. Patterson.

TURNERS LANE HOSPITAL. A special study was made here of diseases of the nerves caused by wounds. It was located near the junction of Twenty-second and Oxford streets. Assistant Surgeon in charge, Charles H. Alden; executive officer, A. A. Surgeon C. B. King; staff, A. A. Surgeons Charles Carter, S. Weir Mitchell, W. W. Keen and J. A. Da Costa.

THE OFFICERS HOSPITAL was located in Camac's Woods near the intersection of Eleventh and Berks streets. Surgeon in charge, William M. Camac. Late in the course of the war this hospital was removed to Twenty-fourth and Chestnut streets.

THE EPISCOPAL HOSPITAL at Front and York streets was in charge of Surgeons Richard A. Cleeman and Robert P. Thomas.

THE BROAD STREET HOSPITAL was opened February 2d, 1862, in the old station building of the Philadelphia and Reading Railway Company on the site now occupied by the Parkway Building. Branches of this hospital were afterward established in the old market house on Broad street below Race street and on Cherry street east of Broad street. Surgeon John Neill was appointed in charge, his staff including Surgeons Thomas Yarrow, Henry Yarrow, Harrison Allen, H. M. Bellows, Henry Eggleton and Thomas Eggleton; Medical Cadets James Tyson, George W. Shields, E. R. Corson, Edward Livezy, J. W. Corson and W. R. D. Blackwood. The ladies actively interested in this hospital were from the many prominent families then resident near by. This hospital was closed when the Mower Hospital was completed but was reopened for a short time after the battle of Gettysburg, the surgeon then in charge being W. V. Keating.

ST. JOSEPH'S HOSPITAL occupied temporary buildings erected on the property of the large Catholic institution of the name at Seventeenth street and Girard avenue. Surgeon incharge, W. P. Moon.

THE MASTER STREET HOSPITAL occupied a manufacturing building at the northwest corner of Sixth and Master streets. It was opened upon July 1st, 1862, and continued until after the Chestnut Hill Hospital (Mower) was in operation, nearly a year later. It was considered one of the most efficient establishments in the city.

Dr. Paul B. Goddard was surgeon in charge; resident surgeons, Kingston Goddard, Jr., A. Hamilton Smith, Matthias K. Knorr; visiting surgeons, Drs. Wm. H. Pancoast, David Gilbert, Joseph Klapp and Samuel Murphy; apothecary, Joseph B. Fox.

The building was subsequently used as a factory for supplying sheets for the hospitals and underwear for the army.

THE GEORGE STREET HOSPITAL occupied the building of the Order of American Mechanics at Fourth and George streets. It was opened June 20th, 1862. Surgeon in charge, Lewis D. Harlow. It was closed on February 23d, 1863.

FIFTH STREET HOSPITAL was established under the direction of Surgeon Thomas G. Morton in the buildings of the Dunlap carriage factory, at Fifth and Buttonwood streets. It was opened in February, 1862, and was discontinued a year later, after which the structures were used as a military prison for Confederates and a barracks for the Provost Guard. The hospital was in charge of Surgeon A. C. Bournonville, assisted by Surgeons R. J. Dunglison and William M. Breed.

THE RACE STREET HOSPITAL occupied the armory of the National Guards on Race street below Sixth street. It was closed March 18th, 1863, the patients being removed to Mower Hospital. Surgeon in charge, A. C. Bournonville.

THE TWELFTH STREET HOSPITAL, at Twelfth and Buttonwood streets, was opened October 22d, 1862, and continued about one year. Surgeon in charge, Thomas G. Morton.

THE FILBERT STREET HOSPITAL was established in the summer of 1862 at the fine State Arsenal building, southeast corner of Sixteenth and Filbert streets. The lower floors were used as a depot for military clothing. Surgeon in charge, Richard A. Dunglison, assisted by Surgeons A. Douglas Hall, John W. S. Norris and S. Weir Mitchell. In February, 1863, this became a convalescent hospital under Surgeon V. P. Hibbard, and later in charge of Surgeons W. S. Forbes and Samuel S. Storrow, consecutively. The assistant surgeons were J. Wilson Magruder, James W. Draper, and A. Douglas Hall.*

THE SOUTH STREET HOSPITAL was located at Twenty-fourth and South streets. From its reputation for amputations it was often called by the soldiers the "stump hospital." The surgeon in charge was Harry C. Hart, who was succeeded in 1864 by Surgeon Henry James. The assistant surgeons were F. F. Maury, E. A. Koerper and A. B. Stonelake.

THE CHRISTIAN STREET HOSPITAL was located on the south side of that street below Tenth street, in Moyamensing Hall. Its proximity to the "Baltimore Railroad station" and to the great refreshment saloons gave it much importance. It was maintained to October 24th, 1864. When opened it was in charge of Surgeon John I. Reese, and later was under Surgeon R. J. Levis. Among those identified with this hospital were Assistant Surgeons S. Weir Mitchell, George R. Morehouse, Charles Holden, W. W. Keen, L. E. Nordmann and John H. Packard.

*A description of this hospital may be found in Dr. Mitchell's first novel, "In War Time." It was here that this distinguished surgeon began his studies of cases of nervous diseases, which he continued later at the Christian Street and Turner's Lane Hospitals.

THE CATHARINE STREET HOSPITAL, at Eighth and Catharine streets, was also convenient to the great highway of military travel across the city, and of great service to passing troops. It was administered by Surgeon Robert R. Taylor.

WOOD STREET HOSPITAL, Twenty-second and Wood streets, was one of the earliest of the in-town hospitals, being continued to February 3d, 1863, when its officials and patients were transferred to the more salubrious environment of the Mower Hospital. Surgeon in charge, Caleb W. Horner; assistant surgeons, S. H. Horner, William H. Gordon and C. B. Voigt.

Among the Philadelphia surgeons who died in the service were:
Albert Owen Stille, Surgeon of the 23d Regiment, died at Fortress Monroe, June 23d, 1862.
James Knighton Shivers, died at Atlanta, 1865.
Joseph Hopkinson, Mower Hospital, died July 11th, 1865.
Charles Baker Riehle, Asst. Surgeon 8th Cavalry, died at Washington, September 14th, 1862.
Edward Donaldson, medical cadet, U. S. A., died at Washington, D. C., May 31st, 1864.

THE CITIZENS' VOLUNTEER HOSPITAL

FOREMOST in extent and capacity among the centrally located hospitals, this beneficent establishment was located opposite the depot of the Philadelphia, Wilmington and Baltimore Railroad, upon the northeast corner of Broad street and Washington avenue. It was especially intended for the reception of the more serious cases of the sick and wounded constantly arriving from the army by train. It was a clearing house from which the patients were gradually distributed to other hospitals. The managers and committees of humane citizens of both sexes maintained volunteer committees in attendance at all incoming trains to not only give instant help to those in need of it, but to protect the soldiers from thieves and harpies, who were ever ready to mislead and rob them. This hospital was opened on September 5th, 1862, and closed on August 11th, 1865. Upon October 12th, 1863, the first anniversary, it was stated that 30,000 soldiers had been cared for, of whom but 80 had died. In its report of May 10th, 1864, it recorded that to that time above 50,000 men had been received. The capacity of this hospital was 400 beds, but at times room was made for 700 men. After great battles the nearby churches were utilized to house the excess arrivals of the wounded. The Methodist Church at Broad and Christian streets, the Presbyterian Church at Broad and

Fitzwater streets, and St. Theresa's (Catholic) Church, upon Broad street, above Catharine street, were all used as temporary hospitals, as were also many of the fire houses.

The cash receipts from contributors aggregated $43,436. Supplies of perhaps greater value were donated. The ground upon which the buildings stood was loaned to the association by Hon. Joseph Randall. When the institution was closed a balance of $4,783.47 remained. This was given to the Soldiers and Sailors Home and other military relief associations.

The Citizens' Volunteer Hospital was in charge of Surgeon R. S. Kenderdine, U. S. V.

President, T. T. Tasker, Sr.; Treasurer, Chas. P. Paret; Secretary, Thos. L. Gifford.

Board of Managers: John Williams, W. L. Clayton, James Evans, John Kilpatrick, Alex. Greaves, Samuel W. Middleton, Frank Bayle, John H, Clayton, John Goorley, Wm. R. Pidgeon, Andrew McFetters, David J. Stevenson, Samuel Bayle, Jos. L. Goff, Edmund Hopper, James D. Doherty, Edward H. Pyle, J. B. Hancock, Wm. J. Verdette, George W. Lott, James L. Moore, David Foy, Henry J. Fox, Wm. H. Taggart, Joseph M. Cardeza.*

WEST PHILADELPHIA GENERAL HOSPITAL, LATER DESIG-NATED THE SATTERLEE U. S. GENERAL HOSPITAL

Capacity, 2,860 Beds

THE project of the extensive hospital located in the Twenty-seventh Ward, West Philadelphia, has been credited to Dr. Isaac I. Hayes, under whose direction it was built and who remained at the head of its administration to the end of the war. The site, now occupied by blocks of attractive, modern homes, was then in the open country. The ground was about 90 feet above tide level, sloping into the valley of a small creek, thus receiving good drainage. The boundaries of the ground occupied extended 1,400 feet northwestward from a point now within Clarence Clark Park, just south of Baltimore avenue, at the intersection of Forty-fourth street. The average width of the reservation was 650 feet. The group of buildings filled the upper space, and these were surrounded by a high fence. The open portion along Baltimore avenue, beyond the ravine of Little Mill creek,

---

*The annual reports of this hospital do not include the names of assistant surgeons or of the many patriotic ladies and citizens who were in attendance here during nearly three years of activity.

was used as a parade, and after the battles of Antietam and Gettysburg was covered with tents for the wounded soldiers.

The Administration Building of two floors occupied the center of the enclosure, flanked by the wards of one floor each, thirty-four in all. These wards were of unequal length. When the group was finally completed by the builder, Wm. L. Sands, under a supplementary contract, in November, 1862, the wards were furnished with 3,124 beds. In addition to the hospital buildings proper quarters were provided for a host of surgeons, attendants, nurses, guards, musicians, cooks, printers and other essential employees.

Dr. Hayes had assumed this task at a great sacrifice of personal interest. Experience with the Second Grinnell Expedition to the Arctic Region six years earlier had led him to further research in that field. When the Civil War began he was absent in the far north upon his schooner "United States." He first learned of the condition of war when arriving at Halifax in October, 1861. He promptly abandoned his scientific plans and tendered his personal services and the use of his ship to the Federal Government. Both were accepted and he was assigned to hospital duty at Philadelphia.

The West Philadelphia U. S. General Hospital was opened for the reception of military patients June 9th, 1862. During the morning of the opening day twenty-five Sisters of Charity reported for duty, having been assigned to the hospital by order of the Surgeon General upon the recommendation, it is said, of Dr. D. Hayes Agnew and Dr. Walter F. Atlee. In the afternoon about one hundred and fifty patients were brought here from other hospitals.

In General Order No. 8, dated July 2d, Dr. Hayes announced his staff as follows:

Resident Surgeons—D. McMurtrie, N. Hickman, H. Hillner, J. A. Buchanan, George H. Deck, L. K. Baldwin, M. S. Perry, W. C. Dixon, W. H. Matlack and C. E. Iddings.

Visiting Surgeons—Alfred Stille, T. Stewardson, E. A. Smith, F. W. Lewis, W. F. Atlee, John G. Tull, R. A. Penrose, J. M. DaCosta, H. West, J. B. Hutchinson, H. L. Lodge, J. H. Packard, E. Crowell, D. H. Agnew, W. C. Halsey, Frank West and Caspar Wistar.

The Cadets were Messrs. Williams, Saunders, Knorr, Cadwell, Lowndes, Byres, Trull, Dickson, Campbell, Keffer and Santee.

In a list printed in the "Hospital Register," a weekly paper printed at the hospital, appear, in addition to the foregoing names, those of Surgeons Joseph Leidy, Ezra Dyer and Edward A. Page. Cadet A. L. Eakin was also added to the staff. In 1864 Surgeon W. H. Forwood, U. S. A., became Executive Officer, succeeding Surgeon John S. Billings.

This hospital, known at first and so designated in official documents as the West Philadelphia U. S. General Hospital, was named, on June 3d, 1863, in honor of Brig.-Gen. Richard Sherwood Satterlee, U. S. A., a noted surgeon, native of Fairfield, Herkimer County, N. Y.,

MOWER U. S. GENERAL HOSPITAL AT CHESTNUT HILL.

(Redrawn from a contemporary lithograph.)

CUYLER HOSPITAL, TOWN HALL, GERMANTOWN.
(From a contemporary photograph.)

and in the regular army service dating from his appointment as Assistant Surgeon in 1822. Throughout the Civil War this officer held the position of Medical Purveyor, with headquarters in New York City.

At the "Satterlee" military discipline was strictly enforced. A company of troops was assigned to guard duty, and as the hospital increased in its invalid population, the guard was reinforced until it numbered 170 rank and file.

A good military band, under Prof. Theodore Hermann, provided daily concerts and music for the dress parades and dirges for the dead. Always hovering above their charges in the hospital wards were the Sisters of Charity, forty-two in number, under the orders of Mother Mary Gonzaga Grace. These nurses were not paid, but the Government reimbursed for their services the order to which they belonged.

Rev. Nathaniel West, D. D., the Protestant Chaplain of the "Satterlee," wrote of these Catholic sister-nurses: "Better nurses, better attendants, more noiseless, ceaseless performers of services in the hospital could not be found. There is probably not a hospital in the public service that would not be glad to have them." Much of the heavier, more trying work at this and other hospitals was done by male assistants known as "contract men."*

The Ladies' Aid Society, Penn Relief Association and Ladies' Association for Soldiers' Relief were all represented in the large numbers of volunteer attendants at this and other hospitals. A number of ladies of the neighborhood, with the aid of the Chaplain, established a hospital library, reading and writing room. Newspapers from all sections of the country were filed here daily. A billiard room and entertainment hall were also maintained. These were upon the southwestern side of the reservation adjoining the still existent homestead of Dr. and Mrs. Louis H. Twaddell, both of whom were active in volunteer work in the often crowded wards.†

A large proportion of the patients sent to this hospital arrived upon steamers which landed at a point just below the old Gray's Ferry bridge, from which the sufferers were taken upon stretchers and in wagons and ambulances along Warrington lane to Baltimore avenue. This now forgotten lane extended across the plateau from the intersection of Gray's Ferry road to the Warrington homestead, which yet stands, surrounded with modern homes, just southward from the site of the Cherry Tree tavern.

Chaplain West states that the full capacity of the hospital was increased to 2,860 beds, in addition to which were 150 large tents to hold

---

*Rev. Nathaniel West, chaplain, died on September 1st, 1864, aged seventy years.

†Under order dated October 29th, 1863, no women were permitted to serve in United States General Hospitals, excepting "matrons," unless provided with a "certificate of approval" or directly appointed by the Surgeon-General. General Order No. 351.

900 more persons. These are said to have been set up along Baltimore avenue opposite and within the space now included in Clarence Clark Park, upon the verge of the ravine. Until the completion of the hospital at Chestnut Hill, this was the largest army hospital in the United States. The Philadelphia Nurses' Corps, the first association of army nurses in the service, was formed at this hospital.* The total number of soldiers and sailors cared for at the "Satterlee" in the course of its operation is believed to exceed 60,000. The Satterlee Hospital was closed upon August 3d, 1865.†

THE MOWER U. S. GENERAL HOSPITAL

Capacity, 4,000 Beds

SELECTING the highest level ground within the city limits, just eastward of Chestnut Hill, where the altitude is 400 feet above the river level, the National Government began the erection, in the fall of 1862, of another vast hospital establishment. The official in charge was Col. Charles H. Greenleaf, U. S. A., who was also Executive Officer. The space covered was 27 acres. The location was bounded by Abingdon and Springfield avenues, the Chestnut Hill track of the Reading Railroad and County Line road. The main frontage was opposite the station now known as Wyndmoor. This was an ideal site for the purpose. The contractor who built the Satterlee Hospital was employed upon this work. The arrangement of the buildings was novel. From a great, flatted, elliptical corridor forty-seven wards, each 175 feet long, radiated outward like the spokes of a wheel. The fence enclosed a space 912 feet wide and 1,037 feet long. The Administration and Medical Department occupied the two-story building in the center. At the far corners were the barracks of the guards. The large commissary building faced the railroad. Kitchens, dining halls, power and heating plants, guard houses and various other structures were grouped in the open central space. A roomy parade and band stand was northeast from

*In December, 1864, Dr. Milton C. Egbert, a wealthy oil producer, of Venango County, Pa., sent, in the name of his wife, $5,000 to be expended upon Christmas dinners for the soldiers and sailors then in the military hospitals of Philadelphia. The sum was apportioned among all of the hospitals excepting the "Mower," which had been otherwise provided for.

†Soon after the close of the war the hospital tract was purchased by a syndicate, which divided it into building lots under the name of "Satterlee Heights." "Sheridan avenue" is now Osage avenue and Fairview avenue is Larchwood avenue. A map of this operation is preserved in a scrap book of the McAllister Collection, Ridgway Library.

the Medical Building. All of the buildings, like those of Satterlee Hospital, were built of wood and rough cast upon the outside. Water was supplied from the Chestnut Hill water works reservoir.

Tramways extended through the corridor and along the center of each ward to facilitate the carrying of patients and food. Many forms of diversion were provided for the soldiers, and here, as in the vicinity of the other hospitals, there was no lack of kindly attention upon the part of the neighboring residents. Invalid and wounded soldiers destined for the Mower Hospital were carried to the railroad station at Ninth and Green streets in fire ambulances and thence in special cars.

The Mower Hospital was opened upon January 17th, 1863. The capacity at that time was 2,820 beds for patients. The Surgeon in charge was Dr. J. Hopkinson; Consulting Surgeon, J. H. B. McClellan; Executive Officer, Col. Chas H. Greenleaf, U. S. A.; Assistant Surgeons, Isaac Norris, Henry C. Primrose, W. George Foggo, C. R. Maclean, J. M. Wallis, J. Wherry, M. L. Lauber, Robert Bolling, Horace Y. Evans, L. W. Bickley, J. A. C. Hanley, J. G. Murphy, Wm. M. Welch, E. A. Koerper, L. S. Morand, J. S. Somerville, A. H. Light, Albert Trego, Rollin T. Baker, Lewis T. Garrett, D. P. Pancoast, C. C. Bonibaugh and Chas. H. Budd.

The employees included one steward, 47 ward masters, 141 nurses and two firemen. The guard, at first, consisted of a company from Wayne County, Pa., under Capt. George W. Hubbell. A full band and drum corps furnished daily music.

Soon after the opening about 1,700 patients were brought here, mainly from a number of the small hospitals in town, which were then discontinued.

The total admissions to the end of 1864 were 17,190. The number was greatly increased near the close of the war.

A KEY TO THE OFFICIAL RECORDS OF THE MILITARY HOSPITALS, UNITED STATES ARMY, LOCATED AT PHILADELPHIA

THE unpublished reports and other documentary papers relating to these Civil War Hospitals are filed at the office of the Adjutant-General, War Department, Washington. An index of these records has been prepared by courtesy of that official for use in this book. In order that it may be permanently accessible, copies of this index have been placed in the libraries of the College of Physicians, the Library Company of Philadelphia and the Historical Society of Pennsylvania. It is understood that information, when important, regarding any individual soldier or sailor who may have been an inmate of those hospitals will be furnished by the Government upon presentation of sufficient data. This should be applied for, to secure attention, through members of Congress representing districts in which applicants reside.

THE UNITED STATES ARMY LABORATORY

THE United States Laboratory, located upon the northeast corner of Sixth and Jefferson streets, in a factory building, was established by direction of Surgeon Gen. Hammond in the summer of 1863, and placed in charge of Prof. John M. Maisch. of which he remained the director during the two and a half years of its existence. Here a staff of chemists and other experts prepared supplies for the medical and surgical requirements of the army and navy at an estimated saving, as compared with previous costs, of $750,000.

THE INVALID CORPS, COMPANIES RECRUITED IN PHILADELPHIA

IN May, 1863, the Government authorized the formation of an "Invalid Corps."* This body was afterward designated the "Veteran Reserve Corps," and was recruited from men of former service who had been sick or wounded but were still fit for garrison and guard duty. Under the direction of the Acting Assistant Provost Marshal of Pennsylvania, twelve companies of these troops were formed at the several army hospitals in Philadelphia, through the efforts of Col. Richard H. Rush. Col. George W. Gile, late of the 88th Regiment, was appointed in command. The "Invalid Corps" was composed of two classes, the more able-bodied companies being employed upon provost duty and

*The Invalid Corps consisted of 158 companies, of which 15 were from Pennsylvania. It was established by order of May 25th, 1863. By a subsequent order, dated March 18th, 1864, the designation was changed to that of the Veteran Reserve Corps.

as guards, the second class being assigned as hospital clerks, cooks and nurses.*

The companies recruited in Philadelphia were designated by numbers, as follows:

46th and 135th, McClellan General Hospital; 51st, 57th and 122d, Satterlee General Hospital; 52d, 133d and 134th, Mower General Hospital; 131st, Summit House Hospital; 162d, Cuyler General Hospital; 54th and 59th, from the minor hospitals.†

PATRIOTIC VOLUNTEER FIREMEN

NO class of citizens responded more promptly to their country's call in the spring of 1861 than the members of the volunteer fire companies of Philadelphia, then eighty-seven in number. They were numerous in all of the early regiments recruited in the city, and composed the greater part of the "23d," Birney's Zouaves, and the "72d," Baxter's Philadelphia Fire Zouaves. The "fire-fighters" were also well represented on the many ships of war built and manned at this port. The heroic records of these men are to be found in the regimental histories of our local organizations, and in the naval reports of the period. During the summer of 1861 the city authorities had acquired, by gift and purchase, a number of fine rifled cannon with caissons and equipments. Later in the year it was proposed to form an artillery regiment composed of firemen. So greatly had the various companies been depleted by enlistments that it was not found practicable. The firemen, however, offered the use of their horses for any emergency service. Twice in the course

*It was the duty of the senior officer of Invalid Corps detachments stationed at General Hospitals to keep a record of all deaths and interments. General Order No. 212.

†These troops are not included in the totals of organizations credited to Philadelphia.

of the war, at the instance of Chief David M. Lyle, the time-honored Hibernia Engine Company sent its steam engine, with a detail of men, to Fortress Monroe and Washington, upon request of the War Department. This powerful steam fire engine was built for the "Hibernias" by Reanie & Neafie, of Philadelphia, and was the pioneer engine of its kind in this city, if not in the United States.

This patriotic company was organized in 1752. It was represented in all of the wars of this country from the formation of the Government. The Hibernia Target Company, formed in 1853, became a company in the Pennsylvania Reserve Corps, this being the first full company of firemen sent out during the Civil War by any fire organization in the United States. The Northern Liberty and Vigilant Fire Companies, also dating from long before the Revolutionary War, were proud of the fact that their members had worn the uniforms of the Continentals as well as of Zouaves. The first organization of local firemen in the field was Capt. Wm. McMullen's "Rangers," a company recruited from the "Moyamensing Hose" for the three months' service, under Gen. Robert Patterson, in 1861.

The total number of Philadelphia firemen who served in the Union Army between 1861 and 1865 is estimated to have been about eleven thousand.

Not less notable is the story of the splendid work accomplished by the firemen of the city through their volunteer ambulance service, which began with the Southwark Hose Company No. 9. These ambulances were thirty-five in number. They were built with money subscribed by the firemen and their friends and were maintained at the houses of the Delaware, Southwark, Washington, Weccacoe, Diligent, Philadelphia (2), Assistance, America, Fairmount, Northern Liberty, United States, Vigilant, Good Intent, Globe, Mechanic, Decatur, Fellowship (2), Monroe, Good Will (2), and West Philadelphia Engine Companies, and the Franklin, Hope, Southwark, Western, Philadelphia, Good Will, Neptune, Cohocksink, Kensington, Independence, Northern Liberty and West Philadelphia Hose Companies. Great rivalry existed between the several companies in the artistic embellishment of their handsome and servicable vehicles. They were kept in readiness for instant call. Upon the arrival of vessels or trains filled with wounded and invalid soldiers the electric call "9-6," repeated three times, was rung upon the bells in the fire towers, and away the ambulances sped for the river front or the depots.

In the five days preceding Christmas, 1862, the ambulances, under the direction of Chief David M. Lyle, carried 2,500 patients from the Citizens' Volunteer Hospitals to others throughout the city.*

In many instances the fire companies invested their funds in Gov-

---

*It is stated in Lossing's History of the Civil War that the Philadelphia fire ambulances carried from the trains to the hospitals and elsewhere one hundred and twenty thousand sick or wounded soldiers.

ernment bonds, and when the sad harvest of battle was brought to our doors the fire houses became temporary hospitals. Many of the dead of the 72d Regiment, who fell at Antietam and Gettysburg, were exhumed from graves upon the fields where they had fought by their brother firemen and given burial in the home cemeteries.

In 1867 the handsome ambulance of the Philadelphia Fire Engine Company was sent to the Exposition Universelle at Paris as a part of the United States Government display, and was exhibited in the Army and Navy section. The company was awarded a bronze medal and a diploma by the Exposition authorities.

For many years after the volunteer fire department had been disbanded the "old timers," when upon their frequent visitations to other cities, generally carried along one or two war ambulances as the most prized of their treasures.*

THE UNION LEAGUE OF PHILADELPHIA

AFTER eighteen months of war the outlook for the final success of the Union cause was far from promising. In Philadelphia the disloyal element openly expressed joy over Confederate victories in the faces of their patriotic neighbors. This exasperating situation was discussed by a group of eminent citizens. It was decided to invite other loyal men to meet at the residence of Mr. Benjamin Gerhard, at 226 South Fourth street, to promote the formation of a Union Club. Referring to that movement years afterward, Mr. George H. Boker wrote:

"So timid and hesitating was the beginning of the Union Club that the notice to certain gentlemen to meet in Mr. Gerhard's house seemed to contain no authority for the assemblage. The receivers of the notes of invitation were informed merely that there would be a meeting of loyal men for a patriotic purpose. There was no signature to these notes, and from the context one might have inferred that Mr. Gerhard, for the nonce, had abandoned his house to the use of his friends.

*The survivors of the old-time fire companies still maintain local organizations in the Veteran Volunteer Firemen's Association, Tenth street above Brown street; the Volunteer Firemen's Association, Eighth and Buttonwood streets, and the Active Volunteer Firemen's Association, at Buttonwood street and Old York road. The Tivoli, William Penn and Taylor Hose Companies also continue their headquarters. These associations include many old soldiers and possess a number of valuable collections of apparatus, relics and pictures.

The original promotors who met in response to the invitation were Judge J. I. Clark Hare, Benjamin Gerhard, George Boker, Morton Mc-Michael, Horace Binney, Jr., and Charles Gibbons. Several meetings were subsequently held at private homes, and it has been stated, in a recent semi-centennial review of the origin of the Union League, that the formation of the club was regarded as a renewal of the historic Wistar parties instituted by Dr. Caspar Wistar in 1798. At the seventh meeting, held at the residence of Dr. John F. Meigs, upon December 27th, 1862, the title of the "Union League" was adopted. The first meeting of the Union League was held in Concert Hall, upon January 22d, 1863. Meanwhile, the large residence of Mr. Hartman Kuhn, at 1118 Chestnut street, had been rented by the club. This house, afterward known as the Baldwin Mansion, stood upon the site now occupied by Keith's Theatre. The first President of the Union League was William Morris Meredith, then Attorney-General of the State. The membership had at this time grown to five hundred and thirty-six. The house was opened for members upon February 23d, 1863, and the Union League became at once a potent center of aggressive Union effort.

The following members were among the subscribers to a fund to form and equip regiments for the national service:

William M. Meredith.	Horace Binney, Jr.	Joseph Allison.
J. Forsyth Meigs.	William Welsh.	Oswald Thompson.
Charles Gilpin.	J. Reese Fry.	Edwin Greble.
John B. Myers.	J. Edgar Thomson.	William Henry Rawle.
George H. Boker.	James H. Orne.	Charles J. Stille.
Henry C. Carey.	H. C. Knight.	Alexander Brown.
Daniel Smith, Jr.	John G. Fell.	William D. Lewis.
James W. Paul.	Adolph E. Borie.	George Trott.
Morton McMichael.	Anthony J. Drexel.	N. D. Browne.
James L. Claghorn.	George W. Childs.	Lindley Smyth.
Daniel Dougherty.	S. V. Merrick.	Clement Barclay.
John Russell Young.	Charles Gibbons.	John W. Field.

The names of these gentlemen were inscribed upon the columns of the Court of Honor of the 33d annual national encampment of the G. A. R., held at Philadelphia in September, 1889, with their help and that of others, the following regiments were organized:

1. 45th Regt. Penna. 90-day Militia, Cols. Wm. D. Whipple and James T. Clancy. Served July 1st to Aug. 29th, 1863.
2. 52d Regt. 90-day Militia. Col. Wm. A. Gray. Served July 10th to Sept. 2d, 1863.
3. 59th Regt. 90-day Militia. Col. George P. McLean. Served July 9th to Sept. 9th, 1863.
4. 183d Regt. Infantry. Cols. George P. McLean, J. F. McCullough, James C. Lynch, George T. Egbert. Served Dec. 24th, 1863, to July 13th, 1865.
5. 196th Regt. Infantry. Col. Harmanus Neff. Served July 20th, 1864, to Nov. 17th, 1864.
6. 198th Regt. Infantry. Col. Horatio G. Sickel. Served Sept. 2d, 1864, to June 4th, 1865.

UNION LEAGUE CLUB HOUSE, 1118 CHESTNUT STREET, February 23d, 1863, to May
11th, 1865. Site now occupied by Keith's Theatre.

BRONZE TABLET IN HONOR OF THE "UNION LEAGUE REGIMENTS," AT
UNION LEAGUE CLUB HOUSE.
(Henry K. Bush Brown, Sculptor.)

7. 213th Regt. Infantry. Col. John A. Gorgas. Served Feb. 24th, 1865, to Nov.
 18th, 1865.
8. 214th Regt. Infantry. Col. David B. McKibbin. Served March 21st, 1865, to
 March 21st, 1866.
9. 215th Regt. Infantry. Col. Francis Wister. Served April 5th, 1865, to July
 31st, 1865.

The Union League also assisted in the formation of the Third Battalion Infantry (Fell's Chasseurs) and of five cavalry companies.

As an inducement to secure recruits the Union League offered, at one time, a bounty of $300, and expended upon the several organizations a total of $108,000.

The Government established Camp William Penn, in Cheltenham Township, Montgomery County, where, under the command of Lieut.-Col. Louis Wagner, of the 88th Regiment, negro recruits of the State were gathered. The Union League expended $33,000 upon their equipment, etc. Each regiment sent out was presented with a stand of colors.

During the war period the Publication Committee constantly issued patriotic circulars and also the *Union League Gazette,* of which 560,000 copies were sent out.

Upon the memorable evening of April 10th, 1865, the news of the surrender of Gen. Robert E. Lee's Confederate force was brought to the Union League by Miss Louisa Claghorn and Mrs. John W. Forney, who had followed an excited telegraph boy to the *Press* office and obtained the dispatch after it had been copied for publication. The original, attested by Mr. J. Gillingham Fell, then President, is still preserved.*

Upon May 11th, 1865, the Union League moved into its new building upon Broad street, which it has occupied to the present time. A bronze tablet placed in the corridor of the Union League clubhouse and a bronze figure of a soldier of the Union army upon its pedestal in front of the building upon Broad street are memorials of the war period in the history of this influential and patriotic organization.†

---

*History of the Union League Club.

†The continued interest of the Union League in the events of the Civil War is evidenced by the group of its members composing "The Pilgrims to the Battlefields of the Rebellion." This organization consists of thirty members, of whom but a minority were soldiers of that period. The "Pilgrims" hold an annual banquet on Lincoln's Birthday, and undertake a visit, each year, to some one or more of the scenes of great battles and campaigns.

Upon the occasion of the semi-centennial of its organization, on February 12th, 1913, a list was published of the following survivors of the nearly three thousand members who were identified with the Club prior to May 5th, 1865. They are, as given in the order of their election, as follows: Edward Smith Kelly, Henry G. Morris, George Rice, J. Edward Addicks, Thomas Dolan, John F. Graff, Capt. S. Emlen Meigs, Charles S. Cramp, Frank H. Wyeth, Wayne MacVeagh, John G. Watmough, William M. Cramp, Judge William H. Armstrong, Henry C. Butcher, Richard A. Lewis, Edgar W. Earle, Thomas S. Harrison, William F. Biddle, Jacob N. Donaldson and James T. Graff.

16

THE INVASION OF 1863. GETTYSBURG

E ARLY in the course of the war the *London Chronicle,* viewing the problem of the American people from a dispassionate standpoint, had said:

"They have to discover, by hard trial, whether they have generals who can command, soldiers who will fight, ministers with ability to organize and a National spirit loyal enough to redeem the heavy burdens, the chilling disappointments and, above all, the wearisome delays inevitable to a state of war. * * * Any temporary sacrifice will be amply repaid if the national energies have been trained and society, in every circle, has learned to set a due value on the possessions which have been gained or preserved at a heavy cost of blood and treasure. If such should be the result of the war, it will have proved the happiest event that ever happened in America. They will have acquired a better title to respect from other nations and, above all, they will have learned better how to respect themselves."

The sober truth of the foregoing estimate possessed the souls of the people in Philadelphia in the early summer of 1863. The color, the thrill and the glory of the war were all of the past. The newspapers became monotonous with their brief daily records of military funerals, of the return of the wounded from the splendid Philadelphia regiments, shattered at Chancellorsville and Fredericksburg. There were signs portent of another draft. The disloyal element of the city, no longer cowed into hiding, became aggressive. They proclaimed the war a failure, they held meetings under the shadow of Independence Hall and their newspaper, the *Age,* defied patriotic people.

But there was no weakening of purpose with loyal Philadelphia. The wives of soldiers to whom pittances, sorely needed, came from husbands at the front, took the little hoards down to Jay Cooke & Co. and bought Government bonds. That was the spirit and the sacrifice of the time in thousands of homes.

Many of the depleted regiments of New England and New York state, whose terms of service were ended, were passing homeward through the city. At the hands of the tired but steadfast men and women of the great refreshment saloons they were, once more, bountifully fed. Now and then a new regiment passed southward, clean in their fresh uniforms and gay with the old spirit of '61.

There were also long gray lines of prisoners, limping, between their guards, down Washington avenue and amazed to find a good meal and kindly attention awaiting them before they embarked for Fort Delaware.

There was a feeling abroad that the war was approaching its conclusion. In the beautiful June afternoons crowds were thronging to Fairmount Park to enjoy the concerts of Birgfeld's popular band. The Union League and the fire companies were busy planning for a great Fourth of July parade, with banquets and fireworks in the evening. Meanwhile, the veterans of Hooker's army were expected to force back the strenuous gray lines of the enemy within the old battle regions so familiar to both armies. But the newspaper dispatches, from day to day, told the story of the unchecked advance of Confederate cavalry toward the Susquehanna River.

On June 15th President Lincoln had called for 100,000 militia to be mustered into the national service and to serve six months. This call was immediately followed by another from Governor Curtin, in the course of which he said: "We must be true to the thirty-five thousand Pennsylvanians who have fallen on the field of battle." Upon the following day Mayor Henry summoned business men to close their places and arm themselves.

At the City Arsenal buildings, Broad and Race streets, the rifles, cannon, harness, fire-arms, uniforms, equipments, tents and commissary utensils, which had been bought and stored by the city, awaited the expected rush of volunteers, and as fast as they came, with the proper requisitions, they were fitted out and sent to the trains. It was said that a full company could be thus metamorphosed from civilians to soldiers in half an hour.

On the 17th and 18th of June many bodies of the city military proceeded to Harrisburg. Within the week following nearly all of the local militia had gone. Several fine regiments from New York and New Jersey (the first of them being the alert "7th" of New York city) had traversed the city and were now upon the line of defence.

It now became evident that somewhere between Hagerstown and Philadelphia Lee's seventy thousand veteran fighters must be turned back or Philadelphia and probably Baltimore and Washington must capitulate.

Despite the general fear of the people Philadelphia hospitality was extended, that week, to a delegation of visiting officials from the City of Cincinnati.

Upon June 29th Mayor Henry again issued an urgent admonition to the citizents. He said: "You number more than fifty thousand able-bodied men. The means to arm and equip yourselves are at hand. Close your manufactories, workshops and stores before the stern necessity for common safety makes it obligatory. Assemble yourselves forthwith for organization and drill. * * * Spurn from you those who would delude you to inactivity or disaffection. * * * Let no one refuse to arm who will not be able to justify himself before man and God in sight of a desolated hearth or of a dishonored family."* Few public utterances of that time were the equal of this stirring call to

---

*As he wrote these fiery words the gray cavalry of Jenkins was within sight of Harrisburg, and another column of raiders, under Rodes, was assessing York, sixty-five miles from Philadelphia, for heavy tribute in shoes, food and money. The nearest corps of Hooker's army was forty miles or more distant from the points thus reached by the enemy.

duty. Business was very good in Philadelphia in the summer of 1863. A large number of establishments were humming with Government contracts. General manufacturing, locomotive and shipbuilding, these and countless lesser undertakings occupied the earnest attention of a large proportion of the "fifty thousand" thus addressed. To literally cease from these activities meant heavy loss or ruin to many, but there was a rousing response.*

That day policemen carried enrollment blanks from house to house, and those who signed were told to go to Independence Square, where the Mayor and the Commanding General awaited them. Here Major-Gen. N. J. Dana instructed them how to organize and where to report for service.†

The Evening Bulletin's versatile local historian, "Penn," recurring to the stress of the week of Gettysburg, as affecting Philadelphia, says:

"On the day when Reynolds took his position at Seminary Ridge and began the main fight, Governor Curtin was in Philadelphia. He communicated to the Philadelphia authorities and to the officers of the Pennsylvania Railroad the principal facts concerning the critical conditions at the State capital and the difficulty of obtaining exact information from the Federal army, now that it was on the point of contact with the advancing forces of the Confederates. It was at this time that he made his memorable speech from the balcony of the Continental; he exhorted all Philadelphians to spring to arms at once, and some men in after years recalled it as the most impressive in its earnestness that was heard here in the course of the war. This was the speech which produced enough enlistments during the next ten hours to make at least five regiments. Before nightfall the city was in the midst of alarms; all business had come to a standstill, and the report that Reynolds had fallen caused, for the moment, a profound depression. Some dispirited citizens doubted whether the Governor would be able to get back to the Capitol, and the thought of the possibility that it might be necessary to set up the State government in Philadelphia entered many minds."

---

*Three regiments of Maine troops whose enlistments of nine months had expired arrived in Philadelphia, homeward bound, on July 1st, 1863. While dining at the Union Volunteer Refreshment Saloon the Rev. Thomas Brainerd and others appealed to them to remain here and assist in the defence of the city. They were offered, upon the part of the city authorities, fifty dollars each if they would stay ten days. A minority of the men and nearly all of the officers were willing to do so, but the majority refused and all finally departed northward. "Life of Rev. Thomas Brainerd."

†The points designated as rendezvous for citizen volunteers were Commissioners' Hall, at Thirteenth and Spring Garden streets; the City Armory, Broad street, below Race street; the Market House, at Twenty-second and Spring Garden streets, and Commissioners' Hall, at Thirty-seventh and Market streets. A stirring instance of the answer made by the people was the appearance of one hundred workmen at Independence Hall, demanding immediate enrollment. These men were employed at the establishment of S. V. Merrick & Sons, then engaged upon machinery for war ships. At this great plant upon Washington Avenue three companies of armed and uniformed infantry from the working force were maintained by the firm. The volunteers thus mentioned were promptly sworn in, sent to Harrisburg and became Company K of the 31st Regiment Emergency Infantry.

LOCAL DEFENCES OF 1863

A S a measure of protection against the threatened advance of the Confederates upon Philadelphia in June, 1863, a Committee of Defence was authorized by City Councils to establish a number of redoubts commanding the principal approaches. The positions of these earthworks were determined by officers of the United States Coast Survey.* They were placed as follows: On the south side of Chestnut street, east of the junction of Darby road; upon the east side of the Schuylkill River, near the U. S. Arsenal; on the west side of the Schuylkill River, below Gray's Ferry bridge; at the east end of Girard avenue bridge; at Hestonville, near Lancaster avenue, and on School House lane, near Ridge road.

The total cost of these defences, as shown by the records of the City Controller, was $51,537.37. The largest of these works, located at the Falls of the Schuylkill and known as "Fort Dana," was created by the gas-works force, and cost only $3,559.47.†

As far as known no guns were mounted, as the danger ended with the battle of Gettysburg. Several of the redoubts remained for a number of years after the war, as reminders of the strenuous, and, as some critics thought, ridiculous, labors of the excited public of the time.

ORGANIZING FOR DEFENCE

T HERE was no sufficient interval of time between the call of the President, upon June 15th, and the clash of the opposed armies at Gettysburg to carry through the plan of an organized force of men enlisted to serve six months. The companies reporting at Camp Curtin were, therefore, formed upon either an "emergency" basis (these troops becoming temporarily a part of the National force) or upon an enlistment of ninety-day militia, the latter serving as State

---

*The officer in immediate charge of the work was Richard Meade Baché, of Philadelphia.

†Readers interested in the Civil War chronicles of the old 21st Ward, covering the Ridge Road Camps and including the Falls of Schuylkill, Manayunk and Roxborough districts, will find the military history of those sections, prepared by Dr. Charles K. Mills, both accurate and comprehensive. It was printed in serial form in the *Weekly Forecast,* published by Ernest E. Carwardine, at the Falls of the Schuylkill, during the summer of 1913. It is on file at the library of the Historical Society of Pennsylvania.

troops. The newly created "Department of the Susquehanna" had been placed under the command of Major-Gen. Darius N. Couch, U. S. A., with headquarters at Harrisburg. The handling of the constantly arriving militia and volunteers was in his charge.

After the battle of Gettysburg the 36th Regiment, ninety-day militia, was sent to that place, and Col. H. C. Alleman was appointed Military Governor, with other organizations in his command. His duty was to forward wounded and prisoners and gather property from the field. In his report he stated that, in addition to a great amount of war material, he had collected from camps and field hospitals twelve thousand and sixty-one wounded Union soldiers, six thousand one hundred and ninety-seven wounded Confederates, three thousand and six Confederate prisoners and large numbers of stragglers. In this work the 51st Regiment, Col. Oliver Hopkinson, assisted.*

The rapid concentration of the scattered divisions of Hooker by his successor, Meade, in the pathway of Lee's army was a surprise to the enemy, and the assemblage of fifty thousand emergency soldiery in reserve was a phenomenon.† Although but one militia regiment had a part in the battle, the moral effect caused by the gathering of the emergency militia greatly impressed the Southern people and their Northern allies everywhere.‡

Among the many companies formed for local defence or emergency service in June and July, 1863, were the following:

The Bridesburg Guard, composed chiefly of employees of Alfred Jenks & Son, Lieutenant Colonel Barton H. Jenks. This fine Battalion made its own muskets and was uniformed by its commander.
Independent Artillery Company, veterans of the Naval Home.
Gymnast City Guard, Captain Hillebrand. This was the fourth Gymnast Company raised by this officer.
Independent Infantry Militia, composed of workmen at the Navy Yard.
Independent Battery, Light Artillery Militia, composed of workmen at the Navy Yard. Captain Wells, U. S. A.
Independent Company of Minute Men from the Baptist churches.

---

*The official report of Major-Gen. Meade, November, 1863, of the battle of Gettysburg, indicates the capture of 3 guns, 41 standards, 24,978 small arms and 13,621 prisoners. Union losses were 2,834 killed, 13,709 wounded, 6,643 missing.

†The State of Pennsylvania furnished for the summer campaign of 1863 thirty-four regiments enlisted for ninety days and about five thousand emergency men in separate companies and battalions. Very few of these troops died in action or from wounds, but one hundred and twelve died from sickness.

‡On the 26th of June a militia regiment, which had been recruited and sent to Gettysburg from Camp Curtin and designated the 26th Emergency Infantry, commanded by Col. W. W. Jennings, had been marched out the Chambersburg pike to delay, if possible, the Confederate advance. This command, numbering 743 men, encountered a battalion of White's (Confederate) Cavalry four miles from Gettysburg. One hundred and seventy-six of the regiment were captured and paroled. The cavalry was finally repulsed and the 26th marched to Harrisburg. Ex-Governor Samuel W. Pennypacker was a private in this regiment (page 764, "Pennsylvania at Gettysburg," Vol. 2).

Independent Company Militia from First Presbyterian Church.
Independent City Guards, Capt. William Milward.
Franklin Guards, composed of clerks in the offices of the Pennsylvania Railroad and Philadelphia and Reading Railway Companies.
Merrick Guards, from the machine works of Merrick & Sons. On duty at Harrisburg and at Cumberland, Maryland.
Independent Co., Infantry Militia, William Penn Hose Co.
Hatters' Guards, Capt. Isaac Williams (attached to the Merchants' Regiment).
Schuylkill Arsenal Company, Capt. W. H. Gray.
Russell Light Infantry, Col. William Mayer.
Pennsylvania Veterans (76 soldiers of 1812).
Norris Rifles, Carnell's iron foundry.
Pennsylvania Railroad employees, from Washington Avenue wharf, Capt. John Whittaker.
United States Mint Company.
Germantown Home Guard, Capt. Marks J. Biddle.
Falls of Schuylkill Company, Capt. John Dobson.
Engineer Corps, students of the Polytechnic College. (Attached to the 3d Regiment Home Guard, on duty at Dupont Powder Works, Wilmington, Del.)
National League Rifles. Capt. G. C. Steinbach.
Wissahickon Cavalry, Capt. Samuel W. Comly.

EMERGENCY MILITIA FROM PHILADELPHIA, 1863

TWENTIETH REGIMENT MILITIA, INFANTRY.

COLONEL WILLIAM B. THOMAS.

971 Officers and Men.

This command was formed from the 3d Regiment of the Philadelphia Home Guard Brigade. It was composed largely of attaches of the Philadelphia Custom House. It had served as the 20th Regiment, Emergency Militia, in the Antietam campaign of 1862. The regiment was mustered into the United States service upon June 17th, 1863, and assigned to guard duty along the Northern Central Railroad, near York, from which it was forced back by the Confederates at Wrightsville, Pa. The "20th" joined the "27th" under Col. Jacob G. Frick, the First Troop Philadelphia City Cavalry and some other commands there fortifying. Having no artillery, after an engagement Col. Frick's force was obliged to retreat across the Susquehanna river to Columbia, burning the bridge behind it.* The "20th" was mustered out upon August 10th, 1863. In the following year the regiment again served for one hundred days as the 192d Infantry Militia, and finally, in 1865, as the 192d Regiment Infantry Volunteers, under an enlistment of one year.
*Historical Sketch, First Troop Philadelphia City Cavalry.

THIRTY-FIRST REGIMENT MILITIA INFANTRY.

COLONEL JOHN NEWKUMET.

716 Officers and Men.

Companies A, B, C, E and K from Philadelphia.

Mustered into United States service at Harrisburg, June 30th, 1863. Discharged August 8th, 1863. Service in the Department of the Susquehanna.

Company K of this regiment, Capt. James B. German, was composed of workmen from the establishment of S. V. Merrick & Sons.

THIRTY-THIRD REGIMENT MILITIA INFANTRY (BLUE RESERVES).
Colonel William W. Taylor.
654 Officers and Men.

Mustered into United States service at Harrisburg June 26th, 1863. Discharged August 4th, 1863. Service in the Department of the Susquehanna. This regiment was generally known as the "Blue Reserves," of the Reserve Brigade. Many of its members had served in the 8th Regiment, emergency troops of September, 1862.

INDEPENDENT COMPANY MILITIA INFANTRY.
Captain William B. Mann.
100 Officers and Men.

Mustered into United States service at Harrisburg June 17th, 1863. Discharged July 24th, 1863. Service in the Department of the Susquehanna. This was the first command from Philadelphia to reach Harrisburg in response to the call of the Governor, in June, 1863.

INDEPENDENT COMPANY MILITIA INFANTRY.
Captain John Spear.
96 Officers and Men.

Mustered into United States service June 17th, 1863. Discharged July 21st, 1863. Service in Department of the Susquehanna. This command was known as the "Henry Guards," and was composed of members of the Philadelphia police force.

INDEPENDENT COMPANY INFANTRY MILITIA.
Captain Thomas E. Campbell.
150 Officers and Men.

Mustered into United States service July 2d, 1863. Discharged September 16th, 1863. On duty in Department of the Susquehanna.

INDEPENDENT COMPANY INFANTRY MILITIA.
Captain William F. Rich.
100 Officers and Men.

Mustered into United States service June 29th, 1863. Discharged July 8th, 1863.

INDEPENDENT BATTERY MILITIA LIGHT ARTILLERY.
Captain Henry D. Landis.
108 Officers and Men.

Originally recruited by Captain Clement Biddle as Company A, Home Guard Regiment of Artillery. This battery was in the field for a short time during the Antietam emergency. It was mustered into the United States service at Harrisburg upon June 19th, 1863, "for the emergency." The battery was effectively engaged in actions at Sporting Hill, a few miles west of Harrisburg, upon June 30th, and at Carlisle, July 1st, when in the early evening the town was shelled by the Confederates. Mustered out July 30th, 1863.

DEFENCE

OF THE

CITY OF PHILADELPHIA

Office of the Mayor of the City of Philadelphia.

BY VIRTUE OF THE AUTHORITY vested in me, by the Act of the General Assembly of the Commonwealth of Pennsylvania, entitled, "An Act relating to the Home Guard of the City of Philadelphia, Approved the Sixteenth day of May Anno Domini one thousand eight hundred and sixty one.

I do hereby require Brigadier General A. J. PLEASONTON, Commander of the HOME GUARD, to order out (and into the service of the City of Philadelphia,) THE WHOLE OF THE SAID GUARD, for the preservation of the public peace AND THE DEFENCE OF THE CITY. And I hereby call upon all persons within the limits of the said City, to yield a PROMPT AND READY OBEDIENCE to the Orders of the said Commander of the HOME GUARD, and of those acting under his authority in the execution of his and their said duties.

In witness whereof, I have hereunto set my hand and caused the Corporate Seal of the City of Philadelphia, to be affixed, this sixteenth day of June, A. D., one thousand eight hundred and sixty-three.

ALEXANDER HENRY,

Mayor of Philadelphia.

BEFORE GETTYSBURG, THE HOME GUARD ON DUTY.

(From a war time poster.)

HEAD-QUARTERS, HOME GUARD, CITY OF PHILADELPHIA,
June 16th, 1863.

Under the authority of an Act of the General Assembly of the Commonwealth of Pennsylvania, entitled "An Act relating to the Home Guard of the City of Philadelphia," approved the sixteenth day of May, Anno Domini, one thousand eight hundred and sixty-one, and of the requirement of the HON. ALEXANDER HENRY, Mayor of the City made pursuant thereto, and hereto prefixed, the undersigned assumes the duties "FOR THE PRESERVATION OF THE PUBLIC PEACE AND THE DEFENCE OF THE CITY."

He invites the support and co-operation of his fellow-citizens, and of all the Authorities, National, State and Municipal, in the performance of his responsible duties.

A. J. PLEASONTON,

Wm. BRADFORD,
Assistant Adjutant General.

Brigadier General Commanding in Philadelphia.

King & Baird, Printers, 607 Sansom Street, Philadelphia.

AT FIFTH AND CHESTNUT STREETS, JUNE, 1863.
(From Frank Leslie's Weekly.)

INDEPENDENT BATTERY MILITIA LIGHT ARTILLERY.

CAPTAIN E. SPENCER MILLER.

102 Officers and Men.

Having been mustered into the United States service upon June 19th, 1863, "for the emergency," this battery was forwarded from Harrisburg to Chambersburg with a column under Brigadier-General Joseph F. Knipe. Retreating before the superior numbers of the enemy to Carlisle, the command was engaged in disputing the approach of Ewell's Confederates toward Harrisburg. At Oyster Point, a few miles west from the State capital, the battery with its infantry support turned back the invading column. This affair, upon June 28th, 1863, was the most northerly point of conflict in the Civil War. The battery was mustered out July 25th, 1863.

FIRST TROOP PHILADELPHIA CITY CAVALRY.

CAPTAIN SAMUEL J. RANDALL.

75 Officers and Men.

With thousands of soldiers hastening to the Susquehanna river, the "First Troop" entrained upon June 18th, 1863, at Mantua and proceeded to Harrisburg. Two days later the troop was engaged in scouting upon the roads in the vicinity of Gettysburg, encountering, at several points, advance parties of the enemy. As the Confederates increased in force the Union advance retreated. The troop passed through York to Columbia, but again recrossed the bridge at that point, and after a skirmish with the enemy retreated, with the small Union force present, across the Susquehanna. A detail of four troopers set fire to the bridge, which was almost entirely destroyed. Upon the 2d a detachment of the troop crossed the river upon scows and rode to York, there learning of the battle of Gettysburg. From July 16th to 30th the troop was upon provost duty at Philadelphia.*

NINETY-DAY MILITIA FROM PHILADELPHIA, 1863†

THIRTY-SECOND REGIMENT PENNSYLVANIA NINETY-DAY MILITIA (GRAY RESERVES), 1863. GETTYSBURG CAMPAIGN.

COLONEL CHARLES SOMERS SMITH.

894 Offiers and Men.

The 1st Regiment, Infantry Militia (Gray Reserves) reported at Harrisburg upon the evening of June 18th, 1863. Mustered June 26th, the "1st" became, for the time being, the "32d" Regiment, Ninety-Day Militia, United States Service. The command assisted in the defence of Harrisburg, at Fort Washington, upon the high western shore of the Susquehanna river. The "32d" reached Carlisle upon

---

*The expense borne by the troop in this campaign for equipping and other essentials was $6,500.

†All the Ninety-Day regiments of militia of 1863 were mustered into the United States service "for the defence of the State of Pennsylvania."

the evening of July 1st, 1863, accompanied by Landis' Battery, being subjected to an artillery fire for several hours from a Confederate battery. One casualty occurred in the "32d." Private Charles W. Colladay, of Company D, was fatally wounded by the fragment of a shell. This soldier is said to have been killed at a point farther north than where any other Union volunteer fell during the war.

None of the Philadelphia troops of the "Ninety-Day" enlistment were present at Gettysburg. The "32d" was ordered, with the brigade of Gen. Brisbane, upon a tour of the South Mountain, in Maryland, and the lower Shenandoah Valley, returning to Philadelphia upon July 27th, where the command was mustered out August 1st.

FORTIETH REGIMENT INFANTRY, NINETY-DAY MILITIA.

Colonel Alfred M. Day.

700 Officers and Men.

Mustered into the United States service at Harrisburg, July 1st, 1863. Discharged, August 3d-4th, 1863. On duty Department of the Susquehanna. This command was known as the "First Coal Trade Regiment."

The Coal Trade of Philadelphia uniformed and armed the 40th and 51st Regiments of 1863, and paid a bounty of $25.00 to each recruit.

FORTY-FOURTH REGIMENT INFANTRY, NINETY-DAY MILITIA.

Colonel Enos Woodward.

1,000 Officers and Men.

Mustered in the United States service July 1st., 1863. Discharged August 27th, 1863. On duty Department of the Susquehanna. This command was designated "The Merchants' Regiment."

FORTY-FIFTH REGIMENT INFANTRY, NINETY-DAY MILITIA.

Colonel James T. Clancy.

Mustered into United States service July 1st, 1863. Discharged, August 29th, 1863. On duty Department of the Susquehanna. This command was designated the "First Union League Regiment."

FORTY-NINTH REGIMENT INFANTRY, NINETY-DAY MILITIA.

Colonel Alexander Murphy.

950 Officers and Men.

Company A and part of Company B from Washington Grays, Company E from Luzerne, Pa.; Company K from Lancaster. Mustered into the United States Service July 14th, 1863. Discharged September 2d-3d, 1863. On duty Department of the Susquehanna. (Second Corn Exchange Regiment.)

FIFTY-FIRST REGIMENT INFANTRY, NINETY-DAY MILITIA.

Colonel Oliver Hopkinson.

783 Officers and Men.

Mustered into United States service July 3d, 1863. Discharged September 2d, 1863. On duty Department of the Susquehanna. This regiment was ordered to Gettysburg following the battle, and assisted in the work of removing the wounded, burying the dead and guarding the military material left upon the field. This command was known as the "Second Coal Trade Regiment."

FIFTY-SECOND REGIMENT INFANTRY, NINETY-DAY MILITIA.

COLONEL WILLIAM A. GRAY.

716 Officers and Men.

Mustered into the United States service July 9th, 1863. Discharged September 1st, 1863. On duty at Philadelphia. This command was known as the "Second Union League Regiment."

FIFTY-NINTH REGIMENT INFANTRY, NINETY-DAY MILITIA.

COLONEL GEORGE P. McLEAN.

718 Officers and Men.

Mustered into United States service July 1st, 1863. Discharged September 9th, 1863. On duty at Philadelphia. This command was known as the "Third Union League Regiment."

SIXTIETH REGIMENT INFANTRY, NINETY-DAY MILITIA.

COLONEL WILLIAM F. SMALL.

361 Officers and Men.

Mustered into United States service June 19th, 1863. Discharged September 8th, 1863. On duty at Philadelphia. This command was known as the "Victualers' Regiment."

INDEPENDENT COMPANY CAVALRY, PENNSYLVANIA NINETY-DAY MILITIA.

CAPTAIN RICHARD W. HAMMELL.

104 Officers and Men.

Mustered into United States service July 2d, 1863. Discharged September 16th, 1863. On duty in the anthracite region of Pennsylvania. This command was known as the "Dana Troop," and was organized largely from late members of the "Anderson" Cavalry, under the direction of a committee of the Union League.

INDEPENDENT BATTERY LIGHT ARTILLERY, NINETY-DAY MILITIA.

CAPTAIN BENONI FRISHMUTH.

104 Officers and Men.

Mustered into United States service June 26th, 1863. Discharged August 1st, 1863. On duty Department of the Susquehanna.

INDEPENDENT BATTERY LIGHT ARTILLERY, NINETY-DAY MILITIA.

CAPTAIN EDWARD FITZKI.

143 Officers and Men.

Mustered into United States service July 6th, 1863. Discharged August 24th, 1863. On duty Department of the Susquehanna.

MONUMENTS, MARKERS AND TABLETS AT GETTYSBURG

Indicating positions of Philadelphia Regiments and Batteries.

INFANTRY

Regiment.	Brigade.	Corps.	Location.
2d Res.	McCandless	5	Ayres ave., East Wheat Field.
12th Res.	Fisher (9 companies)	5	Big Round Top.
23	Shaler	6	Slocum ave., North Culp's Hill.
26	Carr	3	Emmitsburg road, North of Sickles ave.
27	Coster	11	Coster ave.
27	do	11	East Cemetery Hill.
28	Candy	12	Slocum ave., North Culp's Hill.
28	do	12	(Marker) Rock Creek, east of Culp's Hill.
29	Kane	12	Slocum ave., North Culp's Hill.
29	do	12	Slocum ave., South Culp's Hill.
56	Cutler (9 companies)	1	North Reynolds ave.
61	Neill	6	Neill ave., Wolf Hill.
68	Graham	3	Peach Orchard.
68	do	3	Wheat Field road, opposite Peach Orchard.
69	Webb	2	Webb ave., Stone Fence, The Angle.
69	do	2	(Company markers) Webb ave., Stone Fence, The Angle.
71	do	2	Webb ave., Stone Fence, The Angle.
72	do	2	Webb ave., Stone Fence, The Angle.
72	do	2	Webb ave., north of Copse of Trees.
73	Coster	11	East Cemetery Hill.
74	Amsberg	11	West Howard ave.
74	do	11	(Markers) National Cemetery.
75	Krzyzanowski	11	East Howard ave.
75	do	11	National Cemetery.
81	Cross	2	Sickles ave., Wheat Field.
82	Shaler	6	Slocum ave., North Culp's Hill.
88	Baxter	1	Doubleday ave., Oak Ridge.
88	do	1	(Marker) Forney Field, Oak Ridge.
88	do	1	(Marker) North Hancock ave., Ziegler's Grove.
88	do	1	(Marker) South Hancock ave.
90	do	1	Doubleday ave., Oak Ridge.
90	do	1	North Hancock ave., Ziegler's Grove.
90	do	1	(Boulder) South Hancock ave.
90	do	1	(Howell Tablet) Chambersburg Street Lutheran Church.
91	Weed	5	Sykes ave., Summit Little Round Top.
95	Bartlett	6	Wheat Field road, north of Valley of Death.
98	Nevin	6	Field north of Valley of Death.
98	do	6	Sykes ave., north slope Little Round Top.
99	Ward	3	Sickles ave., Devil's Den Hill.
99	do	3	North Hancock ave.
106	Webb	2	Hancock ave., near Copse of Trees.
106	do	2	Emmitsburg road, Codori Buildings.
106	do	2	(Marker) East Cemetery Hill.
109	Kane	12	Slocum ave., South Culp's Hill.
110	De Trobriand (6 companies)	3	Brooke ave., southwest of Wheat Field.
114	Graham	3	Emmitsburg road, Sherfy House.
114	do	3	Central Hancock ave., east of The Angle.
115	Burling	3	Brooke ave., South Wheat Field.
116	Kelly (4 companies)	2	Sickles ave., at The Loop.
118	Tilton	5	Sickles ave., at The Loop (first position).
118	do	5	(Marker) Wheat Field road (second position).
118	do	5	North slope of Round Top (third position).
119	Russell	6	Howe ave., east of Round Top.
119	do	6	North slope of Round Top.
121	Biddle	1	South Reynolds ave.
121	do	1	Central Hancock ave.
147	Candy (8 companies)	12	Geary ave., South Culp's Hill.
147	Candy	12	(Marker) Sykes ave., north slope of Little Round Top.
150	Stone	1	Stone ave., McPherson Ridge.
150	do	1	Central Hancock ave.

252

CAVALRY

Regiment.	Brigade.	Corps.	Location.
2	Provost guard_____	General Head-quarters.	Meade ave.
3	McIntosh_____	Cavalry__	Gregg ave., East Cavalry battlefield.
3	_____do_____	___do_____	Marker on Low Dutch road, extreme right, Army of the Potomac.
6	Merritt_____	___do_____	Emmitsburg road, 1½ miles south of Peach Orchard.
6	Companies E and I__	General Head-quarters.	Meade ave., Meade's Headquarters.
8	Huey_____	Cavalry__	Pleasanton ave.
16	Gregg, J. Irvin_____	___do_____	Deardorff Farm, on right flank.
18	Farnsworth_____	___do_____	Confederate ave., Bushman Woods.

ARTILLERY

Battery.	Commander.	Corps.	Location.
1 (F and G)___	Ricketts_____	Reserve___	East Cemetery Hill.
E_____	Knap_____	12	Slocum ave., North Culp's Hill. (Section.)
E_____	_____do_____	12	Powers' Hill.

MARKERS OF BRIGADES, ARMY OF THE POTOMAC (INDICATING POSITIONS OF BRIGADES, WHICH INCLUDED PHILADELPHIA TROOPS).

INFANTRY

Brigade.	Division.	Corps.	Commander.	Location.
2_____	1	1	Butler_____	North Reynolds ave.
2_____	2	1	Baxter_____	Doubleday ave., north end.
1_____	3	1	Biddle_____	Reynolds ave., south of Springs road.
2_____	3	1	Stone_____	Stone ave., north end.
1_____	1	2	Cross_____	Ayres ave., center.
2_____	1	2	Kelly_____	Sickles ave., near The Loop.
2_____	2	2	Webb_____	Hancock ave., at The Angle.
2_____	1	3	Ward_____	Sickles ave., north of Devil's Den.
3_____	1	3	DeTrobriand_____	Sickles ave., Wheatfield.
1_____	2	3	Carr_____	Sickles ave., near north end.
3_____	2	3	Burling_____	Brooke ave., Wheat Field.
3_____	2	5	Weed_____	Sykes ave., Little Round Top.
1_____	3	5	McCandless_____	Ayres ave., Center.
2_____	1	6	Bartlett_____	Wheatfield road, near Plum Run.
3_____	1	6	Russell_____	Howe ave.
2_____	3	6	Eustis_____	Sedgwick ave., south section.
3_____	3	6	Nevin_____	Lane, north of Crawford ave.
1_____	2	11	Coster_____	Coster ave., center.
2_____	3	22	Krzyzanowski_____	Howard ave., east of Carlisle road.
2_____	2	12	Kane_____	Slocum ave., north end Geary ave.

CAVALRY

Brigade.	Division.	Corps.	Commander.	Location.
Reserve_____	1	Cavalry__	Merritt_____	Emmitsburg road, South Cavalry Field.
1_____	2	Cavalry__	McIntosh_____	East Cavalry battlefield.
2_____	2	Cavalry__	Huey_____	Pleasanton ave.
3_____	2	Cavalry__	J. I. Gregg_____	Near Hanover road, East Cavalry battlefield.
1_____	3	Cavalry__	Farnsworth_____	Section 6, Confederate ave.

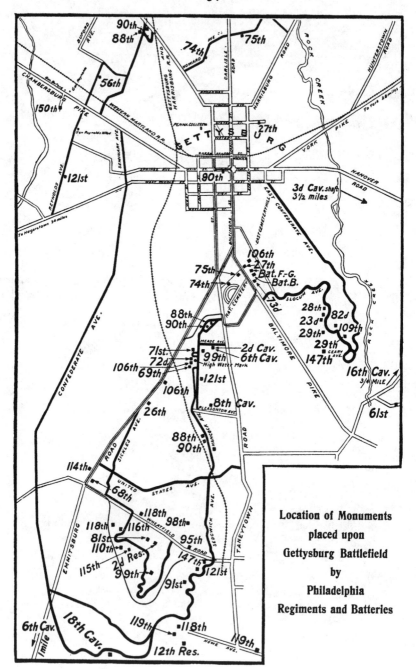

Location of Monuments
placed upon
Gettysburg Battlefield
by
Philadelphia
Regiments and Batteries

MONUMENTS AND MARKERS ERECTED BY THE GETTYSBURG NATIONAL PARK COMMISSION.

Brevet Lieut.-Col. JOHN P. NICHOLSON, Chairman.

ARMY OF THE POTOMAC MONUMENT, HANCOCK AVENUE, AT THE ANGLE.

CORPS OF THE ARMY OF THE POTOMAC

Corps.	Commander.	Location.
1	Doubleday	Reynolds ave., south of Chambersburg pike.
2	Hancock	Hancock ave., north of Meade ave.
3	Sickles	Peach Orchard, northwest corner.
5	Sykes	Little Round Top, north slope.
6	Sedgwick	Sedgwick ave., north of center.
11	Howard	Howard ave., west of Carlisle road.
12	Slocum	Slocum ave., south slope Culp's Hill.
Cavalry	Pleasonton	Pleasanton ave.

DIVISIONS, ARMY OF THE POTOMAC

Division.	Corps.	Commander.	Location.
1	1	Wadsworth	Reynolds ave., north of Chambersburg pike.
2	1	Robinson	Robinson ave., center.
3	1	Rowley	Reynolds ave., north of Springs road.
1	2	Caldwell	Hancock ave., south of center.
2	2	Gibbon	Hancock ave., center.
3	2	Hays	Hancock ave.
1	3	Birney	Peach Orchard, northwest corner.
2	3	Humphreys	Do.
2	3	do	Sickles ave., south of Emmitsburg road.
1	5	Barnes	Sickles ave., south of Wheatfield road.
2	5	Ayres	Knoll east of Ayres ave.
3	5	Crawford	Crawford ave., near Plum Run.
1	6	Wright	Sedgwick ave., south of center.
2	6	Howe	Howe ave.
3	6	Wheaton	Sedgwick ave.
1	11	Barlow	Howard ave., foot of Barlow Knoll.
2	11	Steinwehr	Baltimore pike, opposite National Cemetery Gate.
3	11	Schurz	Howard ave., west of Mummasburg road.
1	12	Ruger	Slocum ave., south section.
2	12	Geary	Slocum ave., south of center.
1	Cavalry	Buford	Reynolds ave., near Reynolds Woods.
2	do	Gregg	East Cavalry Field, on Gregg ave.
3	do	Kilpatrick	Section 6, Bushman's Woods.
	Artillery Reserve.	Tyler	South end, Pleasanton ave.

ARMY AF THE POTOMAC ITINERARY TABLETS.

Nine bronze tablets, Baltimore pike, front of East Cemetery Hill.
Iron tablets:
June 29, 1863, Uniontown, Md.
June 29, 1863, Middleburg, Md.
June 29 and July 3, 1863, Westminster, Md.
June 30 and July 1, 1863, Hanover, Pa.
June 30 and July 1, 1863, Taneytown, Md.

Iron tablets—Continued:
June 30 and July 3, 1863, Manchester, Md.
July 1, 1863, Emmitsburg. Md.
July 1 and 7, 1863, Two Taverns, Pa.
July 2, 1863, Hunterstown, Pa.
July 5, 1863, Littlestown, Pa.
July 6, 1863, Fairfield, Pa.

OTHER MONUMENTS OF SPECIAL INTEREST TO PHILADELPHIANS.

GETTYSBURG—1913

IN the week beginning Sunday, June 30th, 1913, forty thousand survivors of the Union armies met eleven thousand Confederate veterans, sharing with them, in peace and amity, in the semi-centennial celebration of the Battle at Gettysburg. It was an event unique in the history of human affairs. As a renewed affirmation of the principle of national sovereignty, as superior to that of any subordinate part, by a now invincible free people, it was of world-wide importance. Conceding all honor and valor to the veterans of the Southern cause, conceding nothing at variance with the immortal sentences spoken there by Abraham Lincoln, the soldiers of the North took the gray Confederates to their hearts and together they wrote a new and enduring pact and sealed it with the red seal of that field of fields; and where these men, once armed enemies, now comrades under one flag, stood face to face, their aged bodies young once more with patriotic ecstasy, a great temple will arise, and on its walls of marble and bronze will be recited the last chapter of the story which began at Sumter. 'Those who were thus briefly gathered must soon pass to their eternal bivouac, but centuries hence the message to posterity here and then written will stir the souls and inspire the united action of all patriots when our country is endangered from abroad or threatened by dictators from within.

SEMI-CENTENNIAL REUNION AT GETTYSBURG, JULY 1st TO JULY 4th, 1913

THE movement which culminated in the great and impressive gathering of Union and Confederate veterans upon the field of Gettysburg, in celebration of the fiftieth anniversary of the battle at that place, originated at a meeting of citizens of Gettysburg invited by Col. John P. Nicholson, Chairman of the U. S. Gettysburg Battlefield Commission, held for the discussion of the project on the evening of September 8th, 1908. At a subsequent meeting held in the Court House a local committee was organized.

The Fiftieth Anniversary Commission of the Battle of Gettysburg was created by the Pennsylvania Legislature pursuant to an enactment adopted May 13th, 1909.

The Pennsylvania Legislature appropriated the sum of $150,000 for the purposes of the celebration and the United States Government provided a like sum. The details of the preparatory work and the maintenance of the Camp were under the control of the War Department. Subsistence was furnished by the State of Pennsylvania. Representative veterans of nearly all of the States attended the several meetings of the Pennsylvania Commission, their reports resulting in appropriations by the several Commonwealths, with few exceptions, providing for the cost of transportation of veterans to the celebration and return to their homes. The officers of the United States Army detailed to establish the camp, the Pennsylvania Commission, the Commissions of the other States, the Gettysburg Battlefield Commission, the Grand Army of the Republic, the Confederate veteran associations and the citizens of Gettysburg co-operated in a common purpose, to make the event memorable.

The number of veterans of the two armies who were gathered here during the week of beginning June 29th, 1913, is estimated to have been 55,000. Many thousands of civilians were also attracted to the field. The detail of four troops of the 15th U. S. Cavalry posted here for guard duty was materially assisted in the care and guidance of the old

17

soldiers by a large detachment of boy-scouts from Philadelphia and by a portion of the State police force. An extensive system of field hospitals so thoroughly safeguarded the aged guests of the State and nation that the number of deaths during the week (nine) was below the normal average. The railroads transported the vast assemblage to and fro with but little delay and without accident.

The members of the Battle of Gettysburg Commission at the date of the encampment were Col. J. M. Schoonmaker, Chairman; Brevet Brig.-Gen. William D. Dixon, Brevet Col. R. Bruce Ricketts, Corporal Irvin K. Campbell, Capt. William E. Miller, Capt. George F. Baer, Capt. John P. Green; Secretary, Lieut.-Col. Lewis E. Beitler.

Of the original Commission Col. Lewis T. Brown, Adjt. William Penn Lloyd and Major Alexander McDowell died before the period of the celebration. Gen. Louis Wagner, the first chairman, Capt. J. Richards Boyle, D.D., the first Secretary, and Gen. R. Dale Benson resigned.

The vast encampment was planned by Brevet Lieut.-Col. Emmor B. Cope, Engineer U. S. Commission. It was established ready for occupancy by Major James E. Normoyle, U. S. A., and Capt. H. F. Dalton, U. S. A., of the Quartermaster's Department. The U. S. Cavalry was in command of Major Charles O. Rhoades, U. S. A.

Lincoln's Gettysburg Address Memorial

JULY 4TH, 1863

THE late Henry Armitt Brown, Esq., speaking ten years after the event, thus described the suspense of the people of Philadelphia while awaiting messages from the scene of conflict on July 4th, 1863.

"It was the Nation's birthday, but there was no rejoicing. No sounds filled the streets save the rattling of the hurrying wagons and the rapid tramp of marching men. The frightened women gathered in the houses and 'muttered with white lips.' Men talked on the corners in hushed and anxious crowds. The air grew sultry and still. Suspense hung over all as in that breathless moment before the breaking of a storm. Sullenly the great sun sank behind the western hills round as a shield and as red as blood. Men hurried to their homes, but not to sleep. On a sudden there came a sound. Like the rushing of the cooling breeze it grew louder and more loud. The people ran into the streets to clasp each other by the hand. The clamor of many voices rose into the air as wild crowds jostled to and fro, with shouts and rejoicing, only half knowing why. Then, from yon ancient steeple, rang out the long familiar bell. The whole city was frenzied with delight. Rousing herself, Philadelphia held her breath to hear how our own Meade had stood like a lion between her and the foe as the wave of rebellion broke into spray and receded from the heights of Gettysburg."

Far westward, among Pennsylvania's hills, the red sun went down. In the stillness of a deserted battlefield men with lanterns and litters were busy garnering the winrows of death. Slowly the long trains, heavy with shattered survivors of yesterday, crept hitherward, and on the morrow Philadelphia knew the price of her defence.

THE ELLETS AND THE MISSISSIPPI RAM FLEET

CHARLES M. ELLET, Jr., of Philadelphia, was, prior to the Civil War, a civil engineer. Two of his important achievements were the construction of the once famous wire bridge across the Schuylkill River at Fairmount and the first suspension bridge at Niagara Falls. To his fertile mind was due the idea of employing ram steamers upon the Mississippi River and its tributaries for the purpose of destroying the inland navy of the enemy. He argued the project so strongly at Washington that he was given a commission as colonel of engineers in March, 1862, in order to try the experiment. At Pittsburgh and other points on the Ohio River he rebuilt nine steamers. A portion of the several crews were enlisted in Philadelphia. Detachments of sharpshooters were also placed upon the boats, these being volunteers from Illinois regiments under the command of Capt. Alfred M. Ellet. Col. Ellet was mortally wounded in a brilliant naval battle at Memphis, June 6th, 1862. His son, Charles Rivers Ellet, a young physician, then became fleet commander, acting under orders of Admiral Farragut. The vicissitudes of the service undermined his health and he died at Bunker Hill, Ill., October 29th, 1863, in his twenty-first year. Father and son rest in Laurel Hill Cemetery. To their bravery and resource was largely due the end of Confederate power on the lower Mississippi River.*

PHILADELPHIA COMPANIES ENLISTED IN REGIMENTS OF OTHER STATES

A T a period when it became necessary to enforce drafts in order to fill quotas, serious differences existed between the city authorities and the Government officials, stationed in Philadelphia, with regard to the credits due the city upon the numbers of men already serving in the national armies. Apropos of this, a special committee of Councils, of which Joseph Sites was chairman (in charge of the City Relief Fund for the families of soldiers), reported: "We are furnishing relief to about two thousand families of soldiers enlisted in other States. As the average of those seeking relief is one in three, it is estimated that six thousand Philadelphia men are thus serving in regiments of other States."

In the early summer of 1861 notices of the departure of detachments of men for New York City and elsewhere outside of the State of Pennsylvania were very frequent in the Philadelphia papers. Ardent seekers for military glory, witnessing the march of New York troops through the city, hastened to offer their services where there seemed a better prospect of getting to the front. Officers of local companies, tired of delay in the process of acceptance and muster here, took their men where they were eagerly accepted. Philadelphia was already a fertile ground for recruiting agents from adjoining States and continued to be so until it finally became unlawful for outside agents to pick up recruits in this community.†

---

*The Mississippi Marine Brigade, afterward organized to patrol the western rivers, was a separate force of 2,000 men manning a fleet of eight vessels commanded by Gen. Alfred M. Ellet. (History of the Nat. Asso. of Naval Veterans, Simmons.)

†By an ordinance of Councils dated July 14th, 1864, the Mayor was authorized to enforce in the city an Act of the Assembly to punish agents recruiting men for military organizations of other States.

EASTERN TROOPS TO THE ARMY OF THE CUMBERLAND

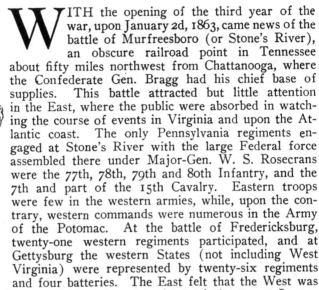

WITH the opening of the third year of the war, upon January 2d, 1863, came news of the battle of Murfreesboro (or Stone's River), an obscure railroad point in Tennessee about fifty miles northwest from Chattanooga, where the Confederate Gen. Bragg had his chief base of supplies. This battle attracted but little attention in the East, where the public were absorbed in watching the course of events in Virginia and upon the Atlantic coast. The only Pennsylvania regiments engaged at Stone's River with the large Federal force assembled there under Major-Gen. W. S. Rosecrans were the 77th, 78th, 79th and 80th Infantry, and the 7th and part of the 15th Cavalry. Eastern troops were few in the western armies, while, upon the contrary, western commands were numerous in the Army of the Potomac. At the battle of Fredericksburg, twenty-one western regiments participated, and at Gettysburg the western States (not including West Virginia) were represented by twenty-six regiments and four batteries. The East felt that the West was abundantly able to take care of its own share of the war. It was distinctly a surprise and a shock, therefore, when, on September 23d, 1863, twenty thousand picked troops were suddenly taken from the Army of the Potomac and hurried westward, under Gen. Hooker, to Chattanooga.* The troops transferred were the Eleventh and Twelfth Corps, which now became a part of the Twentieth Corps.† The 15th Pennsylvania Cavalry, largely composed of Philadelphians, was, up to this time, with the exception of the 7th Cavalry and 9th Veteran Volunteer Cavalry, the only command in the Army of the Cumberland which was of local interest. This regiment, commanded by Col. William J. Palmer, was attached to the Second Division of the Fourteenth Army Corps. The regiments arriving with Hooker, wholly or partly of Philadelphia volunteers, were the 27th, 28th, 29th, 73d, 75th, 109th, 111th and 147th Infantry, and Knap's Ind. Battery E.

The result of the sanguinary battle of Chickamauga, fought Sep-

---

*Of the forty-nine regiments, one company of infantry and seven batteries in the Hooker movement, thirty-five regiments, one company and three batteries were from the eastern States.

†Under General Order No. 72, dated March 24th, 1863, the original Twentieth Army Corps was consolidated with the Twenty-first Corps to form the Fourth Corps, which was placed in command of Major-Gen. Gordon Granger.

tember 19th, 1863, was to "bottle up" the forty thousand men under Rosecrans at Chattanooga. This city is located upon a picturesque bend of the Tennessee River, and is dominated by the lofty cliffs of Lookout Mountain, and the heights of Mission (or Missionary) Ridge. Gen. Bragg had occupied these points of vantage as well as the approaches with a superior force, and had sat down, contentedly, to starve out the Federals. Major-General Hooker's errand was to correct this condition of things.

Upon October 16th, 1863, the several western departments of the army were consolidated into the "Military Division of the Mississippi," and Major-General U. S. Grant was placed in command. His immediate subordinates were Major-General William T. Sherman and Major-General George H. Thomas. The dramatic events which subsequently transpired in the vicinity of Chattanooga and later upon Gen. Sherman's famous march, "one hundred thousand strong," are outlined in the stories of these regiments and that of the 15th Cavalry.

The following memorials stand in testimony of the services rendered by the Philadelphia troops in the vicinity of Chattanooga.

27th Pennsylvania Infantry, Monument, Orchard Knob.
28th Pennsylvania Infantry, Monument on slope of Lookout Mountain.
29th Pennsylvania Infantry, Tablet, palisade of Lookout Mountain.
73d Pennsylvania Infantry, Monument, Missionary Ridge, near tunnel.
75th Pennsylvania Infantry, Monument, Orchard Knob.
109th Pennsylvania Infantry, Monument, Orchard Knob.
147th Pennsylvania Infantry, Monument, near Craven House, Lookout Mountain.
9th Pennsylvania Cavalry, Monument, near Glenn House, Chickamauga National Park.
15th Pennsylvania Cavalry, Monument, Dyer House, Chickamauga National Park.
Knap's Battery E, Monument, Orchard Knob.

THE UNITED STATES SANITARY COMMISSION

BY far the most beneficent of the many civilian organizations formed for the help of the soldiers and alleviation of their sufferings through the Civil War was the United States Sanitary Commission, which originated with a group of ladies in New York City, led by the Rev. Henry W. Bellows. This association was given official status by the Secretary of War upon June 8th, 1861. The members of the United States Sanitary Commission were: Rev. Henry W. Bellows, Chairman; Prof. A. D. Bache, Chief of the U. S. Coast Survey; Prof. Jeffries Wyman; W. H. Van Buren; R. C. Wood, Surgeon-General; Gen. G. W. Cullom, of Gen. Scott's Staff, and Alexander

Shiras. Branches of the Commission were formed in every large northern city. Large sums of money were constantly placed at the disposal of the officers, coming especially from the Pacific Coast. The officials and committees toiled without pay. The Sanitary Commission undertook to handle and forward supplies and comforts to the men at the front, and to assist, by every humane means, in the relief work among the wounded after the great battles. A general hospital directory was published by a Bureau of Information, located at Washington, in order to enable friends and relatives to find soldiers in the army hospitals. A claim agency and pension agency were maintained without cost to the soldiers. More than forty Soldiers' Homes were established, having a daily average of twenty-three hundred inmates. Sixty hospital inspectors constantly visited every portion of the army. Hospital trains were operated over the railroads, and hospital vessels upon the seas. As far as possible the Commission supplied food, medicine and clothing to the prisoners of war held in the South.

It is stated by Lossing, the historian of the Civil War, that the Commission handled gratuitious supplies valued at $15,000,000 and money to the amount of over $5,000,000.

In Philadelphia the local branch, located at 1307 Chestnut street, received cash and supplies to the amount of $1,565,377, eighty per cent. of which was expended outside of the city.

In connection with the battle of Gettysburg the Sanitary Commission expended, in field work, $75,000. The outlay often exceeded $20,000 per diem. The local Commission provided a "lodge" at Thirteenth and Christian streets for the temporary subsistence and shelter of soldiers.

In aid of the Sanitary Commission great fairs were held in New York City, Brooklyn, Chicago, Boston, Albany, Buffalo, Cleveland, Pittsburgh, St. Louis, Cincinnati, Baltimore, Washington and Philadelphia.

In the spring of 1864 the Sanitary Commission projected the Sanitary Fair at Philadelphia, which was opened upon Logan Square on June 7th. The buildings, which were constructed in forty working days, enclosed many of the trees. The main building extended through the center of the square, from Eighteenth to Nineteenth street, and was of Gothic arch design, 540 feet long and 60 feet wide. Single floor buildings extended around the four sides of the square, and were connected by corridors with the central feature called "Union Avenue."* A splendid loan collection of paintings filled the northern corridor. A great variety of displays and amusement features were provided. President Lincoln attended the Fair upon June 16th, accompanied by Mrs. Lincoln. The Fair was open two weeks. The cost of the undertaking

---

*The Art Gallery was kept open to July 6th, when a sale of contributed drawings and paintings was held. During July the buildings were used as barracks for three thousand convalescents gathered to assist in repelling the then threatening Confederate advance into Maryland and Pennsylvania.

was largely derived from popular subscription, and the enterprise netted the Sanitary Commission $1,046,859.*

The New Jersey and Delaware Branches of the Sanitary Commission worked nobly to assist in this splendid result.

The Executive Committee of the United States Sanitary Commission, Local Branch of Philadelphia, was composed of Horace Binney, Jr., Chairman; Matthew W. Baldwin, Rev. H. A. Boardman, John C. Cresson, J. I. Clark Hare, Samuel Powell, Thomas T. Tasker, Edward Hartshorne, Caleb Cope, R. M. Lewis, Charles J. Stille, Fairman Rogers, S. Vaughan Merrick and William M. Tilghman.

The Women's Pennsylvania Branch of the United States Sanitary Commission was organized on February 25th, 1863. The special work of this auxiliary was the relief of soldiers' dependents and the gathering of supplies for the men in the field.†

The officers were Mrs. Caleb Cope, President and Treasurer; Mrs. R. M. Lewis, Secretary. Executive Committee: Mrs. M. B. Grier, Mrs. George Plitt, Mrs. Bloomfield Moore, Mrs. B. Griffith, Mrs. Wm. H. Furniss, Mrs. D. Samuel, Mrs. J. Edgar Thompson, Mrs. Joseph R. Chandler, Miss S. Dunlap, Mrs. Lathrop, Mrs. C. J. Stille, Mrs. T. A. Budd, Mrs. R. M. Lewis, Mrs. M. M. Duane and Mr. Philip P. Randolph.

THE CHRISTIAN COMMISSION

UPON November 15th, 1861, delegates from fourteen branches of the Young Men's Christian Association met in New York City and organized the Christian Commission, electing George H. Stuart, a distinguished citizen of Philadelphia, as permanent chairman. The city, therefore, became the center of a national movement for the moral and spiritual welfare of the soldiers. Of the nearly five thousand agents of the Commission, eventually sent to the army everywhere, the first group was composed of fourteen members of the Philadelphia Y. M. C. A.

For a long period the Government army officers and many of the chaplains tolerated, but did not heartily assist, the Commission's agents.

---

*A blank book, known as the "Record of Honor," was kept at the Sanitary Fair, wherein the friends and relatives of soldiers were permitted to write of their deeds of personal bravery. It was understood that this book was to be deposited at the Philadelphia Library, but it was probably lost.

†The final report of the United States Sanitary Commission of January 1st, 1866, included an estimate showing that Philadelphia furnished during the war a total of 150,000 men. This was evidently based largely on surmise.

GOVERNMENT LABORATORY.
N. E. Corner of Sixth and Jefferson Streets.

U. S. NAVAL HOSPITAL AND HOME.

FAIR OF THE U. S. SANITARY COMMISSION AT LOGAN SQUARE, JUNE 7TH TO 21ST, 1864.

(Redrawn from a war time lithograph.)

Authority to visit and work among the soldiers was officially given in some instances, and refused or revoked in others. Along with its moral propaganda the Commission began to provide material comforts, especially to the sick and wounded in the hospitals. In November, 1863, an arrangement was effected with the Confederate authorities which enabled the Commission to send food, medicine and clothing to the Union prisoners confined at Richmond. It was not until September, 1864, that an order was signed by General U. S. Grant giving the representatives of the Christian Commission full privileges in the camps of the army. In the three and a half years of its activity the Commission performed a noble work.* The entire receipts in that period were $6,291,107.

The Philadelphia offices of the Christian Commission were located at 1011 Chestnut street, where the assistance given to soldiers and sailors and to strangers seeking relatives in the hospitals was constant and important. The Christian Commission established cordial relations with the United States Sanitary Commission, and they co-operated in the cities, camps and on the seas everywhere in the glorious work to which both organizations were devoted. The officers of the Christian Commission were George H. Stuart, President; Joseph Patterson, Treasurer, and Rev. W. E. Boardman, Secretary.

In August, 1864, the activities of the U. S. Christian Commission required an enlargement of its executive *personnel.*. The Executive Committee was increased from five to fourteen, and the general body from twelve to forty-seven. The Philadelphia members of the Executive Committee, under the reorganization, were George H. Stuart, Chairman; Joseph Patterson, Treasurer; Rev. W. E. Boardman, Secretary; John P. Crozer, Jay Cooke, Bishop M. Simpson, D.D., Stephen Caldwell aud H. G. Jones.

THE PATRIOTIC CLERGY AND CHAPLAINS

WITH few exceptions the clergymen of Philadelphia were staunch supporters of the Union cause. Many of them resigned their pastorates to accompany departing regiments as chaplains. Others devoted themselves to exhausting and gratuitous labor in the military hospitals, and led in every humane enterprise for the help of soldiers' families and the care of the orphans of men who had perished while in the armies of the North.

---

*After every great battle the Christian Commission vied with the Sanitary Commission in forwarding to field hospitals material comforts. In the summer of 1864 its agents shipped cargoes of onions to the front, to the great delight of the whole army.

Repeatedly, through proclamations from hundreds of pulpits, the citizens were aroused to defensive action in time of emergency. Many churches were offered and used as temporary hospitals. In the numerous camps of rendezvous within the city limits Sunday services were conducted by the local clergy, assisted by the choirs of their respective churches, and day by day, as military funerals wended their sad course to the cemeteries, it was the task of the minister and the priest to comfort the mourners in thousands of desolated homes. Foremost in connection with the splendid records of the Union Volunteer Refreshment Saloon stands the name of Thomas Brainerd, pastor of the old Pine street church, out of whose congregation one hundred and thirty young men entered the army and navy.*

Among the chaplains of Philadelphia regiments and hospitals were the following:

Reverends William Fulton, James G. Shinn, Charles A. Beck, Charles W. Heisley, Benjamin F. Sewall, Edward C. Ambler, Michael F. Martin, Washington B. Erben, Gamaliel Collins, Ephraim Bast, Ferdinand Miller, E. L. Wittig, Francis Goekeritz, Stacy Wilson, Charles W. Clothier, Horatio S. Howell.† Joseph Welsh, Henry Ginal, John K. Karcher, J. G. Rammel, Charles E. Hill, William O'Neill, B. R. Miller, W. C. Ferriday, Charles Griffin, J. B. H. Janeway, Joseph F. Jennison, David Kennedy, Samuel S. Huff, William J. Stevenson, Francis D. Eagan, J. Pinckney Hammond, Henry S. Spackman, Richard Graham, Nathaniel West, John Long, Alexander Shiras, James Wrigley and Jeremiah W. Asher.‡

---

*The Rev. Thomas Brainerd, a native of Lewis County, N. Y., was a familiar figure in the war period, as he rode the streets on his white horse, bent on errands of patriotic purposes, everywhere and in all kinds of weather. His figure is shown upon the well-known drawing of the Union Volunteer Hospital by Thomas Moran. A tablet at the Pine Street Church contains the names of twenty young men of his congregation who perished in the war. On the occasion of the return of the battle flags to the State of Pennsylvania, on July 4th, 1866, Dr. Brainerd delivered the prayer of thanksgiving. He died six weeks later at Scranton, Pa., aged sixty-two years.

†Captain Horatio S. Howell was killed July 1st, 1863, at Gettysburg (see 90th Regiment).

‡Chaplain Asher died at Wilmington, N. C., from fever contracted in the hospitals (6th U. S. colored troops).

BOUNTIES AND DRAFTS

OF the several general calls for troops issued by President Lincoln in the course of the war, those antedating the call of August 4th, 1862, produced a surplus of volunteers. When men were no longer willing to respond in sufficient numbers without special inducement or compulsion the era of bounties and drafts began. The right of the Government to enforce a conscription was bitterly fought by the Democratic party, and was only confirmed after a Republican had displaced a Democrat in the United States Supreme Court.*

Constantly increasing bounties were offered, when the necessity arose, by the Government, the cities and their various wards. The bounties paid out by the city of Philadelphia, under the last call for troops (December 19th, 1864), amounted to $2,177,879.77, this resulting in a comparatively small accession of recruits.

The final report of the City Bounty Fund Commission (created under an ordinance of Councils, January 3d, 1865) indicates that the city paid out a total of more than $9,000,000 in bounties in order to escape the odium of a draft. The large sums paid for the same purpose by the Ward Committees working to secure the quotas imposed upon them cannot be estimated.

Philadelphia's total recruitment, as stated in the report cited, was 93,323 soldiers and sailors; those to whom bounties were paid numbered 25,300.†

The third call for troops, as issued by the President, brought the total national requisition to 1,100,000 men. The quota of Philadelphia, including the new call, was placed at 33,414. The city was credited, by the Government officials, upon September 15th, 1862, with 29,094 men in service, out of a total enrollment of 100,723 citizens subject to military duty.

Thus, in the midst of the excitement and anxiety attending the week of Antietam, the city was confronted with an apparent shortage of 4,230 men and the probability of a draft. It was to avert this stigma upon the city that to the moderate national bounty the city authorities and the citizens had added so liberally. The municipal bounty gave to every duly certified recruit, at this time, $20.00 for nine monhs men, $30.00 for one year men, and $50.00 for those enlisting for "three years or the war." The ordinance creating the fund for this purpose was approved upon July 26th, 1862. To the $500,000 appropriated by the city the Pennsyl-

---

* In the fall elections of 1863 in Pennsylvania, out of a total vote of 523,697 Governor Curtin was re-elected by the narrow majority of 15,335. The City of Philadelphia saved the Republican party in this State from defeat.

†The number of individuals who enlisted in Philadelphia cannot be definitely stated. Many soldiers served under two and three separate enlistments.

vania Railroad Company added $50,000, and the Philadelphia and Reading Railroad Company $25,000. A Citizens' Bounty Fund was also raised.

The General Committee of this latter fund consisted of the following persons: Alexander Henry, Mayor; James McClintock, City Treasurer; Charles Gibbons; Charles D. Webster; William Welsh; J. Ross Snowden; Adolph E. Borie; S. W. De Courcey; George H. Stuart; Michael V. Baker; George Whitney; James C. Hand; Lorin Blodgett; John V. Addicks; John D. Watson, and James Milliken. Upon September 8th, 1862, the fund created by this Committee and the several Ward Committees aggregated $466,938.

In their estimate of the quota to be supplied by Philadelphia under the third call, the Commissioners, Messrs. William H. Allen and B. Gerhard, accepted the records of Col. Charles F. Ruff, the United States mustering officer, as a basis, deducting from the total 10 per cent. as an allowance for men who had come from outside and enlisted in Philadelphia. They failed to take into account a number of regiments and companies not mustered by that official. They credited to the city local enlistments of sailors and marines, 1,754, and of Philadelphians enlisted in other States, 644. These conclusions aroused the city authorities. A joint committee of Councils was appointed to prepare an estimate through tabulation of the muster rolls of the organizations thus far originating in this city. Upon September 18th they presented a report showing that, exclusive of the eight three-months regiments of 1861, the city had furnished officers and enlisted men to the number of 38,812. This estimate did not include soldiers from Philadelphia serving in other States, sailors and marines and recruits of the regular army taken from this city.

With regard to men from Philadelphia enrolled in the regiments of other States, the Committee stated that there was reason to believe their number to be nearly or quite 6,000. This calculation was probably excessive. The entire report of the Committee was ignored by the draft officials. Upon the petition of the Mayor, the Governor postponed the date for the draft in Philadelphia repeatedly. Strenuous efforts were made in all parts of the city to "fill the quota," and finally, upon November 2d, the Commissioners were able to announce that the quota had been completed.

Very few, if any, Philadelphians went into the army as drafted men. The Philadelphia regiments in the field received, from time to time, large accessions of drafted men who were assembled from other sections of the State, and the frequency of the word "deserted" upon their rolls is chiefly attributable to this fact.

The recurrent announcements of "another draft" was no more welcome in Philadelphia than elsewhere, but public sentiment, backed by the presence of a sufficient military force, was sufficient to overawe the chronic opponents of the Government, and the city was saved from the disgrace of such scenes of riot as affected the city of New York in the summer of 1863. There can be no doubt that, in connection with the matter of drafts, Philadelphia had more than once abundant cause for protest. The estimates of the Federal officials on draft duty in the city were invariably far lower, with regard to credits upon quotas, than those of the city authorities. When the final call was issued the Government demanded from Philadelphia 17,514 men. Through the efforts of city officials and others, foremost of whom was Henry Carey Lea, Esq., the requirement was reduced March 24th, 1865, to 4,457 men, which were furnished. At this time the net pay of volunteers, including their bounties, was, for one year of service, $1,131.00; for two years, $1,687.00, and for three years, $2,145.00. As nearly all of them were discharged within a half year, their per diem compensation equalled a very good wage.

DRAFT AND RECRUITING MEMORANDA.

In 1864 draft brokers in Philadelphia offered "$1,000 and upwards" for veterans re-enlisting as substitutes. In some wards ladies paid for substitutes.

John J. Kromer, 403 Chestnut street, published a pamphlet specifying the diseases and afflictions which gave immunity from the drafts.

By common consent Ward Committees made assessments upon citizens for money to provide substitutes for drafted men.

The congregations of a number of clergymen who were drafted paid for their substitutes.

In July, 1863, a draft was enforced in the Fourth Congressional District, and February and March, 1865, drafts took place in the Third, Fourth, Fifth, Sixth, Seventh, Eighth, Ninth and Twenty-fifth Wards.

On August 8th, 1862, President Lincoln proclaimed that no citizen capable of bearing arms should leave the country until the number of troops called for at that time should have been enlisted.

General Order No. 33 was issued by the Adjutant-General at Washington by instructions of the Secretary of War on April 3d, 1862, under which all recruiting throughout the country was stopped and the recruiting service was ordered to close up its offices and affairs. ("McClellan's Own Story.")

Substitutes were accepted under the Act of Congress of March 3d, 1863. Those thus exempted were given a certificate by the Board of Enrolment.

By General Order No. 163, dated June 4th, 1863, the Government provided that any citizen, non-commissioned officer or soldier who brought a recruit for either the regular or volunteer service to a recruiting rendezvous should receive two dollars. After muster the recruit was to be given one month's pay in advance.

Recruiting in Philadelphia ceased early in April, 1865. In the preceding four months the State had sent to the army three regiments of infantry, 9,133 volunteers and 6,675 drafted men to the old regiments in the field; 75 separate companies and 387 men for the regular army; a total of 25,840 officers and men.

CAMP PHILADELPHIA

A S Philadelphia had been designated as the rendezvous for the drafted levies of the eastern counties of Pennsylvania, a camp, known as "Camp Philadelphia," was established in the fall of 1862 near the western border of the city and a short distance north of Market Street. Within a short time 7,000 men were assembled here. The camp ground covered about ninety acres. Tents were provided by the thousand, and upon the margin of the scene an array of booths were erected by amateur sutlers. Awaiting the slow process of company formation, most of the conscripts, not yet uniformed, suffered greatly from cold weather. Many of them were sent to the hospitals. These men were enlisted for nine months. Some availed themselves of the privilege of enlisting for three years, thereby securing a considerable bounty. Discipline was lax and the men scattered almost at will over the city. The provost guard, under Capt. J. Orr Finnie, was kept busy rounding up the strays and in hunting deserters. It was estimated that fully 3,000 of these conscripts deserted, and afterward some of them wrote to those encamped at Norfolk, Va., ridiculing them for not doing likewise. Many of these skulkers were caught, but large numbers escaped the provosts and left the State. Out of this material was finally created many companies which won honorable records in the service.

CAMP CADWALADER

T HE necessity for a permanent point of assemblage within the city, properly barracked and enclosed, where recruits might be housed and regiments formed, resulted in Camp Cadwalader. This camp was the most important military rendezvous in the city. It consisted of an extensive group of barracks and other buildings enclosed by a high fence and was located upon Islington Lane, east of Ridge Road. It faced the line of Twenty-second Street, the rear being toward Twentieth Street and the south side toward the German Hospital at Twentieth and Norris Streets. At times it was much overcrowded and in the latter period of the war was the subject of many complaints from soldiers and the public (see note following 187th Regiment). The camp of the considerable guard force maintained here was located adjoining, the guards being chiefly of the Invalid Corps. Many regiments were organized and mustered in here and a large proportion of the returning commands were sent here for muster out.

THE ONE-YEAR REGIMENTS, 1864-65

THE one-year regiments were organized to supply the deficiency in the fighting line due to the waste of war among the old three-year regiments, the return of many thousands whose period of enlistment had expired and to take the place of the numerous long-term commands on garrison, provost and guard duty, whose presence was required at the front. These new regiments offered the inducements of liberal bounties and the prospect of a speedy end to the war. They were largely officered by soldiers of experience, and the raw recruits, many of them too young for acceptance at an earlier period, had the advantage of comrades who had shared in the campaigns of the past. When these one-year commands were mustered in they were fit for any service required of them, and the fact that the majority of them experienced little or no fighting was not due to any lack of patriotic ardor.

ONE HUNDRED AND NINETY-SECOND REGIMENT INFANTRY.
COLONEL WILLIAM W. STEWART.
Total Enrollment, 1,000 Officers and Men.

A portion of this regiment had served in 1862 in the 20th Regiment Militia (Emergency), and in 1863 in the 20th Regiment, Pennsylvania Volunteer Infantry. These organizations had been recruited largely from officials and employees of the United States Custom House at Philadelphia. The original 192d Regiment, formed from this source as volunteer infantry, in July, 1864 (see One Hundred-day Regiments), was the basis of the new organization, which was employed in the vicinity of Staunton and Lexington, Virginia, during its term of service, without coming into any notable conflict with the then weakened and scattering Confederates. The regiment was mustered in during February and March, 1865, and discharged August 24th, 1865.

TOTAL LOSSES.
Died from disease .... 16 men.

ONE HUNDRED AND NINETY-EIGHTH REGIMENT INFANTRY.
COLONEL HORATIO G. SICKEL.
LIEUT.-COLONEL JOHN B. MURRAY.
(Fourteen Companies.)
Total Enrollment, 1,640 Officers and Men.

This strong regiment, known as the 6th Union League Regiment, was destined to have an active part in several of the important engagements incident to the last year of the war and to be "in at the death" at

Appomattox. The "198th" left Philadelphia on September 19th, 1864, joining the army as part of the First Brigade, First Division, Fifth Corps, in front of Petersburg, Va. Col. Sickel, who had been commander of the 3d Regiment Reserves, was almost immediately appointed to command of the brigade, being succeeded in the colonelcy by Lieut.-Col. John B. Murray on September 30th. The regiment participated in the battle at Peebles' Farm, and was, later, busily engaged along the South Side Railroad. After a trying march for the destruction of the Weldon Railroad, winter quarters were established near the end of December, and command was assumed by Major Edwin A. Glenn. With the beginning of the campaign of 1865, the Fifth Corps met the enemy, on February 5th, at Hatcher's Run, the First Division, including the "198th," moving toward Dinwiddie Court House. On the following day the "198th" executed two successful bayonet charges with entire success. At the affair of Lewis' Farm the regiment, together with the 185th New York, led by Gen. Sickel, drove the enemy from the field, but at great loss. Twenty-eight officers and men were killed and one hundred and seventeen wounded. Leaving this field on March 31st, the regiment again met the enemy at White Oak Swamp, and on April 1st, at Five Forks, where, at the moment of victory, the commander, Major Glenn, fell mortally wounded. Then began the pursuit of the retreating enemy, following the fall of Richmond, the long, exhausting march ending on April 8th, within view of the remnants of Lee's Army at bay. The surrender took place on the 9th, and the war was over. The 198th was mustered out at Philadelphia, amid an ovation, on June 3d, 1865.

TOTAL LOSSES.

Killed or died from wounds ....officers, 6; men, 67
Died from disease .... "   44

BATTLES, ETC.

In front of Petersburg, Poplar Springs Church, Boydton Road (October 8th), Boydton Road (October 27th), Hatcher's Run, Weldon Railroad, Dabney's Mills, Hatcher's Run, Boydton Road (March 29th), Lewis Farm, White Oak Road. Five Forks, Appomattox Court House.

ONE HUNDRED AND NINETY-NINTH REGIMENT INFANTRY.
(Commercial Regiment.)
COLONEL JAMES C. BRISCOE.
Total Enrollment, 1,462 Officers and Men.

The "199th" joined the "Army of the James" in October, 1865, on the James river, being assigned to the First Brigade, Twenty-fourth Corps, and under the direction of its veteran officers proceeded to fortify, being at the extreme right. On March 27th the First Division crossed the river and, advancing southward, captured by assault, six days later, Forts Gregg and Alexander, important Confederate works.

TYPES OF THE FIRE AMBULANCES.
(From photographs by R. Newell.)

HIBERNIA ENGINE. TWICE IN THE SERVICE OF THE UNITED STATES.

AMBULANCE OF THE PHILADELPHIA FIRE ENGINE COMPANY, EXHIBITED AT
THE PARIS EXPOSITION OF 1867.
(From a painting in possession of the Veteran Volunteer Firemen's Association.)

In this affair, which President Lincoln, who was near-by, characterized as "a most gallant charge," the "199th" lost eighteen killed, including two officers, and ninety-one wounded, including six officers, one being Col. Briscoe, who was brevetted brigadier-general for gallantry and placed in command of the brigade. Incident to the pursuit of the retreating Confederates, early in April, the regiment met the enemy at Rice's Station and on the day preceding the surrender in a skirmish near Appomattox Court House. In these final scenes of combat the regiment lost four killed and eight wounded. The "199th" was afterward placed in camp with the First Division on the border of Richmond, where, on June 28th, the original members were mustered out and the recruits assigned to the 188th (three year) regiment, of which Col. Briscoe was appointed commander (see 188th Regiment).

TOTAL LOSSES.

Killed or died from wounds ....officers, 2; men, 30
Died from disease .... "   52

BATTLES, ETC.

Peebles' Farm, South Side Railroad, Weldon Railroad, Forts Gregg and Alexander in front of Petersburg, Fall of Petersburg, Rice's Station, Appomattox Court House, on duty at Richmond.

TWO HUNDRED AND THIRD REGIMENT INFANTRY.

COLONEL JOHN W. MOORE.

Total Enrollment, 1,364 Officers and Men.

This regiment was recruited in Philadelphia and the counties of Chester, Delaware, Lancaster and Lycoming, and was intended to serve in the division of Major-Gen. David B. Birney as sharpshooters. After the death of that gallant officer the project was abandoned and the command was rated as ordinary infantry. The officers were all veterans who had served in earlier regiments. The regiment left Philadelphia on September 22d, 1864, and was attached to the Second Brigade, Second Division, Tenth Corps, then in front of Petersburg, Va.

The "203d" reached the scene just in time for the actions at Chaffin's Farm and New Market Road, acting upon provost duty in guarding prisoners to the rear. Between October 5th and 28th the command was under fire in various movements much of the time. Upon the reorganization of the Army of the James the "203d" was attached to the Second Brigade, Second Division, Twenty-fifth Corps. Early in December the Second Division was sent as part of an expedition from Fortress Monroe for the reduction of Fort Fisher, at the entrance of the Cape Fear River, North Carolina. The attempt failed for the time being, but was renewed with the same and additional troops under Brig.-Gen. Alfred H. Terry. In the historic assault of January 15th, 1865, made in co-operation with the fleet of fifty-eight warships upon this stronghold, the "203d" was in the lead, fighting like tigers; its heroic Colonel falling, he raised the flag above his head in the hand-to-hand contest. When, long after nightfall, the clamor of the battle ceased, and the fort was in the hands of the Union forces, the "203d" had lost forty-six killed, including Col. Moore, Lieut.-Col. Jonas W. Lyman and two line officers and one hundred and forty-five officers and men wounded. On February 11th, an advance was made upon Wilmington, N. C., which involved considerable fighting, but ended with the occupation of the city. Soon afterward the column met the equally victorious troops of Major-Gen. Sherman near Goldsboro and shared with them in the glory of the capture of the force under the Confederate Gen. Johnston, who surrendered on April 26th, 1865. This ended the final chapter of fighting on the Atlantic seaboard. The "203d" was encamped at Raleigh, N. C., to the date of its muster out on June 22d, 1865.

TOTAL LOSSES.

Killed or died from wounds ....officers, 4; men, 70
Died from disease .... " 72

BATTLES, ETC.

Chaffin's Farm, New Market Road. Fair Oaks, Expedition to Fort Fisher (December, 1864), Capture of Fort Fisher (January, 1865), Sugar Loaf Battery, N. C., Fort Anderson, N. C., Capture of Wilmington, N. C., advance on Goldsboro, occupation of Raleigh, N. C., surrender of Johnston's Army.

TWO HUNDRED AND THIRTEENTH REGIMENT INFANTRY.

(Seventh Union League Regiment.)

COLONEL JOHN A. GORGAS.

Total Enrollment, 1,150 Officers and Men.

This regiment was mustered during February, 1865, and was composed of recruits enlisted in Philadelphia and the counties of Berks, Chester and Juniata. During its entire term of service it was detailed upon guard duty. At first the command was stationed at Camp Parole, Annapolis, Maryland, and at Frederick City, Maryland. Early in April it was posted upon the northern defences of Washington, remaining on duty here through the balance of its term of service. Mustered out November 18th, 1865.

TOTAL LOSSES.

Died from disease .... 18 men.

TWO HUNDRED AND FOURTEENTH REGIMENT INFANTRY.

(Eighth Union League Regiment.)

COLONEL DAVID B. McKIBBIN.

Total Enrollment, 1,400 Officers and Men.

The "214th" was recruited in Philadelphia and the counties of Lancaster and Northampton and mustered in during March, 1865. Prior to July the regiment performed guard and provost duty in the Shenandoah Valley. Then it was stationed at Washington, with the exception of a detachment under Major Washington M. Worrall, located at Annapolis, where that officer commanded the post. This was the last of the Pennsylvania infantry regiments in the National service. It was mustered out March 21st, 1866.

TOTAL LOSSES.

Died from disease .... 24 men.

KEYSTONE BATTERY INDEPENDENT ARTILLERY.

CAPTAIN MATTHEW HASTINGS.

156 Officers and Men.

An infantry company, formed on April 21st, 1861, was eventually enrolled as Company B, 1st Regiment, Philadelphia Home Guard. The Keystone Battery was recruited upon the latter company and was mustered into the United States service for one year August 13th, 1862, being immediately sent to Fort Ethan Allen, defences of Washington. A few weeks later the battery was moved to Union Mills, Va., reporting to Gen. Alexander Hays, remaining hereto the early summer of 1863, in the meantime participating in numerous movements without being engaged in battle. At Gettysburg the battery was in reserve.* It was present in the engagement at Snicker's Gap, following the retreat of Lee. The command was mustered out August 20th, 1863.

ENLISTED FOR NINE MONTHS

ONE HUNDRED AND FIFTY-FOURTH REGIMENT PENNSYLVANIA INFANTRY.

(Three companies), 165 Officers and Men.

Although a full regimental organization was effected before the commissions were issued to officers, seven companies were detached and the remaining three companies, under their respective captains, were mustered in and placed upon provost duty at Philadelphia. These companies were A, Capt. John T. Doyle, succeeded by Capt. Chas. Fair; B, Capt. O. C. Cunningham; and C, Capt. Lemuel Howell; mustered out September 29th and October 21st, 1863. These appear to have been the only volunteer nine months troops originating in Philadelphia.

---

*History of Battery A, Scott.

ENLISTED FOR SIX MONTHS

THIRD BATTALION INFANTRY.
LIEUTENANT-COLONEL T. ELWOOD ZELL.
500 Officers and Men.

Organized at Philadelphia, with assistance of the Union, League, and mustered in during June and July, 1863. Discharged January 29th, 1864. Lieut.-Col. Zell was previously captain of Co. D, 121st Regiment Infantry Volunteers. The battalion was known as the "Pennsylvania Chasseurs." It was engaged during its term of service upon guard and provost duty at various points in the State of Pennsylvania.

WOODWARD'S INDEPENDENT BATTERY.
CAPTAIN W. H. WOODWARD.
150 Officers and Men.

Organized during the impetus of enlistments resulting from the Gettysburg emergency, this battery was accepted for six months' service, being mustered in July 9th, 1863. The command served at various points in Pennsylvania, and was mustered out November 4th, 1863.

ONE HUNDRED-DAY TROOPS—1864-5

T HE alarm caused by the Confederate Cavalry raid into Pennsylvania in June, 1864, incident to which was the burning of Chambersburg, induced the President to issue a call upon Pennsylvania for 12,000 militia or volunteers to serve one hundred days "in the vicinity of Washington."

Governor Curtin, mindful of two stressful summer experiences of the past, sent forth this characteristic and forceful admonition:

EXECUTIVE CHAMBER.

HARRISBURG, Sunday, July 10, 1864.

HON. ALEX. HENRY, Mayor of Philadelphia, and to the People of Pennsylvania:

I refer to my recent proclamations calling for troops on the requisition of the President.

You are not responding freely.

276

The enemies of our Government are active in deterring you, and efforts have been made to dissuade you from the belief that any considerable rebel force is in your vicinity, and many of our most loyal and patriotic citizens have been thus deceived.*

Similar efforts were too successfully made last year at the moment when Lee's army was actually on your border.

Despatches have been this morning received establishing the fact that General Wallace, with 10,000 men, was yesterday compelled to fall back from Frederick. He is believed to be in retreat towards Baltimore.

The communication between this point and Baltimore was cut this morning by the rebels below Cockeysville.†

The authorities of the United States at Washington are so impressed with the necessity of immediate effort, that they have this morning, by telegraph, authorized men to be mustered in by companies, which they had yesterday peremptorily refused.

It is my duty to state to you the fact that your country requires your immediate service, and the safety of your own soil, and of our good neighbors in Maryland, may depend on your promptness.

Recollect that the mode of enlisting men is at the discretion of the Government, and it is the duty of all to obey its requisitions.

It would be disgraceful in you to waste time in objecting to matters of form and detail, or to profess that you would go if called in some different way. Those who want an excuse for skulking may do so, but all who desire to do their duty to their country will scorn such subterfuges.

Turn, therefore, a deaf ear to all mischievous suggestions from any quarter. Do not lend yourselves to a betrayal of your country. Come forward, like men, to aid her. The rebel forces will be easily defeated and driven away if you do your duty, and I pray God so to enlighten you that the honor of the Commonwealth may be maintained.

A. G. CURTIN.

Among the militia responding from Philadelphia were the following:

One Hundred and Ninety-second Regiment Infantry.

Colonel William B. Thomas.

Total Enrollment, 1,500 Officers and Men.

This regiment contained fifteen companies. It originated in the "Revenue Guards" formed by Col. Thomas, then Collector of the Port, from the force of the U. S. Custom House employees at Philadelphia. As the 20th Regiment Pennsylvania Militia these troops had performed emergency service in September, 1862, and were again enlisted as volunteers in June, 1863. The "192d" was, therefore, Col. Thomas' third

---

*A vote of July, 1864, upon a Constitutional amendment in Pennsylvania, intended to enable soldiers in the field to exercise their franchise rights as citizens, resulted in 27,211 in favor of and 9,930 against said amendment.

†Apropos of a third Confederate advance northward, the *Richmond Whig* printed a communication on July 24th, 1864, entitled "The Devoted Band," a part of which is in these words: "Fire and sword must be carried into the houses of those who are visiting these blessings on their neighbors. Philadelphia and even New York are not beyond the reach of a long and brave arm. The moral people of those cities cannot be better taught the virtues of invasion than by the blazing light of their own dwellings."

command. At Camp Cadwalader, during July, 1864, the regiment was mustered and sent at once to camp near Baltimore, soon afterward moving to Fort McHenry, from which the command was ordered to guard duty at the prison camp for Confederate officers at Johnson's Island, Lake Erie. Within a few days the command was dispatched to the Ohio River for guard and patrol duty at Galliopolis. Several companies were here detached and sent to Winston, West Virginia. The regiment returned to Philadelphia and was mustered out upon November 11th, 1864. Few short-term organizations experienced as much varied service as the "192d." After this tour of duty members of the several companies enlisted in a company which, under Captain Thomas McLeester, became Company A, of a second 192d Regiment, which was accepted by the Government for one year. This new regiment was commanded by Col. William W. Stewart and remained in the service until August 24th, 1865. (See One-year Regiments.)

It should be noted that the members of the "Revenue Guards" identified with these several enlistments were aided by their fellow employees in the Philadelphia Custom House, who raised a fund of $4,400 to assist their families during their absence.

One Hundred and Ninety-sixth Regiment Infantry.
(Fifth Union League Regiment.)
Colonel Harmanus Neff.
Total Enrollment, 958 Officers and Men.

This command, under Col. Harmanus Neff, organized with the co-operation of the Union League Committee, was formed at Camp Cadwalader on July 20th, 1864, and sent to the vicinity of Baltimore a week later. From Camp Bradford, at this point, it was ordered to Camp Douglas, Chicago, and employed in guard and exchange duty at the large prison for Confederates. Company H was detailed to provost duty at Springfield, Ill. A brief period prior to the expiration of the term of enlistment was spent on duty at Fort Delaware. Mustered out November 17th, 1864.

One Hundred and Ninety-seventh Regiment Infantry.
(Third Coal Exchange Regiment.)
Colonel John R. Haslett.
Total Enrollment, 932 Officers and Men.

With the assistance of the Coal Exchange of Philadelphia, which had previously aided the 8th and 51st Regiments, State Militia, this regiment was mustered into the United States service at Camp Cadwalader upon July 22d, 1864. Col. John R. Haslett and his associate field officers were experienced soldiers. The companies, with the exception of a part of one company from Montgomery County, were recruited in Philadelphia. Many of the rank and file had served in earlier commands. The regiment was, however, destined to be assigned to the tedious and inglorious duty of guarding the prison camp of Confederates at Rock Island, Ill., and here it remained to the end of its period of enlistment, when, upon return to Philadelphia, it was mustered out November 11th, 1864.

Two Hundred and Fifteenth Regiment Infantry.
(Ninth Union League Regiment.)
Colonel Francis Wister.
Total Enrollment, 1,117 Officers and Men.

This, the last of the regiments sent out from Philadelphia, was commanded by Col. Francis Wister (of the 12th U. S. Infantry). Under the auspices of the Union League it was mustered at Camp Cadwalader in April, 1865, and ordered to duty in Delaware and upon the Eastern Shore of Maryland. Following this service it was stationed at Fort Delaware early in June, and remained there until mustered out upon July 31st, 1865.

Independent Company Infantry, Colored Troops.
Captain Converse Southard.
100 Officers and Men.

Organized at Camp William Penn, July 20th, 1864. Mustered out November 14th, 1864. (See 119th Regiment, U. S. Colored Troops.)

Independent Railroad Troop.*
Captain George D. Stroud.
96 Officers and Men.

Mustered in July 9th, 1864. Mustered out October 31st, 1864.

Keystone Battery, Independent Artillery.
Captain Matthew Hastings.
150 Officers and Men.

Organized July 12th, 1864. Mustered out October 25th, 1864. On duty at Huntingdon, Bloomsburg, Chambersburg, Greencastle, etc., Department of the Susquehanna.

---

*An independent cavalry troop, composed of railroad officials and employees, commanded by Capt. G. D. Stroud, was equipped and mounted by the Pennsylvania and the Northern Central Railroad Companies. This command left Philadelphia for Maryland on July 19th, 1864.

ARMY NECROLOGY

COMMISSIONED OFFICERS FROM PHILADELPHIA KILLED IN BATTLES, OR
WHO DIED FROM WOUNDS AND SICKNESS DURING THE CIVIL WAR.

(Compiled from Bates' History of the Pennsylvania Volunteers, 1861-1865, and
from the Report of the Adjutant-General of Pennsylvania for 1866. It should
be especially noted that this list does not include the names of officers of the
regiments enumerated who were not specified as residents of Philadelphia.)

*For names of general officers killed or who died during the war, see list of
officers of that rank.

11TH REGIMENT.
 Thomas S. Martin, Lieut-Col. Killed at Bull Run, Va., August 30th, 1862.
23D REGIMENT (3 years' service).
 Dr. A. Owen Stille, surgeon. Died at Fortress Monroe, June 22d, 1862.
 Joshua S. Garsed, 1st Lieut., Co. B. Killed at Gettysburg, July 3d, 1863.
 Benj. Thomas, 2d Lieut., Co. D. Died February 9th, 1862.
 John G. Boyd, 2d Lieut., Co. D. Killed at Cold Harbor, June 1, 1864.
 James Johnston, 1st Lieut., Co. E. Killed at Cold Harbor, June 1, 1864.
 Henry A. Marchant, Capt., Co. I. Killed at Cold Harbor, June 1, 1862.
 James G. Williamson, 2d Lieut., Co. K. Died of wounds, June 2, 1864.
26TH REGIMENT (3 years' service). Co. K not included.
 Samuel G. Wregner, Sergeant-Major. Died of wounds received at Gettysburg,
 July 2d, 1863.
 Benj. R. Wright, 2d Lieut., Co. A. Killed at Gettysburg, July 2d, 1863.
 Thomas P. Morris, 2d Lieut., Co. G. Killed at Spotsylvania C. H., May
 12th, 1864.
 Benjamin R. Wright, 2d Lieut., Co. A. Killed at Gettysburg, July 2d, 1863.
 Frank B. Bird, 2d Lieut., Co. H. Died July 31st, 1863, of wounds received
 at Gettysburg.
 John J. Flannery, 2d Lieut., Co. D. Died June 15th, 1864, of wounds received
 at Gettysburg.
 John D. Sloan, Capt., Co. I. Killed at Mine Run, November 28th, 1863.
 David Potts, 2d Lieut., Co. I. Killed at Bull Run, August 29th, 1862.
 William S. Small, Capt., Co. K. Died at Philadelphia, February, 1864.
 Thomas P. Morris, 2d Lieut., Co. H. Died July 31st, 1863, of wounds received
 at Gettysburg.
27TH REGIMENT.
 Peter A. M'Aloon, Lieut.-Col. Died December 7th, 1863, of wounds received
 at Missionary Ridge.
 Walter S. Briggs, Adjutant. Killed at Gettysburg, July 2d, 1863.
 John Kumpel, 1st Lieut., Co. E. Killed at Gettysburg, July 1st, 1863.
 James Hamilton Kuhn, 1st Lieut., Co. G. Killed at New Market Cross Roads,
 June 30th, 1862.
 Frederick Luders, 2d Lieut., Co. K. Killed at Cross Keys, Va., June 8th, 1862.
28TH REGIMENT. Philadelphia Companies C, D, I, K, M and P.
 Robert Warden, Major. Died at Winchester, Va., June 30th, 1862.
 L. F. Chapman, Major. Killed at Chancellorsville, May 3d, 1862.

Peter F. Laws, Capt., Co. C. Killed at Antietam, September 17th, 1862.
William C. Shields, 1st Lieut., Co. G. Killed at Chancellorsville, May 3d, 1863.
George B. U. Martin, Capt., Co. H. Died at Bridgeport, Ala., March 24th, 1864.

29TH REGIMENT.

John J. McKeever, 2d Lieut., Co. A. Killed at Gettysburg, July 3d, 1863.
William Harrington, 2d Lieut., Co. B. Killed by railroad accident, March 4th, 1864.
James Kerr. 2d Lieut., Co. D. Died October 21st, 1864.
Ethan O. Fulce, 2d Lieut., Co. F. Killed at Fayetteville, N. C., March 14th, 1865.
Edward J. Harvey, 2d Lieut., Co. K. Killed at Gettysburg, July 2d, 1863.

31ST REGIMENT (2d Reserves). Philadelphia Companies A, B, C, D, E, G, H and K.

Augustus T. Cross, Adjutant. Killed at Antietam, September 16th, 1862.
James C. Manton, 1st Lieut., Co. B. Died January 13th, 1864.
J. R. Nightingale. 2d Lieut., Co. C. Killed at Charles City Cross Roads, June 30th, 1862.
John B. Fletcher, 1st Lieut., Co. E. Died July 12th, 1862, from wounds received at Charles City Cross Roads, June 30th, 1862.
Robert J. Clark, 1st Lieut., Co. F. Died of wounds May 12th, 1864.
Max Wimpfheimer, 2d Lieut., Co. G. Killed at Antietam, September 17th, 1862.

32D REGIMENT (3d Reserves). Philadelphia Companies E and G.

John Connolly, 2d Lieut., Co. G. Died at Camp Pierpont, December 2d, 1861.

33D REGIMENT (4th Reserves). Philadelphia Companies A, B, D, G and I.

Richard H. Woolworth, Col. Killed at Cloyd Mountain, May 9th, 1864.
Prosper M. Davis, Capt., Co. I. Killed at Cloyd Mountain, May 9th, 1864.
Robert A. Moore, 1st Lieut., Co. I. Died from wounds January 9th, 1863.

36TH REGIMENT (7th Reserves). Philadelphia Companies E, G and K.

Daniel L. Sanders, 1st Lieut., Co. K. Killed at Antietam, September 17th, 1862.

37TH REGIMENT (8th Reserves).

Thomas Jones, surgeon. Died of wounds May 16th, 1864.

43D REGIMENT (1st Light Artillery Reserves). Philadelphia Batteries C, D, G and H.

John G. Simpson, Capt., Battery A. Died at Philadelphia, December 8th, 1864.
F. McLaughlin, 1st Lieut., Battery D. Died June 4th, 1862, from illness contracted upon the Chickahominy.
Mark Kern, Capt., Battery G. Killed at Bull Run, August 30th, 1862.
Thomas Thornton, 2d Lieut., Battery H. Died at Washington, March 26th, 1862.

52D REGIMENT.

George Scott, 2d Lieut., Co. D. Died July 3d, 1864, from wounds received at James Island, S. C.

56TH REGIMENT.

Benjamin F. Young, 2d Lieut., Co. D. Killed May 25th, 1864.

58TH REGIMENT (Infantry).

Theodore Blakley, Capt., Co. B. Killed at Fort Harrison, September 29th, 1864.
Daniel F. Linn, Capt., Co. C. Died from wounds received at Fort Harrison, September 29th, 1864.
Godfrey M. Brinley, 1st Lieut., Co. D. Died at Beaufort, S. C., August 19th, 1863.
Joseph B. Paxon. Died of disease August 14th, 1864.
John F. Wood, Capt., Co. K. Died of disease at Richmond, Va., November 25th, 1865.

59TH REGIMENT (2d Cavalry). Philadelphia Companies A, B, C, E, G and H.
Charles F. Taggart, Major. Died at Warrenton, Va., October 24th, 1863, from wounds in action of October 22d, 1863.
Frank J. Dungan, 2d Lieut., Co. A. Killed at Todd's Tavern, Va., May 8th 1864.
Alfred Biles, 1st Lieut., Co. B. Killed by guerillas, July 26th, 1863.
Jacob H. Martin, 2d Lieut., Co. K. Died of wounds August 18th, 1864.
Albert C. Walker, Capt., Co. M. Died August 3d, 1864.

60TH REGIMENT (3d Cavalry). Philadelphia Companies A, B, C, F, I, K and M.
Walter S. Newhall, Capt., Co. A. Drowned near Rappahannock Station, Va., December 18th, 1863.
George K. Hogg, 1st Lieut., Co. K. Drowned at Nottingham, Md., September 12th, 1861.
James E. Lodge, 2d Lieut., Co. F. Died (date unknown).
Elwood Davis, 2d Lieut., Co. H. Killed near Bull Run, October 15th, 1863.

61ST REGIMENT. Philadelphia Companies G, H and I.
George C. Spear, Col. Killed at Mayres' Heights, May 3d, 1863.
John W. Crossby, Lieut.-Col. Killed at Petersburg, April 2d, 1865.
George W. Wilson, Adjutant. Killed at Spotsylvania, May 9th, 1864.
John Barrett, Capt., Co. G. Killed at Cedar Creek, Va., October 19th, 1864.
Alfred Moylan, 1st Lieut., Co. I. Died July 8th, 1862, from wounds received at Fair Oaks.

65TH REGIMENT (5th Cavalry).
Jonathan J. Phillips, 2d Lieut., Co. D. Died at Fortress Monroe, June 11th, 1864.
William E. Frick, 1st Lieut., Co. F. Died October 11th, 1861.
Samuel M. Williamson, 1st Lieut., Co. H. Killed near Williamsburg, Va., January 15th, 1863.
William H. Cameron, Capt., Co. I. Died June 26th, 1864.
James D. Brown, Capt., Co. K. Died August 9th, 1862.
Dietrich Bruno, 1st Lieut., Co. L. Died August 29th, 1864.

67TH REGIMENT. Philadelphia Companies B and part of E and I.
William E. Tucker, Capt., Co. B. Died November 2d, 1862, from wounds in action.

68TH REGIMENT.
Thomas Hawksworth, Major. Died January 7th, 1863, from wounds received at Fredericksburg.
John Reynolds, 2d Lieut., Co. E. Killed at Gettysburg, July 2d, 1863.
John C. Gallagher, Capt., Co. C. Died April 3d, 1865, from wounds received at Petersburg.
George W. McLearn, Capt., Co. D. Killed at Gettysburg, July 2, 1863.
Andrew Black, 2d Lieut., Co. D. Killed at Gettysburg, July 2d, 1863.
James Shields, 1st Lieut., Co. E. Died May 5th, 1863, from wounds received at Chancellorsville.
Milton C. Davis, Capt., Co. F. Killed at Orange Grove, Va., November 27th, 1863.
Lewis W. Ealer, 1st Lieut., Co. F. Died October 6th, 1863, from wounds received at Gettysburg.
Joseph E. Davis, 2d Lieut., Co. F. Killed at Fredericksburg, December 13th, 1862.
John D. Pauling, Capt., Co. I. Died May 15th, 1863, from wounds received at Chancellorsville.

69TH REGIMENT.
Dennis O'Kane, Col. Killed at Gettysburg, July 3d, 1863.
Martin Tschudy, Lieut.-Col. Killed at Gettysburg, July 3d, 1863.

James Harvey, Capt., Asst. A. G. Killed at Ball's Bluff, October 21st, 1861.
William Whildey, Adjutant. Killed at Cold Harbor, Va., June 3d, 1864.
James Dunn, 2d Lieut., Co. A. Killed at Antietam, September 17th, 1862.
Joseph McHugh, 1st Lieut., Co. D. Killed at Antietam, September 17th, 1862.
James McGinley, 2d Lieut., Co. D. Killed at Hatchers Run, February 5th, 1865.
Andrew McManus, Capt., Co. E. Killed near Falmouth, Va., May 27th, 1863.
George C. Thompson, Capt., Co. F. Killed at Gettysburg, July 3d, 1863.
C. Howard Taylor, 2d Lieut., Co. F. Died of disease November 7th, 1862.
F. VonBierwirth, Capt., Co. G. Killed at Antietam, September 17, 1862.
Bernard Sherry, 1st Lieut., Co. G. Died of wounds May 15th, 1864.
Michael Mullen, 2d Lieut., Co. G. Killed at Gettysburg, Julv 3d, 1863.
Thomas Kelley, Capt., Co. H. Died May 18th, 1864, from wounds received
 at Spotsylvania Court House, May 12th, 1864.
Thomas Carroll, 2d Lieut., Co. H. Died at Philadelphia, June 25th, 1862.
Charles F. Kelley, 2d Lieut., Co. H. Killed at Gettysburg, July 2d, 1863.
Michael Duffy, Capt., Co. I. Killed at Gettysburg, July 2d, 1863.
Josiah Jack, 1st Lieut., Co. K. Killed at Spotsylvania Court House, May 12th,
 1864.

70TH REGIMENT (6th Cavalry). Not including Company G.

Robert Morris, Jr., Major. Died at Libby Prison, Richmond, Va., August
 13th, 1863.
Henry C. Whelan, Major. Died at Philadelphia, March 2d, 1864.
Stephen H. Martin, Adjutant. Killed at Old Church, Va., May 30th, 1864.
Theodore M. Sage, Quarter Master. Killed by guerillas at Elk Run, Va.,
 November 4th, 1863.
Arthur E. Murphy, 1st Lieut., Co. A. Killed at Cold Harbor, May 31st, 1864.
James Magee, 2d Lieut. Killed near Dinwiddie C. H., March 31st, 1865.
Charles B. Davis, Capt., Co. F. Killed at Beverly Ford, Va., June 9th, 1863.
William Sproule, 2d Lieut., Co. F. Died at Belle Plain, Va., May 8th, 1863.
Lewis Miller, 1st Lieut., Co. L. Killed (date unknown).

71ST REGIMENT (First "California" Regiment). Philadelphia Companies A,
 B, C, D, E, F, G, I and partly H and K.

Edward D. Baker, Col. Killed at Ball's Bluff, Va., October 21st, 1861.
John M. Steffan, Capt., Co. A. Killed at Gettysburg, July 3d, 1863.
J. W. Lingenfelter, Capt., Co. B. Killed near Chain Bridge, Va., September
 21st, 1861.
William H. Dull, Capt., Co. B. Killed at Gettysburg, July 3d, 1863.
William Wilson, 2d Lieut., Co. B. Killed at Antietam, September 17th, 1862.
William E. Otter, Capt., Co. C. Killed at Ball's Bluff, Va., October 21st, 1861.
Benjamin F. Hibbs, 2d Lieut., Co. D. Died of wounds received at Fredericks-
 burg, Va., December 13th, 1862.
Joseph D. Williams, 2d Lieut., Co. D. Killed at Ball's Bluff, October 21st, 1861.
Christian A. Schaeffer, 2d Lieut., Co. F. Died at Poolesville, Md., March
 3d, 1862.
E. Carlyle Norris, Capt., Co. G. Died May 1st, 1863, from wounds received
 in action.
James Clark, 1st Lieut., Co. G. Killed in action May 23d, 1864.
Maurice C. Moore, 1st Lieut., Co. H. Killed on picket, June 8th, 1864.
John Convery, 2d Lieut., Co. K. Killed at Antietam, September 17th, 1862.
George W. Kenney, 1st Lieut., Co. N. Killed at Antietam, Md., September
 17th, 1862.

72D REGIMENT (Baxter's Fire Zouaves).

Theodore Hesser, Lieut.-Col. Killed at Mine Run, Va., November 27th, 1863.
Andrew C. Supplee, Major. Died at Philadelphia, July 27th, 1864, from wounds
 and exposure.

DeBenneville B. Shewell, Sergt.-Major. Died July 21st, 1862, of wounds in action.

Charles W. Gonigle, Capt., Co. B. Killed at Savage Station, Va., June 29th, 1862.

Richard L. R. Shreve, Capt., Co. B. Killed at Wilderness, Va., May 6th, 1864.

Peter H. Willitts, Capt., Co. C. Killed at Antietam, September 17th, 1862.

Michael Coste, 1st Lieut., Co. C. Killed at Bristoe Station, Va., October 14th, 1863.

Andrew McBride, Capt., Co. D. Killed at Gettysburg, July 3d, 1863.

Sutton Jones, 2d Lieut., Co. E. Killed at Gettysburg, July 3d, 1863.

Edward G. Roussel, Capt., Co. G. Died October 11th, 1862, from wounds received at Antietam.

James L. Griffith, 1st Lieut., Co. I. Killed at Gettysburg, July 3d, 1863.

R. I. Parks, Jr., 2d Lieut., Co. K. Killed at Antietam, Md., September 17th, 1862.

73D REGIMENT.

John A. Koltes, Col. Killed at Bull Run, August 30th, 1862.

Aug. C. Brueckner, Capt., Co. A. Killed at Bull Run, August 30th, 1862.

Jacob Liebfried, Capt., Co. G. Died at Philadelphia from wounds received at Chancellorsville, May 2d, 1863.

Henry Hess, Capt., Co. H. Died June 19th, 1864, of wounds received at Pine Knob, Ga., June 15th, 1864.

Henry J. Giltinan, Capt., Co. K. Killed at Chancellorsville, May 3d, 1863.

74TH REGIMENT. Philadelphia Company K.

William Roth, 2d Lieut., Co. K. Killed at Gettysburg, July 1st, 1863.

75TH REGIMENT.

Francis Mahler, Col. Killed at Gettysburg, July 1st, 1863.

William J. Sill, 1st Lieut., Co. C. Died July 21st, 1863, from wounds received at Gettysburg.

William Froelich, 1st Lieut., Co. E. Killed at Bull Run, August 30th, 1862.

Louis Mahler, 2d Lieut., Co. F. Killed at Gettysburg, July 1st, 1863.

Adolph Winter, 1st Lieut., Co. I. Drowned in the Shenandoah River, April 15th, 1862.

William Bowen, 2d Lieut., Co. I. Killed at Bull Run, August 30th, 1862.

Christian Wyck, Capt., Co. K. Drowned in the Shenandoah River, April 15th, 1862.

Henry Hauschild, 2d Lieut., Co. A. Killed at Gettysburg, July 1st, 1863.

80TH REGIMENT.

Nicholas A. Wynkoop, Adjutant. Killed at Gallatin, Tenn., August 21st, 1862.

81ST REGIMENT. Philadelphia Companies A, B, C, D, E and F.

H. Boyd McKeen, Col. Killed at Cold Harbor, Va., June 3d, 1864.

Robert M. Lee, Jr., Lieut.-Col. Died (after leaving service) September 21st, 1863.

Charles Wilson, Capt., Co. A. Killed near Farmville, Va., April 7th, 1865.

Peter McGee, 2d Lieut., Co. A. Killed at Ream's Station, Va., August 25th, 1864.

Philip R. Schuyler, Capt., Co. C. Died September 21st, 1862, from wounds received at Antietam.

Clinton Swain, Capt., Co. C. Killed at Fredericksburg, December 13th, 1862.

Horace M. Lee, 1st Lieut., Co. F. Died June 3d, 1862, from wounds received at Fair Oaks.

William H. Van Dyke, 1st Lieut., Co. F. Killed at Antietam, September 17th, 1862.

Zadoc Aydelott, 2d Lieut., Co. F. Died January 5th, 1863, from wounds received at Fredericksburg.

82D REGIMENT (not including Company B).

James B. Grier, Quartermaster. Killed at Malvern Hill, Va., July 1st, 1862.
Robert G. Creighton, 1st Lieut., Co. F. Died June 2, 1863, from wounds received at Cold Harbor, Va.
John H. Delap, Capt., Co. G. Died May 9th, 1863, from wounds received at Mayres Heights.
John F. McKernan, 2d Lieut., Co. G. Died April 18th, 1865.
Mark H. Roberts, 1st Lieut., Co. K. Killed at Malvern Hill, July 1st, 1862.
William H. Myers, 1st Lieut., Co. K. Killed at Sailor's Creek, Va., April 6th, 1865.

88TH REGIMENT. Philadelphia Companies C, D, E, F, G, I and K.

Joseph A. McLean, Lieut.-Col. (Berks). Killed at Bull Run, August 30th, 1862.
Charles H. Kartsher, Adjutant. Killed in battle at Fredericksburg, December 13th, 1862.
John J. Belsterling, Capt., Co. C. Killed at Bull Run, August 30th, 1862.
Thomas J. Koch, Capt., Co. A. Killed at Five Forks, Va., April 11th, 1865.
Harry Hudson, 2d Lieut., Co. C. Killed by a falling bridge near Mitchell's Station, Va., August 18th, 1862.
Daniel G. Lehman, 1st Lieut., Co. E. Died May 20th, 1865, from wounds received at Five Forks, Va.
George B. Rhoads, Capt., Co. F. Killed at White Oak Swamp, Va., June 13th, 1864.
George H. Fulton, Lieut. Killed at Fredericksburg, December 13th, 1862.
Jacob Houder, Capt., Co. H. Killed on Weldon R. R., August 19th, 1864.

89TH REGIMENT (8th Cavalry). Philadelphia Companies C, D, E, F, G, H, I, K, L and part of M.

Peter Keenan, Major. Killed at Chancellorsville, May 3d, 1863.
J. Hazleton Haddock, Adjutant. Killed at Chancellorsville, May 3d, 1863.
George L. Bragg, Com. Sergeant. Killed August 16th, 1864.
William J. Latta, Capt., Co. I. Died at Washington, October 5th, 1862.

90TH REGIMENT.

Horatio S. Howell, Chaplain. Killed at Gettysburg, July 1st, 1863.
Jesse W. Super, 1st Lieut., Co. C. Killed at Spotsylvania C. H., May 10th, 1864.
Wilbur F. Myers, Capt., Co. F. Died at Philadelphia, August 24th, 1864.
James S. Bonsall, 2d Lieut. Killed at Weldon Railroad, August 19th, 1864.
Charles W. Duke, 1st Lieut., Co. K. Killed at Fredericksburg, December 13th, 1862.

91ST REGIMENT.

George W. Todd, Major. Died December 19th, 1862, from wounds received at Fredericksburg.
George W. Eyre, Q. M. Died of disease December 31st, 1862.
Thomas H. Parsons, Capt., Co. C. Died June 26th, 1863, from wounds received at Chancellorsville.
John Stewart, 1st Lieut., Co. C. Died June 22d, 1864, from wounds.
John Edgar, Jr., 1st Lieut., Co. G. Killed at Hatcher's Run, Va., February 6th, 1865.
James H. Closson, Capt., Co. H. Died November 23d, 1864, from wounds received at Chancellorsville.
George Black, 1st Lieut., Co. H. Died May 6th, 1863, from wounds received at Chancellorsville.
Horace B. Faust, Capt., Co. D. Died at Bealeton, Va., December 16th, 1863.
George Murphy, 1st Lieut., Co. I. Killed at Fredericksburg, December 13th, 1862.

92D REGIMENT (9th Cavalry).

Col. Thomas C. James. Died at Philadelphia, January 13th, 1863.

95TH REGIMENT (Gosline's Zouaves).

John M. Gosline, Col. Died June 29th, 1862, from wounds received at Gaines' Mill, Va.
Gustavus W. Town, Col. Killed at Salem Church, Va., May 3d, 1863.
Elisha Hall, Lieut.-Col. Killed at Salem Church, Va., May 3d, 1863.
William B. Hubbs, Major. Died June 29th, 1862, from wounds received at Gaines' Mill, Va.
Eugene D. Dunton, Adjutant. Killed at Salem Church, Va., May 3d, 1863.
James J. Carroll, Capt., Co. A. Killed at Sailor's Creek, April 6th, 1865.
T. D. G. Chapman, Capt., Co. C. Killed at Salem Church, Va., May 3d, 1863.
Hamilton Donohue, 1st Lieut., Co. C. Killed at Gaines' Mill, June 27th, 1862.
David Hailer, 1st Lieut., Co. F. Killed at Salem Church, Va., May 3d, 1863.
Edward Carroll, Lieut.-Col. Killed at the Wilderness, May 5th, 1864.
Thomas Burns, Capt., Co. G. Died October 28th, 1864, from wounds received at Cedar Creek, Va.

97TH REGIMENT.

George W. Hawkins, Lieut.-Col. Died of wounds August 28th, 1864, received at Darbytown Road, Va.
Lewis H. Watkins, 2d Lieut., Co. H. Killed at Green Plains, Va., May 20th, 1864.

98TH REGIMENT.

John B. Kohler, Lieut.-Col. Killed at Cedar Creek, Va., October 19th, 1864.
John W. Beamish, Major. Killed at Cold Harbor, Va., June 1st, 1864.
Edward Schwatlo, Adjutant. Killed at Cold Harbor, June 3d, 1864.
Chas. H. Weidman, 2d Lieut., Co. E. Killed at Wilderness, Va., May 5th, 1864.
Christian A. Gallas, 2d Lieut., Co. F. Killed at Malvern Hill, July 1st, 1862.
William Sehr, Capt., Co. H. Killed at Malvern Hill, July 1st, 1862.
Henry Hohenstein, 1st Lieut., Co. I. Died December 13th, 1861.
George Bush, 1st Lieut., Co. I. Died May 9th, 1863, from wounds received at Salem Heights, Va.
Herman Solbrich, 1st Lieut., Co. I. Died April 4th, 1865, from wounds received at Petersburg.
John Heppler, 2d Lieut., Co. K. Killed at Opequan, September 19th, 1864.

99TH REGIMENT.

J. Wesley Chew, 1st Lieut., Co. A. Died January 18th, 1865.
Matthew N. Heiskill, 1st Lieut., Co. B. Killed at Petersburg, Va., June 18th, 1864.
Frederick Klein, 1st Lieut., Co. B. Died April 20th, 1865.
Harrison Y. Clifton, 1st Lieut., Co. D. Died at Annapolis, Md., from wounds received at Sailor's Creek, Va.
George W. Ellsler, 2d Lieut., Co. F. Killed at Petersburg, Va., September 10th, 1864.
Isador Hirsch, 1st Lieut., Co. G. Killed at Petersburg, Va., June 17th, 1864.
John R. Nice, 1st Lieut., Co. H. Died July 3d, 1863, from wounds received at Gettysburg.
William Fisher, 1st Lieut., Co. H. Killed at Petersburg, Va., October 10th, 1864.
Lewis F. Waters, Capt., Co. I. Killed at Spotsylvania C. H., Va., May 12th, 1864.
Thomas R. Birch, 1st Lieut., Co. K. Died at Alexandria, Va., January 5th, 1862.

104TH REGIMENT.

John M. Gries, Major. Died of wounds June 13th, 1862.

287

106TH REGIMENT.

William L. Curry, Lieut.-Col. Died at Washington, D. C., July 7th, 1864, from wounds received at Spotsylvania C. H., Va., May 11th, 1864.

Ferdinand M. Pleis, Adjutant. Died August 2d, 1863, from wounds received at Gettysburg.

Charles S. Swartz, 1st Lieut., Co. A. Killed at Spotsylvania C. H., Va., May 12th, 1864.

William H. Smith, 2d Lieut., Co. B. Killed at Gettysburg, July 2d, 1863.

Joshua A. Gage, 2d Lieut., Co. D. Killed at Spotsylvania C. H., May 12th, 1864.

S. R. Townsend, 1st Lieut., Co. E. Killed at Cold Harbor, Va., June 5th, 1864.

Francis E. Foliet, 1st Lieut., Co. I. Died April 19th, 1862.

Martin C. Frost, Capt., Co. K.

108TH REGIMENT (11th Cavalry). Company C.

Robert S. Monroe, Major. Killed at Five Forks, Va., April 1st, 1865.

Henry B. Neilson, 1st Lieut., Co. C. Killed at Ream's Station, Va., August 25th, 1864.

Robert S. Monroe, Capt., Co. E. Killed at Five Forks, April 1st, 1865.

William Lancaster, 1st Lieut., Co. E. Killed at Five Forks, Va., April 1st, 1865.

109TH REGIMENT. All Philadelphia Companies excepting two.

Henry J. Stainrook, Col. Killed at Chancellorsville, Va., May 3d, 1863.

James Glendening, 1st Lieut., Co. A. Killed at Wauhatchie, Tenn., October 29th, 1863. (Bates' History.)

Charles W. Norris, 2d Lieut., Co. C. Died June 21st, 1863, from wounds received at Chancellorsville.

110TH REGIMENT. Companies E, F, G and I.

William Stewart, Capt., Co. F. Killed at Fort Steadman, Va., March 25th, 1865.

William A. Norton, Capt., Co. I. Died at Washington, D. C., from wounds received at Petersburg, Va.

W. H. Kochersperger, 1st Lieut., Co. I. Died April 10th, 1862, from wounds received at Winchester.

112TH REGIMENT. Heavy Artillery.

James L. Anderson, Col. Killed at Chaffin's Farm, Va., September 29th, 1864.

John S. Jarden, Capt., Co. C. Died November 9th, 1863.

Louis Fisher, 1st Lieut., Co. K. Died at Petersburg, September 6th, 1865.

113TH REGIMENT. 12th Cavalry.

Milton Funk, 2d Lieut., Co. C. Killed near Winchester, July 24th, 1864.

114TH REGIMENT (Collis' Zouaves).

Joseph S. Chandler, Major. Killed at Chancellorsville, Va., May 3d, 1863.

A. J. Cunningham, Capt., Co. A. Killed at Petersburg, Va., April 2d, 1865.

Henry M. Eddy, Capt., Co. D. Died April 11th, 1865, from wounds received at Petersburg, Va.

Frank A. Elliot, Capt., Co. F. Killed at Chancellorsville, Va., May 3d, 1863.

Charles E. Henkel, 2d Lieut., Co. G. Died at Morrisville, Va., November 24th, 1862.

George M. Cullen, 2d Lieut., Co. G. Killed at Chancellorsville, May 3d, 1863.

Edward T. Marion, 1st Lieut., Co. I. Killed at Petersburg, Va., April 2d, 1865.

H. C. McCarty, 1st Lieut., Co. K. Killed at Gettysburg, July 2d, 1863.

115TH REGIMENT. Companies A, B, C, E, F, H, I and K.

F. A. Lancaster, Col. Killed at Chancellorsville, Va., May 3d, 1863.

James Malloy, 1st Lieut., Co. B. Died of wounds May 3d, 1863.

George Cromley, Capt., Co. C. Killed at Chancellorsville, Va., May 3d, 1863.
Robert M. Jeffries, Capt., Co. F. Killed near Petersburg, Va., June 16th, 1864.
William L. Houpt, Capt., Co. I. Died at Falmouth, Va., January 26th, 1863.
George R. Curtis, Capt., Co. K. Died at Philadelphia, February 16th, 1863.

116TH REGIMENT.

Richard C. Dale, Lieut.-Col. Killed at Spotsylvania C. H., May 12th, 1864.
Christian Foltz, 2d Lieut., Co. A. Killed at Fredericksburg, Va., December 13th, 1862.
Henry D. Price, 1st Lieut., Co. C. (Brevet Major). Killed near Petersburg, Va., October 27th, 1864.
Garrett Nowlen, Capt., Co. D. (Brevet Major). Killed at Ream's Station, Va., August 25th, 1864.
Eugene Brady, 1st Lieut., Co. D. Killed at Five Forks, Va., March 31st, 1865.
Samuel Taggart, Capt., Co. I. (Brevet Major). Killed at Ream's Station, Va., August 25th, 1864.
Robert B. Montgomery, 2d Lieut., Co. I. Died December 21st, 1862, from wounds received at Fredericksburg, Va.
Capt. George Halpin, Co. A. Died at close of war from disease contracted in a Confederate prison.
George H. Bibighaus, 2d Lieut., Co. D. Died at Washington, August 25th, 1863.
Henry Keil, 2d Lieut., Co. E. Killed at Spotsylvania C. H., May 21st, 1864.
Robert T. McGuire, 1st Lieut., Co. B. Died at close of war from wound received at Fredericksburg.
Patrick Casey, 1st Lieut., Co. K. Died November 9th, 1862, at Philadelphia, from wounds received in action.

117TH REGIMENT (13th Cavalry).

Nathan S. Sneyd, Capt., Co. D. Killed at Hatcher's Run, Va., February 6th, 1865.
John Cline, Capt., Co. H. Killed at Hawes' Shop, Va., May 28th, 1864.

118TH REGIMENT (Corn Exchange Regiment).

Dendy Sharwood, Capt., Co. C. Died at Philadelphia, November 21st, 1863.
John Conahey, 2d Lieut., Co. E. Killed at Peeble's Farm, Va., September 30th, 1864.
John Scott, Capt., Co. F. Killed at Dabney's Mills, Va., February 6th, 1865.
Daniel L. Ware, 1st Lieut., Co. F. Died June 23d, 1864, from wounds received at Cold Harbor, Va.
Courtland Saunders, Capt., Co. G. Killed at Shepherdstown, W. Va., September 20th, 1862.
Richard W. Davis, Capt., Co. G. Killed at Gettysburg, July 2d, 1863.
J. Rudhall White, 2d Lieut., Co. G. Killed at Shepherdstown, W. Va., September 20th, 1862.
Joseph W. Ricketts, Capt., Co. K. Killed at Shepherdstown, W. Va., September 20th, 1862.
Charles M. Young, Capt., Co. K. Died October 29th, 1864, from wounds received at Peeble's Farm, Va.
J. Mora Moss, Jr., 2d Lieut., Co. K. Killed at Shepherdstown, W. Va., September 20th, 1862.
Arthur Steel, 2d Lieut., Co. G. Killed at Pegram's Farm, Va., September 30th, 1864.

119TH REGIMENT (Gray Reserves).

Henry P. Truefitt, Jr., Major. Killed at Spotsylvania C. H., Va., May 12th, 1864.
John D. Mercer, Adjutant. Killed at Petersburg, Va., April 2d, 1865.
John R. Laurens, Lieut., Co. C. Died May 4th, 1864, of wounds received at Wilderness.

William C. Moss, Capt., Co. D. Died at Washington, February 11th, 1864.

Edward E. Coxe, 2d Lieut., Co. D. Died November 22d, 1863, from wounds received at Rappahannock Station, Va.

George C. Lovett, 2d Lieut., Co. G. Died May 30th, 1863, from wounds received at Wilderness, Va.

Edward Ford, Jr., 2d Lieut., Co. I. Killed at Spotsylvania C. H., May 10th, 1864.

Charles P. Warner, Capt., Co. K. Killed at Spotsylvania C. H., May 12th, 1864.

Robert Reaney, 2d Lieut., Co. E. Killed at Rappahannock Station, November 7th, 1863.

Peter W. Rodgers, Capt., Co. B. Killed at Salem Church, Va., May 3d, 1863.

Cephas M. Hodgson, Capt., Co. B. Killed at Rappahannock Station, Va., November 7th, 1863.

George C. Humes, Capt., Co. B. Killed at Cold Harbor, Va., June 3d, 1864.

121ST REGIMENT.

Thomas M. Hall, Major. Died at Philadelphia, November 6th, 1864.

John Iungerich, Adjutant. Died at Philadelphia, June 24th, 1864, from wounds received at Jerico Ford, Va.

Samuel B. Haines, Q. M. Died of disease February 23d, 1863.

George W. Brickley, 1st Lieut., Co. A. Killed at Fredericksburg, Va., December 13th, 1863.

Joseph Frank Sterling, Capt., Co. C. Died November 6th, 1863, from wounds received at Gettysburg.

George W. Powell, 2d Lieut., Co. D. Died November 9th, 1863.

M. W. C. Barclay, 2d Lieut., Co. G. Killed at Fredericksburg, Va., December 13th, 1862.

William W. Dorr, Capt., Co. K. Killed at Spotsylvania C. H., May 10th, 1864.

147TH REGIMENT. Philadelphia Companies M and P, from 28th Regiment.

Wm. H. Hughes, 2d Lieut., Co. D. Killed at Chancellorsville, May 3d, 1863.

Thos. C. Baker, 2d Lieut., Co. D. Died July 5th, 1863, of wounds received at Gettysburg.

Henry Elliott, 2d Lieut., Co. D. Died August 28th, 1864.

Wm. Tourison, 1st Lieut., Co. E. Killed at Gettysburg, July 3d, 1863.

150TH REGIMENT (2d Bucktails). Philadelphia Companies A, B, C and F.

H. Chancellor, Jr., 1st Lieut., Co. B. Died August 7th, 1863, from wounds received at Gettysburg.

Cincinnatus Topham, 1st Lieut., Co. B. Died at Washington, November 8th, 1862.

Charles P. Keyser, 2d Lieut., Co. B. Killed at Gettysburg, July 1st, 1863.

160TH REGIMENT (15th Cavalry).

A. G. Rosengarten, Major. Killed at Stone River, Tenn., December 29th, 1862.

Harvey S. Lingle, 1st Lieut., Co. G. Died December 29th 1863, from wounds received at Mossey Creek, Tenn.

Evan W. Grubb, 2d Lieut., Co. G. Killed at Stone's River, Tenn., December 31st, 1862.

Washington Airey, Capt., Co. L. Captured and died August 12th, 1865, from consequent hardships.

180TH REGIMENT (19th Cavalry). Not including Companies L and M.

Edward Freeman, 1st Lieut., Co. C. Died at Philadelphia, December 26th, 1864.

James E. Wenrick, Capt., Co. E. Died while a prisoner of war at Columbia, S. C., October 23d, 1864.

181ST REGIMENT (20th Cavalry).

John C. Henry, Capt., Co. G. Died August 20th, 1864, from wounds received at Winchester, Va.

19

183D REGIMENT.

John M. Ottinger, 1st Lieut., Co. A. Killed at Spotsylvania C. H., January 13th, 1864.

Charles H. Hamm, 1st Lieut., Co. B. Died March 26th, 1865.

Benjamin B. Lathbury, 1st Lieut., Co. C. Died at Richmond, Va., June 27th, 1864, from wounds received in action.

Alexander Campbell, Capt., Co. F. Died at Philadelphia, June 20th, 1864.

Joseph R. Smith, Capt., Co. G. Killed at Cold Harbor, Va., June 3d, 1864.

John Digman, Capt., Co. H. Died at Danville, Va., December 21st, 1864.

John H. Hutt, Capt., Co. K. Killed at Spotsylvania C. H., Va., May 12th, 1864.

188TH REGIMENT.

Herman C. Moeller, Capt., Co. C. Killed at Cold Harbor, Va., June 1st, 1864.

William Dieterlie, 1st Lieut., Co. C. Killed at Cold Harbor, Va., June 1st, 1864.

Adam W. Mattice, 2d Lieut., Co. C. Killed at Cold Harbor, June 3d, 1864.

Hiram R. Shinkel, Capt., Co. E. Died at Richmond, Va., from wounds received at Drury's Bluff, May 16th, 1864.

Henry E. Breel, Capt., Co. I. Died September 22d, 1864, from wounds received at Cold Harbor.

192D REGIMENT (6 months' service).

William E. Tyndale, 1st Lieut., Co. B. Drowned October 21st, 1864.

198TH REGIMENT.

Edwin A. Glenn, Major. Died at City Point, Va., April 11th, 1865, from wounds received at Five Forks.

Charles I. McEwen, Major. Died from wounds received at Lewis Farm, March 31st, 1865.

George W. Mulfrey, Capt., Co. C. Died from wounds received at Lewis Farm, Va., March 31st, 1865.

Andrew A. Pomeroy, Capt., Co. I. Killed at White Oak Road, Va., March 31st, 1865.

Charles W. Frasier, 1st Lieut., Co. L. Died February 7th, 1865, from wounds received at Hatcher's Run.

199TH REGIMENT.

Patrick O'Murphy, Capt., Co. D. Killed at Fort Gregg, Va., April 2d, 1856.

Robert McMillan, 1st Lieut., Co. I. Killed at Fort Gregg, Va., April 2d, 1865.

203D REGIMENT.

John W. Moore, Col. Killed at Fort Fisher, N. C., January 15th, 1865.

Jacob T. Smallwood, Capt., Co. C. Killed at Fort Fisher, N. C., January 15th, 1865.

R. W. Hemphill, 1st Lieut., Co. H. Died of wounds February 13th, 1865.

210TH REGIMENT.

William Sergeant, Col. Died April 11th, 1865, from wounds received at Five Forks, Va.

INDEPENDENT BATTERY A (3 years' service).

Philip Secker, 2d Lieut. Died at Philadelphia, July 30th, 1862.

INDEPENDENT COMPANY, ENGINEERS.

Albert S. White, Capt. Died at Philadelphia, March 29th, 1863.

THE MISSISSIPPI RAM FLEET.

Charles Ellet, Col., U. S. Engineers, Commander. Died June 21st, 1862, from a wound received near Memphis during a naval engagement.

Charles Rivers Ellet, Col., Mississippi River Marine Brigade. Died at Bunker Hill, Ill., October 16th, 1863.

291

U. S. ARMY

13TH U. S. INFANTRY.
Archibald Hill Engle, Major. Killed at Resaca, Ga., May 14th, 1864.
Charles H. Brightly, U. S. A., Capt., 4th U. S. Infantry. Died June 9th, 1864, from wounds received in the Wilderness.
Charles Lombaert Kneass, Brevet Major, U. S. Army. Killed at Stone River, Tenn., December 31st, 1862.

1ST U. S. ARTILLERY.
William K. Pollock, 2d Lieut. Died at Fort Macon, N. C., August 4th, 1863.

2D U. S. ARTILLERY.
John Trout Greble, Lieut. Killed at Big Bethel, Va., June 10th, 1861.
Ulric Dahlgren, Col. of Cavalry. Killed during a raid under Gen. Kilpatrick, near Richmond, March, 1864.
Caesar Rodney Fisher, U. S. A., 1st Lieut., Cavalry. Died May 12th, 1864, from wounds received at Upperville, Va.
Charles Douglas Waterman, Lieut. U. S. Engineer Corps. Died September 28th, 1864, at Bordentown, N. J.
J. Penrose Ash, Brevet Lieut.-Col., 5th U. S. Cavalry.

8TH U. S. COLORED INFANTRY.
Charles W. Fribley, Col. Killed at Olustee, Fla., February 20th, 1864.

15TH REGIMENT ENGINEERS, NEW YORK.
Walter Scott, 2d Lieut. (Date of death unknown.)

40TH REGIMENT, NEW YORK VOLUNTEERS.
Washington Peel, 1st Lieut. Killed before Petersburg, 1864.
Orlando G. Wagner, Brevet Capt., U. S. A. Died from wounds received at Yorktown, April 21st, 1862.

6TH REGIMENT, U. S. COLORED INFANTRY.
Rev. Jeremiah Asher, Chaplain. Died at Wilmington, N. C.
Fred. Meyer, Lieut., Co. B. Killed at Chaffin's Farm, Va., September 29th, 1864.
Henry Herbert, Capt., Co. G. Died at Goldsboro, N. C., May 15th, 1865.

DETACHED VOLUNTEER OFFICERS.

Henry J. Biddle, Capt. and A. A. G., Pennsylvania Reserve Corps. Died while prisoner at Richmond, July 20th, 1862.
William D. Kirk, 1st Lieut. (Commissary). Died at Alexandria, Va., June 28th, 1864, from wounds received at Todd's Tavern.
Thomas H. Elliott, Capt. and A. A. G., formerly 1st Lieut., Co. H, 28th Infantry. Killed near Atlanta, July, 1864.

The following commanding officers of Philadelphia regiments were killed or died after separation from the regiments by reason of promotion or who were not citizens of Philadelphia and therefore are not included in the foregoing list:

23D REGIMENT.
David B. Birney, Brig. Gen. Died October 18th, 1864.

61ST REGIMENT.
O. H. Rippey, Colonel. Killed at Fair Oaks, May 31, 1862.

75TH REGIMENT.

Henry Bohlen, Brig.-Gen. Killed at Freeman's Ford, Va., August 22d, 1862.

81st REGIMENT.

James Miller, Colonel. Killed at Fair Oaks, May 31st, 1862.

88TH REGIMENT.

Joseph A. McLean, Colonel. Killed at second Bull Run, August 30th, 1862.

110TH REGIMENT.

James D. Crowther, Colonel. Killed at Chancellorsville, May 3d, 1863.

116TH REGIMENT.

Richard C. Dale, Lieut.-Col. Killed at Spotsylvania, May 12th, 1864.

183D REGIMENT.

J. F. McCullough, Colonel. Killed in action, May 31st, 1864.

CITIZENS OF PHILADELPHIA WHO GAINED THE RANK OF GENERAL OFFICERS

(With Dates of Commissions)

REGULAR ARMY.

McCLELLAN, GEORGE B., Major-General, Commander Armies of the United States, November 5th, 1861.

MEADE, GEORGE G., Major-General, Commander Army of the Potomac, June 28th, 1863.

BRIGADIER-GENERALS.

Blake, George Alexander H........................March 13th, 1865
Barnes, Joseph K., Surgeon-General.................August 22d, 1864.
Hardin, Martin D..................................March 13th, 1865.
Meigs, Montgomery C., Quartermaster-General.......May 15th, 1861.
McKibbin, David Bell..............................March 13th, 1865.

VOLUNTEER ARMY.

MAJOR-GENERALS.

Patterson, Robert . . . .April 16th, 1861.
Birney, David B. (Died October 18th, 1864).........May 20th, 1863.
Cadwalader, George . . ..April 25th, 1862.
Crawford, Samuel Wylie............................August 1st, 1864.
Franklin, William B...............................July 16th, 1862.
Heintzelman, Samuel P.............................July 16th, 1862.
Humphreys, Andrew A. . . ..July 8th, 1863.
*Parke, John Grubb . . ..July 18th, 1862.
Reno, Jesse L. (Killed at South Mountain, Md., September 14th, 1862) . . . .August 20th, 1862.
Smith, Andrew J. . . ..May 14th, 1864.
Smith, Charles Ferguson (Died April 25th, 1862)....March 22d, 1862.

BREVET MAJOR-GENERALS OF VOLUNTEERS.*

Collis, Charles H. T.............................March 13th, 1865.
Gregory, Edgar M................................August 9th, 1866.
Gwyn, James....................................April 1st, 1865.
Kane, Thomas Leiper............................March 13th, 1865.
Mindil, George Washington......................March 13th, 1865.
Mulholland, St. Clair A.........................March 15th, 1865.
Neill, Thomas H................................March 13th, 1865.
Pennypacker, Galusha (Major-General, U. S. A., March
    2d, 1867)...................................March 13th, 1865.
Sickel, Horatio Gates..........................March 13th, 1865.
Tyndale, Hector................................March 13th, 1865.

BRIGADIER-GENERALS OF VOLUNTEERS.

Bohlen, W. Henry C. (Killed at Freeman's Ford, August
    22d, 1862).................................April 28th, 1862.
Brisbin, James S...............................May 3d, 1865.
Brooke, John Rutter............................May 12th, 1864.
Campbell, Charles T............................March 17th, 1863.
Hays, Alexander (Killed in the Wilderness, May 5th,
    1864)......................................September 29th, 1862.
Haupt, Herman (Appointment vacated September 5th,
    1863)......................................September 5th, 1862.
Keim, William H. (Died May 18th, 1862)..........December 20th, 1861.
Meredith, Sullivan A...........................November 29th, 1862.
Naglee, Henry M................................February 4th, 1862.
Owen, Joshua T.................................November 29th, 1862.
Patterson, Francis E. (Died November 27th, 1862)...April 15th, 1862.
Porter, Andrew.................................May 17th, 1861.
Sully, Alfred G................................September 6th, 1862.
Von Schimmelfennig, Alexander (Died September 7th,
    1865)......................................November 29th, 1863.
Wistar, Isaac J................................November 29th, 1862.
Williams, David H..............................November 29th, 1862.

BREVET BRIGADIER-GENERALS.

Ballier, John F................................July 13th, 1864.
Bassett, Isaac C...............................December 12th, 1864.
Baxter, DeWitt C...............................March 13th, 1865.
Biles, Edwin R.................................March 13th, 1865.
Bodine, Robert L...............................March 13th, 1865.

---

*GENERAL ORDER No. 72.

WASHINGTON, March 24th, 1863.

An Act to authorize the brevetting of volunteer and other officers in the United States Service: Be it enacted, etc., That the President of the United States be, and hereby is authorized, by and with the advice and consent of the Senate, to confer brevet rank upon such commissioned officers as have been or may hereafter be distinguished by gallant actions or meritorious conduct, which rank and title shall not entitle them to any increase of pay or emoluments.

By order of the Secretary of War.

E. D. TOWNSEND,
    Assistant Adjutant General.

Briscoe, James C....................................March 13th, 1865.
Clark, Gideon . . . .March 13th, 1865.
Clay, Cecil ....March 13th, 1865.
Cummings, Alexander . . ..April 18th, 1865.
Ely, John. . ...April 15th, 1865.
Flynn, John. . . ..May 13th, 1865.
Foust, Benezet F...................................March 13th, 1865.
Frink, Henry A............•••••....................August 15th, 1865.
Fritz, Peter, Jr. . ...March 13th, 1865.
Gile, George W.....................................May 6th, 1865.
Gilbert, Charles Champion..........................September 9th, 1862.
Gallagher, Thomas F...........••••••...............March 13th, 1865.
Herring, Charles P.................................March 13th, 1865.
Hofmann, J. William................................August 1, 1864.
Huey, Pennock . . ..March 13th, 1865.
Irwin, William H...................................March 13th, 1865.
Knowles, Oliver B.............••••••...............March 13th, 1865.
Lynch, James C.....................................March 13th, 1865.
Leech, William Albert..............................March 13th, 1865.
Lewis, William D., Jr..............................March 13th, 1865.
Lyle, Peter..March 13th, 1865.
McCormick, Charles C....••••.......................March 13th, 1865.
Markoe, John.......................................March 13th, 1865.
Merrill, Lewis, U. S. A............................March 13th, 1865.
Morton, James St. Clair, U. S. A. (Killed at Peters-
    burg, Va., June 17th, 1864)....................March 13th, 1865.
Morehead, Turner G.................................March 15th, 1865.
Murphy, John K.....................................March 13th, 1865.
Palmer, William J..................................November 6th, 1864.
*Potter, Carroll Hagedorn·.........................March 13th, 1865.
Price, Richard B...................................March 13th, 1865.
Prevost, Charles M.................................March 13th, 1865.
*Patterson, Robert Emmett..........................March 13th, 1865.
*Reno, Marcus A....................................March 13th, 1865.
Ruff. Charles Frederick............................March 13th, 1865.
Selfridge, James L.................................March 13th, 1865.
Thompson, Robert . . ..March 13th, 1865.
Tilghman, Benjamin C...............................March 13th, 1865.
West, Robert M.....................................April 1st, 1865.
Wagner, Louis. . . ..March 13th, 1865.
Wister, Langhorne. . . ••••.........................March 13th, 1865.
Winslow, Robert E..................................March 13th, 1865.
Zulick, Samuel M...................................March 13th, 1865.

PROMOTIONS BY BREVET IN PHILADELPHIA REGIMENTS, BELOW THE RANK OF BRIGADIER-GENERAL.

(Compiled from the annual reports of the Adjutant-General of Pennsylvania for the years 1865 and 1867.)

Anderson, William, First Lieut., 99th Infantry; brevet captain April 6th, 1865.
Armor, William C., Capt., 28th Infantry; brevet major March 13th, 1865.
Ashbrook, Joseph, Capt., 118th Infantry; brevet major July 6th, 1864.
Ashurst, Richard L., Adjutant, 150th Infantry; brevet major March 13th, 1865.
Ayres, Peter B., First Lieut., 90th Infantry; brevet captain April 6th, 1865.

*Graduates of the U. S. Military Academy.

Banes, Charles H., Capt., 72d Infantry; brevet captain and assistant adjutant-general May 15th, 1863.

Benson, R. Dale, First Lieut., 114th Infantry; brevet captain and major March 13th, 1865.

Binney, Horace, Capt., 118th Infantry; brevet major March 13th, 1865.

Bonnaffon, Sylvester, Jr., Capt., 99th Infantry; brevet major and lieutenant-colonel March 13th, 1865.

Brady, James, Lieut.-Col., 1st Artillery; brevet colonel March 13th, 1865.

Brinton, Robert M., Major, 2d Cavalry; brevet lieutenant-colonel April 1st, 1865.

Brinton, Joseph P., Lieut.-Col., 2d Cavalry; brevet colonel August 1st, 1864.

Breitenbach, J. R., Capt., 106th Infantry; brevet major and lieutenant-colonel March 13th, 1865.

Brooke, William Rawle, Capt., 3d Cavalry; brevet major March 13th, 1865.

Cadwalader, C. N., Capt., 2d Artillery; brevet major and lieutenant-colonel March 13th, 1865.

Cavada, Frederick F., Capt., 23d Infantry; brevet captain and assistant adjutant-general July 14th, 1862.

Casner, John F., Capt., 91st Infantry; brevet major October 27th, 1864.

Cassells, John, Major, 11th Cavalry; brevet lieutenant-colonel March 13th, 1865.

Clark, Charles P., Capt., 99th Infantry; brevet major and lieutenant-colonel March 13th, 1865.

Clark, William, Capt., 82d Infantry; brevet major September 19th, 1864.

Clark, William, Major, 82d Infantry; brevet lieutenant-colonel April 6th, 1865.

Clarke, Gideon, Lieut.-Col., 119th Infantry; brevet colonel April 2d, 1865.

Carpenter, J. Edward, Capt., 8th Cavalry; brevet major March 13th, 1865.

Cosslett, Charles, Capt., 116th Infantry; brevet major March 13th, 1865.

Crosby, J. W., Major, 61st Infantry; brevet lieutenant-colonel July 12th, 1865.

Colwell, James, First Lieut., 82d Infantry; brevet captain April 6th, 1865.

Davis, Charles L., Capt., 82d Infantry; captain Signal Corps, U. S. A., March 3d, 1863.

Dechert, Robert P., Major, 29th Infantry; brevet lieutenant-colonel March 13th, 1865.

Dutton, James, First Lieut., 119th Infantry; brevet captain April 6th, 1865.

Fagan, Maurice E., Capt., 19th Infantry; brevet major and lieutenant-colonel March 13th, 1865.

Fayman, B. J., First Lieut., 91st Infantry; brevet captain, major, lieutenant-colonel and colonel August 18th, 1864.

Foering, John O., First Lieut., 28th Infantry; brevet captain March 13th, 1865.

Frink, West, Major, 121st Infantry; brevet lieutenant-colonel April 1st, 1865.

Ford, Edward L., Capt., 99th Infantry; brevet captain and aide-de-camp, Tenth Corps, September 3d, 1864.

Fry, William H., Major, 16th Cavalry; brevet lieutenant-colonel March 13th, 1865.

Glenn, E. A., Major, 198th Infantry; brevet major and lieutenant-colonel April 1st, 1865.

Givin, Alexander W., First Lieut., 114th Infantry; brevet captain March 13th, 1865.

Goodman, Samuel, Adjt., 28th Infantry; brevet captain, major, lieutenant-colonel, colonel March 13th, 1865.

Goodman, William E., Capt., 147th Infantry; brevet major March 13th, 1865.

Gordon, David, Capt., 95th Infantry; brevet major April 6th, 1865.

Gray, William C., Major, 119th Infantry; brevet lieutenant-colonel April 6th, 1865.

Griffith, Orlando B., Capt., 82d Infantry; brevet colonel March 13th, 1865.

Gunther, William L., Capt., 198th Infantry; brevet major April 1st, 1865.

Harper, John, Major, 95th Infantry; brevet lieutenant-colonel October 19th, 1864.

Harper, John, Lieut.-Col., 95th Infantry; brevet colonel April 6th, 1865.

Hand, Charles H., First Lieut., 118th Infantry; brevet captain September 30th, 1864.

Hand, Charles H., Capt., 118th Infantry; brevet major April 1st, 1865.

Hamersly, G. W., Quartermaster, 186th Infantry; brevet captain and major August 15th, 1865.

Hartley, James, First Lieut., 114th Infantry; brevet captain April 9th, 1865.

Hassinger, David S., First Lieut., 119th Infantry; brevet captain April 6th, 1865.

Hill, William H., Capt., 99th Infantry; brevet first lieutenant, Signal Corps, U. S. A., March 3d, 1863.

Hindmarsh, Henry E., Lieut., 95th Infantry; brevet captain and major April 6th, 1865.

Hughes, Robert B., Lieut.-Col., 199th Infantry; brevet colonel April 2d, 1865.

Ivers, Albert, Capt., 82d Infantry; brevet major April 6th, 1865.

Jones, D. D., Lieut. and Quartermaster, 88th Infantry; brevet captain July 17th, 1862.

Kimball, J. W., Capt., 198th Infantry; brevet major April 1st, 1865.

Knight, William H., Capt., 82d Infantry; brevet major April 6th, 1865.

Landell, E. A., Capt., 119th Infantry; brevet major December 5th, 1864.

Landell, E. A., brevet lieutenant-colonel April 6th, 1865.

Lambert, William Harrison, 15th Cavalry (and adjutant 33d N. J. Infantry); brevet major March 13th, 1865.

Lambdin, J. Harrison, First Lieut., 121st Infantry; brevet captain and A. A. G. May 18th, 1865.

Latta, James W., Capt., 119th Infantry; brevet captain and A. A. G. April 20th, 1864.

Lentz, David H., Quartermaster, 91st Infantry; brevet captain and A. Q. M. May 8th, 1864.

McCalla, Theodore H., Major, 95th Infantry; brevet lieutenant-colonel March 13th, 1865.

Mead, James P., Capt., 88th Infantry; brevet major and lieutenant-colonel March 13th, 1865.

Meade, George, Second Lieut., 6th Cavalry; brevet captain and aide de camp to Genl. Meade May 22d, 1863.

Mitchell, S. B. Wylie, Surgeon, 8th Cavalry; brevet lieutenant-colonel March 13th, 1865.

Mitchell, James H., Capt., 81st Infantry; brevet major March 13th, 1865.

Mitchell, R. W., First Lieut., 6th Cavalry; brevet captain and aide de camp to Genl. Reynolds April 25th, 1863.

Morris, Thomas, First Lieut., 119th Infantry; brevet captain April 6th, 1865.

Morrow, A. J., Lieut.-Col., 6th Cavalry; brevet colonel March 13th, 1865.

Neiler, James R., Lieut.-Col., 82d Infantry; brevet colonel April 6th, 1865.

Newlin, Alfred S., Capt., 114th Infantry; brevet major April 9th, 1865.

Newhall, Frederick C., Capt., 6th Cavalry; brevet major and aide de camp to Gen. Sheridan May 3d, 1864.

Nicholson, John P., Quartermaster, 28th Infantry; brevet captain, major and lieutenant-colonel March 13th, 1865.

Northrop, B. T., First Lieut., 82d Infantry; brevet captain April 6th, 1865.

Nowlen, Garrett, Capt., 116th Infantry; brevet major August 25th, 1864.

O'Brien, John T., Capt., 82d Infantry; brevet major and lieutenant-colonel April 6th, 1865.

O'Neil, Henry, Major, 118th Infantry; brevet lieutenant-colonel December 2d, 1864.

Orr, Robert L., Capt., 61st Infantry; brevet major September 22d, 1864.

Orr, Robert L., Lieut.-Col., 61st Infantry; brevet colonel April 2d, 1865.

Paul, Frank W., First Lieut., 2d Artillery; brevet captain March 13th, 1865.

Paul, H. W., Capt., 5th Cavalry; brevet major April 5th, 1865.

Prenot, Louis F., Capt., 82d Infantry; brevet major September 17th, 1864.

Reen, Charles, Lieut.-Col., 95th Infantry; brevet colonel April 2d, 1865.

Roberts, Joseph W. P., First Lieut., 82d Infantry; brevet captain April 6th, 1865.

Rosengarten, Adolph G., Major, 15th Cavalry; brevet colonel December 29th, 1862.

Rosengarten, Joseph G., First Lieut., 121st Infantry; brevet captain March 13th, 1865.

Saylor, Benjamin, Capt., 119th Infantry; brevet captain and commissary April 20th, 1864.

Sacriste, Louis J., Capt., 116th Infantry; brevet major March 13th, 1865.
Sellers, Alfred J., Major, 90th Infantry; brevet lieutenant-colonel and colonel March 13th, 1865.
Shermer, Benjamin C., Capt., 114th Infantry; brevet major April 9th, 1865.
Silas Crispen, Capt. of Ordnance, U. S. A.; brevet lieutenant-colonel March 13th, 1865.
Smith, Charles Ross, Lieut.-Col., 6th Cavalry; brevet colonel March 13th, 1865.
Street, William L., First Lieut., 88th Infantry; brevet major March 13th, 1865.
Taylor, Samuel W., First Lieut., 26th Infantry; captain and aide de camp to Gen. Hooker May 21st, 1864.
Todd, George W., Major, 91st Infantry; brevet lieutenant-colonel December 13th, 1862.
Treichel, Charles, Major, 3d Cavalry; brevet lieutenant-colonel March 13th, 1865.
Veale, Moses, Capt., 109th Infantry; brevet major March 13th, 1865.
Vezin, Henry A., Capt., 5th Cavalry; brevet major and lieutenant-colonel April 9th, 1865.
Vogel, T. K., First Lieut., 198th Infantry; brevet captain April 9th, 1865.
Walters, A. H., Capt., 118th Infantry; brevet major July 6th, 1864.
Warner, Henry C., Capt., 119th Infantry; brevet major April 2d, 1865.
Wessels, Francis, Capt., 106th Infantry; brevet major and lieutenant-colonel March 13th, 1865.
White, C. A., Adjt., 8th Cavalry; brevet captain March 13th, 1865.
Whitehead, G. Irvine, First Lieut., 6th Cavalry; brevet major and judge advocate March 11th, 1863.
Wilson, William, Lieut.-Col., 81st Infantry; brevet colonel March 13th, 1865.
Wilson, James B., Capt., 118th Infantry; brevet major September 30th, 1864.
Weidersheim, Wm. A., Capt., 119th Infantry; brevet major April 6th, 1865.
Williams, John W., First Lieut., 6th Cavalry; brevet captain and A. A. G. April 14th, 1862.
Woodward, Evan M., Adjutant, 2d Reserves; brevet captain March 13th, 1865.
Woodeard, George W., Private, 15th Cavalry; brevet captain and A. A. G. February 8th, 1865.
Wrigley, Samuel, Capt., 198th Infantry; brevet major March 13th, 1865.

REGIMENTS LOSING FIFTY OR MORE KILLED OR FATALLY WOUNDED*

ABOVE TWO HUNDRED.

Second Heavy Artillery; 61st, 72d and 81st Infantry.

ABOVE ONE HUNDRED AND FIFTY.

Forty-third (1st Artillery Reserves); 28th, 69th, 95th, and 116th Infantry.

ABOVE ONE HUNDRED.

Seventh, 11th, 16th, 17th Cavalry; 41st Infantry (12th Reserves), 23d, 26th, 29th, 56th, 71st, 73d, 82d, 88th, 90th, 91st and 188th Infantry.

ABOVE FIFTY.

Second, 5th, 8th, 9th, 13th, 14th, 18th Cavalry; 31st (2d Reserves), 32d (3d Reserves), 33d (4th Reserves), 36th (7th Reserves), 58th, 67th, 68th, 74th, 75th, 104th, 109th, 114th, 147th, 183d, 187th and 203d Infantry.

*Dyer's Compendium.

BATTLES IN WHICH PHILADELPHIA TROOPS SUSTAINED THE GREATEST LOSSES OF ANY COMMANDS IN ACTION.*

		Killed, Wounded and Missing.
Fair Oaks	61st Regiment	263
Shepherdstown	118th Regiment	269
Fort Stevens, D. C.	98th Regiment	36
Strawberry Plains	110th Regiment	31
Fort Fisher	203d Regiment	191
Sailor's Creek	82d Regiment	89
Brandy Station	6th Cavalry	29
Wilson's Raid	11th Cavalry	183
White Sulphur Springs	14th Cavalry	102
Shepherdstown (July, 1863)	16th Cavalry	24

BOY SOLDIERS OF '61-'65

IN the course of a recent editorial in the *Saturday Evening Post* it was stated that the Union Armies of the Civil War included eight hundred and forty-six thousand boys sixteen years of age or less, one million one hundred and fifty thousand of eighteen years or less, and that ninety thousand boys died in battle or from disease while in the service. Every boy wanted to be a soldier. Thousands of mothers trembled as they watched the martial fever lay hold upon the veins of their school-boy sons. Thousands of these children wept as the mustering officer turned them away from the doors of the recruiting stations. In every vacant lot infant officers were drilling their puerile squads. It was hard in those stirring days to be so young, when the best one could do was to march along abreast of the stunning bands of the never-ending regiments of other and older boys, on their way to the waiting military trains at Broad and Prime streets, or to go down to the Navy Yard and see the ships sail away. It was great to grow big enough and tall enough to get into even the Home Guards.

At the High School it was ordained that any pupil, in the highest grade, who enlisted was entitled to graduate with his class, although

---

*These figures, from Fox's "Regimental Losses," vary, in some instances, from other accepted records.

They do not include the losses of the 6th and 8th Regiments, U. S. Colored Troops, at Chaffin's Farm, Va., and Olustee, Florida, of which records have not been published.

absent on duty. Of twenty students who were examined for the position of third assistant engineer in the navy none were rejected.

"The Boys' Own Infantry" was enrolled in the Home Guard Brigade, and in Col. Eakins' Third Regiment of the same organization a company of engineer cadets from the Polytechnic College served in guarding the great Du Pont Powder Works on Brandywine Creek.

Major G. Eckendorf, a well-known tactician, was engaged at many of the public schools in drill instruction. This officer also drilled officers of boy companies and regiments in evolutions and the manual of arms. Military schools, in which the pupils wore uniforms, were numerous and popular. The students of the Pennsylvania Military Academy and the Courtland Saunders Cadets repeatedly gave exhibition drills at the Academy of Music and at Musical Fund Hall before admiring audiences. The latter organization, sixty strong, under Capt. N. Browne, Jr., was especially remarkable for its perfect discipline. It originated at the Saunders Institute in West Philadelphia, and was named in honor of the son of the principal, the youthful captain of Company G, 118th Regiment, who was one of the many Philadelphia boys of the "Corn Exchange" Regiment, sacrificed by reason of military mischance at Shepherdstown, West Virginia, upon that fateful September 20th, 1862. Post 21, G. A. R., continues to keep alive the memory of the lamented Capt. Courtland Saunders.

A fine battalion of boy cadets was connected with the Hlasko Institute at 219 South Broad street, and was frequently to be seen in parades.

Another favorite company was the Wyers' Academic Cadets, which is on record as having paraded down Chestnut street on September 13th, 1863.

Southwark was proud of its Lyle Cadets, some of whom were but seven years old. They were drilled by Capt. Hincken, who commanded the Pulaski Guards.

The "Minute Guards" of the Jefferson Grammar School, Philadelphia Cadets, Pennsylvania Cadets and National Guard Cadets were connected with Gen. Pleasonton's Home Guard Brigade. Naturally, Zouave Cadet companies and Zouave gymnastics appealed strongly to the youthful imagination, and the red-legged cohorts of juveniles lent color to many a public display of martial character, and many a recruit for the 23d, 72d and 95th Regiments was gained from among these juvenile organizations. Several companies of Zouaves went to the war from Capt. Louis Hillebrand's gymnasium at Ninth and Arch streets. (23d Regiment.)

The Philadelphia Sketch Club, composed of young artists and art students, was represented in the Union Army at different times by several of its older members, one of whom was killed in battle; others of the club were active in painting battle flags and transparencies of patriotic design.

Every ship of war that slid from its cradle into the Delaware River, every ship that came into port proudly, with prizes and to mend the scars of conflict, carried away boys of Philadelphia, and many, many indeed, never came home when the blockading and the sea fighting was done. The sailors have few monuments to mark the place where they fought and died for their flag and the country.

No accurate record can be made, from any reliable material, of the number of our Philadelphia boys who perished by reason of the war, but the loss to this community, in its natural rate of increase, is suggested in the fact that in the decade ending with 1860 the population gained twenty-nine per cent. In the decade following the gain was but nineteen per cent., an increased proportion of which was of foreign origin. The loss of its native stock is a heavy part of the price of this city, in common with the country at large, paid as tribute to the cause of the National Union.

GRADUATES AND STUDENTS OF THE CENTRAL HIGH SCHOOL WHO SERVED IN THE ARMY AND NAVY

THE Central High School of Philadelphia was represented in the Union service, upon land and sea, in its roll of graduates and students by one hundred and sixty-seven commissioned officers, one hundred and fourteen non-commissioned officers and privates in the volunteer and regular armies, and by sixty commissioned officers in the Navy and nineteen in the Marine Corps, a total of three hundred and sixty. Of these thirty-nine were killed or died in the service.*

Among those most distinguished for service were Robert Porter Dechert, James W. Latta, Charles H. Banes, Samuel B. Roney, Frederick Williams, Albert L. Magilton, Charles Parham, William J. Palmer, Gustavus W. Town, George W. Mindil, Edwin R. Biles, Charles Kochersperger, Frederick F. Cavada, William A. Leech, Robert B. Potter, Henry Pleasants, Frederick E. Crosman, Lewis H. Pelouze, Thomas H. Addicks, James T. Bates, Andrew J. Town, Theodore McMurtrie, Cyrus S. Detre, Louis G. Sacriste, Richard J. Levis (surgeon), William H. Gobrecht (surgeon), S. B. Wylie Mitchell, Thomas H. Town, Elisha Hall, John S. Jarden, Silas Crispin, Thomas I. Leiper, Cornelius Widdis, William A. Wiedersheim, Charles H. Brightly, Charles H. Gibson, William H. Harrison, Lemuel B. Norton, Frederick A. Sorber, John T. Greble (first Union officer killed), Orlando G. Wagner, Edward E. Coxe, Joshua S. Garsed, William R. Peddle, Robert J. Park, Jr., James F. McElhone, Edwin Ford, Joseph Mora Moss and Edwin Walton.

*A complete list may be found in a small brochure printed in 1864, entitled: "Contribution of the Central High School of Philadelphia to the War," compiled by Nicholas H. Maguire, Principal.

U. OF P. IN WAR

THE "Alumni Register," University of Pennsylvania, has recently published (1913) a list of the Alumni and students of the University who served in the armies of the North and South in the course of the Civil War. The compiler, Dr. Ewing Jordan, has recorded 927 names, and there yet remain a large number not tabulated. Nearly 500 of those already listed came from the medical department, having served as surgeons or surgical assistants.

The notables in the surgical department of the Confederate Army were largely University of Pennsylvania men. John Clifford Pemberton, of Philadelphia, Lieut.-Gen. in the Confederate Army, was a graduate of the University. Distinguished Alumni among Union officers included Major-Gens. George B. McClellan, John Grubb Parke, Samuel Wylie Crawford, Brigadier-Gens. Leslie, Cadwalader, Roberts, Meredith, Tilghman, West, Patterson, Tevis, Neill, Morton, La Motte, Clay, Markoe and Leiper.

A mural tablet at the University of Pennsylvania contains the names of the following University of Pennsylvania men who fell in the Union service: John Richter Jones, Francis Engle Patterson, Henry Jonathan Biddle, Thomas S. Martin, William Platt, Jr., Albert Owen Stille, Charles Frederick Taggart, Charles Iszard Maclean, Henry Courtland Whelan, Daniel P. Buckley, James Hamilton Kahn, Charles Baker Riehle, John Haseltine Haddock, George McClelland Bredin, Francis Gordon Dalton, Archibald Hill Engle, Robert Patterson Engle and George William Powell.

GIRARD COLLEGE IN THE ARMY

THOUGH Girard College was founded but thirteen years before the outbreak of the Civil War, and though no students could be admitted into the College who were over ten years of age, the institution was well represented in the armies for the Union, both from the lists of those who had gone out to apprenticeships in advance of the outbreak of the war, and those who left the College to go to the service of their country.

A total of one hundred and eighty-five names are reported as having enlisted. Of these the verification of service has been made up to this time of one hundred and twenty-four men; of these twelve saw service as commissioned officers, twenty-eight as non-commissioned officers, eighty-one as privates and three as musicians.

Of the foregoing, seventeen are known to have died in service, and of the total of one hundred and eighty-five reported twelve additional are said to have lost their lives.

Among those most distinguished in service were Henry M. Steel, William H. Kilpatrick, George H. Bartram, Joseph Blascheck, Daniel W. Bussinger, David Chambers, Theodore L. DeBow, Enoch E. Gilbert, William F. Hilton, William Miller, Thomas Orr, Charles W. Raphun, Charles N. Vollum, Henry E. Wrigley and Henry T. Crosby.

A PENNSYLVANIA MONUMENT AT COLD HARBOR

THE State of Pennsylvania has caused to be placed upon the battlefield of Cold Harbor, Va., a monument dedicated to the commands of the Commonwealth which participated in the operations from May 31st to June 12, 1864, incident to and during the battle at that point.

The organizations inscribed include two batteries of light artillery, two regiments of heavy artillery, eleven regiments of cavalry and sixty-five regiments of infantry. The Philadelphia troops thus honored are the 2d Heavy Artillery, the Second Provisional Heavy Artillery, 61st, 67th, 68th, 69th, 71st, 72d, 81st, 82d, 88th, 90th, 91st, 95th, 98th, 99th, 106th, 110th, 114th, 115th, 116th, 118th, 119th, 121st, 150th, 157th, 183d, 187th and 188th Infantry.

RECRUITING STATIONS IN PHILADELPHIA—1861-65

(Compiled from the Poster collection, preserved at the Ridgway Branch of the Philadelphia Library.)

19th Regiment, Co. H, Capt. William C. Rush, 432 North Second street.
19th Regiment, Co. D, Capt. J. B. De Haven, 605 Arch street.
118th Regiment, Co. D, Capt. Chas. H. Fernald, 340 North Third street.
118th Regiment, Co. I, Capt. C. M. O'Callahan, southeast corner Second and Walnut streets.
81st Regiment, Co. E, Capt. William Wilson, 620 Chestnut street.

90th Regiment, Co. A, Capt. John T. Durang, northwest corner Sixth and Chestnut streets.

119th Regiment, Co. H, Capt. Henry H. Edwards, Barley Sheaf Hotel, Second street, below Vine street.

144th Regiment (Irish Legion), Col. George Crookes, Connelly's Hotel, opposite State House.

146th Regiment, Col. John D. C. Johnson, 519 Arch street.

156th Regiment, Col. Charles Ermenwein, 533 Chestnut street and at Camp Morton, Islington lane.

157th Regiment, Col. Wm. A. Gray, 527 Chestnut street.

157th Regiment, Co. D, Capt. William N. Rowland, 450 Walnut street and 218 North Third street.

215th Regiment, Co. D, Capt. Richard C. Wilson, National Guard Hall.

52d Regiment (Ninety Day Militia), Co. F, Capt. C. A. Thomas, 921 North Tenth street.

Keystone Battery, Capt. Samuel C. Thompson, Race street, below Broad street.

Pennsylvania Sharpshooters, Col. Charles R. Doron, Quinton Hotel, Manayunk.

Second Regiment, Irish Brigade, Col. Robert E. Patterson, 1215 Market street.

Irish Volunteers, Col. Joshua T. Owen, 421 Walnut street.

First Pennsylvania Cavalry, Col. J. C. Hess, 221 Race street and 110 South Sixth street.

Second Pennsylvania Cavalry, Col. R. Butler Price, northwest corner Third and Chestnut streets.

Philadelphia Light Cavalry, Col. Richard Henry Rush, 833 Market street and northwest corner Third and Chestnut streets.

Independent Troop, Russell Light Cavalry (Co. M, 2d Cavalry) Capt. John C. Gallagher, Seventh street, above Chestnut street.

117th Regiment, Co. I (13th Cavalry), Capt. Timothy A. Byrnes, Ridge avenue, below Poplar street.

112th Regiment (2d Heavy Artillery), Co. A. A. Gibson, U. S. A., 611 Chestnut street.

Flying Artillery, Co. I (Col. J. E. Peyton's Continental Cavalry), Capt. John W. Massey, 735 Market street, northwest corner Broad and Fitzwater streets, northwest corner Eleventh and Oxford streets.

Washington Legion, Col. Frederick Harvey, 528 Market street.

Buena Vista Rangers, Capt. Joseph C. Costello, southwest corner Sixth and Chestnut streets.

Washington Cavalry, Co. A (14th Cavalry), Capt. J. W. Hall, Farmers' Hay Market, Seventh and Oxford streets; Thornley's Hotel, Holmesburg; Seven Stars Hotel, Frankford.

Independent Mounted Rangers (8th Cavalry), Col. Ernest G. Chorman, 1128 Market street.

Continental Light Cavalry, Col. J. E. Peyton, Richards House, Eighth street, below Spring Garden street.

Pennsylvania Cavalry, Col. Campbell, 232 North Fourth street.

Staunton Cavalry (19th Cavalry), 22 South Fourth street.

Cameron Dragoons, 428 Coates street.

Thomas A. Scott Regiment, 2312 Chestnut street.

2d Regiment Rifles, Co. C (9th Regiment Militia), Capt. George K. Carrie, Thirty-eighth and Bridge streets, Mantua.

2d Regiment, Reserve Brigade, Co. C, Armory, Board of Trade Building, 505 Chestnut street.

3d Regiment, Reserve Brigade, Col. C. M. Eakin, Armory, Thirteenth and Filbert streets.

3d Regiment, Reserve Brigade, Co. B, Market, Twenty-second and Spring Garden streets.

3d Regiment, Reserve Brigade, Co. C, Commissioners' Hall, Thirty-seventh and Market streets.

Battery F (3d Artillery), Capt. J. F. Blake, 329 Chestnut street.

5th Regiment Infantry, Baker's Brigade (106th Regiment), Co. A, Capt. Lewis Bartleson, Franklin Place, Chestnut street, above Third street.

5th Regiment Infantry, Baker's Brigade, Co. F, Crozier Guard (106th Regiment), Capt. R. H. Ford, 207 South Fourth street.

20th Regiment Militia, Col. William B. Thomas, 533 Chestnut street.

Birney's Zouaves (23d Regiment), 602 Arch street.

Philadelphia City Guard for 88th Regiment, Col. J. Reeside White, Fifth street, above Prune street.

28th Regiment, Lieut.-Col. John Flynn, 204 Dock street.

1st Coal Regiment (197th Regiment), Col. John R. Haslett, Walnut street, below Dock street.

2d Coal Regiment, Col. Alfred M. Day, 108 Walnut street.

2d Army Corps, 134 South Fourth street.

Philadelphia Light Infantry (121st Regiment), Col. Chapman Biddle, 337 Chestnut street.

Union Guards (Co. E, 187th Regiment, six months' service), Capt. Wm. F. Robinson, 247 Arch street and Eighteenth and South streets.

Battery H (3d Heavy Artillery), Capt. Gilbert S. Clark, 741 South Front street.

Rathbun Guards (183d Regiment), Col. George P. McLean, New Market and Laurel streets.

118th Regiment, Co. A (Corn Exchange), 727 Market street.

Blue Reserves, Co. E, Eighth and Callowhill streets.

32d Regiment, Co. F, Capt. Washington Richards, Pennsylvania Hotel, Second street, below Pine street.

Governor's Guards, Co. F, Capt. Thomas Bringhurst, William Penn Hose House.

Gray Reserves, Co. F, Capt. J. N. Piersol, Armory, northeast corner Second and Race streets.

Gosline's Zouaves, Co. B (95th), Capt. Enos Baldwin, northwest corner Sixth and Chestnut streets, fifth floor.

Gosline's Zouaves, Co. K (95th), Capt. Harry W. Hewes, 603 Chestnut street.

Imperial Zouaves, 533 Chestnut street.

Hamilton Rifles (2d Company), Capt. Joseph L. Davis, Saunders Institute, West Philadelphia.

4th Reserves (33d), Capt. John C. Chance, 510 Richmond street, Kensington.

4th Union League Regiment, Lieut.-Col. Arthur Maginnis, 434 Chestnut street.

Hancock's Corps, James Boldman, 826 Market street.

Independent Company, Emergency, Capt. Samuel J. Malone, Front and Vine streets.

Fire Zouaves, F. Louis Gimber, 333 Chestnut street.

5th "California" Regiment (106th), S. B. Munger, 209 South Fourth street.

2d Cavalry, Capt. Joseph Archambault, 106 South Sixth street.

Germantown Home Guard, Co. C, Capt. M. J. Biddle, at Armory.

Board of Trade Rifle Regiment (156th), Col. Chas. Ernenwein, northwest corner Seventh and Chestnut streets.

Durrell's Battery, John M. Gries, 206 South Fourth street.

Columbia Guards, Columbia Engine Co., Capt. H. M. Thomas, Filbert street, above Eleventh street.

Dallas Guards, Capt. A. M. Mooney, Old Church, Crown street, above Race street.

Zouaves d'Afrique, Capt. E. R. Bowen, Third and Gaskill streets.

Cameron Light Guard (88th), Capt. John D. Schoch, 804 Market street.

Cameron Light Guard (88th). Capt. Wm. F. Powell, Western Hose House and Falstaff Hotel, Sixth street, above Chestnut street.

Read Guard, Capt. R. Haslett, Richmond and Ann streets.

Philadelphia Guards, Capt. Samuel Davies, 516 South Fourth street.

"Colonel Heenan's Regiment," Co. M, Capt. Thomas A. Murray, southwest corner Sixth street and Girard avenue.

Jefferson Guards, Capt. John Moore, 2130 Market street.

Blue Reserves, Co. C, Capt. S. M. Janney, Armory, 505 Chestnut street, fourth floor.

Blue Reserves, Co. D, Capt. Charles Naylor, 505 Chestnut street, fifth floor.

"Colonel Staunton's Regiment," Co. F, Capt. George W. Kite, northwest corner Fourth and Walnut streets.

Invalid Corps, Capt. Edwin Palmer, Provost Marshal, 1214 Locust street.

"Thomas A. Scott Regiment," Co. F, Capt. John T. O'Brien, Sixth and Minor streets.

National Guard Regiment, Co. K, Capt. Paul L. Lewis, northeast corner Ninth and Shippen streets.

Dana Troop, J. L. Anderson, R. W. Hammell, J. Tyndale, T. C. Babb, H. W. Arnold, committee, 1010 Chestnut street.

Curtin Light Guard (109th), Co. H, Lieut. Richard Young, 602 South Broad street.

Philadelphia Zouave Cadets, Capt. Daniel F. Gillen, southwest corner Eighth and Sansom streets.

"Washington Guard, 1st Regiment," Co. G, Col. Wm. F. Small, Capt. John Smith, 112 Marion street.

Washington Guard, Co. L, Capt. D. W. Donopley, Reliance Engine House, New street, above Second street.

"Washington Gray Regiment," Col. Alexander Murphy, Capt. Caleb Needles, League House, northeast corner Broad and Race streets.

Twenty-third Ward Troop, Capt. Jacob B. Sacket, Jolly Post Hotel, Frankford.

"Young Men's Company for City Defence," Capt. Robert J. Craig, Kirchenmann's Columbia Hall, 1729 Germantown road.

"Union Guard Regiment," Co. F, Col. John B. Adams, Capt. William Stewart, Lombard street, below Broad street.

Independent Naval Battery, Lieut. Frank Barr, Union Volunteer Refreshment Saloon.

"Regiment, Men of Color," Col. John W. Taggart, 1210 Chestnut street.

"Garibaldi Legion, Captain Hagen's Company," northwest corner Fifth and Prune streets.

"Artillery Company, for Col. J. Richter Jones' Regiment,'" Capt. Paul T. Jones, 138 South Fourth street.

"First Heavy Artillery" (112th), Col. Charles Angeroth, Sr., 506 Vine street.

Marine Artillery, Battery L, Col. Segebarth, Lieut. Joseph C. Ferguson, Frankford road and Columbia avenue.

Baxter Fire Zouaves, 527 Chestnut street.

"Independent Company Bushwhackers," Capt. B. F. Johnston, 721 South Front street.

Bucktail Brigade, Capt. Charles Buckley, 335 Walnut street.

Cooper Guards, Capt. John W. Smith, northwest corner Front and Pine streets.

20

"Col. Gregory's Regiment," (91st), Co. D, Capt. Joseph H. Sinex, Broad and South streets.

Gosline's Zouaves (95th), Capt. McCullough's Company, Eighth street above Race street.

3d Regiment Reserve Brigade, Militia, Col. C. M. Eakin, Capt. Alfred Driver (Camp Du Pont, Del), Saunders Institute.

"Second Corps, recruits wanted," Capt. George D. Whitecar, American and Master streets.

2d Heavy Artillery, Lieut. J. N. Abbey, 138 South Fourth street.

Harlan Cavalry,. Capt. John D. Struthers, Struthers & Sons' marble yard, Market street, between Tenth and Eleventh streets.

Irish Brigade, Col. Robert E. Patterson, 14 South Eighth street.

Governor's Guard, 219 Lodge street.

Federal Guards, Capt. Charles Parkham, northeast corner Third and Arch streets, Union Bank.

Gymnast Zouaves, Capt. P. V. Smith, 37 South Third street.

Philadelphia Brigade, Richard L. Shreve, 416 Library street.

U. S. REGULARS.

U. S. Cavalry, 603 Sansom street.

10th Infantry, northwest corner Front and Dock streets and 419 Walnut street.

11th Infantry, Third and Dock streets.

12th Infantry, 229 South Front street.

14th Infantry, 47 South Third street.

17th Infantry, 318 South Front street.

19th Infantry, 134 South Fourth street.

U. S. Marine Corps, Lieut. W. Stokes Boyd, 311 South Front street.

SOME LOCAL ASSOCIATIONS FOR THE AID AND COMFORT OF THE SOLDIERS

ALL through the war period numerous patriotic and helpful associations were existent in Philadelphia. Many of them were connected with the churches, others of secular origin, but all provided some form of assistance to the soldiery of the Union cause. The services of a large proportion of the devoted men and women, thus organized, cannot be adequately estimated. In some instances, printed reports were made, copies of which have been preserved in libraries, and these afford an outline of many deeds accomplished.

Probably the first local association of women who "wanted to help" was that of the "Ladies' Union Relief," which organized on April 20th, 1861, "to provide garments for soldiers, work in hospitals and take care of soldiers' families." Could any charter cover a broader field of patriotic intent? So eager were the women of Philadelphia to find beneficiaries that the whole country was none too large. For instance, the ladies of

St. Luke's Episcopal Church sent, in May, 1861, nine hundred pairs of shoes to the Missouri Volunteers. On July 28th, 1862, a number of ladies met at the office of Edward Brady, Esq., 135 South Fifth street, and formed "The Ladies' Association for Soldiers' Relief." Mrs. Mary A. Brady became President and Mrs. M. A. Dobbins, Treasurer. At first, this association devoted its efforts to providing special dinners to the occupants of the local army hospitals. Later they seem to have made a specialty of the Sixth Corps, and the most successful relief expedition that ever went out of Philadelphia (from the soldiers' point of view) was welcomed in the camps of those Philadelphia warriors when Mrs. Brady and her associates appeared, one day, at the front with a wagon load of good plug and smoking tobacco. The ladies of this association hastened to the bloody fields of Antietam and Gettysburg, and there, amid sickening surroundings, emulated the English nurses who had, but a few years before, followed Florence Nightingale to the Crimea. On May 27th, 1864, Mrs. Brady died at her home, 406 South Forty-first street, West Philadelphia, as a result of her persistent labor in the cause to which she had been so long devoted.

The "Penn Relief Association" was founded "to assist sick soldiers in and out of hospitals and to aid their families." The officers and Executive Comittee included many women identified with the Society of Friends. These were: President, Anna M. Needles; Vice-Presidents, Hannah J. Jenkins, Hettie W. Chapman, Elizabeth B. Garrigues; Secretaries, Anna P. Little and Sallie R. Garrigues; Treasurer, Mary M. Scranton; Lucy Black, Sarah J. Webb, Elizabeth F. Williams, Helen L. Deacon, Mary S. Pancoast, Elizabeth E. Allen, Lydia S. Truman, Margaret L. Skillman, Martha P. Stotesbury, Deborah B. Haines, Sarah G. Yarnall, Helen P. Mansfield, Elizabeth Pearce, Mary A. Tyson, Julia A. Cook and Mary B. Breed.

The first institution in the United States to receive children of men who desired to enlist and of deceased soldiers was the "Northern Home for Friendless Children and Associated Institute for Soldiers' and Sailors' Orphans," located at Twenty-third and Brown streets. This institution was aided liberally, through the efforts of Mrs. E. W. Hutter, by Dr. Albert G. Egbert, a wealthy oil operator of Mercer County, Pa. Above thirteen hundred children of soldiers were housed and educated at this home.

The Board of Trustees in the Civil War period was composed of Thomas Earp, President; Thomas S. Mitchell, Treasurer; William R. Stockton, Secretary; Isaac Collins, John M. Ogden, James J. Barclay, J. Fisher Leaming, John W. Claghorn, Thomas Robinson, William S. Perot, Isaac Baker, Henry Perkins, Joseph Jeanes, H. W. Safford, A. V. Murphey and Charles Keen.

The following ladies formed the Board of Managers:

Mrs. E. E. Hutter, President; Mrs. John W. Claghorn, Vice-President; Miss Mary Jeanes, Vice-President; Miss Susan O'Neill, Recording

Secretary; Mrs. George Duffield, Jr., Corresponding Secretary; Mrs. R. Hammett, Treasurer; Mrs. Eliza Ann Brown, Mrs. Emma W. Shepherd, Mrs. S. A. Clark, Mrs. Eliza S. McClure, Mrs. Wilson Jewell, Mrs. Maria Wood, Mrs. Sarah M. Grant, Mrs. Mary Potter, Mrs. Mary C. Hibbler, Mrs. A. L. Raymond, Mrs. I. F. Baker, Mrs. James L. Claghorn, Mrs. Emma S. Cameron, Mrs. Ann Woodward, Mrs. W. J. Chaplain, Mrs. Hiram Ayers, Mrs. A. V. Murphey, Miss Agnes Y. McAllister and Miss Lucy Sulger.

The Lincoln Institution, incorporated in 1866, was founded in order to provide a home for the sons of white soldiers who had fallen in the course of the war. Major-Gen. George G. Meade was active in this beneficence and became its first President. The institution was and continues to be located upon 11th street, below Spruce street. The Educational Home for Boys, opened at 49th street and Greenway avenue in 1873, was essentially a branch of the parent institution. This was continued until recent years, when the property was sold and the Educational Home was merged with the Lincoln Institution. At these well-conducted homes hundreds of boys were educated, sustained while learning trades and sent out into the world well equipped to win success. At a later period the management admitted Indian boys and girls to both institutions, under an arrangement with the Government.

The first "Board of Counsellors" of the Lincoln Institution included the following persons:

President, Major-Gen. George Gordon Meade; Vice-President, William G. Boulton; Secretary, John L. Redner; Treasurer, Morton McMichael, Jr.; Managers, Rev. Richard Newton, D. D., Jay Cooke, Caleb Cope, Lemuel Coffin, Thomas Sparks, William P. Cresson, Charles Platt, J. Vaughan Merrick, William Ellis, Charles J. Stille, George C. Cresson, Edward S. Buckley, A. H. Franciscus, Lewis J. Redner, Francis Wells, William Struthers, Rev. J. W. Robins, George T. Lewis, F. Ratchford Starr, Ezra Bowen, M. J. Mitcheson, R. M. Lewis, Charles E. Lex, Edward Shippen, William B. Robins and Joseph Harrison, Jr.

LADIES' BOARD OF MANAGERS.

Miss McHenry, Mrs. William Ellis, Mrs. George T. Lewis, Miss M. A. Lennig, Miss Anna Blanchard, Mrs. George G. Meade, Miss N. W. Fisher, Mrs. George W. Norris, Mrs. James W. Robins, Mrs. C. W. Paul, Mrs. C. J. Stille, Mrs. James C. Fisher, Mrs. Morton McMichael, Jr., Mrs. J. Edgar Thompson, Mrs. George C. Carson, Mrs. C. T. Platt, Mrs. J. B. Moorhead, Mrs. A. D. Jessup, Mrs. E. K. Mitchell, Miss Emily Norris, Miss M. Cadwalader, Mrs. J. R. Fry, Mrs. Ezra Bowen, Miss Mary Milligan, Mrs. William G. Boulton, Mrs. William Palmer, Miss G. Bowen, Miss Annie Frazer and Mrs. George F. Tyler.

The "Ladies Aid Society" undertook to furnish prompt aid in supplies for local army hospitals and those in the field. Mrs. Joel Jones was President; Mrs. Stephen Colwell, Treasurer, and Mrs. John Harris, Secretary, of this organization.

The "Ladies Association of West Philadelphia" was active in raising money for soldiers' families in 1863. Prominent ladies interested were Mrs. John Cotton, Mrs. Thomas Hunter, Mrs. John Sweeney, Miss Caroline Harvey and Mrs. J. A. Covell.

A modest but popular enterprise of war days, in Philadelphia, was the "Soldiers' Reading Room," maintained, for several years, on Twentieth street below Market street, in a building formerly the Brickmakers' Baptist Church. Here soldiers were always welcome. A considerable library, magazines and games, files of newspapess from many cities, writing material, a piano and a smoking room were at the free disposal of all soldiers and sailors. Hot lunches were provided at five cents, or without charge, if occasion required. Lectures were given in the evenings and religious services on Sundays. The average attendance was about one hundred per diem. Those identified with this beneficence were Dr. Frank W. Lewis, President; William P. Cresson, Secretary; George T. Lewis, Treasurer. The managers were C. J. Stille, L. H. Redner, Alexander Brown, F. R. Starr, E. M. Hopkins, Daniel Dougherty, Joseph L. Harrison, Joseph R. Fry, John H. Atwood, J. Heatly Dulles, George P. Smith and Edward S. Clark. Board of Lady Visitors: Mrs. George T. Lewis, Mrs. F. R. Starr, Mrs. George W. Norris, Mrs. Joseph R. Fry and Misses Mary McHenry and S. Field.

The "Union Temporary Home" was established to provide a shelter for the children of soldiers in the field and of men who wished to enlist. The Board of Managers included Miss Susan J. O'Neill, President; Mrs. John Mason, Vice-President; Mrs. C. J. Peterson, Treasurer, and Mrs. Thos. Mott, Secretary.

In 1864 the Ladies' First Union Association was active, with rooms at 537 North Eighth street, in subsisting a large number of the families of soldiers.

Among still other enterprises prompted by patriotic sympathy were the Freemasons' Soldiers' Relief Association at 204 South Fourth street, and the New England Soldiers' Relief Association, on Chestnut street near Thirteenth street. Most of these helpful centers continued to the close of the war.*

---

*In May, 1863, an exhibition of paintings contributed by Philadelphia artists for the benefit of soldiers' families was displayed at Earle's Galleries on Chestnut street.

With the crumbling of the Confederate Army great numbers of people swarmed from the South into Philadelphia. Public meetings were held to organize relief. They were fed, clothed and given work. Philadelphia's charity toward her late foes was as broad as her patriotism.

In 1866, as a means of raising money with which to supply widows and orphans of deceased soldiers with coal, war maps and portraits were advertised by relief committees.

RELIEF FROM THE CITY

THE final report of the Commission for the Relief of Families of Philadelphia Volunteers in the Army and Navy, acting under authority of Councils, indicates that financial assistance was given in the course of the war to 48,707 families. The total sum thus expended was $2,596,307.87. In addition, $15,000 was repaid to the Trustees of the Philadelphia Gas Works for sums disbursed to dependents of employees who had enlisted. The Commission met the funeral expenses of 780 soldiers or members of soldiers' families. The members of the Commission were: Hon. Alexander Henry, President; Charles P. Trego, Vice-President; Peter Wilson, Treasurer; Samuel C. Dawson, Secretary; Theodore Cuyler, Charles E. Lex, Thomas Potter, William Loughlin, Archibald McIntyre, Henry Davis, John Robbins, Matthew W. Baldwin, James S. Watson, Caleb Cope, Robert Coane, William Baird and Charles S. Close.

WHEN RICHMOND FELL

AT eleven o'clock A. M., April 3d, 1865, the *Philadelphia Inquirer* posted a bulletin proclaiming the fall of Richmond. Further dispatches related to the occupation of that city by Union troops. Summoned by the bell of Independence Hall, the population thronged to the heart of the city. Within an hour jubilant processions, led by the fire companies, were parading the streets. From the navy yard thousands of workmen, headed by the Marine Band, paraded to the business section, hurrahing wildly as they passed the newspaper offices and the Mayor's office, at Fifth and Chestnut streets. Clearly, above the clamor around the old "State House," a single voice began the stately words, "Praise God from whom all blessings flow." The singer was an old white-locked man. Instantly the mass of excited people bared their heads and thousands joined in the beautiful lines of the Doxology. The public schools were dismissed and the children, with songs and flags, marched through their respective neighborhoods. A mass meeting of joy was held in front of the Custom House. The Union League flung out every flag; indeed, the whole city was soon brilliant with red, white and blue. Until late at night the brilliantly illuminated streets were crowded with scores of military bands leading impromptu processions from the suburbs, and the clamor of that day of great rejoicing only ended with the utter exhaustion of the happy people; soon, Johnnie would "come marching home."

THREE SUNDAYS

From Joy to Mourning

GEN. ROBERT E. LEE surrendered to Gen. U. S. Grant at Appomattox on Palm Sunday, April 9th, 1865. The news reached Philadelphia the same date about 9.40 P. M. From the Mayor's office it was telegraphed to various parts of the city, and within an hour the streets downtown, usually dark and deserted, were crowded with rejoicing citizens. The windows of the several morning newspaper offices were illuminated. Over the portals of the Union League flashed the word "Victory." Bells rang everywhere. A score of fire companies brought their hose carriages to Independence Hall and added to the din of the hour. Great crowds, mad with joy, surged around the old Cradle of Liberty. In thousands of homes thanks were breathed to Heaven that long absent fathers, husbands and sons would soon be home from the war and in the enjoyment of the firesides they had left, so long ago, to fight for their country's flag. Down on Washington avenue the historic little cannon, the watchdog of the Union Volunteer Refreshment Committee, stirred up all Southwark by barking out thirty-six rounds of good Union powder, a bark for every State. Upon Monday no one thought of business or work. At sunrise the bells were ringing again and a band was playing patriotic airs in the tower of Independence Hall. Flags were flying from ten thousand windows. At nine o'clock A. M. school children marched down Chestnut street, unmindful of the rain. At noon the Union League Battery fired two hundred rounds at Broad and Market streets, and at sunset, by order of Mayor Henry, one hundred rounds were fired at Nineteenth and Hamilton streets.

That spring Monday was the beginning of a week of joy all over the North, and not less in the camps of the Federal armies. Never did a people know a greater transition from gladness to sorrow and despair. Never were two Sundays the scenes of more diverse emotions. The world knew on the morning of Sunday, April 16th, that Abraham Lincoln had been murdered, at Ford's Theatre in Washington, the evening before. Men came to their doors that placid morning, picked up and opened their newspapers and went mad at the black words they saw there. Again the people crowded to the heart of the old town. But those who were prone to covert abuse of the great President and the cause of which he was the leader (and there were some, as every soldier knew) such men stayed indoors, for vengeance was abroad waiting hungrily to find action.

Upon that memorable Sunday and early on Monday morning all of the black goods in the stores of Philadelphia and in a hundred thousand homes were brought out and draped upon the buildings. None who then lived in Philadelphia have forgotten those sombre streets or the look frozen upon the silent faces of the people who crowded around the newspaper offices as one bulletin from Washington followed another. Thousands of soldiers, the ink hardly dry upon their discharges, crowded around their old officers and begged to be led back to the South and a new campaign of revenge. But the honorable people of the South repudiated the conspirators and their deeds, and the war, although not officially ended (by President Johnson's proclamation nearly a year later), was not conducted along lines of reprisal. The 8th Union League Regiment arrived in Washington, south-bound, upon the day of the great crime, and it was as late as April 26th when the Union League sent away its 215th Regiment to relieve the returning veterans. This was the last body of soldiery to go out from Philadelphia in the course of the war. Grant had said: "Let us have peace," but peace came slowly.

The funeral services of the late President were held in Washington, at noon, on April 19th, four years, to the hour, from the fateful incident at Baltimore, where the first soldiers of the Republic were slain. At the same hour, in churches in every loyal city and State, the people were gathered in testimony of their love for the martyred leader.

The body of the President reached Philadelphia April 22d and was followed by a great escort of soldiers and citizens from Broad and Prime streets to Independence Hall, and all that night—all the following Sunday—the people trod reverently through the silent, dimly-lighted room of Independence Hall to look upon his careworn, peaceful face. At three o'clock Monday morning the "First Troop" and the 187th Regiment, with muffled drums and arms reversed, escorted him to the waiting funeral train which was to take him to other cities and mourners on the long way to his resting place at Springfield, Illinois.*

---

*Mayor Henry, the City officials and police wore crepe upon their sleeves thirty days following the date of the ceremonials incident to the departure of the Lincoln funeral train.

RETURN OF THE COLORS. INDEPENDENCE SQUARE, JULY 4TH, 1866.
(From a contemporary lithograph.)

CIVIL WAR MEMORIAL, FAIRMOUNT PARK.

TABLET ON SITE OF CAMP, 88TH REGIMENT, FAIRMOUNT PARK.

THE WELCOME HOME, 1865

BEGINNING with May 21st, 1865, when the 114th Regiment, Penna. Vols. (Collis Zouaves) arrived home, the Philadelphia regiments and companies returned at frequent intervals, and generally without advance information necessary for the arrangement of suitable receptions. It was, therefore, decided by the city authorities, with the concurrence of the higher military officers, to organize a Grand Review and thus afford the public a glimpse of the veterans and give expression, to the soldiers, of the honor in which they were held. The Review took place June 10th, 1865, in the midst of a heavy rain storm. The reviewing stand was erected on the west side of Broad street, between Market and Filbert streets. Here were assembled a great throng of officials, officers and distinguished guests. Another stand, situated upon the east side of Broad street, below Market street, contained the sick and wounded veterans and their families. On a third stand, north of Filbert street, five hundred young ladies were placed, to sing patriotic songs. Many other private stands bordered the route. For this event every effort had been made to secure the return of as many of the local regiments as possible. The route of the parade extended from Camp Cadwalader, far out Ridge avenue, to the Volunteer Refreshment Saloons at the foot of Washington avenue, where a much-appreciated dinner awaited every soldier. At the head of the review rode Major-General George Gordon Meade and a brilliant staff, accompanied by the First Troop Philadelphia City Cavalry. The veterans were escorted by delegations from the city fire companies. The Military Division included detachments of the following regiments and batteries: 81st, 17 men; 91st, 59 men; 99th, 62 men; 114th, 227 men; 116th, 124 men; 118th, 220 men; 119th, 230 men; 121st, 193 men; 183d, 17 men; 198th, 910 men, and Battery D, 2d Penna. Heavy Artillery, 140 men. The cavalry was represented by detachments, marching dismounted, of the 2d, 3d, 5th, 6th, 8th, 11th, 12th, 13th, 14th, 15th, 16th, 18th, 19th and 20th Regiments. In the rear of the military came the sailors and marines from the United States ships in port.

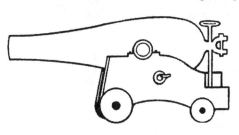

313

FAMOUS WAR SONGS

A NUMBER of the most stirring songs popular in the Civil War period originated in or were identified with Philadelphia. One of the most prolific lyrists of the time was Sep. Winner, who gave to the camps "The Arms of Abraham," "Give Us Back Our Old Commander," "Baxter's March" and the "Zouave Quickstep."

The author of "When Johnny Comes Marching Home," Thomas Brigham Bishop, of Wayne, Maine, lived, in his later years, at 807 North 63d street, where he died on May 15th, 1905. His grave is in Mount Peace Cemetery.*

Many versions have been printed with regard to the "John Brown Song." The score is included in a collection published by Oliver Ditson & Co., of Boston, in 1861, under the title "John Brown's Ghost."

In 1863 the Supervisory Committee for Recruiting Colored Regiments printed the words with the statement that the author of the original version was H. H. Brownell, of Hartford, Conn. The facts concerning this, the most popular of all songs of the camp and march, have been compiled by Gen. Oliver C. Bosbyshell, who has written, for this book, the true story. He says:

"Mr. William Steffe, who resided many years on 36th street, below Chestnut street, wrote the music to which the "John Brown Song" was afterward attached. Some years before the Civil War a Charleston, S. C., fire company visited Philadelphia and engaged Mr. Steffe to compose an air to a song beginning "Say, Bummers, Will You Meet Us?" The Methodists afterward applied the catchy tune to "Say, Brothers, Won't You Meet Us," adding the chorus, "Glory, Glory, Hallelujah!"

In 1861, while Col. Fletcher Webster's 12th Massachusetts Regiment was encamped at Fort Warren, it included the Brockton Military Band. Four members of the regiment formed an excellent quartette. One of them named John Brown was the butt of much wit, due to the similarity of his name to that of the famous abolitionist. From this circumstance were evolved the ringing words which were fitted to Steffe's music and including the Methodist "Glory, Hallelujah!" The Brockton band adopted the song, and, when superseded by Patrick Gilmore and his band, the latter took it up and played it on all occasions. Gilmore afterward published the march.

With Gilmore and his band in the lead, the 12th Massachusetts Regiment marched down Broadway, New York City, every one of

---

*For the information relating to this and several other war songs the writer is indebted to Miss Jane Campbell.

314

its thousand men singing the great song thus strangely evolved. They sang it through Philadelphia and the length of Pennsylvania avenue in Washington, and its echo was heard wherever loyal citizens gathered or soldiers of the Union grouped around the fires of a thousand camps. Thus the music written in Philadelphia for the firemen of a Southern citadel of disunion became an inspiration, a paen of victory for the loyal North."

It was a Philadelphian, Private A. D. Frankenberry, of the 15th Cavalry, who, with the signal corps on Kenesaw Mountain, sent Sherman's message by flag over the heads of the Confederates to Corse's defenders at the supply depot of Allatoona Pass, which inspired P. P. Bliss to thrill the nation with "Hold the Fort, for I am Coming."

RETURN OF THE COLORS

NEVER before was Philadelphia so gorgeously panoplied with the red, white and blue, as upon July Fourth, 1866, for upon that memorable day the soldier sons of Pennsylvania were to consign to the loving care of their mother State the flags which they had followed into a hundred battles and over thousands of miles of southern roads. Broad, Market and Chestnut Streets were embowered with a bewildering blaze of streamers and massed flowers. With the coming of daylight the throb of drums pulsed upon the air. By every incoming railroad train fresh thousands of soldiers and civilian onlookers poured into the already crowded streets. At Independence Hall, upon the spot facing its shaded square where, ninety years before John Nixon had read the "Declaration" of defiance to Great Britain, a great ampitheatre had been erected, large enough to seat five thousand people. Early to arrive were the children of the Soldiers' Orphan Schools, for whom seats to the right and left of the "Court of Honor" had been provided. Behind them, still sombre in their mourning garb were gathered the "invited guests," nearly all from the families of fallen soldiers. High up in the shadow of the old tower were placed the singers and the military band, A little lower in front stood the speaker's platform flanked by tables for the press. Long before the coming of the veterans every foot of ground within sight held its waiting citizen. Every window commanding the scene had its group of guests.

Promptly at ten o'clock in the morning the march began. The head of the column was formed upon Broad Street above Arch Street. The route of the parade was down Broad Street to Market Street, to Twelfth Street, to Chestnut Street, to Second Street, to Walnut Street, to Independence Square.

First came Major-Gen. Winfield S. Hancock, his staff and escort, followed by the "First Defenders." Closely behind these came a garden of banners, each war-worn flag carried by a sergeant and escorted by six corporals. What cheering! What a tumult of glorious color flaunting in the breeze! What tears from pent-up emotions of patriotic joy! It was thus that the Colors came to the waiting War-Governor of the Commonwealth.

ORDER OF THE PARADE.

MAJOR-GENERAL WINFIELD S. HANCOCK and staff escorted by the First Troop, Philadelphia City Cavalry, and the Henry Guards.

FIRST DIVISION.

MAJOR-GENERAL JAMES S. NEGLEY.

The "First Defenders," composed of detachments from the Logan Guards, of Lewistown; Allen Guard, of Allentown; Washington Artillery, of Pottsville; National Light Infantry, of Pottsville, and Ringgold Light Artillery, of Reading.

SECOND DIVISION. .

MAJOR-GENERAL ROBERT PATTERSON.

Detachments and color guards of the 23d, 26th, 28th, 29th, 31st, 32d, 33d, 36th, 41st, and 43d Artillery Reserves, 58th, 69th, 71st, 72d, 73d, 78th, 81st, 88th, 90th, 95th, 97th, 98th, 99th, 106th, 114th, 115th, 116th, 118th, 119th, 121st, 139th, 152d, 183d, 192d, 198th and 199th Regiments, Pennsylvania Volunteers.

THIRD DIVISION.

BRIGADIER-GENERAL CHARLES T. CAMPBELL.

Detachments and color guards of the 1st, 2d and 3d Artillery Regiments.

FOURTH DIVISION.

MAJOR-GENERAL DAVID McM. GREGG.

Detachments and color guards of the 2d, 3d, 5th, 6th, 8th, 15th and 16th Cavalry Regiments, escorting

MAJOR-GENERAL GEORGE GORDON MEADE and staff.

FIFTH DIVISION.

MAJOR-GENERAL JOHN W. GEARY and staff.
Provisional troops.

SIXTH DIVISION.

MAJOR-GENERAL S. WYLIE CRAWFORD.
Soldiers' orphans in carriages, escorted by firemen.

SEVENTH DIVISION.

MAJOR-GENERAL JOHN R. BROOKE.
City militia regiments.

Upon the massing of the veteran troops at Independence Square, the color guards were gathered in the Court of Honor, and with impressive oratory the flags were presented by Major-General Meade to Governor Andrew G. Curtin, who accepted them upon behalf of the State of Pennsylvania.

PROGRAMME.

Music, "Triumphal March" ....Birgfield's Band.
Prayer, Rev. Thomas Brainerd, D. D.
Music, "The Star Spangled Banner"..................Handel and Haydn Society.
Presentation of the Colors to Governor Andrew G. Curtin by Major-General George Gordon Meade.
Acceptance by His Excellency the Governor.
Music, "Thanks to Almighty God for Victory and Peace."
Music, "Old Hundred"................................Handel and Haydn Society.
Music, "Coronation March" ....Birgfield's Band.
Benediction.

At the close of these exercises artillery stationed in Washington Square fired a salute.

Few scenes in our National history have been attended with so much that was dramatic, even pathetic, as that witnessed when each war-worn group of veterans parted from its faded flags, to uphold which, in the face of the enemy, so many of their comrades had fallen.

In the course of the day the National Union Club fired one hundred guns at the Penn Squares, and the Keystone Battery, under the direction of the Union League, delivered a similar salute at the forts in Fairmount Park. The celebration ended with fire-works at the Penn Squares. In charge of the Henry Guards the battle flags were stored in Sansom Street Hall under guard and upon the following day were taken to Harrisburg. They number, with some subsequently deposited, three hundred and thirty standards. They have long been exhibited in glass cases at the building of the State Library, but provision has been made for their permanent array in the corridors of the new State Capitol Building.

The Official Catalogue, revised by the State Librarian, the Hon. Thomas L. Montgomery, for this book, contains the complete list of flags borne by the Pennsylvania Regiments in the Civil War, now in possession of the State of Pennsylvania.

COLORS AND STANDARDS OF THE VARIOUS PENNSYLVANIA REGIMENTS AND BATTERIES DEPOSITED IN THE CAPITOL BUILDINGS AT HARRISBURG.*

Organization.	No. Flags	Organization.	No. Flags	Organization.	No. Flags
11th Regiment	2	28th	3	32d (3d Reserves)	2
23d	1	29th	2	33d (4th Reserves)	2
26th	1	30th (1st Reserves)	2	34th (5th Reserves)	2
27th	2	31st (2d Reserves)	2	35th (6th Reserves)	2

*From souvenir, "Return of the Colors," July 4th, 1866, published by William D. Moore.

Organization.	No. Flags		Organization.	No. Flags		Organization.	No. Flags
36th (7th Reserves)	1		96th	1		158th	1
37th (8th Reserves)	2		97th	2		159th (14th Cavalry)	1
38th (9th Reserves)	2		98th	2		160th (15th Cavalry)	1
39th (10th Reserves)	2		99th	1		161st (16th Cavalry)	1
40th (11th Reserves)	2		100th	3		162d (17th Cavalry)	2
41st (12th Reserves)	2		101st	1		163d (18th Cavalry)	0
42d (1st Rifles)	2		102d	3		165th	1
43d (1st Artillery)	1		103d	1		166th	1
44th (1st Cavalry)	2		104th	2		167th	3
45th	2		105th	5		168th	1
46th	3		106th	1		169th	1
47th	2		107th	2		171st	3
48th	2		108th (11th Cavalry)	1		172d	1
49th	2		109th	2		173d	2
50th	3		110th	3		174th	0
51st	8		111th	3		175th	1
52d	2		112th (2d Artillery)	3		176th	1
53d	3		113th (12th Cavalry)	1		177th	3
54th	0		114th	1		178th	1
55th	2		115th	1		179th	1
56th	3		116th	4		180th (19th Cavalry)	0
57th	3		117th (13th Cavalry)	1		181st (20th Cavalry)	0
58th	2		118th	4		182d (21st Cavalry)	1
59th (2d Cavalry)	1		119th	1		183d	3
60th (3d Cavalry)	2		121st	3		184th	2
61st	3		122d	1		185th (22d Cavalry)	1
62d	1		123d	4		186th	2
63d	2		124th	1		187th	1
64th (4th Cavalry)	3		125th	1		188th	2
65th (5th Cavalry)	2		126th	1		190th	2
67th	3		127th	1		191st	1
68th	3		128th	1		192d	2
69th	2		129th	2		193d	1
70th (6th Cavalry)	1		130th	1		194th	1
71st	1		131st	1		195th	1
72d	1		132d	3		196th	0
73d	3		133d	1		198th	3
74th	1		134th	2		199th	2
75th	2		135th	1		200th	1
76th	4		136th	1		201st	1
77th	3		137th	1		202d	3
78th	4		138th	2		203d	2
79th	2		139th	1		204th (5th Artillery)	2
80th (7th Cavalry)	3		140th	2		205th	1
81st	2		141st	3		206th	2
82d	1		142d	2		207th	1
83d	3		143d	4		208th	2
84th	3		145th	1		209th	2
85th	2		147th	2		210th	2
87th	1		148th	3		211th	1
88th	3		149th (2d Bucktails)	3		212th (6th Artillery)	2
89th (8th Cavalry)	1		150th (3d Bucktails)	2		213th	3
90th	1		151st	1		214th	3
91st	2		152d (3d Artillery)	2		215th	1
92d (9th Cavalry)	2		153d	2		32d Prov. Cavalry	1
93d	2		155th	2		Ringgold Battery, 1861	2
95th	3		157th	2			

The Law of the Standards.

Reverence for the standard has been elemental from the earliest times in the training of the soldiers of the English-speaking race. Ceremony, salute, respect has ever attended its presence. On the regimental colors were inscribed battles, skirmishes and affairs-at-arms, a remembrance of the glories of the past, and as an incentive to valor in the future. So immediately had a spirit of militarism seized our people that recognition of this tradition found forceful expression within the month following the opening of hostilities in the passage by the Legislature of Pennsylvania of the following:

JOINT RESOLUTION

Relative to the providing of Standards for the several Regiments of Pennsylvania called or to be called into the service of the United States.

SECTION 1. *Resolved, by the Senate and the House of Representatives of the Commonwealth of Pennsylvania in General Assembly met,* That the Governor of the Commonwealth be requested to ascertain how the several regiments raised in Pennsylvania during the War of the Revolution and the War of 1812 and the War with Mexico were numbered, among what divisions of the service they were distributed, and where the said regiments distinguished themselves in action. That having ascertained the particulars aforesaid he shall provide regimental standards to be inscribed with the numbers of those regiments respectively, on which shall be painted the arms of this Commonwealth and the names of the actions in which said regiments distinguished themselves. That the standards so inscribed shall be delivered to the regiments now in the field or forming corresponding to the regiments of Pennsylvania in former wars.

SECT. 2. That the Governor do procure regimental standards for all the regiments formed or to be formed in Pennsylvania beyond the numbers in former wars, upon which shall be inscribed the number of the regiment and painted the Arms of the Commonwealth, and that all these standards, after the present unhappy rebellion is ended, shall be returned to the Adjutant-General of the State, to be further inscribed, as the valor and good conduct of each particular regiment may have deserved, and that they be carefully preserved by the State to be delivered to such future regiments as the military necessities of the country may require Pennsylvania to raise.

ELISHA W. DAVIS,
Speaker of the House of Representatives

LOUIS W. HALL,
Speaker of the Senate.

APPROVED the sixteenth day of May, Anno Domini one thousand eight hundred and sixty-one.

A. G. CURTIN.

Pamphlet Laws of 1861, page 776.*

---

*Of the regimental, battalion and separate company organizations enlisted in the National service during the Civil War, numbering 3,559, Pennsylvania furnished 383, being exceeded, numerically, only by Missouri and New York. The Missouri organizations, however, averaged only 244 men. Pennsylvania was, therefore, only second to New York in the number of officers and men furnished.

MAJOR-GEN. CHARLES FERGUSON SMITH

IN the impressive array of names of distinguished officers of the army whose lives were cut short in the course of the Civil War, while serving their country, none among those from Philadelphia, perhaps from the country at large, is more deserving of remembrance than that of Major-Gen. Charles Ferguson Smith. The career of this officer began as a cadet in 1820. He was born in Philadelphia, grandson of John Blair Smith, D. D., second pastor of the Pine Street Church.

Charles Ferguson Smith won honors for gallantry in the principal battles of the Mexican War. He was stationed, as commandant, at the United States Military Academy during the cadetship of U. S. Grant, and when they were brought together in the western army in the early operations of General Grant he did not hesitate to avail himself of General Smith's advice.

In his memoirs General Grant makes frequent mention of his admiration for General Smith's abilities, which had then gained for him the rank of major-general.* His death on April 25th, 1862, was due to exposure after the capture of Fort Donelson. He was buried, with an imposing military funeral, at the Laurel Hill Cemetery, on May 6th, 1862.†

THE DAHLGRENS

JOHN A. DAHLGREN, VICE-ADMIRAL U. S. NAVY.

SON of a Swedish merchant resident in Philadelphia, John A. Dahlgren was born upon November 13th, 1809. He entered the navy in 1826, and at the opening of the Rebellion was stationed at the Washington Navy Yard. When his superior officer, Capt. Franklin Buchanan, resigned to join the Southern cause, Lieutenant Dahlgren took command and was largely instrumental in saving that important navy yard from capture by the enemy. He was advanced to the rank of captain and appointed chief of the Bureau of Ordnance. In 1863, co-operating with Vice-Admiral Gilmore, he silenced the Confederate guns of Fort Sumter and opened the harbor of Charleston. An

---

* The statement is made in "Under the Old Flag" (Wilson) that Gen. Smith would probably have become the commanding general of the armies had he lived. Gen. William T. Sherman is credited with having held that opinion.

† A full description of this funeral may be found in The History of the First Regiment N. G. P., Latta.

accomplished master of gunnery, he succeeded in linking his name with improved types of cannon, ranging from boat howitzers to the heaviest guns then made for the armament of war ships and forts. Subsequently, with the rank of rear admiral, he commanded the South Pacific Squadron. In 1870 he was again placed in command of the navy yard at Washington, where he died upon July 12th of that year.

COLONEL ULRIC DAHLGREN.

The name of Ulric Dahlgren has ever recalled to veterans of the cavalry service one who was an ideal leader, and whose tragic end was mourned by all who had known and followed him. He was the son of Capt. (afterward Rear Admiral) John A. Dahlgren of Philadelphia. His first service was in the navy, but upon the opening of the war, at the age of nineteen years, he ranked as captain of artillery in the United States service. Endowed with great energy, bravery and good judgment, he was in demand as an aide and so served upon the staffs of Generals Stahl, Sigel, Hooker and Meade. Before and after the battle of Gettysburg he undertook important services. Upon July 8th, 1863, in a cavalry charge upon the retreating Confederates, at Hagerstown, Md., he was wounded, resulting in the loss of a leg. After leaving the hospital he again became active. As second in command, under General Kilpatrick, he participated in the historic cavalry raid of March, 1864, intended for the release of the Union prisoners at Richmond. Detaching five hundred men, he was sent forward by Kilpatrick and reached the James River. The treachery of a guide involved a loss of time, and his small force was surrounded. At the head of one hundred horsemen he attempted to fight his way out. He was killed, with many of his men, and the balance were captured. Colonel Dahlgren's body was eventually brought, with the help of friendly Virginians, within the Union lines. It was laid in state at Independence Hall, from which, under military escort, the body of the young hero was conveyed to Laurel Hill Cemetery.

THOMAS BUCHANAN READ

Although the fame of this lyrist rests upon a single contribution to the poetry of the Civil War, his "Sheridan's Ride," he wrote a number of stirring war poems and recited often in the camps at the front. He was born in Chester County but lived much of his life in Philadelphia, being a cigar maker by trade and, later, a student of art abroad. His patriotic verses were published in book form in 1865. He died in New York City in 1872.

JAMES E. MURDOCH

A MONG the patriotic civilians of Philadelphia, the services of James E. Murdoch, actor and orator, are recalled by thousands of old soldiers. Stately and picturesque, his powerful war lyrics were a feature of enlistment meetings, in the camps at the front and the wards of the military hospitals. Especially favorite with him were the inspiring verses of a group of poets closely identified with Philadelphia and its vicinity, which included Thomas Buchanan Read, Bayard Taylor, Lucy Hamilton Hooper, Francis De Haes Janvier and George H. Boker.

Colonel Forney is credited with the opinion that Professor Murdoch's presence in a camp as an inspiration to weary and home-sick soldiers was as good as an added regiment of troops. This gifted man lost one son at Chickamauga, and another came out of the war in a disabled condition.

MILITARY ORDER OF THE LOYAL LEGION

THE Military Order of the Loyal Legion of the United States had its inception on that saddest day, at the conclusion of the Civil War, when humanity throughout the world was shocked by the death of Abraham Lincoln. "In honor of that illustrious leader and of the great cause for which we had fought; in recognition of the affectionate friendship which had been inspired among the officers of the Army then about to disband; in historic recollection of the Society of the Cincinnati, which had embraced the officers of the Revolutionary Army, it was determined to form this Order; and at a meeting of a few officers in the city of Philadelphia the initial steps were that day taken for its organization. It was the first of the military societies which followed, or rather accompanied, the close of the War."*

On April 15th, 1865, a meeting was held at the office of Lieut.-Col. Thomas Ellwood Zell, in Philadelphia, to take action for the officers and ex-officers of the Army and Navy to act as a guard of honor to the remains of the President. It was determined by those present to call a meeting of those who had served in the Rebellion on April 20th, when Col. Zell presented a motion, which was adopted, that a society should be formed to commemorate the events and principles of the War for the Union, then drawing to a close, and that measures should be adopted to promote that object. Subsequent meetings of those interested were held and a provisional organization was effected at a meeting held May

*From General Charles Devens's Twenty-fifth Anniversary Oration.

31st in the room in Independence Hall where the first Senate and House of Representatives of the United States assembled and in which Washington was inaugurated. (From "The Organization of the Loyal Legion," by Col. Zell, in "United Service Magazine," February, 1889.)

Brevet Lieut.-Col. Samuel Brown Wylie Mitchell, Lieut.-Col. Thomas Ellwood Zell, and Capt. Peter Dirck Keyser are designated as the founders of the Order, Col. Mitchell's insignia and diploma being No. 1.

The plan of a permanent organization having been perfected, the Commandery of the State of Pennsylvania was organized November 4th, 1865, to date from April 15th, commemorating the day of the first meeting. Major-Gen. George Cadwalader was elected Commander, and Col. Mitchell, Recorder; both served also as Acting Commander-in-Chief and Acting Recorder-in-Chief, respectively, until their deaths in 1879. The Commandery of the State of Pennsylvania continued to be the Acting Commandery-in-Chief until October 21st, 1885, when the Commandery-in-Chief was organized. Major-Gen. Winfield Scott Hancock having become Acting Commander-in-Chief, in 1879, was elected the first Commander-in-Chief, serving until his death in 1886. The successive Commanders-in-Chief have been: Gen. Philip Henry Sheridan, 1886; Brevet Major-Gen. Rutherford Birchard Hayes, 1889; Brig.-Gen. Lucius Fairchild, 1892; Major-Gen. John Gibbon, 1895; Rear Admiral Bancroft Gherardi, 1896; Lieut.-Gen. John McAllister Schofield, 1899; Brevet Major-Gen. David McMurtrie Gregg, 1903; Major-Gen. John Rutter Brooke, 1905; Major-Gen. Granville M. Dodge, 1907; Lieut.-Gen. John C. Bates, 1909; Rear Admiral George W. Melville, 1911; Lieut.-Gen. Arthur McArthur, 1912; Col. Arnold A. Rand, 1913. Brevet Lieut.-Col. John Page Nicholson succeeded Colonel Mitchell as Acting Recorder-in-Chief in 1879, and in 1885 became Recorder-in-Chief, serving continuously to the present time.

Among Commanders of State Commanderies have been: Major-Gen. George Cadwalader, Brevet-Major Gen. D. McM. Gregg, Major-Gen. John R. Brooke, Pennsylvania; Gen. Ulysses S. Grant and Admiral David G. Farragut, New York; Gen. Philip H. Sheridan, Illinois; Ex-President Rutherford B. Hayes and Benjamin Harrison, and Gen. William T. Sherman, Ohio; Lieut.-Gens. John M. Schofield, Nelson A. Miles and Samuel B. M. Young, California.

All legislative power is vested in the Congress of the Order, composed of three representatives from each Commandery, which meets quadrennially.

The executive and judicial power is vested in the Commandery-in-Chief, which consists of the Commanders, ex-Commanders, Vice-Commanders, ex-Vice-Commanders, Recorders and ex-Recorders of the various Commanderies. It meets annually.

Six meetings yearly is the average among the Commanderies; the proceedings generally include business meeting, collation and reading of a historical paper. Many volumes of these contributions to the history of the Rebellion have been published. A majority of the Commanderies maintain permanent headquarters and possess valuable collections of books, pictures and relics pertaining to the War period.

COMMANDERY OF THE STATE OF PENNSYLVANIA. Headquarters, Philadelphia. Instituted April 15th, 1865. Acting Commandery-in-Chief, 1865 to 1885. Commander, Gen. Charles G. Sawtelle. Recorder, Col. John P. Nicholson. In 1888 the largest in membership; since that year has been second in number of members. Original, 688; Hereditary and Second Class, 405; Third Class, 1; total, 1095.

This Commandery is now permanently located in a spacious suite of rooms upon the fifth floor of the Flanders Building, southeast corner of Fifteenth and Walnut streets, including in its treasured possessions an extensive collection of Civil War portraits, prints and relics, and a comprehensive military and naval library.

In addition to his duties as Recorder-in-Chief, Col. Nicholson is also Chairman of the Gettysburg National Park Commission and Vice-President of the Valley Forge Park Commission.

DAMES OF THE LOYAL LEGION.

The Dames of the Loyal Legion Society of Pennsylvania is composed of the wives and daughters of Union Officers who served in the Civil War. The present officers are: Mrs. Frank A. Hutchinson, President; Mrs. Arthur A. Scott, Senior Vice-President; Mrs. Robert Wetherill, Junior Vice-President; Mrs. Clarence W. Bispham, Recorder; Mrs. William Irish, Treasurer; Mrs. Thompson F. Edwards, Registrar; Miss Frances R. Edwards, Color Bearer.

THE GRAND ARMY OF THE REPUBLIC*

MILE upon mile of dusty, tattered, but glorified regiments; hour after hour of martial music, of scenes that were full of cheering, of ecstasy and of sobbing. So the armies of the Union marched through Washington, passing in review before the statesmen and military chiefs of the Nation. Behind them were the graves of the fallen, before them the renewed problems of civil life. A few

*The discharged officers and soldiers of the United States Army, residing in Philadelphia, held a meeting, the presiding officer being Lieut.-Col. Henry A. Cook, of Baxter's Fire Zouaves, and proposed to secure a charter for a society of veterans and to establish branch organizations throughout Pennsylvania. Army and Navy Journal, May, 1865.

This was one of the many now forgotten movements which, a year later, found solution in the organization of the Grand Army of the Republic.

more days of drums, breeze-tossed flags, of fervent oratory, as each group of survivors came to its own community, and the rifles were stacked in the armories, the swords and sashes placed above domestic mantels. The war was over.

Beside the camp-fires, from the Potomac to the Mississippi, men had dreamed and talked of the preservation of comradeship. Many plans were suggested. Politicians were alert to a great opportunity. But it was an army surgeon in the home city of the martyred War President who showed the way to success.

Having organized the first post of the Grand Army of the Republic at Decatur, Ill., on April 6th, 1866, the founder of the order, Dr. Benjamin F. Stephenson, called together representative soldiers from all sections of the State, and submitted, with explanations, the principles upon which the Grand Army of the Republic was destined to build the greatest association of veteran soldiery known to history. This meeting was held at Springfield, Ill., on July 12th, 1866. As commander-in-chief, Dr. Stephenson called through Adjutant-Gen. J. C. Webber and Major Robert M. Woods, the first National Encampment to convene at Indianapolis, Ind., on November 20th, 1866. At this time Wisconsin and Iowa and posts in Pennsylvania had been organized, and during the encampment Indiana joined the movement.

The fifth State to organize a department, and the first of the seaboard States, was Pennsylvania.

The Second National Encampment was held at Philadelphia, January 15th, 16th and 17th, 1868, Major-Gen. John A. Logan being elected commander-in-chief. The institution of an annual Memorial Day was introduced by Gen. Logan. The purposes of the order are epitomized in the words "Friendship, Charity and Loyalty." Former rank is not officially recognized in the order. All honorably discharged soldiers, sailors and marines are eligible to membership, the commander of an army corps and the private soldier being upon an equality in the post-room.

Membership in the order passed beyond one hundred thousand in 1883 and reached its zenith at four hundred and nine thousand four hundred and eighty members, in good standing, in 1890. The national membership in 1911 was one hundred and ninety-one thousand three hundred and forty-six. The membership in that year (fifty years after the opening of the Civil War), in the State of Pennsylvania, was nineteen thousand two hundred and ninety-eight.

PAST COMMANDERS-IN-CHIEF FROM PHILADELPHIA AND VICINITY.

John F. Hartranft	1875-1876
Louis Wagner	1879
Robert B. Beath	1883
J. P. S. Gobin	1897
Thomas J. Stewart	1902

SENIOR VICE COMMANDER-IN-CHIEF.

Joshua T. Owen..1868

PAST DEPARTMENT COMMANDERS FROM PHILADELPHIA.

Louis Wagner 1866-1867
A. R. Calhoun 1870
Robert B. Beath 1873
A. Wilson Norris 1874
James W. Latta 1876
S. Irvin Givin.. 1877
John Taylor 1881
John M. Vanderslice 1882
William Emsley 1894
James F. Morrison 1899
Lewis W. Moore 1910

SESSIONS OF THE NATIONAL ENCAMPMENT, GRAND ARMY OF THE REPUBLIC, HELD IN PHILADELPHIA.

January 15th, 1868 ....Second Encampment.
June 30th 1876 ....Tenth Encampment.
September 6th 1899 ....Thirty-third Encampment.

POSTS OF THE GRAND ARMY OF THE REPUBLIC IN ORGANIZATION IN PHILADELPHIA JANUARY 1st, 1912.

No.	Post.	Location.	Meetings.
1.	Gen. George G. Meade	Parkway Building	Monday.
2.		667-669 N. Twelfth Street	Thursday.
5.	Gen. U. S. Grant	1706 South Street	Tuesday.
6.	Ellis	Town Hall, Germantown	Thursday.
7.	Capt. Walter S. Newhall	Girard Ave. and Eyre Street	Tuesday.
8.	Gen. E. D. Baker	1417 Columbia Avenue	Thursday.
10.	Lieut. John T. Greble	721 Wharton Street	Monday.
12.	Hetty A. A. Jones	Roxborough	Monday.
14.	Col. Ulric Dahlgren	2434 Kensington Avenue	First and third Tuesday.
15.	Gen. G. K. Warren	Carson Street, Manayunk	Thursday.
18.	Col. Wm. L. Curry	317 N. Twentieth Street	Thursday.
19.	Col. Fred. Taylor	1431 Brown Street	Thursday.
21.	Courtland Saunders	Thirty-ninth St. above Market street	Monday.
24.	Admiral DuPont	Broad and Federal Streets	Second and fourth Monday.
27.	John W. Jackson (Colored)	409 S. Eleventh Street	First Wednesday.
35.	The Cavalry	Parkway Building	First Thursday.
46.	Col. Gus. W. Town	1421 South Street	Wednesday.
51.	Capt. Philip R. Schuyler	Sepviva and Norris Streets	Thursday.
55	Gen. Phil. Kearny	4604 Frankford Avenue	Monday.
56.	Col. John W. Moore	3930 Lancaster Avenue	First and third Friday.
63.	Gen. D. B. Birney	Germantown Avenue and Diamond Street	Wednesday.
71.	Gen. John F. Reynolds	1226 S. Eighth Street	Wednesday.
77.	(no name)	524 N. Sixth Street	Second Friday.

No.	Post.	Location.	Meetings.
80.	Robert Bryan (Colored)	S. W. Cor. Eleventh and Fitzwater Streets	Tuesday.
94.	Anna M. Ross	Girard Avenue and Hutchinson Street	Monday.
103.	Charles Sumner (Colored)	1224 N. Eleventh Street	Second and fourth Wednesday.
114.	Winfield Scott	2054 Ridge Avenue	Monday.
115.	Gen. John A. Logan	1231 S. Seventeenth Street	Wednesday.
160.	Gen. Hector Tyndale	1365 Ridge Avenue	Saturday.
191.	Penna. Reserve	S.W. Cor. Fifth and Chestnut Streets	Wednesday.
228.	John A. Koltes	236-238 George Street	First Sunday, 3 P. M.
275.	Gen. Robert Patterson	1131 S. Broad Street	First and third Wednesday.
312.	Lieut. Edw. W. Gay	2214 Germantown Avenue	First and third Wednesday.
334.	Col. James Ashworth	Frankford	Wednesday.
363.	Gen. T. C. Deven	Parkway Building	First Thursday.
400.	The Naval	132 S. Eighth Street	Wednesday.

IMPORTANT EVENTS IN THE LOCAL HISTORY OF THE GRAND ARMY OF THE REPUBLIC.

October 17th, 1866.—Organization of a Post of the G. A. R. Commander Clayton McMichael (designated Post 1).

October 29th.—Organization of a Post of the G. A. R. Commander, S. B. Wylie Mitchell (later designated Post 2).

January 16th, 1877.—A permanent department of the Department of Pennsylvania, organized at Philadelphia. Gen. Louis Wagner, Commander.

January 15th, 1868.—Second Annual National Encampment convened at Independence Hall, Philadelphia. Gen. Louis Wagner, Commander.

May 31st, 1868.—First annual observance of Memorial Day by Posts of the G. A. R. and the public.

June 30th, 1876.—Tenth National Encampment convened at the headquarters of Post 2, Thirteenth and Spring Garden Street, Philadelphia.

May 16th, 1877.—General U. S. Grant was mustered into George G. Meade, Post 1, by special dispensation, at the office of Mr. George W. Childs in the Public Ledger building. Reception at Independence Hall.

July, 1877.—The Grand Army Posts were organized as veteran emergency regiments to preserve order in the city during the railroad riots.

October 19th, 1877.—First observance of "Grand Army Day." Parade of the Posts and review at the Permanent Exhibition in Fairmount Park by Commander-in-Chief J. C. Robinson, Governor John F. Hartranft, Gen. George B. McClellan, Gen. S. P. Heintzelman, Gen. D. McM. Gregg and other distinguished officers.

December 12th, 1879.—Magnificent welcome to ex-President U. S. Grant by the veteran soldiers of the city, upon his return from his tour of the world. Reception at the Academy of Music.

September 16th, 1887.—Grand Army Day of the Centennial Celebration of Adoption of the National Constitution.

September 4th-9th, 1899.—Thirty-third Annual National Encampment G. A. R., held at Philadelphia. An event of nation-wide notice, attended by a general suspension of business, splendid public and private decorations and an imposing parade of the veterans of the Union Army and Navy, escorted by the local military.

October, 1898.—Peace Jubilee. Led by Gen. Nelson A. Miles, chief marshal. The Posts of the Grand Army of the Republic joined with the National Guard of Pennsylvania in honoring the heroes and volunteers who served in the war with Spain.

October 9th, 1908.—"Historical Day" of the Founders' Week Celebration, a leading feature of which was the parade of local and visiting G. A. R. Posts and of the Sons of Veterans, the latter uniformed and armed to represent the departing regiments of the Civil War. The details of this last great parade of the Grand Army of the Republic in the City of Philadelphia was in charge of a committee from the Grand Army Association, consisting of Comrade Robert B. Beath, Chairman; John D. Worman, Secretary; James W. Latta, St. Clair A. Mulholland, Joseph R. Craig, Charles A. Suydam and Henry I. Yohn.

June 30th to July 4th, 1913.—Fiftieth anniversary of the Battle of Gettysburg. As guests of the Commonwealth of Pennsylvania, the States, North and South, and of the National Government, this remarkable and unique event was attended by a host of veterans of the Union and the Confederate armies, meeting under one flag and pledged to renewed loyalty to the Government of the United States.

MEMORIAL DAY IN PHILADELPHIA

ANNUALLY during a period of forty-five years the members of the Grand Army of the Republic all over the country have assembled pursuant to official orders at their Post headquarters and, after appropriate services, have marched to the burial places of their departed comrades to mark their graves with flowers. Veterans of the naval service cast their wreaths upon the waters of the seas. Armed escorts of Post Guards and Sons of Veterans discharge volleys over the dead, and the grandchildren of the veterans gone and yet to go march with the ever-lessening lines to the solemn dirge of bands and the beat of muffled drums.

The duties of this day are divided, in Philadelphia, among the several Posts, each taking charge of the ceremonies, as a rule, year after year at the same cemeteries. The assignments are as follows:

Post 1. North, South and Central Laurel Hill.

Post 2. Monument Cemetery.

Post 5. Mt. Moriah (Philadelphia portion), St. James Cemetery, Sixty-ninth Street and Woodland Avenue, and the grave of Anna M. Ross at Monument Cemetery.

Post 6. All cemeteries in Germantown and Chelten Hills. (Camp No. 9, Sons of Veterans, Holy Sepulchre and Ivy Hills Cemeteries.)

Post 7. Palmer and Hanover Cemeteries and Walter S. Newhall monument.

Post 8. Glenwood Cemetery.

Post 12. Leverington, St. Timothy's Presbyterian, Lutheran and St. Mary's, Roxborough, Cemeteries. Hetty Jones' monument.

Post 15. German Reformed, St. David's, St. John's, German Catholic, Westminster and Presbyterian (Manayunk) Cemeteries.

Post 18. Fernwood and Col. W. L. Curry's grave at South Laurel Hill.

Post 19. Odd Fellows' Cemetery.

Post 21. Woodland, Cathedral, Quaker (at Darby), Melrose and Baptist (Blockley) Cemeteries.

Post 24. Hebrew Cemetery.

Post 27. Merion and Eden Cemeteries.

HEADQUARTERS GRAND ARMY OF THE REPUBLIC, DEPARTMENT OF PENNSYLVANIA, AT FIFTH AND CHESTNUT STREETS, PHILADELPHIA.

(From a photograph made during 33d National Encampment, September, 1899.)

MASSED SCHOOL CHILDREN. A BEAUTIFUL FEATURE OF THE 33D NATIONAL ENCAMPMENT OF THE G. A. R., SEPTEMBER, 1899.

BREVET MAJOR-GEN. ST. CLAIR A. MULHOLLAND AND STAFF, VETERAN DIVISION, FOUNDERS' WEEK PARADE, OCTOBER, 1908.

Post 35. West Laurel Hill and McClellan monument.

Post 46. Ronaldson, Philanthropic, St. Peter's (Third and Pine Streets), Old Pine Street Church Cemeteries, the graves of Commodore Stephen Decatur, Capt. Ross of First Troop, Philadelphia City Cavalry, George M. Dallas and William Hurry (who, the tradition is, rang the State House bell when the Declaration of Independence was proclaimed).

Post 51. Franklin, St. Ann's, Bellevue, St. Peter's, Holy Redeemer Cemeteries, and the grave of Capt. Philip R. Schuyler, at Monument Cemetery.

Post 55. St. Joachim's, Cedar Hill, North Cedar Hill, Cheltenham, Oxford Church, Pennypack, Bridesburg, Magnolia and Bustleton Cemeteries.

Post 56. Mt. Moriah (west side) and Graceland Cemeteries.

Post 63. Oakland and Knights of Pythias' Cemeteries and the grave of Gen. David B. Birney.

Post 71. Old Swedes' (Gloria Dei), Union and Mutual Cemeteries and the Reynolds monument.

Post 77. Olney Cemetery.

Post 80. Wilmot and Bethel Cemeteries.

Post 94. American Mechanics' Cemetery.

Post 103. Olive Cemetery.

Post 114. Mt. Vernon and St. James the Less Cemeteries.

Post 115. Trinity Lutheran Cemetery.

Post 160. Mt. Peace Cemetery and the grave of Gen. Hector Tyndale at North Laurel Hill.

Post 191. Fifth and Arch Streets, Fernwood, Christ Church Cemeteries and the tomb of Robert Morris.

Post 228. German Lutheran Cemetery and the grave of Col. John A. Koltes at Glenwood Cemetery.

Post 275. St. Mary's and Philadelphia Cemeteries and grave of Gen. Francis E. Patterson at Laurel Hill.

Post 312. Northwood, Milestown Baptist and Methodist Cemeteries and the grave of Lieut. E. W. Gay.

Post 334. Methodist, Presbyterian, Mt. Sinai, Hedge Street (Holmesburg), All Saints' (Collegeville) and German Hill (Torresdale) Cemeteries and the grave of Col. James Ashworth at Cedar Hill.

Post 363. National Cemetery, Germantown.

Post 400. Mt. Moriah (naval plot) and St. Mary's (Fourth and Pine streets) Cemeteries.

NATIONAL CEMETERY AT PHILADELPHIA

THIS cemetery is located in the suburb of Pittville, at the intersection of Haines Street and Limekiln Pike. The soldiers, both Union and Confederates, who died at the several military hospitals of the city in the course of the war, are buried here, having been removed from the local cemeteries to this beautiful tract. The total interments to June 30th, 1913, are 3,288 of identified soldiers and 40 of those unknown. This includes 180 known and 4 unknown Confederates. A monument to these Southern soldiers was recently dedicated by the local Chapter, Daughters of the Confederacy. All but 40 of the 444 bodies of soldiers remaining in Mt. Moriah Cemetery are in charge of the Superintendent of the National Cemetery.

GRAND ARMY ASSOCIATION

THIS central organization of the Grand Army of the Republic in Philadelphia was formed July 26th, 1895, as a responsible medium for the relief of indigent veterans and widows of soldiers of the Civil War, and also for the advancement of the interests of the Grand Army of the Republic in all honorable particulars. It is formed from four delegates, elected annually, from each post in Philadelphia and Camden, N. J. Regular monthly meetings are held at the southwest corner of Fifth and Chestnut streets, in the room in which met the first Supreme Court of the United States. The Grand Army Association undertakes to relieve the local posts from the annoyance of impostors, to assist soldiers in securing pensions, to see that deceased soldiers and soldiers' widows receive proper burial, and to dispense charity to all having a proper claim. It has thus paid out since its organization above $10,000, the majority of the male beneficiaries not being members of the Grand Army of the Republic. Annual reunions are held at Willow Grove Park which attract thousands of veterans, their families and friends. The first president was Hon. G. Harry Davis of Post 1 (deceased); second president, Joseph R. Craig, Post 2 (deceased); third president, Col. R. B. Beath, Post 5, Past Commander-in-Chief of the Grand Army of the Republic; fourth president (present incumbent), Joshua R. Field, Post 19. Secretary, dating from organization, Henry I. Yohn, Post 1;* first treasurer, Edwin Walton (deceased); second and present treasurer, C. F. Gramlich.

REGIMENTAL ASSOCIATIONS

THE spirit of fraternity and loyalty to soldierly traditions among the veterans who had again assumed the duties of civil life naturally prompted the organization of regimental associations for the perpetuation of friendships and for mutual aid in the years to come. Strong in numbers and enthusiasm in the earlier years of their existence, many of these associations, whose survivors are now

---

*Comrade Henry Irvin Yohn, a sturdy representative of Pennsylvania Dutch stock, joined the Union Army when fourteen years old, in 1862. The following year he was transferred to the 1st U. S. Cavalry, and had the distinction of being the youngest cavalryman then in the ranks of the regular army. His enlistment being for a term of five years, he accompanied his regiment to the far West, and as sergeant served in the campaigns against the Apache Indians in Arizona. He has long held the position of Chief Deputy, Bureau of Delinquent Taxes, Philadelphia.

few and scattered, have ceased to exist; others continued to be a rallying point and refuge, in their old age, to their ever-lessening list of adherents. Could the individual records of these minor societies be printed, it would afford an impressive story of fidelity of the strong to the weak. In the weary march along the devious road of life none have been left helpless and abandoned to their fate. Some of the more active of the regimental associations have made and continue to enjoy annual excursions to the scenes of their campaigns as soldiers. In some instances members of wealth have left sums of money for this purpose. By far the most important of the many things accomplished by the associations is seen in the beautiful and costly monuments erected, with state assistance,* and dedicated upon the site of their positions on the battle line, marking for all time the scenes where they fought, notably at Antietam, Gettysburg and around Chattanooga.† These memorials have been committed to the care of the National Government, an exception being the superb monument of the Philadelphia Brigade at Antietam, which is left to the guardianship of the City of Philadelphia, which provided the fund for its erection.

Among the most active of the veteran associations still existent in this city are those of the 23d, 26th, 28th, 29th, 50th, 68th, 71st, 72d, 73d, 75th, 88th, 90th, 91st, 95th, 106th, 109th, 114th, 118th, 119th and 121st Infantry, the Reserve Corps Association, the Philadelphia Brigade Association, the 3d, 5th, 6th, 15th and 20th Cavalry, the 2d Heavy Artillery.

ORGANIZATIONS OF NAVAL VETERANS

THE pioneer organization of Union veterans of the naval force was the Farragut Naval Veteran Association No. 1, formed at Philadelphia within two years after the close of the war. Subsequently, similar independent associations were organized in other cities, but it was not until 1887 that the project, often discussed, of a union of these scattered bodies was realized. In that year the National Association of Naval Veterans of the United States of America was formed at New York City. The order includes, as eligible, any officer or enlisted man who served in the United States Navy, Marine Corps or Revenue Marine during any portion of the period from April,

*The earliest battle monuments erected in the South were dedicated by Massachusetts and Pennsylvania troops at Bull Run and Groveton, Va., June 12th, 1865.

†The State of Pennsylvania awarded to each regiment the sum of $1,500 to pay the cost of battlefield monuments. Nearly all of those erected were far more expensive, the additional outlay being met by the Regimental Associations.

1861, to August, 1865. The Second National Convention met at Philadelphia in the hall of Naval Post 400, in September of the following year. Generally, the annual conventions of the order have been held at the same places and coincidentally with the National Encampments of the Grand Army of the Republic, with which the majority of the navy veterans are identified and which includes three posts, composed exclusively of seamen, one of which, Post 400, organized in 1883, is located in Philadelphia.

An independent association, which is still existent in Philadephia, is the Naval Veteran Legion, which is closely allied to Naval Post 400. The Legion originated in a reunion of the survivors of the crew of the U. S. Sloop-of-War *Jamestown,* who were shipwrecked during a voyage around the world in the course of the Civil War.* The Philadelphia Naval Veteran Association No. 32, once strong in numbers, still musters about fifty surviving members. The present officers of this local association are Commander William J. McEwan, Lieut.-Commander Solomon Asher, Lieut. Louis E. Keen, Surgeon Charles W. Karsner, Paymaster Albert T. Young; Secretary, Jacob Teal; Assistant Secretary, Charles Shotwell; Chaplain, Charles F. Dyce.

THE ASSOCIATION OF UNION EX-PRISONERS OF WAR, PHILADELPHIA

THE Union Ex-Prisoners of War Association of Philadelphia was chartered on the eighth day of October, 1883, by C. C. Shanklin, President of the National Association of the Union Ex-Prisoners of War, at Cleveland, Ohio, and, although its ranks are being rapidly depleted by the ravages of time coupled with the disabilities resulting from imprisonment in the military stockades of the South, its members maintain the loyal and fraternal spirit which united them at its inception.

During the first year of the war no formal agreement for the exchange of prisoners existed, captives being exchanged by mutual consent of the opposing commanders. But, as the operations of the armies extended, it became apparent that a better method should be devised, hence a cartel of exchange was agreed upon on July 22d, 1862, between Gen. John A. Dix and Gen. D. H. Hill, the former representing the United States Government, the latter the Southern Confederacy. By its

*The voyage of the U. S. S. Jamestown, covering a period of three years, is the subject of an entertaining little volume written by Shipmate Isaac K. Arthur.

terms all prisoners of war were to be discharged on parole in ten days, the surplus on either side to be held from service until duly exchanged.

For a year after the cartel was agreed upon exchanges progressed without any serious friction. Then dissatisfaction began to develop into a more serious rupture, hence, many of those comprising this association, who had been captured by the enemy, were incarcerated for many months, suffering terrible privations, owing to the unfortunate conditions which culminated in the entire cessation of the exchange of prisoners.

The following ex-prisoners are recorded on the charter of the association: David T. Davis, Edmund A. Maas, Louis R. Fortescue, Alexander F. Nicholas, Herman J. Hambleton, Henry E. Rulon, William H. Blanks, Robert Stewart, James Reid, Daniel B. Meany, James Mc-Caulley, Chas. E. Tipton, George S. Neill, Joseph Burnes, Lewis F. Schiebler, Joseph E. Preston, Benjamin F. Skeen, Frank E. Moran, Rufus S. Read, James Noon, George L. Brown, James H. Ward.

THE WOMEN'S RELIEF CORPS

THE Seventeenth Annual National Encampment of the Grand Army of the Republic, held at Denver, Colorado, in July, 1883, conferred official standing upon this organization of patriotic women as a National Auxiliary to the G. A. R. The Women's Relief Corps was formed from a large number of local and State corps, generally composed of the female relatives of soldiers and informally attached to various posts. The several New England corps were united under a Union Board, and at the Denver gathering the members of the Executive Committee of said Board were elected officers of the New National Corps. Mrs. E. Florence Barker, of Massachusetts, became the first President, the Senior Vice-President being Mrs. Kate B. Sherwood, of Ohio, who had been largely instrumental in promoting the national body. All loyal women were now eligible to membership. The officers and delegates were accorded every courtesy by the Grand Army of the Republic and were invited to witness the installation of Comrade Robert B. Beath as Commander-in-Chief.

The objects of the Woman's Relief Corps as set forth in the preamble are: "To specially aid and assist the members of the Grand Army of the Republic and to perpetuate the memory of the heroic dead; to inculcate lessons of patriotism and love of country, not only among our membership, but also among our children."

ARMY AND NAVY MEDAL-OF-HONOR MEN
Resident in Philadelphia

M OVED by appreciation of individual deeds of exceptional bravery and devotion shown by soldiers in the Union army, an Act was passed by the Senate and House of Representatives of the United States and approved by the President upon July 12th, 1862, authorizing the Executive "to cause two thousand 'Medals of Honor' to be prepared, with suitable emblematic devices, and to direct that the same be presented in the name of Congress to such non-commissioned officers and privates as shall most distinguish themselves by their gallantry in action and other soldier-like qualities during the present insurrection."

By a further Act approved March 3d, 1863, commissioned officers were included among those eligible for heroism in action for the distinction of the Medal of Honor.

Under an Act approved December 21st, 1861, the Secretary of the Navy was authorized "to cause two hundred Medals of Honor to be prepared, with suitable emblematic devices, 'for presentation to such petty officers, seamen, landsmen and marines' as shall most distinguish themselves by their gallantry in action and other seaman-like qualities during the present war." Under a further Act approved July 16th, 1862, seamen "distinguishing themselves in battle or by extraordinary heroism in the line of their profession" were eligible to promotion to forward warrant officers or acting master's mates, "as they were best qualified, upon recommendation of their commanding officer, approved by the flag officer and the Department," and such promotion carried with it the right to the "Medal of Honor."

By virtue of these Acts Medals of Honor were presented to those found to be worthy of them in the Federal army during the Civil War and to those entitled to them for service in the navy in the same period. These army and navy medals were distinctive in design, but in 1905 a new and uniform design was adopted by the Government, in conformity with which new medals were issued to the army branch of the service.

By later enactment Congress has provided for awarding Medals of Honor to soldiers, sailors and marines who have distinguished themselves in the service subsequent to the Civil War or may do so hereafter.

At Washington, D. C., upon April 23d, 1890, veterans of the army and navy holding "Medals of Honor" met and organized a military and naval order entitled the "Medal-of-Honor Legion of the United States of America."

The constitution of the order provided for companions of the first class, these being the holders of such medals, and companions of the second class, composed of the eldest or other son nominated by a member, or, on failure of sons, the eldest or other daughter so nominated, these companions to be entitled upon arrival at the age of twenty-one years to enjoy all privileges and rights of voting existing in the order. Upon the death of the original holder of the "Medal of Honor" the son or daughter of his kin, then a companion of the second class, becomes, by right, a companion of the first class, thus perpetuating the membership of the order. A large proportion of the men thus distinguished by the nation identified themselves with the order.

The Military Order of the Medal of Honor.

This additional body of the holders of Medals of Honor was formed in New York City upon November 30th, 1909, membership being confined, in the first class, to those who have been awarded medals authorized by Congress "for distinguished gallantry in action," and, in the second class, to one lineal descendant of deceased members of the first class.

PHILADELPHIANS WHO SERVED IN THE CIVIL WAR TO WHOM THE MEDAL OF HONOR HAS BEEN PRESENTED BY CONGRESS.

*Orson W. Bennett, Captain, 102d U. S. C. T.
*Charles M. Betts, Lieutenant-Colonel, 15th Penna. Cavalry.
*Richard Binder, Sergeant., U. S. Marine Corps.
*Henry H. Bingham, Brevet-Brigadier-General, U. S. Volunteers.
William R. D. Blackwood, Surgeon, 48th Penna. Infantry, Brevet-Lieutenant-Colonel, U. S. V.
Sylvester Bonnaffon, Jr., Captain, 99th Penna. Infantry, Brevet-Lieutenant. Colonel, U. S. Volunteers.
Charles H. Clawson, 61st Penna. Infantry.
Louis H. Carpenter, Brigadier-General, U. S. A., retired.
Daniel Caldwell, First Lieutenant. 13th Penna. Cavalry.
*James G. Clark, Private, 88th Penna. Infantry.
*Charles H. T. Collis, Colonel, 114th Penna. Infantry, Brevet-Major-General, U. S. Volunteers.
Richard Connor, Private, 6th N. J. Infantry.
Michael Dougherty, 13th Penna. Cavalry.
*Edmund English, First Lieutenant and Adjutant, 7th U. S. Vet. Vol. Infantry, Brevet-Captain, U. S. Volunteers.
*John B. Fassitt, Captain, 23d Penna. Infantry.
*Joseph Fisher, Corporal, 61st Penna. Infantry.
*Frank Furness. Captain, 6th Penna. Cavalry (Rush Lancers).
Edward L. Gilligan, Captain, 88th Penna. Infantry.
*William E. Goodman, Captain, 147th Penna. Infantry, Brevet-Major, U. S. Volunteers.
Henry S. Huidekoper, Lieutenant-Colonel, 150th Penna. Infantry.

Note.—Star indicates members deceased to time of publication.

John C. Hunterson, 3d Penna. Cavalry.
*Wallace W. Johnson, Sergeant, 6th Penna. Reserves.
*William H. Lambert, Captain, 33d N. J. Infantry, Brevet-Major, U. S. Volunteers.
John H. Lawson, Landsman, U. S. Flagship Hartford.
*John F. Mackie, First Sergeant, U. S. M. C.
Sylvester H. Martin, Captain, 88th Penna. Infantry.
James Miller, Master's Mate, U. S. S. Marblehead.
*George W. Mindel, Colonel, 27th and 33d N. J. Infantry, Brevet-Major-General, U. S. Volunteers.
*St. Clair A. Mulholland, Colonel, 116th Penna. Infantry, Brevet-Brigadier-General and Major-General, U. S. Volunteers.
Peter McAdams, Lieutenant, 98th Penna. Infantry.
Michael McKeever, Sergeant, 5th Penna. Cavalry.
*Jacob G. Orth, Corporal, 28th Penna. Infantry.
*Robert L. Orr, Colonel, 61st Penna. Infantry.
*William J. Palmer, Colonel, 15th Penna. Cavalry, Brevet-Brigadier-General, U. S. Volunteers.
Robert Penn, Fireman, First Class, U. S. Navy.
*George C. Platt, Private, 6th U. S. Cavalry.
Noble D. Preston, Captain, 10th N. Y. Cavalry, Brevet-Lieutenant-Colonel, N. Y. S. Volunteers.
*Martin E. Scheibner, Private, 90th Penna. Infantry.
*Alfred J. Sellers, Major, 90th Penna. Infantry, Brevet-Colonel, U. S. Volunteers.
*J. Wallace Scott, Captain, 157th Penna. Infantry.
George D. Sidman, 16th Michigan Infantry.
*George H. Stockman, First Lieutenant, 6th Missouri Infantry.
John H. R. Storey, Sergeant, 109th Penna. Infantry.
*Hampton S. Thomas, Major, First Penna. Cavalry, Brevet-Colonel, U. S. Volunteers.
John M. Vanderslice, Private, 8th Penna. Cavalry.
Moses Veale, Major, 109th Penna. Infantry.
*J. Henry White, Private, 90th Penna. Infantry.
Ellwood N. Williams, First Sergeant, 28th Illinois Infantry.
William J. Wray, 23d Penna. Infantry, Sergeant, First Vet. Volunteer Reserve Corps.
Nathan H. Edgerton, Captain, 6th Regiment, U. S. Colored Troops.

ABRAHAM LINCOLN, at Lemon Hill, Fairmount Park.
(Photos by Charles R. Pancoast.)

LEADERS OF THE UNION ARMIES IN BRONZE.
GRANT.   McCLELLAN.
REYNOLDS.   MEADE.
(Photos by Charles R. Pancoast.)

THE SONS OF VETERANS, UNITED STATES OF AMERICA

WHEN the Grand Army of the Republic, yet in the fullness of its numerical and physical strength, realized the importance of creating a junior body to become the worthy heir of its principles and traditions, the medium through which the story of the trials, losses and achievements of its members might be transmitted to oncoming generations, it encouraged the organization of the Sons of Veterans of the United States of America. This movement originated in the year 1879, when a Cadet Corps attached to Anna M. Ross Post, No. 94, G. A. R., at Philadelphia (organized the preceding year), was constituted Anna M. Ross Camp, No. 1, Sons of Veterans. Other existing cadet organizations affiliated with local posts soon adopted the new title and the obligations of the order. In the meantime similar movements have gained strength in Pittsburgh and elsewhere, acting independently. It was only after years of controversy that personal ambitions were subordinated to the interests of concerted effort and the order, spread through other States, became truly national in its scope. The amalgamation of the different elements was accomplished in 1886.

At the present time (1913) the strength of the order throughout the nation is in excess of forty-eight thousand, in the State of Pennsylvania above fifteen thousand, and in the City of Philadelphia thirty-five hundred men. The twenty-two camps located in Philadelphia are affiliated with the local posts of the G. A. R., as follows:

CAMP	POST	CAMP	POST
1 Anna M. Ross	94	27 Moore	56
2 Fred Taylor	19	29 5th Regiment	27
3 MacFayden	15	40 Newhall	7
4 J. F. Reynolds	71	80 Bryan	80.
5 U. S. Grant	5	82 Curry	18
7 Pennsylvania Reserve	191	114 Scott	114
9 Ellis	9	123 Cavalry	35
9 Clegg	12	228 Koltes	228
10 Greble	10	236 Cocker	55
13 Birney	63	277 Baker	8
21 Saunders	21	299 Post 2	2

An auxiliary body, numbering in Pennsylvania about three thousand, and in Philadelphia one thousand, assists the Sons of Veterans in its patriotic functions, which include the yearly recurring exercises and duties of Memorial Day.

The Sons of Veterans Reserve, organized as an uniformed and equipped military body, constitutes, in Pennsylvania, a brigade of nearly three thousand officers and men, which may be counted upon, like the historic militia of *ante-bellum* days, to serve as a nucleus for a strong and well-drilled force for State or National defence.

22   337

PRINCIPAL MEMORIALS OF THE CIVIL WAR LOCATED IN PHILADELPHIA

WITH few exceptions the monuments related to the Civil War period thus far placed in Philadelphia have been erected at private cost. The monument to the soldiers and sailors of Philadelphia in the Civil War, which it is proposed to place in Logan Square and for which an appropriation has been made, will be erected at the expense of the City.

Existing memorials are the following:

IN THE CITY.

Equestrian Statue, Major-Gen. John F. Reynolds, north plaza, City Hall. Sculptor, J. Q. A. Ward.

Equestrian Statue, Major-Gen. George B. McClellan, north plaza, City Hall. Sculptor, Elliott.

Statue, Artillery Corps, Washington Grays, Washington Square. Sculptor, John Wilson.

Statue, First Regiment Infantry (Gray Reserves), in front of Union League Club House. Sculptor, Henry K. Bush Brown.

Bronze Tablet, Union League Regiments, corridor Union League Club House. Sculptor, H. K. Bush Brown.

Monument, Alumni and Cadets of Girard College who served in the Union forces during the Civil War.

Monument, Soldiers and Sailors of the Civil War, Market Square, Germantown.

Monument, Soldiers and Sailors, Mt. Moriah Cemetery.

IN FAIRMOUNT PARK.*

Monument, Abraham Lincoln, Lemon Hill.

Monumental Memorial (Richard Smith bequest). Centennial Concourse.† The military and naval figures placed upon this imposing and costly work are: Equestrian Statue, Major-Gen. Winfield S. Hancock; sculptor, J. Q. A. Ward. Equestrian Statue, Major-Gen. George B. McClellan; sculptor, Edward C. Potter.

Statue, Major-Gen. George Gordon Meade. Sculptor, Daniel Chester French.

Statue, Major-Gen. John F. Reynolds. Sculptor, Charles Grafly.

Bust, Admiral David D. Porter. Sculptor, Charles Grafly.

Bust, Major-Gen. John F. Hartranft. Sculptor, A. Stirling Calder.

---

*A number of these bronzes were contributed by the Fairmount Park Association.

†This noble work, costing $500,000, was designed by James H. and John T. Windrim.

Bust, Admiral John A. Dahlgren. Sculptor, George E. Bissel.
Bust, Major-Gen. S. Wylie Crawford. Sculptor, Bessie O. Potter.
Bust, Gen. James A. Beaver. Sculptor, Katharine M. Cohen.
Bust, Governor Andrew G. Curtin. Sculptor, M. Ezekiel.

Equestrian Statue, Gen. U. S. Grant, East Park River Drive. Sculptors, Daniel Chester French and Edward C. Potter.*
Equestrian Statue, Major-Gen. George Gordon Meade, Lansdowne Drive. Sculptor, Alexander M. Calder.
Statue, Soldier of the Civil War (Courtland Saunders Post 21, G. A. R.), near George's Hill.
Tablet, site of First Camp, 88th Regiment Infantry Volunteers, East Park Drive, Falls of Schuylkill.

PUBLIC SQUARES AND SMALL PARKS NAMED IN HONOR OF PERSONS OR PLACES IDENTIFIED WITH THE CIVIL WAR.

"Greble Plot," 3d street, near Moyamensing avenue.
"Birney Post Park," 6th street and Germantown avenue.
"Thomas J. Powers," Ann, Mercer and Almond streets.
"Anna M. Ross," 10th street and Glenwood avenue.
"Baker Post," Rising Sun avenue and York road.
"Reynolds Post," Snyder avenue, Passyunk avenue and 17th street.

REORGANIZATION OF THE NATIONAL GUARD OF PENNSYLVANIA†

SO completely weary of war and its panoplies were the people of Pennsylvania after the return of the surviving veterans, that the Adjutant-General reported in November, 1865, only eight companies of militia in the State, including those in Philadelphia. The necessity for an efficient armed force of State soldiery required prompt action. Under the training of veteran officers and men, the number of

*Part of cost was defrayed by the City of Philadelphia.

†The chaotic status of the State militia force, due to the depletion of Pennsylvania's fighting blood, was the inducement, probably, for an Act passed by the Legislature May 4th, 1864, for the reorganization of the militia of the Commonwealth, somewhat along the old lines of enrollment. After a discouraging period of effort to obey instructions, Brigadier-General Lemuel Todd, State Inspector General, wrote, in a report to Governor Curtin (Report of Adjutant-General, State of Pennsylvania, for 1866) as follows:

"It is in vain to issue orders and call upon the people to voluntarily assume such labors. The day of voluntary gratuitous service for the State seems to have passed away forever."

The glamour of military glory had faded away. The sight of thousands of crippled veterans, the sorrow in countless homes, bereft of bread-winners fallen companies increased in 1867 to thirty-eight, of which twenty-six were in Philadelphia.

The Frst Division, National Guard, in 1868, included the First Troop Philadelphia City Cavalry, Artillery Corps Washington Grays, Keystone Battery, Philadelphia Veteran Light Artillery Regiment, 2d Regiment (National Guard), 4th Regiment (Philadelphia Fire Zouaves), Philadelphia Zouaves and the Montgomery Guards, also the Reserve Brigade, composed of the 1st Regiment (Gray Reserves) and the 3rd Regiment (Philadelphia Light Guard) Infantry.

Five years after the close of the war the city contained at least a dozen regiments of State troops of varying numerical strength and efficiency.

A LIST OF PHILADELPHIA OFFICERS IN THE NATIONAL GUARD OF PENNSYLVANIA, SUBSEQUENT TO 1865, WHO SERVED IN THE CIVIL WAR

MAJOR-GENERALS.

Bankson, John P.
Bowman, Wendell P.
Brinton, Robert M.

Latta, James W.
Prevost, Charles M.
Snowden, George R.

BRIGADIER-GENERALS.

Baxter, DeWitt Clinton.
Benson, R. Dale.
Bosbyshell, Oliver C.
Bonnaffon, Sylvester, Jr.
Coxe, John R.
    (Commissary General).
Dechert, Robert P.

Hofmann, J. William.
Loud, Edward D. C.
Matthews, E. Wallace.
Muirheid, Henry P.
Wagner, Louis.
Ward, Joseph R. C.
Wiedersheim, Theodore E.†

COLONELS.

Ballier, John F.
Fritz, Peter.
Herring, Charles P.
Lyle, Peter.
Leech, William A.
McMichael, William.
Maginniss, Thomas H.

Maxwell, John.
Neff, Harmanus.
Norris A. Wilson
    (Judge Advocate General).
Sellers, Alfred J.
Smith. Thomas J.†
    (Commissary General).

---

on Southern soil, the widespread sentiment of covert hostility to all that the war party stood for, were the chief causes of this reaction through the State. But, in the end, under the leadership of veteran officers and with seasoned rank and file, the National Guard was destined to rise to a degree of effectiveness and system never before attained, and to become a model which other States might well strive to emulate.

†Under the provisions of the 45th section of the Act for the organization. discipline and maintenance of the National Guard of Pennsylvania, approved May 5th, 1911 (Pamphlet Laws, page 131), the State authorities recognize the services of the militia in the campaigns of 1862 and 1863 as a war service, and the officers who are indicated, as above, in the text all appear in the official records as having been engaged in either one or both of these campaigns.

LIEUTENANT-COLONELS.

Clark, J. Ross.†
Denney, John P.
Gilpin, Washington H.
Gorgas, John A.
Greene, Charles S.
Hassinger, D. Stanley.
Huffington, Thomas E.

Knight, Charles C.
Mears, J. Ewing
(Surgeon)
Morris, Galloway C.†
Randall, Edmund.
North, George H.
Mitchell, S. B. Wylie.

MAJORS.

Allen, William W.†
Chew, W. Wesley.
Ide, Charles K.†
Keyser, James D.†
Kollock, John W.
(Surgeon).
Ladner, Louis J.
Lewis, Samuel N.

O'Callaghan, C. M.
Potter, Harry C.
Rizer, Martin.
Ryan, John W.
Starr, James.
Stewart, William S.
Witherup, William A.
Worman, Charles H.

CAPTAINS.

Addis, Isaac.
Barry, David S.
Biles, Edwin R.
Brady, James.
Bregy, F. Amedee.
Cadwalader, C. G.
Chadwick, Peter B.
Collins, Stephen B.†
Cosslet, Charles.
Davis, Jacob M.
Durang, John T.
Donaldson, Frank A.
Fergusson, Alexander C.†
Furey, Thomas.
Glading, Norwood P.
Grubb, E. Burd.
Hailstock, Charles A.
Hewes, Harry W.
Hoguet, Francis.
Hoyt, Henry F.
(Chaplain).
Jacobus, Peter H.

Kennard, John T.
Koons, Frederick.
Landell, Edwin A.
Laudenslager, Jacob.†
Martin, J. Parker.
McCook, Henry C.
(Chaplain).
McGovern, John.
Muldoon, James.
Mullen, Dennis.
Packer, Edward E.
Peck, Henry T.
Rhinehart, C.
Rose, Charles A.†
Simpson, George W.
Smith, Charles W.
Stafford, Maurice C.
Thompson, John C.
Walters, Albert H.
Ward, William C.
White, John R.
Wilson, J. Lapsley.†

HISTORIES OF COMMANDS IDENTIFIED, WHOLLY OR IN PART, WITH PHILADELPHIA IN THE PERIOD OF THE CIVIL WAR

(Copies of these volumes may be seen at the Philadelphia Library or at the Library of the Historical Society of Pennsylvania.)

CAVALRY.

60th Regiment, 3d Cavalry. Regimental Committee. 1905.
60th Regiment, 3d Cavalry. "A Memoir." Walter S. Newhall. 1864.
60th Regiment, 3d Cavalry. Address, Gettysburg, John C. Hunterson, September 5th, 1890.
60th Regiment, 3d Cavalry. (History of Company H.) 1878.

70th Regiment, 6th Cavalry. S. L. Gracey. 1868.
70th Regiment, 6th Cavalry. Dedication of monument at Gettysburg, October, 14, 1888.
80th Regiment, 7th Cavalry. William B. Sipes. 1905.
80th Regiment, 8th Cavalry. "Sabre Strokes of the Pennsylvania Dragoons." T. F. Dornblaser. 1884.
89th Regiment, 8th Cavalry. Pennock Huey. 1885.
89th Regiment, 8th Cavalry. Pennock Huey. "True History of the Charge of, at Chancellorsville." 1885.
89th Regiment, 8th Cavalry. J. Edward Carpenter, "List of Battles," etc. 1886.
108th Regiment, 11th Cavalry. Register of Commissioned Officers and Historical Memorandum of the Regiment. 1886.
*160th Regiment., 15th Cavalry (and the "Anderson Cavalry"). Charles H. Kirk. 1906.
160th Regiment, 15th Cavalry. John A. B. Williams, "Leaves from a Trooper's Diary." 1869.
163d Regiment, 18th Cavalry. Publication Committee, Regimental Association. 1909.

ARTILLERY.

112th Regiment, 2d Heavy Artillery. George W. Ward. 1904.
Keystone Battery (Battery A). Logan Howard-Smith and J. F. Reynolds Scott. 1912.

INFANTRY.

23d Regiment, Birney's Zouaves. William J. Wray. 1904.
28th and 147th Regiments. Hector Tyndale. 1871.
28th and 147th Regiments and Battery E, Light Artillery. John P. Nicholson. 1882.
28th Infantry. Samuel P. Bates.
31st Regiment, 2d Reserves. E. M. Woodward, "Our Campaign." 1865.
32d Regiment, 3d Reserves. E. M. Woodward. 1883.
61st Regiment. A. T. Brewer. 1911.
69th Regiment, Infantry. Anthony Wayne McDermott. 1889.
72d Regiment. A. S. Webb, Address at Gettysburg. 1883.
88th Regiment. John D. Vautier. 1894.
95th Regiment, Gosline's Zouaves. G. Norton Galloway. 1884.
99th Regiment, Infantry. C. H. Fasenacht. 1886.
103d Infantry. L. S. Dickey. 1910.
106th Regiment. Joseph R. C. Ward. 1906.
The Philadelphia Brigade, 69th, 71st, 72d and 106th Regiments. Charles H. Banes. 1876.
109th Regiment. Address at Gettysburg, September 11, 1889.
109th Infantry (Veteran). Moses Veale. 1890.
111th Regiment. John Richards Boyle, "Soldiers True." 1903.
114th Regiment. Frank Rauscher, "Music on the March." 1892.
114th Regiment. Charles H. T. Collis. 1891.
116th Regiment. St. Clair A. Mulholland. 1903.
118th Regiment. John L. Smith, "Antietam to Appomattox." 1905.
118th Regiment. A. G. Cattell, address at unveiling of a monument erected by the Commercial Exchange of Philadelphia to the Corn Exchange Regiment, at Gettysburg, September 8, 1884.
118th Regiment. H. T. Peck, Historical Sketch read at Gettysburg, September 8, 1884.
121st Regiment. Survivors' Association. 1893.
121st Regiment. Narrative by Col. Alexander Biddle and address by Walter C. Biddle, at Gettysburg, July 3, 1886.

343

150th Regiment. Thomas Chamberlin. 1895.
155th Infantry. McKenna.
187th Regiment (and First Battalion). James M. Gibbs. 1905.
192d Regiment. John C. Myers, "Daily Journal." 1864.
198th Regiment. E. M. Woodward.
Keystone Battery. T. L. Marshall. 1892.
Pennsylvania Reserve Corps. J. R. Sypher, complete record of the organization of Companies, Regiments and Brigades. 1865.
Martial Deeds of Pennsylvania. Samuel P. Bates. 1875.
Commonwealth Artillery Company. Muster Out Roll.
Pennsylvania at Chickamauga and Chattanooga. Ceremonies at the dedication of monuments erected by the Commonwealth of Pennsylvania. Captain George W. Skinner, editor and compiler. 1897. This volume contains addresses and historical essays delivered at the dedication of monuments of the 27th, 28th, 29th, 75th, and 147th Regiments of Infantry; the 7th, 9th and 15th Cavalry Regiments, and of Lighty Battery E, not elsewhere published.
Pennsylvania at Gettysburg. Edited and Compiled by Lieut.-Col. John P. Nicholson. Two vols. 1893. These volumes contain addresses and historical essays delivered at the dedication of monuments of the 26th, 27th, 28th, 29th, 31st (2d Reserves), 41st (12th Reserves), 56th, 61st, 68th, 69th, 71st, 72d, 73d, 74th, 75th, 81st, 82d, 88th, 90th, 91st, 95th, 98th, 99th, 106th, 109th, 110th, 115th, 116th, 118th, 119th, 121st, 147th and 150th Regiments Infantry. The 2d, 3d, 6th, 8th, 16th and 18th Cavalry. Battery G (served under Ricketts at Gettysburg), 1st Artillery, Battery H, 3d Heavy Artillery, Independent Battery E (Knap's).

MILITIA ORGANIZATIONS.

First Troop Philadelphia City Cavalry. Joseph Lapsley Wilson.
1st Regiment Infantry (Gray Reserves). James W. Latta. 1912.

TO FIND NAMES AND RECORDS OF OFFICERS AND ENLISTED MEN, 1861-1865

All volunteer, militia and emergency organizations of Pennsylvania with names of all officers thereof. Annual Report of the Adjutant General, State of Pennsylvania, 1866.
All volunteer, militia and emergency organizations of Pennsylvania with names and records of all officers and enlisted men, 1861—1865. History of Pennsylvania Volunteers, Samuel P. Bates, 5 vols.
Record of all military organizations in the service of the United States during the Civil War. A compendium of the War of the Rebellion. Frederick H. Dyer.
Regimental Histories, see list. These works may be consulted by any person by application at the rooms of the Historical Society of Pennsylvania and of the Library Company of Philadelphia.

A PARTIAL LIST OF WORKS CONSULTED BY THE AUTHOR

Series of Brigade, Regimental and Company Histories of the Pennsylvania Volunteers.
History of the Pennsylvania Volunteers. Samuel P. Bates.
A Compendium of the War of the Rebellion. Frederick H. Dyer.
Report of the Adjutant General of Pennsylvania, 1866.
Pennsylvania at Gettysburg. Edited by Lieut.-Col. John P. Nicholson.
Pennsylvania at Chickamauga and Chattanooga. Edited by Capt. George W. Skinner.
History of the Grand Army of the Republic. Col. Robert B. Beath.

Register of the Military Order of the Loyal Legion, Commandery of the State of Pennsylvania. Compiled by Lieut.-Col. John P. Nicholson.
History of the First Regiment Infantry N. G. P. Maj.-Gen. James W. Latta.
History of the First Troop Philadelphia City Cavalry. Edition of 1874.
Life of Jay Cooke. Oberholtzer.
History of the National Association of Naval Veterans. Simmons.
American Bastile. Marshall.
"U. S. Bonds." Handy.
McAllister Collection Civil War Scrap-books. Ridgway Library.
Pamphlet and Report Collections at the Library of Philadelphia, the Library of the Historical Society of Pennsylvania, of the College of Physicians, and of the Military Order of the Loyal Legion.
Files of the Philadelphia Inquirer, 1861-1865.

WAR CHRONOLOGY—PHILADELPHIA, 1861

January 2d. Philadelphia Cadets formed at National Guards' Hall.
"Minute Men of '76" fired salutes in honor of Delaware loyalty.
January 3d. A day of national fasting and prayer.
Patriotic resolution passed at a meeting of the Board of Trade.
January 4th. Recruiting commenced for a regiment by Capt. George P. McLean at a meeting held at Franklin and Buttonwood streets.
January 5th. Mayor Alexander Henry issued a proclamation against persons engaged in disloyal activity in the city.
Salute of thirty-three guns in honor of Delaware by Shiffler Hose Comapny.
At a meeting of the Board of Trade Judge Ellis Lewis, representing the Bell and Everett faction, denounced coercion of the South and upheld the right of secession. In the evening a great Union demonstration was held at National Hall. Republican Invincibles adopted patriotic resolutions.
January 7th. A meeting was held at Ladner's Military Hall, Third and Green streets, to organize the Monroe Guards, Minute Men of '76, Curtin Guard, American True Blues and Union Guard into a regiment under the command of William F. Small.
January 8th. Jackson Day. Jackson Zouaves, of New York, visited the Philadelphia Zouaves. Parade of National Guards.
Anderson Light Guard formed at 717 North Second street.
January 12th. "Yankee Doodle" hissed by Southern students at the Academy of Music.
January 16th. A secession meeting was held at National Hall.
January 19th. American and German regiments met at Military Hall and formed a brigade to be commanded by William F. Small.
State Guard attached to 1st Artillery Regiment.
January 23d. National Guard Cadets organized and drilled by Col. Peter Lyle.
January 26th. Working men held a Union demonstration in Independence Square.
January 28th. Six companies of Col. F. E. Patterson's artillery regiment drilling at their armories with "Quaker cannon."
January 29th. Twenty carloads of rifles shipped from Frankford Arsenal "to Washington."
February 4th. Berry Light Guard formed by Capt. Casper Berry.
February 10th. Continental Guards formed, at Nineteenth and South streets, as artillery.
February 12th. A steamer loading at Willow street with heavy guns for the defence of Washington.
February 21st. Hon. Abraham Lincoln, President-elect, arrived. He addressed the people from the balcony of the Continental Hotel. He was accompanied by Mrs. Lincoln, Col. Ward H. Lamon, Col. E. E. Ellsworth and several army officers.

February 22d. At daybreak the President-elect raised an American flag upon Independence Hall, leaving later for Harrisburg. He returned at night by special train and, unknown to any one excepting a few railroad and Government officials, left Broad and Prime Streets Station for Washington.

February 25th. U. S. S. Pawnee sailed for Washington.

March 4th. Great crowds assembled in front of newspaper offices to await the news of Lincoln's inauguration.

March 19th. Philadelphia banks resumed specie payments.

April 10th. Sudden activity at the Navy Yard.

April 12th. The arrival of reports of the Confederate assault upon Fort Sumter in Charleston Harbor and the news that Major Anderson had capitulated created immense excitement and at once aroused the patriotic element.

April 15th. Riotous crowds in some sections of the city led Mayor Henry to denounce treason and declare for peace and good order in the city.

Volunteering active in response to the first national call for troops.

Office of the *Palmetto Flag* in Chestnut street threatened by excited citizens.

April 18th. The 6th Massachusetts Regiment arrived at the foot if Walnut street and marched to the Girard House amid stirring patriotic scenes.

April 19th. The 6th Massachusetts Regiment and Gen. Wm. F. Small's "Washington Brigade" (the latter without arms or uniforms) left at an early hour for Washington. During the day the 8th Massachusetts Regiment reached Philadelphia.

City Councils voted to arm Home Guards and to provide money to support families of volunteers during their terms of service.

City Councils appropriated $1,000,000 for sustenance of soldiers' families.

April 20th. Ladies' Union Relief Corps formed.

The 7th New York Regiment arrived and, with the 8th Massachusetts Regiment, proceeded southward by steamers for Annapolis, Md., leaving from the foot of Washington avenue.

The Baltimore attack upon the 6th Massachusetts Regiment created intense excitement.

Col. A. J. Pleasonton appointed commander of the Home Guard.

April 21st. Recruits were drilled in all public squares. A State military clothing factory was opened in the Girard House (then vacant), many leading ladies assisting in the work.

April 22d. The 6th Regiment Infantry, Col. James Nagle, arrived from Pottsville and were quartered in the P., W. & B. R. R. depot, where they remained until May 7th.

George Leisenring, of Gen. Small's command, died at the Pennsylvania Hospital from stab wounds inflicted upon him at Baltimore. He was the first Philadelphia soldier to die in the Civil War.

April 23d. Responding to published appeals, large numbers of ladies reported at the Girard House (then closed as a hotel) and began to make uniforms.

April 24th. The Commonwealth Artillery Company, of Philadelphia, was sent to reinforce the garrison at Fort Delaware.

April 25th. Meeting of loyal Baltimore citizens who had escaped to Philadelphia.

April 30th. An address of confidence was sent to Lieut.-Gen. Winfield Scott, which was signed by Mayor Alexander Henry, Horace Binney, Richard Vaux and others.

May 9th. The 1st Regiment Artillery (17th Regiment), Col. Francis E. Patterson, recruited in Philadelphia, proceeded South. These were the first Philadelphia soldiers to reach Washington, where the command was reorganized as the 17th P. V. Infantry.

Two Ohio regiments encamped at Suffolk Park.

May 13th. First Troop Philadelphia City Cavalry mustered in at Point Breeze Park.

May 14th. The 18th, 19th and 22d Regiments left for the Sou. These regiments were organized in Philadelphia under Cols. Wm. . . Lewis, Jr., Peter Lyle and Turner G. Morehead, respectively, to serve for three months.

Major-Gen. Cadwalader and staff accompanied the Philadelphia regiments to Baltimore.

Before the troops departed young ladies of the High School presented a silk flag to the 19th Regiment (National Guards).

Garibaldi Legion attached to 32d Regiment Pennsylvania Reserve Corps.

May 15th. University Light Infantry drilling upon Fourth street, above Arch street.

May 16th. Pupils of Zane Street Grammar School gave a concert at the Academy of Music for the benefit of the volunteers.

An Act of Assembly approved for the establishment of a Home Guard Brigade in Philadelphia.

May 18th. The 24th Regiment, Col. Joshua T. Owen, encamped at Hestonville.

May 20th. Alfred Jenks & Son, Bridesburg, received a contract for 32,000 rifles.

May 22d. The Military Department of Pennsylvania formed, with headquarters in Philadelphia. This included Delaware and a part of Maryland.

May 24th. Scott Legion, 20th Regiment, encamped at Suffolk Park. These troops had previously quartered at the building adjoining the Custom House upon the west.

May 25th. Col. Ballier's regiment encamped at Suffolk Park.

May 27th. and 28th. Col. Wm. F. Small's regiment, 26th P. V. Infantry, mustered in.

May 28th. 21st and 28th Regiments encamped at Suffolk Park.

May 29th. 31st Regiment, Col. W. B. Mann, marched to Easton.

The 21st, 24th and 26th Regiments, P. V. Infantry, left for the South.

May 30th. The 31st Regiment (2d Reserves) left for the Reserves' Camp at Easton, Pa.

Scott Legion Regiment proceeded to Chambersburg and the First Troop P. C. Cavalry to Carlisle.

June 1st. The tide of returning regiments sets in with the passage through the city of the New York 7th Regiment.

June 7th. Four companies of infantry, commanded by Capt. J. C. Chapman, Capt. John H. Taggart, Capt. C. S. Preall and Capt. Casper Martino, mustered into State service and moved to Camp Curtin.

June 11th. 29th Regiment accepted by the Government.

June 13th. The 27th Regiment in camp near Camden.

June 14th. Funeral of Lieut. John Trout Greble, U. S. A., the first Union officer of regulars to fall during the war. This officer of artillery was killed at the Battle of Big Bethel, Va., June 10th, 1861.

June 17th. 26th Regiment moved to Washington and the 27th Regiment to Chambersburg.

June 29th. 71st Regiment (1st California Regiment), Col. Edward D. Baker, arrived from New York and camped at Suffolk Park.

July 3d. 71st Regiment moved to Baltimore.

July 4th. The Home Guards paraded with the Gray Reserves.

July 16th. The 33d Regiment (4th Reserves) left Easton, Pa., for Baltimore.

July 21st. 36th Regiment Infantry (7th Reserves) left West Chester for Washington.

July 22d. Intense excitement in the city, due to news of defeat of the Union Army at Bull Run.

July 23d. Return of the 23d Regiment.

July 25th. Return of the 17th Regiment.

City Councils appropriated $100,000 for relief of soldiers' families.

July 29th. Return of the 18th, 21st and 22d Regiments.

July 30th. Return of the Scott Legion (20th Regiment) and Commonwealth Artillery.

July 31st. Return of the 19th Regiment (National Guards).

August 2d. Walter W. Smith, a Confederate prize master, confined, with his crew, in Moyamensing Prison, was convicted of piracy. This led to threat of retaliation by the Confederates upon Federal prisoners held in Richmond.

August 3d. 29th Regiment left for Sandy Hook, Md.

August 14th. Return of First Troop Philadelphia City Cavalry.

August 17th. The Zouaves d'Afrique, Capt. Charles H. T. Collis, were sent for duty at Fort Delaware.

August 22d. 65th Regiment (3d Cavalry) left for Washington.

Office of the *Christian Observer* (disloyal) seized and closed by the U. S. Marshal Milward, who also seized copies of the *New York Daily News* arriving by train.

August 31st. The 2d Regiment escorted body of Gen. Lyon (killed at the Battle of Wilson's Creek, Mo.) through the city.

September 1st. Great activity by many concerns in manufacture of fire arms, swords, cannon, baggage wagons, uniforms and other war material.

September 16th. 72d Regiment (Fire Zouaves) left for the front.

September 17th. Military parade in honor of the 74th anniversary day, adoption of the Federal Constitution.

September 24th. The 73d Regiment left for Washington.

September 26th. 75th Regiment left for Washington.

September 27th. The 23d Regiment (Birney's Zouaves) left for Washington.

September 30th. The 98th Regiment left for Washington.

October 1st. Confusion resulting from soldiers' vote in the camps.

October 4th. The 89th Regiment (8th Cavalry) left for the front.

October 5th. The 88th Regiment left for Alexandria, Va.

October 12th. The 95th Regiment left for the South.

October 14th. Harlan's Light Cavalry (11th Cavalry) left for the South.

October 31st. The 106th Regiment left for the South.

November 7th. The body of Col. E. D. Baker, commanding the 71st Regiment (California Regiment), killed at Ball's Bluff, Va., was laid in state at Independence Hall.

November 15th. Launch of the U. S. S. Miami at Philadelphia Navy Yard, where 2,400 men were then employed.

December 4th. Spectacular parade of the 6th Cavalry Regiment, "Rush's Lancers."

December 6th. The 6th Cavalry, Rush's Lancers, with the 58th, 67th, 90th and 91st Regiments, were presented with colors by the State and the Society of the Cincinnati.

December 7th. Magnificient silk flag, made by the crew of the U. S. S. Hartford on voyage home from China, was presented to the city and raised upon the staff above Independence Hall with an imposing demonstration.

Gunboat *Itasca* left the port.

Steamer *Delaware,* built at Wilmington, was bought by the Government.

Sloop of war *Tuscarora* sailed for New York to receive her guns.

December 8th. The "Soldiers' and Sailors' Relief Association of the Episcopal Church" was formed.

December 10th. Departure of a part of the 6th Cavalry (Rush's Lancers).

December 30th. Philadelphia banks suspended specie payment.

December 31st. The Volunteer Refreshment Committees reported having supplied meals, since opening, to soldiers en route to or from the South aggregating 143,394.

The fateful old year was ended and the new year ushered in by the people of Philadelphia with general patriotic observances in all parts of the city.

WAR CHRONOLOGY—1862.

January 1st. To this date the City Treasurer had paid to the families of soldiers $336,612, and had spent for war munitions $138,506.36.

January 2d. The 67th Regiment was encamped at Camac's Woods.

January 10th. The 113th Regiment, Col. Wm. Frishmuth, camped on Ridge avenue.

January 17th. It was stated that more than 10,000 women were employed by the Schuylkill Arsenal authorities in making uniforms.

January 21st. The 91st Regiment left Camp Chase for Washington.

January 31st. U. S. S. *St. Louis* sailed for duty in Mediterranean Sea.

February 3d. Thirty-eight prisoners taken from Confederate privateers were removed from Moyamensing Prison to Fort Lafayette.

February 3d. The 115th Regiment camped at Hestonville.

March 8th. The 58th Regiment left for Fortress Monroe.

March 20th. Sloop of war *Juniata* launched at the Navy Yard.

March 31st. The 90th Regiment (National Guard) left Philadelphia for Baltimore.

April 17th. Steam engine and hose carriage of Hibernia Fire Company was sent to Fortress Monroe accompanied by eight members.

April 21st. Yearly meeting, Society of Friends, warned its members to refuse military service or payment of taxes or other money intended for military use upon penalty of expulsion.

April 23d. Lieut.-Col. W. Brooks, U. S. A., assumed military command of the Department of Philadelphia.

May 1st. Corps of Philadelphia surgeons and nurses left for the Virginia peninsula to aid Federal sick and wounded soldiers of Pennsylvania.

May 10th. 109th Regiment left for Washington.

Iron-clad *New Ironsides* was launched at yard of Cramp & Sons.

May 25th. Governor Curtin called upon the State militia to muster for active service in the Federal army.

Exchanged prisoners from the "California Regiment" (Baker's 71st Regiment) ordered to join their command.

June 2d. Hibernia Engine returned from Washington.

June 9th. The West Philadelphia U. S. Army Hospital was opened.

June 10th. During the week several ships arrived with large numbers of sick and wounded soldiers.

June 17th. Provost guard active searching for deserters and men absent from their commands.

June 18th. Councils made first move to induce the Government to establish a navy yard at League Island.

June 20th. Two monitor gunboats nearly completed by Reaney & Archbold at Chester.

U. S. Hospital opened at Fourth and George Streets (American Mechanics' Hall).

June 26th. New Municipal flag was raised at Independence Hall.

July 4th. Children of the public schools sent large quantities of ice cream to the army hospitals.

July 10th. U. S. S. *Monongahela* launched at the Navy Yard.

July 21st. Under the President's call for 300,000 more troops, the Governor of Pennsylvania fixed the quota of Philadelphia at 50 companies of 100 men each.

July 26th. Councils appropriated $500,000 for a bounty fund. For the same purpose the Pennsylvania Railroad Company subscribed $50,000, Philadelphia and Reading Railway Company $25,000 and private citizens gave $158,000. This amount was largely increased within another month. Citizens had also contributed to the U. S. Sanitary Commission $17,000. Members of the Corn Exchange voted $10,000 toward equipping a regiment to be known as the Corn Exchange Regiment.

July 28th. Collis Zouaves (114th Regiment) camped at Germantown avenue and Nicetown lane.

August 5th. Corn Exchange Regiment in camp at Indian Queen Lane, Falls of the Schuylkill.

August 10th. Following the President's call for a conscription, many persons were prevented by the provost troops from leaving the port of Philadelphia for other countries.

August 31st. 118th (Corn Exchange) Regiment left for the front.

September 1st. Collis Zouaves (114th Regiment) left for Washington.

September 2d. The 68th, 116th and 119th Regiments left for the South.

September 3d. Several hundred recruits for the old regiments left to join their commands.

Children in public schools worked at picking lint.

September 4th. Twenty-five hundred sick and wounded soldiers arrived at Washington Street Wharf.

September 5th. 121st Regiment went South.

September 6th. Estimate published showing that Philadelphia had furnished 31,400 soldiers to that date.

September 8th. Citizens' Bounty Fund, to date, $466,938.

Exchanges and business places closed at 3 P. M. Citizens drilling daily in the streets.

Great recruiting camp established in Independence Square.

Many wounded and sick soldiers were placed, upon arrival, in down-town churches near the Prime Street Station.

September 10th. Intense excitement due to the advance toward Pennsylvania of the Confederates.

A committee of two hundred and fifty leading citizens tendered a splendid ovation to the 6th Massachusetts Regiment, which had re-enlisted and was enroute South.

September 11th. Governor Curtin telegraphed to Philadelphia to send 20,000 emergency troops to Harrisburg.

September 12th. Mayor Henry called upon all citizens to meet at the precinct houses in the twenty-five wards to organize for defence. This plan was frustrated by a heavy rain. Many citizens organized, however, including workmen in large establishments.

September 13th. Numerous trains of emergency men were sent to Harrisburg.

September 17th. Battle of Antietam.

Steam fire engine of the Hibernia Fire Company was taken to Washington with seven men.

September 20th. Rejoicing over retreat of the enemy, and gloom because of heavy losses in Philadelphia regiments, stirred the city.

October 6th. Capt. J. Orr Finnie became Provost Marshal.

October 8th. Flag presentation at Satterlee General Hospital, West Philadelphia.

October 10th. Extraordinary activity in recruiting to avoid draft in the city.

October 14th. Alexander Henry the "War Mayor," was re-elected.

October 22d. Army hospital opened at Twentieth and Buttonwood streets.

October 24th. Independent Battery, Capt. E. Spencer Miller, ordered to Harrisburg.

October 25th. Camp for conscripts established near Haddington, called "Camp Philadelphia."

October 27th. Draft postponed one week.

November 2d. Draft commissioners reported the quota of Philadelphia filled without a draft.

November 3d. Nearly 7,000 conscripts from eastern counties of the State assembled at Camp Philadelphia, Haddington.

November 15th. Hospital for officers completed at Camac's Woods.

November 20th. Total capacity of the military hospitals in the city 6,543 beds.

November 25th. Imposing funeral of Brig.-Gen. Francis E. Patterson.

November 27th. 174th, 175th and 176th Regiments left Camp Philadelphia for the front.
November 28th. Thanksgiving Day. Citizens provided excellent dinners at all of the army hospitals.
December 3d. Companies A and B of the "Continental Cavalry" mustered in.
December 8th. U. S. S. *Shenandoah* launched at the Navy Yard.
December 9th. 157th Regiment broke camp and embarked for garrison duty at Fort Delaware.
Battalion of drafted men left Camp Philadelphia.
December 23d. First of the "Monitors" built at Wilmington arrived at the Navy Yard.
December 25th. Christmas Day. Special dinners and entertainments at the army hospitals.

CHRONOLOGY, 1863.

January 1st. Report of City Treasurer showed that during 1862 the City had paid for defence, $80,392.64; for bounties, $367,105.00, and for relief of soldiers' families, $657,223.90.
January 2d. General rejoicing among colored people regarding the emancipation of slaves.
January 5th. Young ladies of the High School presented a flag to Col. Lyle's regiment, 90th Pennsylvania Volunteers.
January 6th. Local receptions to Major-Gen. B. F. Butler and Major-Gen. George B. McClellan.
January 14th. Mower U. S. General Hospital at Chestnut Hill was opened.
January 17th. Battery "A," Roberts Artillery Regiment, left camp at Germantown for Fortress Monroe.
January 19th. Launch of Monitor *Lehigh* at Chester, Pa.
Departure of Batteries "A" and "C," of Segebarth's Heavy Artillery, for Fortress Monroe.
January 27th. Battalion of Provost Guard formed and barracked in Swanson street.
January 29th. Philadelphia *Evening Journal* suppressed for seditious publications.
February 23d. The Provost Guard of 500 men paraded and were barracked at the former hospital at Fifth and Buttonwood streets.
February 26th. Numbers of Confederates, having taken oath of allegiance, were seeking work in the city.
March 10th. A Union Freedman's Relief Association was organized by colored residents.
March 11th. Lieut.-Col. Wm. D. Whipple, U. S. A., assumed command of the Department of Pennsylvania.
Young Men's Democratic Club, of which George M. Wharton was President, bitterly assailed President Lincoln and advocated "State Rights." Members generally wore, as badges, old copper pennies showing the head of Liberty. Hence the term "Copperhead."
March 23d. A movement was commenced to send colored recruits to the Massachusetts colored brigade and to form a similar brigade in Pennsylvania.
March 26th. A detachment of Connecticut cavalry arrived to perform patrol duty in Philadelphia.
April 6th. A number of merchants were detected in shipping contraband goods via Baltimore to the South, and an order was issued by the Provost Marshal requiring all shippers sending goods south of New Castle, Delaware, to take the oath of allegiance.
April 8th. "Union Leagues" were being formed in several of the wards in order to stimulate loyal sentiment.
April 9th. Several leaders of a disloyal secret organization were brought to the city from Bucks County for trial.

April 10th. The First Troop, Philadelphia City Cavalry, was incorporated.

April 23d. Col. John F. Ballier of the 98th Regiment, who had been suspended, was restored to the command of his regiment.

April 28th. Col. Charles F. Ruff, long acting as State mustering officer, was appointed State Provost Marshal.

April 30th. General observance of a National Fast Day.

May 1st. Disabled soldiers held a meeting to plan the establishment of an invalid brigade for provost and garrison duty.

May 4th. Brig.-Gen. Pleasanton, of the Home Guard, reported the expenditures of the city for defences to date at $124,650.00.

All telegraphic service was placed, temporarily, under control of the military authorities, creating much apprehension.

May. 7th. Gunboat *Tacony* was launched at the Navy Yard.

May 9th. The *Age*, a new Democratic newspaper, located adjoining the post-office, was threatened by soldiers and citizens for disloyal utterances.

May 10th. Large numbers of rebel prisoners were guarded through the city en route to Fort Delaware.

May 12th. Gunboat *Wyalusing* was launched by William Cramp & Sons.

May 15th. U. S. Steamer *Pontiac* was launched by Birely, Hillman & Co.

May 24th. Many illuminations were shown in honor of the victories gained by Gen. U. S. Grant in the southwest.

May 25th. Preparations were begun by Capt. Wm. E. Lehman, U. S. Provost Marshal, at 245 South Third street, for a new draft.

June 3d. Splendid reception, by the German societies, of the 29th Regiment, N. Y. volunteers, en route home. Six companies of this regiment were recruited in Philadelphia.

June 9th. Twenty-four hundred rebel prisoners arrived, under Ohio guards, from Vicksburg. The train upon which they arrived was said to have been the longest that ever entered the city.

June 15th. The city was excited by the report that rebel cavalry had entered Chambersburg, Pa. Governor Curtin once more summoned help to Harrisburg. The President called for 100,000 volunteer militia to serve six months.

June 16th. Governor Curtin called for militia to defend the State. An alarm was sounded upon the bell of Independence Hall.

June 17th. Several regiments and independent companies of Philadelphia militia and home guards were moved to Harrisburg.

June 18th. First Troop, P. C. Cavalry, entrained for Harrisburg. The New York 7th Regiment passed through, followed soon afterward by other New York and New Jersey regiments.

June 27th. Major-Gen. N. J. Dana, U. S. V., assumed command in Philadelphia.

June 29th. Proclamation by Mayor Henry, and great rally of citizens at Independence Square.

June 30th. Two hundred ministers volunteered to work upon the city defences.

July 1st. Great demonstration in honor of Gov. Curtin in front of the Continental Hotel. Led by a blind singer, the people sang the "Star Spangled Banner."

July 2d. The city greatly excited by conflicting rumors from the Cumberland Valley.

July 3d. "Camp Rendezvous" established upon Islington Lane.

July 4th. The Bridesburg Guards, Lieut.-Col. Barton H. Jenks, paraded. Crowds around newspaper offices awaiting news from Gettysburg. Conflicting reports kept the multitude in a condition of constant excitement.

July 5th. Military bands paraded through the streets to stimulate enlistments. Definite news received of the rebel defeat.

July 6th. Force of gas works employees at work upon a fort at School Lane and Ridge road. Other forts under construction in West Philadelphia.

July 7th. The Union League celebrated the victory at Gettysburg by marching, with Birgfeld's Band, to Independence Hall.

Great rejoicing over the retreat of the rebels from Pennsylvania.

The First Union League Regiment, Col. Wm. D. Whipple, presented with colors and left for Camp Curtin.

July 9th. Second Keystone Battery, Capt. Edward Fitzki, left for Harrisburg.

July 10th. Second Union League Regiment received colors and proceeded to Camp Curtin.

Hospitals filled with wounded soldiers from Gettysburg.

July 12th. Trainloads of the wounded constantly arriving.

July 13th. Announcement of the beginning of the new draft in the city.

To this date from July 1st the city had placed 10,683 emergency troops in the field.

July 14th. The 34th and 46th Regiments, Pennsylvania Militia, and other troops brought to the city in anticipation of draft riots.

July 20th. Major-Gen. George Cadwalader, U. S. V., detailed to command of the military at Philadelphia.

Draft barracks established at Twenty-second and Wood streets.

July 27th. Reception of the Gray Reserves, Blue Reserves and 20th Regiment, ninety-day militia, upon return from emergency service.

August 1st. Tenth N. J. Regiment Militia was encamped at Jefferson Square.

August 13th. Col. Tilghman's regiment, 3d U. S. Colored troops, left upon transports for Charleston Harbor.

August 14th. Capt. Hastings' Keystone Battery returned to the city.

August 22d. The 2d Keystone Battery returned home.

August 23d. First and 2d Union League Regiments and the Merchants' Regiment returned.

August 25th. The 2d Coal Regiment, Col. Hopkinson, returned.

August 27th. Second Corn Exchange Regiment, Col. Alex. Murphy, returned.

August 29th. Payments to families of soldiers from the Volunteer Relief Fund averaged, at this time, $3,500 per diem. Total paid out to date, $1,443,707.68.

August 31st. Review of colored troops and flag presentation at Camp William Penn.

September 1st. Grand review at Camp Cadwalader.

September 3d. Battalion of five companies of sharp-shooters sent to Pottsville.

September 10th. Return and muster out of the 3d Union League Regiment (59th Regiment, Pennsylvania ninety-day Militia).

September 11th. The Dana Troop returned from service in Schuylkill County.

September 13th. Detachment of drafted men sent to the 118th Regiment, P. V.

September 21st. Battalion of U. S. Cavalry, composed of 280 Confederate prisoners from Fort Delaware, paraded in Philadelphia and left for Baltimore.

September 24th. Woodward's Independent Battery encamped at the U. S. Arsenal upon Gray's Ferry Road.

September 28th. At a meeting of the Pennsylvania Historical Society plans were discussed for establishing a memorial park at Gettysburg.

September 29th. U. S. Gunboat *Kansas* was launched at the Navy Yard.

October 10th. Parade and mass meeting of "Wide Awake" Clubs, National Union party.

October 12th. First anniversary celebration of the opening of Citizens' Volunteer Hospital.

A number of ex-Confederates who had taken the oath of allegiance and found employment in the city were arrested for attempted fraudulent voting.

October 14th. Sixth U. S. Colored Regiment, Infantry, left Camp William Penn for Fortress Monroe.

October 17th. President Lincoln called for 300,000 volunteers to serve three years.

October 19th. The 1st Pennsylvania Chasseurs, Col. Zell, three companies, returned from service in the coal region.

October 25th. Death of Col. Chas. P. Dare, late of the 23d Regiment, Pennsylvania, three months' service, from illness.

October 29th. The captured rebel ram *Atlanta* was placed on exhibition at Washington Street Wharf for the benefit of the Union Volunteer Refreshment Saloon.

November 2d. The 19th Regiment, Cavalry, left Camp Stanton, paraded and started for the front.

November 8th. A detachment of 260 drafted men, barracked at Twenty-second and Wood streets, was sent South.

November 12th. Fourth Union League Regiment encamped at Frankford.

November 13th. United States Christian Commission began sending clothing, medicine and other supplies to the Union prisoners confined at Richmond.

November 14th. The 9th Regiment, Invalid Corps, Col. G. W. Gile, was sent to Washington.

Many Philadelphia men going to New Jersey to enlist, attracted by larger bounties. The Philadelphia bounty at this time was $250, national bounty in addition $402.

November 19th. Dedication of the Soldiers' Cemetery at Gettysburg.

December 5th. Councils appropriated $1,000,000 for bounties.

December 23d. The 29th Regiment, P. V., Col. Wm. Rickards, Jr., returned on furlough. This was the first of the three years' regiments to arrive home.

December 25th. Special celebrations and dinners at all of the military hospitals.

December 29th. School for the instruction of proposed officers of colored regiments opened at 1210 Chestnut street.

CHRONOLOGY, 1864.

January 1st. It was announced that the quota of Philadelphia had been filled and bounties for enlistments were discontinued.

January 8th. The 91st Regiment arrived home.

January 10th. The 28th Regiment returned.

January 14th. A portion of the 31st Regiment (2d Reserves) returned.

January 16th. The re-enlisted men of the 95th Regiment (Gosline's Zouaves) paraded.

January 17th. The 8th Regiment, U. S. Colored Troops, departed for the front.

January 24th. The 75th Regiment arrived.

January 26th. The 72d Regiment returned.

January 29th. Gen. Gantt, late of the Confederate army, appeared at the Academy of Music in behalf of the Union men of the South.

February 3d. The 98th Regiment arrived.

February 5th. The 89th Regiment (8th Cavalry) arrived.

February 9th. Numerous regiments of New York State and New England passed through the city homeward bound.

February 10th. The 22d Regiment, U.S. Colored Troops, left for the South.

February 12th. The 99th Regiment arrived.

The 88th Regiment returned.

February 22d. Washington's Birthday parade of all the troops in the city.

February 23d. The 183d Regiment (4th Union League Regiment) left for the front.

February 29th. The 29th Regiment re-enlisted and was sent to Chester barracks.

Delaware slave owners applied for the bounties of slaves enlisted in Philadelphia.

March 2d. Twelve hundred Confederate prisoners en route to Fort Delaware were fed at the refreshment saloons.

23

March 3d. The southern guerilla chief, Basil Duke, a prisoner, was lodged at the Continental Hotel and cheered by disloyal citizens.

March 7th. The 69th Regiment returned.

March 10th. The 113th Regiment (12th Cavalry Regiment) returned.

March 13th. The 56th Regiment returned.

March 15th. The President ordered a new draft for 200,000 men for April 15th. Philadelphia's quota for the drafts of February and April, 1864, was estimated at 17,500 men.

March 18th. Many of the schools were busy raising money for the proposed Sanitary Fair.

The Naval Committee visited League Island.

March 19th. Launch of the U. S. S. *Yantic* at the Navy Yard.

March 22d. Lieut.-Gen. U. S. Grant and staff were at the Continental Hotel.

March 30th. The 99th Regiment (re-enlisted) left for the front.

April 15th. The 69th Regiment (re-enlisted) left for Chester barracks.

May 3d. The 188th Regiment being organized from surplus volunteers of the 3d Regiment, Artillery.

May 12th. Parade of colored troops from Camp William Penn.

May 18th. Governor Curtin called for the formation of militia regiments in Pennsylvania, subject to call for 100 days' service as U. S. Volunteers.

May 21st. The old Washington Guard being reorganized by Col. Wm. F. Small as the 60th Regiment, P. M.

May 31st. Arrival of the 27th Regiment.

June 7th. The 1st, 2d and 7th Reserves were welcomed home with special honors.

The Sanitary Fair opened in Logan Square.

June 16th. The 7th Reserves returned.

June 17th. President Lincoln visited the Sanitary Fair.

The 71st Regiment arrived home, being accorded many honors.

June 25th. Close of the Sanitary Fair.

July 1st. The 58th Regiment returned on furlough. The re-enlisted men numbered 243.

July 4th. Salutes by Philadelphia Union Artillery at Nineteenth and Callowhill streets, by Gray Reserves at the Navy Yard, by warships in port. Parade of sailors and marines. Review and fireworks at Camp William Penn. Flag-raising by the "Houser Cadets" in the First Ward. Receptions at the National Union and Union League Clubs.

July 10th. Proclamation by Governor Andrew G. Curtin calling for emergency volunteers was posted on the streets and read from pulpits of all churches.

July 11th. Battalions of the 43d and 45th Regiments, U. S. Infantry, colored troops, left for the front.

July 12th. Confederate raiders cut off train and telegraphic service between Philadelphia and Baltimore. Great activity at armories. A field battery of marines and volunteers rushed to Havre de Grace.

July 18th. Arrival of the 95th Regiment.

July 19th. Stroud's Independent Company of Cavalry (Railroad Troops) left for the South.

July 23d. The 192d Regiment (Custom House troops) left for Baltimore.

July 28th. Departure of the 196th Regiment (National Guards) for Baltimore and Chicago.

July 29th. The 197th Regiment (3d Coal Regiment) left for Rock Island, Ill.

August 1st. Reports of the burning of Chambersburg by the Confederate cavalry aroused the city to greater activity in projects for defence.

August 4th. A day of national humiliation and prayer.

August 5th. The Keystone Battery left for Huntingdon County, Pa.

August 12th. The 72d Regiment (Baxter's Fire Zouaves) was welcomed home with a great demonstration of troops and firemen.

August 20th. The 3d Cavalry (60th Regiment) returned, being escorted by military in an extended parade.

August 22d. The 58th (veteran) Regiment returned, under re-enlistment, to the front.

August 25th. The arrival of the 23d Regiment was attended by another great reception by the firemen and citizens.

August 29th. Return of the 106th Regiment. The escort included the Baxter Fire Zouaves, the Henry Guards and other local troops.

September 6th. Arrival of the 82d Regiment. Reception postponed to following day.

September 7th. Three Philadelphia companies of the 61st Regiment arrived home.

September 18th. Departure of the 198th Regiment (6th Union League Regiment) and of Stroud's Troop (Railroad Cavalry), the latter going to Easton, Pa.

September 21st. Departure of the 203d Regiment.

September 28th. The 127th U. S. (colored) Regiment left from Camp William Penn.

September 30th. The 199th Regiment left for the front.

October 7th. Hastings' Keystone Battery returned.

October 13th. The 47th U. S. (colored) Regiment left Camp Cadwalader.

October 17th. Launch of U. S. S. *Chattanooga* at Cramp's Ship Yard.

October 21st. Military funeral of Gen. David B. Birney.

October 30th. The 192d Regiment (the Custom House Regiment) arrived.

November 1st. It was announced that Philadelphia had filled the quota under the July call for troops without a draft.

November 5th. The 196th Regiment left for duty at Fort Delaware.

A provisional Brigade from the Army of the Potomac, consisting of the 93d, 104th, 119th and 138th Pennsylvania Infantry, of the Sixth Corps, were encamped in Philadelphia to prevent Copperhead riots during the national election.

A large number of bounty-jumpers marched, in irons, through the streets and were sent to the army.

November 6th. Great factional disorder preceding the national elections.

November 16th. Fireworks display at the Union League.

November 17th. Many furloughed soldiers returned to their commands.

November 22d. General U. S. Grant visited Philadelphia.

November 24th. Thanksgiving festivities and patriotic services in the churches.

November 28th. Recruiting started for the "2d Fire Zouave Regiment."

November 30th. A portion of the 90th Regiment returned.

December 6th. A large number of parolled soldiers from southern prison pens arrived, many in a dying condition.

December 7th. Headquarters Military Department of Pennsylvania removed to Philadelphia.

The colored population celebrated the end of slavery in Maryland.

December 13th. Philadelphia merchants gave a banquet to Captain J. A. Winslow, U. S. N., commander of the *Kearsarge.*

December 15th. City bounties stopped. Total of bounties paid by City Treasurer to date $6,796,600.

December 25th. Christmas dinners provided at the military hospitals to about 12,000 men through donation of the "Mrs. M. G. Egbert Fund."

CHRONOLOGY—1865.

January 1st. Donation dinners were provided at all of the military hospitals.

January 10th. A meeting of citizens was convened in behalf of the suffering poor of Savannah. Ga.

January 18th. The Keystone Battery celebrated the capture of Fort Fisher with one hundred guns.

January 20th. A delegation of working women employed in connection with work at the Schuylkill Arsenal visited President Lincoln to protest against the contract system.

356

January 24th. The Officers' Hospital was moved from Camac's Woods to a brick building at Twenty-fourth and Chestnut streets.
February 18th. At a meeting of the Corn Exchange it was decided to raise a "Birney Brigade" of three infantry regiments.
February 19th. News received that Charleston, S. C., had been evacuated by the Confederate forces.
February 23d. A draft was commenced in the Third, Fourth, Fifth, Sixth, Seventh, Eighth, Ninth and Tenth Wards.
March 11th. The 213th Regiment broke camp and started southward.
March 23d. A mass meeting was held at the Academy of Music to promote assistance to deserters from the rebel army.
March 30th. The University Light Artillery was organized by the literary department of the University of Pennsylvania.
April 1st. The Thirteenth, Fourteenth, Twenty-first, Twenty-second and Twenty-fourth Wards had raised their quota of troops under the pending requisition. The balance of the city was still short 3,580 men.
April 3d. General rejoicing, parades and illuminations upon receipt of news that Richmond had fallen.
April 4th. The Union League marched to Independence Hall and held a patriotic demonstration.
April 8th. The 214th Regiment, P. V., departed for the South.
April 10th. Dispatches announcing the surrender of General Lee's army resulted in great rejoicing through the city.
April 15th. The announcement of the murder of President Lincoln the previous evening, at Washington, resulted in scenes of wild excitement.
April 22d. The body of the late President was escorted to Independence Hall by an imposing military and civic procession.
April 24th. The remains of Mr. Lincoln were taken to New York City.
April 26th. The 215th Regiment (9th Union League Regiment) left for the South. This was the last organization of volunteers to go out from Philadelphia.
May 2d. The 24th Regiment (colored troops) left for southern service.
May 3d. Lieut.-Gen. U. S. Grant and family moved into the residence upon Chestnut street which had been presented to them by citizens.
May 14th. The Union League opened its new club house upon Broad street.
May 16th. The Pennsylvania Home for Invalid Soldiers and Sailors was inaugurated at the Academy of Music.
May 21st.,The 114th Regiment (Collis Zouaves) arrived home.
June 10th. Grand review of the returning veterans, in a heavy rain.
June 24th. Reception to Gen. U. S. Grant at the Union League.

NOTE.—By July 1st nearly all of the Philadelphia regiments had returned to the city. The records of their dates of arrival are so conflicting that they cannot now be definitely ascertained. The 95th Regiment reached home on July 19th and the 75th on September 12th. At the end of 1865 the only Pennsylvania regiments still in the service were the 58th, 195th and 214th Infantry, the 2d Artillery and one battalion of the 19th Cavalry.

ERRATA

The second paragraph, page 224, should read:
"In the course of the first year of the war, before the hospital service became efficient, the general mortality in the army was 1.72 per cent. from battle casualties and 5.04 per cent. from disease. In the Atlantic Division, Army Medical Department, the mortality from disease was 3.34 per cent., and in the Central Division 8.21 per cent."

GENERAL INDEX

The names of Philadelphia officers below the rank of captain who died in the service are included in the list upon pages 280 to 291.

Adams, H. A., 200.
Addis, Isaac, 341.
Agnew, D. Hayes, 227, 232.
Ahl, Thos. J., 57, 58, 59.
Airey, Washington, 289.
Alden, Chas. H., 228.
Allen, Harrison, 200, 228.
Allen, Wm. W., 341.
Ames, John W., 189, 190.
Anderson, Jas. L., 150, 287.
Anderson, Wm., 294.
Angeroth, Chas., Sr., 150, 157.
Angeroth, Chas., 27, 54.
Armor, Wm. C., 294.
Ashbrook, Joseph, 294.
Asher, Jere. W., 190, 266, 291.
Ashton, F. M., 200.
Ashurst, R. L., 294.
Averill Wm. W., 157.
Ayres, Peter B., 294.

Bailey, Wm., 169.
Baird, Geo. W., 193.
Baker, E. D., 85, 86, 87, 89, 91, 113, 283.
Baldwin L. K., 232.
Ballier, John F., 36, 116, 293, 340.
Banes, Chas. H., 295.
Bankson, John P., 340.
Barnes, J. K., 292.
Barrett, John, 79, 282.
Barry, David S., 341.
Bassett, I. C., 51, 104, 293.
Bavington, John, 40.
Baxter, DeWitt C., 86, 91, 92, 293, 340.
Beale, Joseph, 200.
Beath, Robert B., 190, 326, 328, 330.
Beamish, J. W., 286.
Belsterling, J. J., 106, 285.
Benson, Edwin N., 22.
Benson, R. Dale, 258, 295, 340.
Betts, Chas. M., 177, 178, 335.
Bewley, Chas. H., 79.
Bickley, L. W., 235.
Bickell, J. M., 40.
Biddle, Alex., 135.
Biddle, Chapman, 23, 135.
Biddle, Craig, 17.
Biddle, H. J., 21, 65, 291.
Biddle, Mark G., 40.
Biles, Edwin R., 118, 119, 341.
Binney, Horace, 295.
Birney, D. B., 21, 49, 122, 125, 291, 292.
Bingham, H. H., 335.
Bishop, D. B., 49.
Blake, Geo. A. H., 22, 292.
Blakiston, Jos. B., 24.
Blakeley, Theo., 281.
Blanchard, Wm., 22.
Bodine, Robt. L., 52, 53, 293.
Bohlen, Wm. H. C., 98, 99, 100, 292, 293.
Bolinger, H. C., 72.
Bolling, Robt., 235.

Bonnaffon, S., Jr., 119, 295, 335, 340.
Borthwick, D., 200.
Bosbyshell, O. C., 340.
Bournonville, A. C., 229.
Bowen, E. R., 125.
Bowen, Geo. K., 145, 272, 273.
Bowman, Wendell P., 340.
Brady, Eugene, 288.
Brady, James, 147, 295, 341.
Brainerd, Thos., 266.
Breed, Wm. M., 229.
Breel, H. C., 290.
Bregy, F. Amadee, 341.
Breitenbach, J. R., 295.
Breuckner, Aug., 284.
Brightly, Chas. H., 291.
Briner, Wm., 69.
Brinton, Robt. M., 295, 340.
Brinton, Joseph P., 155, 156, 295.
Brisbin, Jas. S., 293.
Briscoe, J. C., 145, 146, 271, 272, 294.
Brooke, John R., 293, 323.
Brooke, Wm. R., 295.
Brown, J. D., 282.
Brown, Wm. R., 200.
Brown, Orlando, 192.
Bryan, T. M., Jr., 180.
Buchanan, J. A., 227, 232.
Burns, W. W., 89, 91, 93.
Burnett, Robt. L., 22.
Buschbeck, A., 54, 96.

Cadwalader, Chas. E., 24.
Cadwalader, C. G., 341.
Cadwalader, George, 31, 43, 196, 292, 323.
Cadwalader, C. N., 295.
Camac, Wm. M., 228.
Calhoun, A. R., 326.
Cameron, Wm. H., 228.
Campbell, Alex., 290.
Campbell, Chas. T., 147, 293.
Campbell, John, 224.
Campbell, Thos. E., 248.
Campbell, David, 160.
Cantador, L., 54.
Carpenter, John C., 82, 83.
Carpenter, J. E., 295.
Carroll, Edw'd, 114, 286.
Carroll, Jas. G., 115, 286.
Carson, E. F., 200.
Cash, John C., 200.
Casner, John F., 295.
Cassells, John, 295.
Cavada, F. F., 125, 295.
Chadwick, Peter B., 341.
Chamberlin, Thos., 139.
Chandler, Jos. S., 125, 287.
Chantry, A. W., 81.
Chapman, T. D. G., 286.
Chapman, John C., 72.
Chauncey, Chas., 24.
Chew, W. Wesley, 341.
Chorman, E. G., 165.
Clancy, Jas. T., 240, 250.

Clark, Chas. P., 295.
Clark, Gideon, 133, 294, 295.
Clark, J. Ross, 341.
Clay, Cecil, 77, 78, 294.
Cleeman, R. A., 227, 228.
Cline, John, 288.
Cochrane, Geo., 200.
Collis, Chas. H. T., 124, 293, 335.
Colwell, Jas., 295.
Connor, Eli T., 102.
Cooke, Jay, 220, 221, 223.
Coppee, Henry, 65.
Corrie, Wm. A., 165.
Corson, Robt., 208, 224.
Cosslett, Chas., 129, 295, 341.
Craig, Joseph R., 328, 330.
Couch, Darius N., 43.
Crawford, S. Wylie, 66, 292.
Cresson, C. C., 96, 97.
Cromley, Geo., 288.
Crosby, John W., 79, 80, 282, 295.
Crowther, Jas. D., 122, 292.
Cummings, A. B., 200.
Cunningham, A. J., 126, 287.
Cunningham, O. C., 275.
Curry, Wm. L., 93, 95, 287.
Curtis, C. B., 77.
Curtis, Geo. R., 288.

DaCosta, J. A., 228.
Dahlgren, John A., 200, 291, 320.
Dahlgren, Ulric, 291, 321.
Dale, R. C., 129, 288, 292.
Dare, Chas. P., 32, 37, 40, 43, 49.
Darrach, J., 228.
Davis, Chas. B., 283.
Davis, G. H., 326.
Davis, Jacob M., 110, 341.
Davis, Richard W., 288.
Davis, Wm., 87, 88.
Dawson, Wm. M., 79.
Dechert, Rob't P., 295, 340.
Deck, Geo. H., 232.
De Korpenay, G., 57.
Delph, John H., 104, 285.
Denney, John P., 341.
Dixon, W. C., 232.
Donaldson, F. A., 130, 341.
Dorr, W. W., 289.
Doyle, John T., 275.
Draper, J. W., 229.
Donnelly, V. P., 79.
Doubleday, U., 194.
Duffy, Michael, 283.
Duke, Chas. W., 109.
Durang, John T., 341.
Dutton, Jas., 295.
Dull, Wm. H., 283.
Dungan, F. J., 284.
Dunglinson, R. J., 229.
Dunne, John P., 127.

Eakin, C. M., 18, 19, 218, 219.
Eddy, H. M., 287.
Edgerton, N. H., 336.
Egbert, H. C., 24.
Egbert, Geo. T., 141, 240.

357

Originally published in 1913
This edition ©2014 Westholme Publishing
ISBN: 978-1-59416-205-3
Also available as an eBook

Westholme Publishing, LLC
904 Edgewood Road
Yardley, Pennsylvania 19067
Printed in the United States of America